W. H. Davenport (William Henry Davenport Adams

A book of earnest Lives

W. H. Davenport (William Henry Davenport Adams

A book of earnest Lives

ISBN/EAN: 9783743324633

Manufactured in Europe, USA, Canada, Australia, Japa

Cover: Foto ©ninafisch / pixelio.de

Manufactured and distributed by brebook publishing software (www.brebook.com)

W. H. Davenport (William Henry Davenport Adams

A book of earnest Lives

A BOOK OF EARNEST LIVES.

EARNEST LIVES. JOHN HOWARD. [Face Title.

A

BOOK OF EARNEST LIVES.

BY

W. H. DAVENPORT ADAMS.

> "Servants of God! or sons
> Shall I not call you? because
> Not as servants ye know
> Your Father's innermost mind,
> His, who unwillingly sees
> One of His little ones lost—
> Yours is the praise, if mankind
> Hath not as yet in its march
> Fainted, and fallen, and died."
> —MATTHEW ARNOLD.

London:
W. SWAN SONNENSCHEIN & CO.,
PATERNOSTER SQUARE.
1884.

INSCRIBED,

WITH CORDIAL REGARDS,

TO THE

REV. F. T. SWINBURN, D.D.,

VICAR OF ACOCK'S GREEN,

WHO, IN HIS PARISH AS ELSEWHERE,

HAS ALWAYS

PROVED HIMSELF A "GOOD SAMARITAN."

PREFACE.

THE stern critic from his Rhadamanthine chair has of late been pleased to fulminate against what he stigmatizes as "compilations;" yet I put forward the present volume as avowedly a "compilation" only,—I hope as one which will have some interest and attraction for the general reader. The number of persons who will have the leisure and means to refer to original sources, or, referring to them, will have the tact and skill to use them properly, must always be limited, and if "compilations" are to be prohibited, a very large class of readers will be deprived of all facilities for acquiring knowledge on a vast variety of subjects. The work of the compiler, if humble, is by no means easy; he must be able to analyse and compare, and to place the facts he collects in a lucid order and agreeable form. In truth, he does not so much *compile* as *condense*, and in a single volume is often called upon to present the results obtained from the patient study of half a hundred.

However this may be, I am ready to acknowledge that in the following pages I have been indebted to a considerable number of authorities, from whom I have endeavoured to glean what would best serve my object, and enable me to place before the reader some striking illustrations of Christian chivalry, of heroic effort and enterprise in the fields of religious progress and the charities of civilization. I have brought together a goodly company of educational reformers, of Christian missionaries, of philanthropists, of Good Samaritans; men and women who have dedicated their lives to the great work of making their fellow-creatures better, purer, happier. These are examples which we all may imitate in our different spheres. Studying their noble careers, we may learn to appreciate aright the law of human kindness, and to understand how, if it were universally acted upon, the vast sum of human misery would gradually be reduced; and this will lead us to do, each in his own little circle, what it may be in our power to do, for the ignorant and the afflicted, the strangers who fall among thieves and lie by the wayside, bleeding from their many wounds. O reader, do not pass them by! Do not be deaf to the voice of pain and sorrow! "Shrink from no offices of love, even though they should be painful and perilous," always doing unto others as thou wouldst that others should do unto thee, and, unostentatiously but earnestly, following in the steps of the Good Samaritan.

W. H. D. A.

CONTENTS.

BOOK I.

WORK AND WORKERS IN THE EDUCATIONAL FIELD . . 11

Theories of Education—Importance of Religious Element in Education—Dean Colet—Roger Ascham—Progress of Education in England—Female Education in the 18th Century—Lady Mary Montagu—Dean Swift—Sunday Schools—Robert Raikes—The Monitorial System—Dr. Bell—Joseph Lancaster—National Education—Lord Brougham—Elementary Education Act, 1870—Public School Education—Dr. Arnold—Infant Schools—John Frederick Oberlin—Industrial Schools—Mary Carpenter.

BOOK II.

WORK ON BEHALF OF THE SLAVE 147

Abolition of the Slave Trade—William Wilberforce—Emancipation of the Slave—Sir Thomas Fowell Buxton.

BOOK III.

WORK AND WORKERS IN THE **MISSION FIELD** . . . 191

John Eliot: A Missionary and Leader of Men—David Brainerd—Henry Martyn: Type of the Modern Missionary—John Williams, The "Martyr of Erromanga."

BOOK IV.

PRISON REFORM 273

Condition of our Prisons in the 18th Century — John Howard — Mrs. Elizabeth Fry.

BOOK V.

"THE POOR ARE ALWAYS WITH US" 339

Vincent de Paul: his Labours on behalf of the Poor— English Sisters of Mercy: Miss Sieveking, Mrs. Mompesson — An English Gentleman among the Poor: Edward Denison — Among the Sick: Sister Dora.

BOOK I.

WORK AND WORKERS IN THE EDUCATIONAL FIELD

THEORIES OF EDUCATION.
IMPORTANCE OF THE RELIGIOUS ELEMENT IN EDUCATION.
DEAN COLET.
ROGER ASCHAM.
PROGRESS OF EDUCATION IN ENGLAND.
FEMALE EDUCATION IN THE 18TH CENTURY:—LADY MARY MONTAGU; DEAN SWIFT.
SUNDAY SCHOOLS:—ROBERT RAIKES.
THE MONITORIAL SYSTEM:—DR. BELL; JOSEPH LANCASTER.
NATIONAL EDUCATION:—LORD BROUGHAM.
ELEMENTARY EDUCATION ACT:—1870.
PUBLIC SCHOOL EDUCATION:—DR. ARNOLD.
INFANT SCHOOLS:—JOHN FREDERICK OBERLIN.
INDUSTRIAL SCHOOLS:—MARY CARPENTER.

WORK AND WORKERS IN THE EDUCATIONAL FIELD.

IT is recorded to have been the opinion of Socrates that the duty of man is to learn how to do good and avoid evil, ὅττι τοι ἐν μεγάροισι κακόντ' ἀγαθόντε τέτυκται. In a similar spirit, Dr. Johnson remarks, in his "Life of Milton," that the great aim and end of education is to enable us to live as true men; that is, to live purely, truthfully, and manfully, with our feet in the straight path and our eyes towards the light. We fear, however, that in a very large number of our English schools this end and aim is not kept very constantly in view. Indeed, the common notion of education seems to be realized by the provision of a certain amount of instruction, more or less elementary, in certain branches of knowledge—not including, however, that self-knowledge which the old Greek sage thought of so much importance; and if in our high-class "academies" a separation be made between the "classical" and "commercial" divisions, and young gentlemen are specially prepared for the Civil Service and other examinations; or if in our schools for the poor a master can show that 80 or 90 per cent. of his pupils have passed successfully in "Standard III.," it is assumed that education is really flourishing amongst us, and that we have really got hold of the great secret for making the next generation wiser and better than the present. I think it probable, however, that the compilers of our Church Catechism were nearer the truth when they proposed to teach the young "their duty towards God, and their duty towards their neighbour." The Church bids us learn "to hurt nobody by word or deed, to be true and just in all our dealings, to have neither malice nor hatred in our hearts, to keep our body in temperance, soberness, and chastity;" but the Legislature steps in with the injunction that none of these things shall be taught, and substitutes the latest edition of the Revised Code.

To those who adopt Dr. Arnold's view of education, and hold that it applies equally to mind, and heart, and soul,—that something more is necessary than the mere discipline of the intellect to prepare the young student for playing a noble part in the battle of life, the general tone of public discussion on this subject cannot but be mortifying. The public, and the men who write for the public, seem incapable of rising above the commonplaces of Utilitarianism, and argue as if an acquaintance with reading and writing, and Latin and mathematics, were all that it is necessary for the young mind to gain. In this sense a "good education" means nothing more than just enough learning to pass a competitive examination, or to fit a youth for entering one of the great professions, or, in the humbler walks of life, for a stool in a merchant's counting-house, or a post behind a tradesman's counter. And hence we find the "principals" of our high-class establishments boasting, not that they have educated their pupils in the honour of the Queen and the love of God; not that they have made them good citizens and good Christians; not that they have taught them to love all that is true and just, generous and hospitable, and to despise the false, the mean, and the selfish; but that so many have "passed" at this or that examination, have distinguished themselves at Woolwich or Sandhurst. We do not say that such success is not very desirable and creditable, but that it is by no means a proof or a consummation of a "good education." And, in like manner, we feel that whatever may be said in favour of the Government educational secret of "payment by results," it cannot be pretended that one of these results is to train up a generation of men and women to believe in the Christian faith and to live the Christian life. We hold that in our higher schools as in our lower, the education given is too pretentious, and, therefore, too superficial; that it aims at too much, and therefore, accomplishes too little; that it is worldly in tone and worldly in object; that it dwells too largely upon words, and too little upon things; that it is addressed too exclusively to the intellect, at the expense of the affections and the imagination; and, above all, that it is wholly and completely a failure, when and so far as it is not based upon religion, or inspired with a religious spirit.

The reader will not be displeased, perhaps, if I pause to examine very briefly Milton's loftier and more generous idea of education as it is developed in his celebrated "Letter to Mr. Hartlib," and to see whether the great Puritan poet and thinker can help us to any useful general principles. He describes it as a "voluntary idea of a better education, in extent and comprehension far more large, and yet of time far shorter, and of attainment far more certain, than hath been yet in practice." Such an idea is surely worth considering at a time when education, so called, is more expensive than ever it was, and yet, by common consent, is also more inefficient; when our scholarship is daily growing more imperfect, and a system of "cramming" is rapidly taking the place of careful intellectual and moral training; when all that comes of greater educational facilities and revised codes is an increase of materialistic belief, a constant disregard of the rules and canons of political economy, and a lamentable indifference to Christian doctrine; when all that comes, among the higher classes, of a vast machinery of collegiate institutions, academies, special classes, courses of lectures, and the like, is a superficial acquaintance with many studies and a competent knowledge of none; musicians who cannot play, and artists who cannot draw; linguists who are ignorant of their own language, and can read and write no other; a taste for the meretricious in art, the chimerical in science, and the sensational in literature; a constant yearning after luxury and pleasure, and a cowardly shrinking from self-denial and pain; in short, an abandonment of the old paths trodden by the feet of the great and good, for new ways that lead only into cloudland and confusion. This, of course, is speaking generally; but that the indictment is, on the whole, a true one, must be admitted by all who consider the present pursuits of our young patricians, or the condition of the modern stage, or the popularity of an unwholesome and unclean literature, or the amusements of fashionable society, or, in fact, any of the straws on the surface, which show the direction of the great currents of thought and feeling among us.

The principle which formed the corner-stone of Milton's educational system was thoroughness. He was no advocate of the art of beating out a thin leaf of gold to cover with deceptive tissue the greatest possible amount of insincerity and unreality. And, therefore, in teaching languages, he would have the teacher go at once to the best books in those languages, and use them as his manuals, instead of wasting years upon Delectuses and Graduses and Thesauruses. He strongly protests against the ambitious folly of "forcing the empty wits of children to compose themes, verses, and orations, which are the acts of ripest judgment, and the final work of a head filled, by long reading and observing, with elegant maxims and copious invention." What would Milton have said if he had seen boys of twelve years old required to furnish an analysis of Shakespeare's *Macbeth?* Nothing more strongly moves his indignation, nothing does he more severely censure, than the pretentiousness which plunges the young into the study of complex sciences in order that the "curriculum" may look imposing in the "prospectus." "Latin, Greek, French, Natural Philosophy, Chemistry, Logic"—when we see this goodly enumeration figuring on a sheet of elegantly printed, hot-pressed "post," we cannot but commiserate the unfortunate tyro who has been crammed to the throat with so indigestible a mixture, and with the poet we wonder,

"How one small head could carry all he knew!"

In a strain of lofty eloquence Milton compassionates the novices who having but newly left the "grammatic flats and shallows," where they stuck unreasonably to learn a few words "with lamentable construction," are suddenly transported under another climate, "to be tossed and turmoiled with their unballasted wits in fathomless and unquiet deeps of controversy." The result is, that they for the most part grow into hatred and contempt of learning, until they are called upon to choose their future career. Then, some by the influence of friends, take to "an ambitious and mercenary, or ignorantly zealous, divinity." Some are allured to the trade of law, "grounding" their purposes not on the prudent and heavenly contemplation of justice and equity, which was never taught them, but on the promising and pleasing thoughts of "litigious terms, fat contentions, and flowing fees." Others betake themselves to State affairs; while others, "knowing no better," abandon themselves to "the enjoyments of ease and luxury, living out their days in inglorious idleness."

What Milton insists upon is, that things should be taught,

rather than words; that a sound foundation should be laid before any attempt is made to rear the superstructure, and that both teacher and taught should address themselves to their task in a spirit of conscientious earnestness. He aims at education rather than instruction; and we may infer the scope of his plan from the fact that he purposes to allow about twenty tutors to one hundred and thirty scholars. Though our readers may feel that such a proportion is impracticable in our modern schools, they cannot but own that the class-system so popular now-a-days is fatal to effective and thorough culture. It may be worked successfully by an Arnold, by men with a keen insight into the human heart, and a quick appreciation of differences of character; but in ordinary hands it must always be a failure. To allot thirty or forty pupils to a single teacher is to ensure the application to all of a method of teaching which will be adapted only to two or three. Hence, as a consequence, the two or three will push ahead, carry off prizes, figure at examinations, and maintain "the reputation of the school," while the great majority linger in the rear, hopeless or indifferent, the despair of their teachers, and a burden to themselves. It may be granted that the class-system is useful to a certain extent, and that it enables a given amount of information to be imparted to the maximum of number in the minimum of time; but it effectually prevents the schoolmaster from acquiring a knowledge of the idiosyncrasies of his pupils— from making himself familiar with, and adapting his method to, their individual peculiarities. All are placed on the same Procrustean bed, which is too short for some, and for many too long. The teacher works in a permanent groove—after a prescribed pattern; and the influence of such teaching is injurious not only to the pupil, but to the teacher himself, who gradually loses his early enthusiasm and earnestness, and finds his labour growing daily more irksome as it grows more mechanical. If it be enough that a boy, on leaving school, shall be able to read and write, to express himself in tolerable English, and to have some knowledge, grammatical rather than critical, of Homer and Virgil, with a smattering of French and a vague idea of geography and history, the class-system may be considered successful; but it will never, can never give the education dreamed of by Bacon, Milton, or Arnold; the education that combines full and accurate information with careful mental and moral discipline; the education that if it do not make every man a scholar, will, at all events, direct him towards a just and lofty ideal of life.

How high a standard Milton had conceived we learn from his noble counsel to the teacher to use "all books, whatsoever they be," which may serve to stir up his pupils "with high hopes of living to be brave men and worthy patriots, dear to God and famous to all ages." How seldom, nowadays, we have language like to this! Masters there are, no doubt, whose hearts respond to its elevated meaning; who act upon it and by it and in its spirit; but will any one pretend that the leading principle in English education is to make "brave"—that is, true and Christian —"men and patriots"? Who will assert that even the majority of English parents regard the bringing up of their children from this high point of view? The best proof of the low tone of our educational system is to be found in the low tone of our social, and we cannot raise the latter until we have raised the former.

Contrary to the opinion of the educational philosophers of the present day, who have discovered a panacea for all human ills in what they euphemistically term "secular education," who appear to believe that when every child in Great Britain is taught to read and write and "cipher," a millennium will break upon a happy and favoured nation, Milton anxiously provides that his scholars shall be instructed in religion. The entire scope of their teaching must be religious; their duty towards God and towards their neighbour must be kept always before their eyes; their teacher must make a constant effort to fill their minds with high and holy thoughts, and to put before them the examples of men who have lived high and holy lives. We cannot doubt but that Milton himself, in his brief experience as a schoolmaster, never began his daily task without prayer to that "Eternal Spirit who can enrich with all utterance and knowledge, and who sends out His Seraphim, with the hallowed fire of His altar, to touch and purify the lips of whom He pleases." Puritan as Milton was, he would have shrunk from that strange modern Puritanism, which, in its professed dread of denominational schools, would eliminate the religious element from our national education, and make it a breach of the law to begin, with the hallowing influences of prayer and praise, the daily task of instructing the youthful mind, or to supplement the lessons of history by the precepts and monitions of the Bible. He would have protested against the new ideal of a liberal education, which banishes the Gospel of the Cross into the background, and subordinates "Faith, Hope, and Charity," the Apostolic triad, to the great commercial triad of £ s. d.

In truth, we can judge of the importance which Milton attached to the religious element in education from the provision he makes in his ideal system, that "after evening repast, till bed-time, the thoughts of the scholar" shall be devoted to "the easy grounds of religion, and the story of Scripture." But then Milton's object was one which apparently does not commend itself to the majority of teachers nowadays. He was not so solicitous about instruction as he was about discipline; he looked to culture rather than to information. Instead of aiming at a reputation for "passing" candidates in examinations, he laboured that the young might learn "to despise and scorn all their childish and ill-taught qualities, and to delight in manly and liberal exercises;" he desired to infuse "into their young breasts an ingenious and noble ardour." And we are persuaded that if we adopted Milton's principles; if we held it to be the aim and purpose of all true education to strengthen and purify the soul as well as to improve the mind,—to foster a love of truth and justice,—to inculcate the duty of living a Christian life,—to set before young eyes the example of the heroic dead, and to encourage them in imitating it,— then, "these ways would try all their peculiar gifts of nature, and if there were any secret excellence among them, would fetch it out, and give it fair opportunities to advance itself by, which could not but mightily redound to the good of this nation, and bring into fashion again those old admired virtues and excellences, with far more advantage now in this purity of Christian knowledge." No doubt, an education set in this high key is given in some of our public and in not a few of our private schools; but that it is exceptional will be admitted by all who have had their attention closely directed to the subject.

And the reason why it should be so is not far to seek. A complete education means a religious education; and a religious education is the bugbear of the modern philosophical school. But a religious education means something more than the present class-reading of a portion of the Bible every day—a mode of teaching which, as often practised, is positively harmful, tending to place the Bible in the category of ordinary school-books, and depreciating it to their level in the pupil's estimation; something more than an occasional lesson in the catechism, or the dull stereotyped repetition of hymns and collects; it means that every branch of knowledge shall be taken up and pursued in a religious spirit; that all the appliances of intellectual cultivation shall be wielded with a determination to make them useful, also, for the purposes of moral discipline. We do not want our schoolmasters to teach theology. But they can teach the lessons suggested by the life of Christ; they can teach the lessons written in legible characters on the page of history; they can teach the truths that are embodied in the career of every good and great man; they can teach the wisdom that is manifest in the flowers of earth and the stars of heaven. This teaching involves the use of the Bible, but does not meddle with dogmatic theology. It is, however, in the broadest sense, a religious education, designed to operate upon the moral nature, and to supply a constant motive and stimulus to holy living. And the teacher who approaches his solemn task in a right spirit will soon discover that every department of study supplies material for building up the superstructure of such an education. Do not the annals of great nations furnish abundant opportunities for illustrating and enforcing the providential government of the universe? Does not geography, with its laws of climatic zones and the distribution of animal and vegetable life,—or geology, with its marvellous records of the past, its testimony of the rocks, and its "medals of creation," bring into light the wisdom and power, no less than the benevolence, of the Supreme God? And was not the poet right when he exclaimed—

"An undevout astronomer is mad"?

For, from astronomy, cannot the teacher deduce the existence and attributes of Him in Whom we live and move and have our being?

We admit that it is not the province or the duty of the schoolmaster to teach theology. That is, *sectarian* theology,—the differences of construction and interpretation which have rent, and still rend, the Church of Christ. But, on the other hand, there is a theology which every wise-minded teacher will lose no opportunity

of impressing upon the minds and hearts of his pupils. The
creation of Man in the likeness of his Heavenly Father; the
supernatural gift of His spiritual presence in our souls; the loss of
that precious gift through pride and self-consciousness and
disobedience; the wonderful scheme of love and mercy which
wrought out our redemption; the assumption by God the Son
of the "vesture of the flesh"; the glorious sinless Life which
in its exquisite beauty has extorted the admiration even of
His enemies; the sacrifice of the cross; the mystery of the
atonement; Christ's personal intercession for the sinner; the
tender watchfulness of the Holy Ghost over the Church; the
promise of the salvation and restoration of fallen humanity; the
light which is thus thrown on the future of man, and the assistance
which is thus given to each of us in working for the welfare of our
race; the certainty of a future judgment, and of an eternity in
which the counsels of the Almighty will be revealed and fulfilled;
these are the leading points of a theology accepted more or less
fully by all Christian believers, and of a theology that should
underlie every educational system.

Only in the radiance of such a theology can the "dark places"
of history and the "oppositions of science" and the apparent
mysteries of life be made clear. Only by means of such a
theology can we hope to make the young mind understand all
that is grand and beautiful in the government of the world and
the phenomena of nature.

The dervish, in the fanciful Eastern tale, on rubbing his eyes
with a precious ointment, given to him by the genii, sees shining
diamonds and glowing rubies, emeralds, topazes, and carcanets,
where, before, he had seen nothing but bare rock and sterile earth.
He treads no longer on unfruitful soil, but a pavement set with
precious stones. In like manner the religious element in education transforms for us into beauty that which before seemed
commonplace, and into lucidity that which before was obscure.
It is an expansive, and, at the same time, an elevating force. In
the hands and heart of an able, conscientious teacher, it invests
everything with a new importance, a fresh interest; it clothes all
life, all history, all nature in a pure and healthy atmosphere, just
as the sun by its rising beams converts a sombre landscape into
a scene of freshness and of luminous splendour, steeping hill and

valley and plain in golden light. The starting-point of the teacher in every class, and in every school, and whoever may be his pupils, should be that one pregnant saying of our Lord's: "Blessed are they that hear the word of God, and keep it,"—the word of God as set forth by prophets, evangelists, and apostles; as illustrated by the changes of human history and the aspects of human life; as glorified by the works of human genius in art and science and literature. It is in this way that religion constitutes the axis or pivot on which every well-balanced educational system naturally revolves.

The education of a nation is unquestionably a subject to which the attention of its rulers and statesmen should be directed. Prior to the Reformation, it was left in England almost entirely to the Church, and every large monastery had its schools which provided some kind of instruction for the children of the poorer classes. After the Reformation, it was taken up by the Government, and in the reigns of Edward VI. and Elizabeth a considerable number of Grammar Schools were established and endowed, in which was taught a curriculum as comprehensive as the wants of the time required. They derived their origin from the impulse given by Dean Colet, the first, and not the least able, of the educational reformers of England, who, in 1510, expended his private estate in the foundation of St. Paul's Grammar School. Colet's ideal of education was a religious education, and over the master's chair in his new school he caused to be set up an image of the Child Jesus, with the words "Hear ye Him" inscribed beneath it. He superseded the old and effete methods of instruction by fresh grammars specially composed by Erasmus and other scholars; and at its head placed William Lilly, an Oxford student, who had studied Greek in the east. The scholastic logic which had so long cramped and confined the wits of men found no favour in the eyes of the reformer, who aimed at combining rational religion with sound learning. His example was happily followed by many imitators, and a system of middle-class education was organised, which, by the end of the 16th century, "had changed the very face of England."

A letter addressed to Thomas Cromwell, afterwards Earl of Essex, by his son's tutor, furnishes an interesting account of the course of education adopted by the more liberal and enlightened teachers:—" After that it pleased your mastership," he says, "to give me in charge, not only to give diligent attendance upon Master Gregory, but also to instruct him with good letters, honest manners, pastyme of instruments, and such other qualities as should be for him meet and convenient, pleaseth it you to understand that for the accomplishment thereof I have endeavoured myself by all ways possible to excogitate how I might most profit him. In which behalf, through his diligence, the success is such as I trust shall be to your good contentation and pleasure, and to his no small profit. But for cause the summer was spent in the service of the wild gods (*i.e.*, the sylvan gods, or gods of the field and wood and river), and it is so much to be regarded after what fashion youth is brought up, in which time that that is learned for the most part will not be wholly forgotten in the older years, I think it my duty to ascertain your mastership how he spendeth his time. And first, after he hath heard mass, he taketh a lecture of a dialogue of Erasmus' colloquies, called *Pietas Puerilis*, wherein is described a very picture of one that should be virtuously brought up; and for cause it is so necessary for him, I do not only cause him to read it over, but also to practise the precepts of the same. After this he exerciseth his hand in writing one or two hours, and readeth upon Fabyan's *Chronicle* as long. The residue of the day he doth spend upon the lute and virginals. When he rideth, as he doth very oft, I tell him by the way some history of the Romans or the Greeks, which I cause him to rehearse again in a tale. For his recreation he useth to hawk and hunt and shoot in his long bow, which frameth and succeedeth so well with him that he seemeth to be thereunto given by nature."

In a subsequent letter the tutor speaks of his pupil as learning French, eytmology, casting of accounts, playing at weapons, and other similar exercises.

John Colet was the eldest son of Sir Henry Colet, twice Lord Mayor of London, and was born in 1466. After completing his education at Magdalen College, Oxford, he travelled in France and Italy, forming the acquaintance of Erasmus, Budæus, and other illustrious scholars, gaining a knowledge of the Greek language and literature, and feeling the full influence of the revival of learning. But the strength and sobriety of his mind prevented him from being tainted by the Platonic mysticism or neo-paganism of which the group of scholars round Lorenzo di Medici made profession. Their literary enthusiasm was equally unable to disturb his religious convictions. He studied Greek, not because it was the language of Homer and Thucydides, but because it was the key to the oracles of God as revealed in the New Testament. The mission which he had undertaken was speedily made clear when, in 1498, he took up his residence at Oxford and began to lecture upon St. Paul's Epistles. In these bold and luminous discourses, marked by a breadth of view which gave its tone to Anglican theology, he set aside the trivialities of scholasticism, and brought his hearers face to face with the Apostle's "living mind." To a priest who sought from him some direction in his studies, he said: "Open your book, and we will see how many and what golden truths we can gather from the first chapter only of the Epistle to the Romans." It has been well said that it was more after the manner of the 19th than the 16th century that he loved to indicate the personal features in St. Paul's writings: his "vehemence of speaking," which left him no time to perfect his sentences; the skill and prudence with which he adapted his words to the necessities of the different classes he addressed; his "modesty," "toleration," self-denial, and courtesy; and the force and directness with which many of his sayings applied to the circumstances of the times. Colet was prompt to recognise the principle of "accommodation" in Scripture, as in the Mosaic narrative of the creation and the Pauline theory of marriage. In his doctrinal conclusions he shook himself free from Augustinianism; and while dwelling strongly on the necessity of Divine grace, avoided the extreme tenet of the bondage of the will. The simple facts of the Apostles' Creed became to him the *summa Christianæ theologiæ*. To the young theological students who came to him in despair, tempted to abandon theological study altogether, because it involved so many vexed questions, and afraid lest they should be pronounced unorthodox, he was wont to say:—" Keep firmly to the Bible and the Apostles' Creed, and let divines, if they like, dispute about the rest." His faith, as Mr. Green remarks, "stood simply on a vivid realization of the person of Christ." And in the importance which was thus given to the moral life, in his free criticism of the elder Scriptures, in his evident partiality for simple and intelligible formularies, Colet "struck the key-note of a mode of religious thought as strongly in contrast with that of the later Reformation as with that of Catholicism itself."

Of the spirit in which he regarded the coarser aspects of the Roman religion his behaviour at a later time before St. Thomas à Becket's great Canterbury shrine enables us to judge. It was the Puritanic spirit, stern and uncompromising. Its glow of precious stones, its exquisitely wrought sculptures, its elaborate metal work, drew from Colet the bitter sarcasm that a saint so lavish to the poor in his lifetime would assuredly wish them to possess the wealth accumulated round him since his death.* In like manner he refused to kiss the saint's shoe, angrily exclaiming: "What, do these idiots want us to kiss the shoes of every good man?" And some rags, which were preserved as relics, he touched with the tips of his fingers in great disgust, and contemptuously put them down, "making, at the same time, a sort of whistle."

Austere was the new teacher's life, frugal his table, simple his attire. His character was distinguished by its integrity, his conversation by its vivacity, his manners by a frank cordiality which more than made amends for the quickness of his temper. His friends and pupils loved while they reverenced him. As for his lectures at Oxford, they drew multitudes of eager listeners. He had not taken any degree in theology; yet was there no doctor of the law or divinity, no abbot or dignitary, who did not hasten to hear him. For the first time his auditors found themselves taught to see in the Gospels a living record of the teaching of their adorable Redeemer. He told them with courageous plainness, that he had not discovered in Scripture a number of absurd propositions to which he could yield his

---

* Erasmus, who accompanied Colet on his visit to Canterbury (see his *Peregrinatio religionis ergo*), represents him as saying to the attendant priest : " When the saint was so liberal to the poor while he was poor himself, and had need of money for the supply of his bodily wants, can you suppose that he would be displeased now, when he is rich and has need of nothing, if a poor widow who has starving children at home, or daughters whose virtue is in danger from the want of a dowry, or a husband lying on the bed of sickness and destitute of the means of support, having first asked his permission, should take a mere trifle from this vast wealth . . . either as a free gift, or a loan to be repaid?" . . He added :—"I am sure that the saint would be glad if, now that he is dead, he relieved by his wealth the wants of the poor."

assent only under compulsion; but a Person whom he could take as "his leader on the heavenly road," whom he could love with a love far stronger than that given to the best beloved of human beings, and to whom he could devote himself in mind, body, and spirit.

That religious and intellectual revival which we call the reformation, Colet, as Dean of St. Paul's, indirectly but largely assisted, though he did not openly separate from the Church of Rome. In 1512, he was appointed by Archbishop Warham to preach to the Convocation of the Clergy, and his sermon was remarkable for its outspokenness. "Would that for once," cried the vehement preacher, "you would remember your name and profession, and take thought for the (reformation) of the Church! Never was it more necessary, and never did the state of the Church call for more vigorous effort. . . . We are troubled with heretics; but their heresy is far less fatal to us and to the people at large, than the vicious and depraved lives of the clergy. That is the worst heresy of all!" First of all was needed, he said, a reform of the bishops; then must come that of the clergy, leading to a revival of religion among the people generally. The accumulation of benefices must be abandoned; the priesthood must cast off its worldliness and luxury; its low standard of morality must be raised; only worthy persons ordained and promoted. Such teaching as this exposed Colet to a charge of heresy; but Warham protected him, and King Henry encouraged him to go on. "Let every man have his own doctor," said Henry, after a long interview with him; "but this man is the doctor for me!" He appointed him as chaplain and preacher-in-ordinary, and continued his favour to him until his death, in 1519, in the fifty-third year of his age.

Colet was the author of "Rudimenta Grammaticus," "Epistola ad Erasmuson," and of a collection of Devotional Pieces, written for the use of St. Paul's School. The last named included the "Institutes of a Christian Man;" which Erasmus pleased himself by turning into Latin verse, as a proof of his regard for "a man, than whom, in my opinion," says the Dutch scholar, "the realm of England has not another more pious, or who more truly knows Christ." Great was the grief of Erasmus at the death of his friend. "O true theologian!" he writes; "O wonderful preacher of evangelical doctrine! with what earnest zeal did he drink in the philosophy of Christ! How eagerly did he imbibe the spirit and feelings of St. Paul! How did the purity of his whole life correspond to his heavenly doctrine!" And to Bishop Fisher he writes: "I know it is all right with him who, escaped from this evil and wretched world, is in present enjoyment of that Christ whom he so loved when alive. I cannot help mourning in the public name the loss of so rare an example of Christian piety, so remarkable a preacher of the Christian truth."

Of the evening of this good man's life, Mr. Seebohm has collected some interesting particulars. In 1518, England suffered terribly from the ravages of the sweating sickness, which struck down its victims with terrible rapidity. It was usually fatal on the first day. "If the patient survived twenty-four hours he was looked upon as out of danger. But it was liable to recur, and sometimes attacked the same person four times in succession. This was the case with Cardinal Wolsey: whilst several of the royal retinue were attacked and carried off at once, Wolsey's strong constitution carried him through four successive attacks." Colet was three times its victim; he survived, but the injury to his constitution was so great that he began to prepare for his approaching end. Part of his work was to revise and complete the rules and statutes for the government of his school of St. Paul's; in this he showed his devotion and purity of motive. He made no effort to impress his own particular views on its constitution, though, as its founder, he was free to do so; but anxiously left it open for adaptation in future generations, to the changing necessities of the time. He entrusted its charge, we may remark, "to the most honest and faithful fellowship of the Mercers of London;" not of a bishop, or chapter, or ecclesiastical dignitaries, but of "married citizens of established reputation." In defining the duties and salaries of the masters, he provided expressly that they too might be married men: but they were to hold their office "in no room of continuance and perpetuity, but upon their duty in the school." He wisely gave power to the Mercers to amend and alter the statutes as from time to time might prove expedient, knowing that finality cannot be predicated of any human institution.

The statutes of his school completed, he introduced certain

reforms into St. Paul's Church, and made ready a simple tomb for the reception of his remains at the side of the great cathedral choir, inscribing upon it no other legend than the words, "Johannes Coletus."

Next among our educational reformers we may name **Roger Ascham**, the author of "The Schoolmaster," the first treatise on education written in the English language.

Roger Ascham was born about 1515, at Kirkby **Wiske, near** Northallerton, in Yorkshire. He was the third son of **John** Ascham, house steward in the family of Lord Scrope, by his **wife** Margaret, who **came of an** ancient stock. It is recorded of **his** parents that, **after a** happy married life of forty-seven years, they **died on the same** day, and nearly at the same hour. Young **Roger was** early taken into the family of Sir Anthony Wingfield, **and educated** together with his sons. "This worshipful man," said Ascham afterwards, "hath ever loved and used to love **many** children brought up in learning in his house, amongst whom I myself was one, for whom at these times he would bring down from London both bow **and** shafts. **And when** they should play he would go with them **himself** into the field, see them shoot, and he that shot fairest should have the best bow and shafts, and he that shot ill-favouredly should be mocked of **his** fellows till he shot better. Would to God all England had used or would **use to** lay the foundation of youth after the example of this **worshipful** man in bringing up children in the Book and **the** bow; **by which** two things the whole commonwealth, both in peace **and war, is** chiefly valid and defended withal." Sir Anthony taught them **archery in** obedience to **the** law, which **then** required all boys **between seven** and seventeen **to** be equipped with a long bow and two arrows.

In 1530, **still at Sir** Anthony's expense, Ascham was sent to **St. John's** College, Cambridge, and placed **in** charge of Mr. **Hugh** Fitzherbert. In February 1534 he took his degree of B.A., **and in March** was elected a Fellow; in 1537, **he** became a college lecturer in Greek. The new learning and the new religion were **at this** time working their way into Cambridge, as they had done **a** quarter of a century before into Oxford, and to both Roger Ascham proclaimed his adhesion. As a writer of Latin and a teacher of Greek, **he** quickly obtained distinction; and **on the** resignation of Sir John Cheke, who was appointed tutor to Prince Edward,* Ascham was made Public Orator of the University. In this capacity he wrote his letters of compliment and formal communications. These were not less admired for their penmanship than their elegance of composition; and he acquired so much renown as a caligraphist that he was appointed writing-master, as we should say, to Prince Edward, the Princess Elizabeth, and the two sons of the courtly and chivalrous Brandon, Duke of Suffolk. Eventually, on the death of Grindal, he was promoted to take charge of the Princess Elizabeth's education.

In 1544 Ascham produced his "Toxophilus the Schoolmaster, or Partitions of Shooting," in two books; dedicating it to Henry VIII., who was then on the point of invading France He was allowed, in the following year, to present it to the king, who rewarded him with a pension of ten pounds per annum. It is the work of a man, not only thoroughly conversant with his subject, but an enthusiast about it; and is well worthy of the palmy times of England's national weapon. Philologus and Toxophilus, the *dramatis personæ*, converse through two books on the advantages and pleasures of archery, and on the art of shooting with the long-bow, an art in which Ascham would have men to excel, because in peace it triumphs over effeminate and ignoble recreations, and in war increases largely a nation's strength.

The book is valuable and interesting as a monument of our early English literature. It is written in English, says its author, because he desired to see it in the hands of the gentlemen and yeomen of England; and he proceeds to put forward a plea for the use of English by English writers. "He that will write well in any tongue," he says, "must follow this counsel of Aristotle, to speak as the common people do, to think as wise men do; and so should every man understand him, and the judgment of wise men allow him. Many English writers have not done so, but using strange words, as Latin, French, and Italian, do make all things dark and hard. Once I communed with a man which reasoned the English tongue to be enriched and increased

---

* This is Milton's "Sir John Cheke" (Sonnet XI.), who taught "Cambridge, and King Edward, Greek."

thereby, saying: 'Who will not praise that feast where a man shall drink at a dinner both wine, ale, and beer?' 'Truly,' quoth I, 'they be all good, every one taken by himself alone; but if you put malmsey and sack, red wine and white, ale and beer, and all in one pot, you shall make a drink neither easy to be known, nor yet wholesome for the body.'"

"Toxophilus" is written with an evident love and mastery of the subject: its drier details are relieved by philosophical digressions, one of which, dealing with the value of recreation and its place in the educational system, is very interesting.

In 1548 Ascham was appointed tutor to the Princess Elizabeth at Cheston; but, quarrelling with her steward, he gave up the post, and returned to his college home. In 1550, through the intervention of Sir John Cheke, he accompanied Sir Richard Morissine, or Morison, ambassador at the Court of Charles V., as secretary. He spent some time at Augsburg, using his faculties of observation and insight to good effect,—the result being, in 1553, the publication of a "Report and Discourse of the Affairs and State of Germany and the Emperor Charles his Court, during certain years while Roger Ascham was there."

During his absence in Germany, Ascham's friends procured his appointment as Latin Secretary to Edward VI. On the death of the young king, fearing for the loss of his pension as well as his office, he at once returned to England; but, though his attachment to the reformed religion was known, he secured the favour and esteem of Queen Mary's advisers, retained his pension, and was employed to write official letters and despatches. His influence seems to have been considerable, and to have been exercised in defence of the interests of learning and religion; for it was said by his contemporaries that he hindered those who dined on the Church from supping on the Universities. On the occasion of Mary's unfortunate marriage to Philip of Spain, he wrote within three days as many as forty-seven letters to foreign princes, of whom the lowest in rank was a Cardinal.

In 1554 Ascham married Mistress Margaret Hour, a lady who brought him some fortune, came of a good family, and appears to have possessed some intellectual gifts. On the accession of Elizabeth he was made Latin Secretary, and also reader in the learned languages,—a post which brought him much about the

Queen's person. He was liberally rewarded for his services; and, in 1559, received the prebend of Westwang, in the cathedral of York. The Archbishop had previously conferred it on a nominee of his own; so that Ascham did not get the revenue without the vexation of a lawsuit.

The book to which he chiefly owes his reputation, "The Schoolmaster," was written in 1563,—the year of the plague, when Elizabeth had taken refuge at Windsor. At his apartments in the castle, Sir William Cecil had invited a number of "ingenious men" to dine with him, and among them was Roger Ascham. Cecil communicated to his guests the news of the morning, that several Eton lads had run away on account of their master's severity; which the great minister condemned as a grievous error in the education of youth. Sir William Petre, a man of harsh temper, advocated the contrary view, and was all in favour of the rod and the "whipping-block." Dr. Walter agreed with the minister, and Sir John Mason jested at both. Mr. Haddon supported Petre, and asserted that the then best schoolmaster in England was the hardest flogger. Ascham, intervening, warmly protested that if such a schoolmaster turned out an able scholar, the credit was due not to his birch, but to the boy's genius. When Ascham was retiring after dinner to read to the Queen one of the orations of Demosthenes, Sir Richard Sackville* took him aside, and told him that though he had been silent during the discussion, yet would he on no account have missed it; that he knew only too well the truth of what Ascham had maintained; for it was the perpetual flogging of a tyrannical pedagogue which had given him an unconquerable aversion to study. As he was anxious to prevent this defect in his own grandchildren, he besought Ascham to "put in some order of writing the chief points of their talk, concerning the right order of teaching and honesty of living, for the good bringing up of children and of young men." Ascham represents him as saying: "Seeing it is but in vain to lament things past, and also wisdom to look to things to come, surely, God willing, if God lend me life, I will make this, my mishap, some occasion of good hap to little

---

* Father of Thomas Sackville, one of the authors of "Gorboduc" (1561), our first English tragedy.

Robert Sackville, my son's son. For whose bringing up, I would gladly, if it so please you, use specially your good advice. I hear say you have a son much of his age; we will deal thus together. Point you out a schoolmaster who by your order shall teach my son and yours, and for all the rest I will provide you, though they then do cost me a couple of hundred pounds by year, and besides you shall find me as fast a friend to you and yours as perchance any you have." "Which promise," adds Ascham, "the worthy gentleman surely kept with me until his dying day."

The "Schoolmaster" was not published, however, until after its author's death. Always afflicted with delicate health, Ascham suffered much during the last years of his life from the scholar's disease—dyspepsia. Between dinner and bedtime he was unable to pursue his studies; the curse of sleeplessness fell upon him; and, prematurely worn out, he died on the 30th of December, 1568, at the comparatively early age of fifty-three. It is said that his closing years were also obscured by poverty, and slanderers have ascribed the poverty to his love of gaming and cock-fighting. As regards the former, the calumny is wholly without foundation; and with respect to the latter we must remember that, in Elizabeth's time, it was a popular sport. Fuller quaintly sums up the scholar's character in the following terse phrases: "He was an honest man and a good shooter. Archery was his pastime in youth, which, in his old age, he exchanged for cock-fighting. His 'Toxophilus' is a good book for *young* men, his 'Schoolmaster' for *old*, his 'Epistles' for *all* men."

"The Schoolmaster" was published by Ascham's widow, in 1570, with a dedication to Sir William Cecil, in which she solicits him to undertake its defence, "to avaunce the good that may come of it by your allowance and furtherance to publike use and benefite, and to accept the thankefell recognition of me and my poor children, trustyng of the continuance of your good memorie of Master Ascham and his, and dayly commendyng the prosperous estate of you and yours to God, whom you serve, and whose you are, I rest to trouble you."

In Dr. Johnson's opinion, the method of instruction elaborated in this treatise is perhaps the best ever laid down for the study of languages. Certain it is that Ascham's general principles, as enunciated in the first book, are sound and sagacious, and should be carefully considered by every person engaged in educational work. He particularises certain qualities, or, as he calls them, "plain notes," which will indicate "a good wit in a child for learning,"—borrowing them from Socrates. 1, Euphues; 2, good memory; 3, attachment to learning; 4, readiness to undergo pains and labour; 5, willingness to learn of another; 6, freedom in questioning; and 7, delight in well-earned applause. As the first of these qualities may not be readily understood by every reader, we transcribe Ascham's description, with the remark that the character embodying it obviously suggested John Lyly's celebrated "Euphues."

According to Ascham:—"Euphues (Εὐφυὴς) is he that is apt by goodness of wit, and appliable by readiness of will, to learning, having all other qualities of the mind and parts of the body that must another day serve learning, not troubled, mangled, and halved, but sound, whole, full, and able to do their office: as a tongue not stammering, or over hardly drawing forth words, but plain and ready to deliver the meaning of the mind; a voice not soft, weak, piping, womanish, but audible, strong, and manlike; a countenance not wirish and crabbed, but fair and comely; a personage not wretched and deformed, but tall and goodly: for surely a comely countenance, with a goodly stature, giveth credit to learning and authority to the person; otherwise, commonly, either open contempt or privy disfavour doth hurt or hinder both person and learning. And even as a fair stone requireth to be set in the finest gold, with the best workmanship, or else it loseth much of the grace and price, even so excellency in learning, and namely divinity, joined with a comely personage, is a marvellous jewel in the world. And how can a comely body be better employed than to serve the greatest exercise of God's greatest gift?—and that is learning. But commonly the fairest bodies are bestowed on the foulest purposes."

As a specimen of Ascham's style we extract from "The Schoolmaster" his well-known description of his interview with Lady Jane Grey, prior to his German mission:—

"Before I went into Germany," he says, "I came to Broadgate, in Leicestershire, to take my leave of that noble lady Jane Grey, to whom I was exceedingly much beholden. Her parents, the duke and the duchess" [of Northumberland], "with all the household, gentlemen and gentlewomen, were hunting in the park. I found her in her chamber reading *Phædon Platonis* in Greek, and that with as much delight as some gentlemen would read a merry tale in Boccace. After salutation and duty done, with some other talk, I asked her why she would lose such pastime in the park. Smiling, she answered me: 'I wis, all their sport in the park is but a shadow to that pleasure that I find in Plato. Alas! good folk, they never felt what true pleasure meant.'

"'And how came you, madam,' quoth I, 'to this deep knowledge of pleasure? And what did chiefly allure you into it, seeing not many women, but very few men, have attained thereunto?' 'I will tell you,' quoth she, 'and tell you a truth which, perchance, ye will marvel at. One of the greatest benefits that ever God gave me, is, that He sent me so sharp and severe parents, and so gentle a schoolmaster. For when I am in presence either of father or mother, whether I speak, keep silence, sit, stand, or go, eat, drink, be merry or sad, be sewing, playing, dancing, or doing anything else, I must do it, as it were, in such weight, measure, and number, even so perfectly as God made the world, or else I am so sharply taunted, so cruelly threatened, yea, presently, sometimes with pinches, nips, and bobs, and other ways, which I will not name for the honour I bear them, so without measure misordered, that I think myself in hell, till time come that I must go to Mr. Elmer (John Aylmer, afterwards Bishop of London); who teacheth me so gently, so pleasantly, with such fair allurements to learning, that I think all the time nothing, whiles I am with him. And when I am called from him, I fall on weeping, because, whatever I do else, but learning, is full of grief, trouble, fear, and whole misliking unto me. And thus my book hath been so much my pleasure, and bringeth daily to me more pleasure and more, that in respect of it, all other pleasures, in very deed, be but trifles and troubles unto me.'"

Ascham's comments on the advisability of consulting the natural bias and tendencies of a youth in selecting for him his life's vocation are eminently judicious:—

"This perverse judgment of fathers, as concerning the fitness and unfitness of their children, causeth the commonwealth [to] have many unfit ministers: and seeing that ministers be, as a man would say, instruments wherewith the commonwealth doth work all her matters withal, I marvel how it chanceth that a poor shoemaker hath so much wit, that he will prepare no instrument for his science, neither knife nor awl, nor nothing else, which is not very fit for him. The commonwealth can be content to take at a fond father's hand the riffraff of the world, to make those instruments of wherewithal she should work the highest matters under heaven. And surely an awl of lead is not so unprofitable in a shoemaker's shop, as an unfit minister made of gross metal is unseemly in the commonwealth. Fathers in old time, among the noble Persians, might not do with their children as they thought good, but as the judgment of the commonwealth always thought best. This fault of fathers bringeth many a blot with it, to the great deformity of the commonwealth: and here, surely, I can praise gentlewomen, which have always at hand their glasses to see if anything be amiss, and so will amend it; yet the commonwealth, having the glass of knowledge in every man's hand, doth see such uncomeliness in it, and yet winketh at it. This fault, and many such like, might be soon wiped away, if fathers would bestow their children always on that thing whereunto nature hath ordained them most apt and fit. For if youth be grafted straight and not awry, the whole commonwealth will flourish thereafter. When this is done, then must every man begin to be more ready to amend himself than to check another, measuring their matters with that wise proverb of Apollo, *Know thyself*: that is to say, learn to know what thou art able, fit, and apt unto, and follow that."

We have alluded to the numerous grammar schools which were founded in the reigns of Edward VI. and Elizabeth. These, and their successors, were no part of a scheme of national education, such as the farseeing policy of John Knox initiated in Scotland, but were simply designed to furnish a selected few, who were unable to bear the cost, with gratuitous instruction of the highest order. Up to the time of the Revolution, however, they represented the only educational system which England possessed. The growth of the commercial classes then led to its expansion; and free-schools were established, in which the education given was adapted to their needs. Mr. **Knight** remarks that during the progress of education in recent years, reformers have spoken somewhat contemptuously of these schools and of the instruction they afforded, **but** the censure seems undeserved. With **a** comparatively small population, they were, so it seems to us, praiseworthy pioneers of a national system. While the grammar schools developed **the** sons of the professional classes and the **more opulent tradesmen** into lawyers, divines, or physicians, the **free schools** took up the sons of the mechanics and the labourers, **and** made them clever handicraftsmen and prosperous burgesses. A good work was also done by the parochial charity schools, which found an active supporter **in** Queen Anne. Mainly through **the** efforts of the **Society for** the Promotion of Christian Knowledge, about 2,000 **of these** schools spread over Great Britain and Ireland, between **1698 and** 1741.

At the beginning of the 18th century, however, we take it that the educational standard in England was infinitely lower than in the reign of Elizabeth or the earlier Stuarts. The upper classes were essentially ignorant, and to a large extent were proud of their ignorance. Their principal pabulum was provided by the weekly news-writer. It is clear from the **tone** of the essayists, the *Tatler*, the *Spectator*, the *Guardian*, that the number of those who read was very limited, and that it was necessary to **cater** for **them** very carefully, dealing with every question in the lightest **and most** familiar manner. Writing in 1713, Addison laments that "**there** should be no knowledge in **a** family. For my own part," he adds, " I am concerned when I **go** into a great house **where perhaps** there is not a single person that can spell, unless it **be by chance the** butler or **one** of the footmen. What a figure is **the young heir** likely to make, who is a dunce both by father's **and mother's** side!" **The** ignorance of the women was worse **even than that** of their brothers and husbands. Most of them, **according to the** *Tatler*, spent their hours in an indolent state of **body and mind**, without either recreations or reflections. " I **think**," says Steele, "most of the misfortunes in families arise from the trifling way the women have in spending their time, and gratifying only their eyes and ears instead **of** their reason and understanding." Swift wrote a remarkable paper on the " Education of Ladies," which **is** not without value even for our own day.

"There is a subject of controversy," he says, "which I have frequently met with in mixed and select companies of both sexes, and sometimes only of men—whether it be prudent to choose a wife who has good natural sense, some taste of wit and humour, able to read and relish history, books of travels, moral or entertaining discourses, and be a tolerable judge of the beauties in poetry? This question is generally determined in the negative by women themselves, but almost universally by we men."

Of course, a higher ideal of education was formed by many intelligent women, and the views held, for example, by Lady Mary Wortley Montagu would almost satisfy the warmest advocate of female culture in our own day. "Every woman," she writes, "endeavours to breed her daughter a fine lady, qualifying her for a station in which she will never appear, and at the same time incapacitating her for that retirement to which she is destined. Learning, if she has a real taste for it, will not only make her contented, but happy in it. No entertainment is so cheap as reading, nor any pleasures so lasting. She will not want new fashions, nor regret the loss of expensive diversions, or variety of company, if she can be amused with an author in her closet. To render this amusement complete, she should be permitted to learn the languages. . . There are two cautions to be given on this subject: first, not to think herself learned when she can read Latin, or even Greek. Languages are more properly to be called vehicles of learning than learning itself, as may be observed in many schoolmasters, who, though perhaps critics in grammar, are the most ignorant fellows upon earth. True knowledge consists in knowing things, not words. I would no further wish her a linguist than to enable her to read books in their originals, that are often corrupted, and are always injured by translations. Two hours' application every morning will bring this about much sooner than you can imagine, and she will have leisure enough besides to run over the English poetry, which is a more important part of a woman's education than it is generally supposed. . . .

"You should encourage your daughter to talk over with you what she reads; and as you are very capable of distinguishing, take care she does not mistake pert folly for wit and humour, or rhyme for poetry, which are the common errors of young people, and leave a train of ill consequences. The second caution to be given her,—and which is most absolutely necessary,—is to conceal whatever learning she attains, with as much solicitude as she would hide crookedness or lameness: the parade of it can only serve to draw on her the envy, and consequently the most inveterate hatred, of all he and she fools, which will certainly be at least three parts in four of her acquaintance. The use of knowledge in our sex, beside the amusement of solitude, is to moderate the passions, and learn to be contented with a small expense, which are the certain effects of a studious life; and it may be preferable even to that fame which men have engrossed to themselves, and will not suffer us to share. At the same time I recommend books, I neither exclude work nor drawing."

This was not altogether an unsatisfactory sketch for the studies of a young girl, but to most of Lady Mary's contemporaries it would have seemed the dream of a visionary or the folly of an enthusiast.

I have referred to Dean Swift's essay on the "Education of Ladies." He has also a paper on "Modern Education," which treats of that of gentlemen, and he shows, with characteristic force, that in his own time it was sadly neglected. "The very maxims set up to direct modern education are enough," he says, "to destroy all the seeds of knowledge, honour, wisdom, and virtue among us. The current opinion prevails that the study of Greek and Latin is loss of time; that public schools, by mingling the sons of noblemen with those of the vulgar, engage the former in bad company; that whipping breaks the spirits of lads well-born; that universities make young men pedants; that to dance, fence, speak French, and know how to behave yourself among great persons of both sexes, comprehends the whole duty of a gentleman." A similar opinion is still held, we fear, by many.

"There is one circumstance," continues Swift, "in a learned education which ought to bear much weight, even with those who have no learning at all. The books read at school and college are full of incitements to virtue and discouragements from vice, drawn from the wisest reasons, the strongest motives, and the most influencing examples. Thus young minds are filled early with an inclination to good, and an abhorrence of evil, both which increase in them according to the advances they make in literature; and although they may be, and too often are, drawn, by the temptations of youth, and the opportunities of a large fortune, into some irregularities, when they come forward into the great world, yet it is ever with reluctance and compunction of mind, because their bias to virtue still continues. They may stray sometimes, out of infirmity or compliance; but they will soon return to the right road, and keep it always in view." It may be doubted whether this is, indeed, the special merit of a "learned education." The classics have their uses; but we should hardly be disposed to regard them as incentives to the practice of the higher virtues, and are inclined to think that the study of Christ's Gospel will have an infinitely greater influence for good on the minds and hearts of the young.

The first outlines of a national system of education were laid down by Robert Raikes in 1780, when he started Sunday schools. That they supplied a want is proved by the rapidity with which they spread. In less than forty years England possessed 5,000 of these schools, attended by 452,000 children. In 1833 the number of Sunday school children had increased to a million and a half, and it must now be nearer three millions; though these schools have lost something of their popularity, and their place is to some extent being supplied by improved agencies. The sum of good which they have accomplished cannot well be over-estimated. Many a mind has owed to them its first conceptions of knowledge; many a soul has first been awakened by them to a sense of the love and wisdom of Jesus Christ. They have guided the feet of thousands and tens of thousands into the paths of peace and righteousness; they have saved thousands and tens of thousands from succumbing to the evil influences of the world. Society has been perceptibly purified and elevated by them; they have confirmed and extended,—have supplemented, and in some cases been an effective substitute for, the work of the preacher and the teacher. The establishment of Sunday schools seems to me one of the noblest efforts of a wise philanthropy; and among the world's Good Samaritans, Robert Raikes, their founder, must ever hold a foremost place.

Robert Raikes, the son of "Raikes the printer," long well known as the proprietor and conductor of the *Gloucester Journal*, was born in a house in Palace Yard, Gloucester, on the 14th of

September, 1735. He was fortunate in both his parents; for while his father was a man of enlightened mind and generous character, his mother was a woman of exemplary piety and many acquirements. He received a liberal and yet a practical education, with the view of fitting him for a journalistic career; and through the death of his father in 1757, found himself, at the age of twenty-two, plunged into it, as well as into the management of an extensive printing and publishing establishment. His ability, diligence, and firmness fully maintained and consolidated the large business he had inherited, and he soon took up a leading position among the influential men of his native city.

His first essay as a philanthropist was made in connection with the city prisons; for in the work of prison reform he preceded John Howard. The condition of the prisoner, whether he was a felon or only an unfortunate debtor, was a disgrace to the boasted humanity of England. He was half-starved, ill-clad, harshly treated; his cell was loathsome and pestiferous; and nothing was done to provide him with useful employment. At Gloucester Castle from forty to sixty prisoners were received every week; yet for this large number only one court was available. The day-room for men and women felons measured twelve feet by eleven. The unhappy wretches imprisoned for debt were huddled together in a den fourteen feet by eleven; it had no windows, and light and air struggled in through a hole broken in the plaster wall. In the upper part of the building was a close dark room, called "the main," the floor of which was in such a ruined state that it could not be washed; this was the sleeping apartment of the male felons, and directly opposite the stairs which led to it a large dunghill gave forth its reeking odours. The whole place was steeped in infection, and ten to twelve victims were slaughtered by it monthly. As for the debtors, that any of them returned to the outer world alive was matter of surprise; for they received no allowance either of food or money, nor was any opportunity furnished them of earning the smallest pittance. If unable to pay for beds, they lay at night on litters of straw; for clothing as for food they were thrown upon their own means or on the charity of the benevolent, and hence it followed that the most honest and deserving—those who had given up all their property to their creditors—were the most wretched. Even the felons were better treated, for they received beds and clothing, and every two days a sixpenny loaf. It is needless to say that the indiscriminate association of felons and debtors, the criminal and the unfortunate, men and women, the hardened offenders and the involuntary or repentant trespassers, was productive of the greatest evil, and that few left such a *cloaca* without being hopelessly degraded and polluted. Every new inmate on his entrance was forced to pay a sum of money, called "garnish," which was immediately spent in beer, supplied by the gaoler, whose chief emoluments were derived from this contraband traffic. In a word, the pictures drawn by Fielding in his " Jonathan Wild " and Smollett in his " Peregrine Pickle," by Dickens in his " Pickwick Papers," and Besant and Rice in their " Chaplain of the Fleet," do not in any wise exaggerate the awful condition of the English prisons at the time that Raikes began his labour of reform in Gloucester.

His earliest efforts were necessarily tentative, and were limited to providing the imprisoned debtors with the necessaries of life ; and for this purpose he made personal application to his friends and addressed the public through the medium of his newspaper. As early as 1768, paragraphs like the following appeared in the *Gloucester Journal* :—

"The prisoners confined in the Castle, without allowance and without the means of subsistence by labour, most humbly entreat some little assistance from those who can pity their wretchedness. The favours they have heretofore received will ever be remembered with gratitude."

"The unhappy wretches who are confined in our county gaol for small crimes which are not deemed felonies (for felons have an allowance of bread), are in so deplorable a state that several of them would have perished with hunger but for the humanity of the felons, who have divided with them their little pittance. A person who looked into the prison on Saturday morning was assured that several had not tasted food for two or three days before. Were a county Bridewell established they might then work for their subsistence. The boilings of pots or the sweepings of pantries would be well bestowed on these poor wretches. Benefactions for their use will be received by the printer of this journal."

The exertions of Raikes were not confined to the relief of the physical distresses of the **prisoners;** this Good Samaritan was not less solicitous about **their moral** and spiritual condition. He supplied **them** with wholesome reading, and strove to find for **them** some kind of occupation, knowing the therapeutic **value** of **honest** industry. Dr. Glam tells us that if among the prisoners he found one able to read, he gladly made use of him to instruct his companions, encouraging him to be diligent and faithful **in** the work by pecuniary rewards. And frequently **he** had the pleasure of hearing them thank God that, through their imprisonment, they had had opportunities afforded them of **learning** that good which otherwise **they** would probably have never **known** in their whole lives. The selection of books being carefully made, and religious **instruction being** blended with secular, the teacher himself **was often taught by** his teaching others, **and** the very nature of **his employment** exercised **a** salutary influence **on his** mode **of living.**

But Mr. Raikes did not restrict himself merely to the business of literary improvement; it was part of his object to inspire these men with sentiments of good-will and mutual kindness, to subdue in them that savageness of disposition **and** behaviour which added to the hardships of their situation. And observing, says Dr. Glam, that idleness was the parent of much mischief among them, "and that they quarrelled with one **another** because they had nothing else to do, he endeavoured to procure employment for such as were willing, or were permitted, to work."

In due time the task of prison reform was undertaken by **Howard,** who ever found in Raikes a **vigorous** and appreciative **supporter.** In 1784, Gloucester Castle **and its site** were ceded by the **Crown** to the county of Gloucester, **and** shortly afterwards, thanks to the energy of Howard and Sir George Paul, and the cordial co-operation of Raikes, the old county prison was swept away, **and a new and** commodious one, clean and well-ventilated, erected in its place.

We now come to the **work with** which Raikes's **name is** indissolubly **connected.** It is **true that** he was not **the "founder of** Sunday-schools," if we limit the word "founder" to **the** person who first conceived the idea of imparting instruction to the young on the Lord's Day; but it was he by whose untiring energy **the** system **was** spread over the length and breadth of the country. It was he who converted a local practice into a national one. It was he who, finding the institution in existence in a few small towns and villages, recognized its merits, its potency for good, and by his strenuous advocacy of it, secured its adoption throughout the kingdom, by Nonconformists as well as by the Church of England. In the same sense in which we speak of James Watt as the inventor of the steam-engine, or of William Wilberforce as the emancipator of the slaves, we may justly speak of Raikes as the founder of Sunday-schools. As early as the sixteenth century, the sainted Carlo Borromeo, Archbishop of Milan, established Sunday schools in various parts of his diocese. Towards the close of the seventeenth century, the Rev. Joseph Alleine, of Taunton, a well-known Nonconformist divine, and author of the "Alarm to the Unconverted," introduced the plan into his own congregation. The monument to the memory of Mrs. Catherine Bovey, in Flaxley Church, Gloucestershire, records the fact of her "clothing and feeding her indigent neighbours and teaching their children, some of whom every Sunday by turns she entertained at her house and condescended to examine them herself. . . . Six of the poor children by turns dined at her residence on Sundays, and were afterwards heard say the Catechism."

A Sunday-school was established at Cuttinits, in Yorkshire, in 1764; and another, on an humbler scale, at Little Levor, near Bolton, by a poor man named James Hey, or, as he was popularly called, "Old Jemmy o' th' Hey." "Old Jemmy" spent his week days in winding bobbins for weavers, and his Sundays in teaching the boys and girls of the neighbourhood to read. His scholars assembled twice each Sunday in a neighbour's cottage; the hour of assembling being made known not by a bell, but by an old brass pestle and mortar. Sympathizing with his object, Mr. Adam Compton, a paper manufacturer, began to supply him with books; others sent him subscriptions in money; and he was thus enabled to form three branches, the teachers of which were paid one shilling each per Sunday for their services. Thus, it is evident that Mr. Raikes was not the inventor of Sunday-schools, though he may well claim the honour of having developed the system.

It seems certain that, so far as he was concerned, the work came upon him as a necessary sequence of his philanthropic labours in the Gloucester gaols. Painful experience must have taught him in what an arduous Sisyphus-like toil he was engaged, while endeavouring to subdue the natures of wretches long inured to fierce and savage habits. Painful experience must have impressed upon him the sluggishness and dulness of scholars unaccustomed to any honest or useful exercise of the mind, and the lack of receptivity on the part even of those who were willing to learn. He must often have reflected on the unwisdom and improvidence of society in allowing the young to grow up in an atmosphere of evil, and have been startled by the ignorance of their most obvious duties displayed by the lower classes. And every Sunday he must have observed with regret that multitudes of the rising generation of the poor were growing up in the same atmosphere, victims of an equal ignorance.

"The streets," says his biographer, "were full of noise and disturbance every Sunday, the churches were totally unfrequented by the poorer sort of children, and very ill-attended by their parents: they were nowhere to be seen employed as they ought to be. Had they been disposed to learn or attend to anything that was good, their parents were neither willing nor able to teach or to direct them; they were therefore a perpetual nuisance to the sober part of the community. They were riotous, impudent, and regardless of all authority whatsoever in their mode of behaviour, disrespectful in the extreme, and frequently detected in such petty offences as plainly indicated that they were on the high road to perdition, unless something could be done to rescue them. It occurred to him, and to a worthy clergyman (Mr. Stock), to whom he complained of the dissolute state of these poor children, that infinite would be the benefit, to the community as well as to themselves, if any method could be contrived of laying them under some proper restraint and instilling some good principles into their minds.

"The foundation, they well knew, must be laid in the fear and love of God, in a reverence for the duties of religion, and for all things relating to the Divine honour and service. Mr. Raikes soon began to make known his intentions to the parents, and without much difficulty obtained their consent that their children should meet him at the early service performed in the Cathedral on a Sunday morning. The numbers at first were small, but their increase was rapid. The gentleness of his behaviour towards them; the allowance they found him disposed to make for their former misbehaviour, which was merely from a want of a better information; the amiable picture which he drew for them when he represented kindness and benevolence to each other as the source of real happiness, and wickedness, malice, hatred, and ill-will as the cause of all the misery in the world; the interest which they soon discovered him to have in their welfare, which appeared in his minute inquiries into their conduct, their attainments, their situation, and every particular of their lives: all these circumstances soon induced them to fly with eagerness to receive the commands and be edified by the instruction of their best friend."

The first Sunday-school in Gloucester seems to have been established in St. Catherine's parish by Raikes in the month of July, 1780; and almost at the same time one was opened in St. John's parish by his zealous coadjutor, the Rev. Thomas Stock, M.A., then head-master of the Cathedral Grammar School. "The beginning of the scheme," according to Raikes himself, was owing to accident. Some business leading him one morning into the suburbs of the city, where the lowest of the people, who were principally employed in the pin manufactory, chiefly resided, he was greatly moved by the sight of a group of wretchedly ragged children at play in the streets. He inquired whether the children belonged to that part of the town, and lamented their misery and idleness. "Ah, sir!" replied the woman whom he had been addressing, "if you could take a view of this part of the town on a Sunday, you would be shocked indeed; for then the street is filled with multitudes of these wretches, who, released that day from employment, spend their time in noise and riot, playing at 'chuck,' and cursing and swearing in a manner so horrid as to convey to any serious mind an idea of hell rather than any other place. We have a worthy clergyman," she continued, "the curate of our parish, who has put some of them to school, but upon the Sabbath day they are all given up to please their own inclinations without restraint, as their parents, totally abandoned themselves, have no idea of instilling into the minds of their children principles to which they themselves are entire strangers."

On this hint Raikes acted. The conversation suggested to him the probable advantages of some "little plan" devised to check this deplorable Sabbath desecration. He inquired, therefore, if there were any decent, well-disposed women in the neighbourhood who kept schools for teaching to read. He was told of four; and with these he made an agreement that they should receive on Sundays as many children as he should send, and instruct them in reading and the Church Catechism. Their remuneration was fixed at one shilling for the day's work. Mr. Raikes afterwards waited on the clergyman (the Rev. Mr. Stock) to whom the old woman had referred, and explained his plan. He was so much pleased with it that he undertook to visit the schools every Sunday afternoon to examine into the progress made, and enforce decorum and order.

Out of this arrangement grew what we may designate the Sunday-school proper, established, as we have said, in St. Catherine Street, in July 1780. The second was started by Mr. Stock, in the parish of St. Mary the Crypt; the third, in St. John the Baptist's; the fourth, in St. Aldate's; and several others rapidly sprang up all over the city. In November 1783, the good work which had been so quietly organised was brought to the notice of the public in Mr. Raikes's newspaper. And thenceforward, for several years, he gave it vigorous and efficient journalistic support. Before the close of 1784, he had stimulated the establishment of eleven prosperous Sunday Schools in different parts of Gloucestershire. The beneficial effects were speedily discernible, and called forth a spontaneous tribute of approval from the Gloucestershire magistrates at the Easter Quarter Sessions of 1786. Earl Ducie was soon induced to become their warm and generous patron, under circumstances which Mr. Raikes described in his journal:—" A nobleman," he says, " to whom a title and large estate in this county lately descended, was present at the parish church near his seat a few Sundays ago, where he saw the aisles filled with a great number of the poorest children in the parish. He observed silence and good order prevail among them, and that, at the close of the service, instead of running promiscuously and hastily out of church, they took their ranks and walked in order two and two like a disciplined body, to the number of more than a hundred. Inquiring into this singular regulation, he learnt that with the view to keep the children out of mischief—to which the Sunday was formerly entirely devoted—

the minister of the parish assembled them in little seminaries, where the day was spent in the improvement of their minds, in learning the catechism, and in attending public worship. His lordship inquired how far their general behaviour was affected by this institution, and expressed great pleasure in hearing that a remarkable alteration in their conversation and manners had been the result; nor were the children alone benefited, for the parents were observed to be less vile and profligate since attention had been paid to the improvement of the children. With this information his lordship appeared sensibly affected, and immediately determined to give the measure all possible countenance and encouragement."

By degrees the movement spread beyond the borders of Gloucestershire. Raikes made it known in the *Gentleman's Magazine*, also in the *European Magazine*; and it so commended itself to good men and women as a simple and effective remedy for a great evil, that it everywhere met with a God-speed. Adam Smith said of it: "No plan has promised to effect a change of manners with equal ease and simplicity since the days of the Apostles." Cowper averred that he knew no nobler means of accomplishing the reformation of the lower classes. John Wesley exclaimed: "I verily think these schools are one of the noblest specimens of charity which have been set on foot in England since the time of William the Conqueror." Bishop Porteous (in 1786) devoted to it an episcopal charge, and vowed that experience had but confirmed the favourable opinion he was originally inclined to entertain of them. "The next generation," he said to his clergy, "if not the present, will probably, in consequence of these benevolent exertions of yours, perceive an astonishing change in the manners of the common people. And they who live to see so desirable a reformation will not, I trust, forget (most assuredly your Heavenly Father will not forget) to whose kindness and to whose labours they stand indebted for such substantial benefits."

A few years later it was estimated that in the Sunday schools throughout the kingdom were no fewer than 300,000 scholars. The "grain of mustard seed" had extended its branches everywhere, and these branches were sound and vigorous. They showed no sign of decay; it was clear that they possessed an abundant vitality. Royalty itself took the new movement under its patronage. At Christmas, 1787, Queen Charlotte sent for Mr. Raikes, and desired him to give her an account of its position and of the good it had already effected. The Sunday-schools at Brentford were visited by George III. Literature, as represented by Mrs. Trimmer and Hannah More—two names of far greater influence in their own day than in ours—was highly favourable to it. In 1785 a new impetus was given by the organization, through the exertions of William Fox, Jonas Hanway, Henry Thornton, Samuel Hoare, and other philanthropists, of the " Society for the Establishment and Support of Sunday-schools throughout the Kingdom of Great Britain ;" and the extent of the work done by it may be inferred from the fact that in the first year of its existence it founded five schools in London, and in ten years had distributed 91,915 spelling-books, 24,232 Testaments, and 5,360 Bibles. At first the Sunday-school teachers were *paid* from 1*s.* to 2*s.* each per Sunday for their services. In many localities the want of funds for this purpose hindered the growth of the schools, and led to the introduction of *gratuitous* teaching, which may be regarded as having insured the permanent success of the system. A further reform, however, has yet to be effected before it can accomplish all the good that lies within its power, and become as mighty and beneficial a factor in the education of the people as it ought to be,—the teachers must be *trained*.

In 1803 was formed the Sunday School Union; an association still in healthy life, prosperous, and largely helpful in the great work of religious education.

It may interest the reader to glance for a moment at the method adopted by Mr. Raikes in the schools under his immediate supervision. We find it explained in letters addressed to various correspondents. Thus he writes to Colonel Towerley:—

"It is now about three years since we began, and I could wish you were here to make enquiry into the effect. A woman who lives in a lane where I had fixed a school told me some time ago that the place was quite a heaven upon Sundays, compared to what it used to be. The numbers who have learnt to read and say their catechism are so great that I am astonished at it. Upon the Sunday afternoons the mistresses take their scholars

to church—a place into which neither they nor their ancestors
had ever before entered with a view to the glory of God. But
what is yet more extraordinary, within this month these little
ragamuffins have in great numbers taken it into their heads to
frequent the early morning prayers which are held every morning
at the Cathedral at seven o'clock. I believe there were nearly
fifty this morning. They assemble at the house of one of the
mistresses, and walk before her to church, two and two, in as
much order as a company of soldiers. I am generally at church,
and after service they all come round me to make their bow, and,
if any animosities have arisen, to make their complaints. The
great principle I inculcate is, to be kind and good-natured to
each other; not to provoke one another; to be dutiful to their
parents; not to offend God by cursing and swearing; and such
little plain precepts as all may comprehend. . . .

"The number of children at present thus engaged on the
Sabbath is between two and three hundred, and they are increas
ing every week, as the benefit is universally seen. I have
endeavoured to engage the clergy of my acquaintance that reside
in their parishes. One has entered into the scheme with great
fervour. . . .

"I cannot express to you the pleasure I often receive in discovering genius and innate good dispositions among this little
multitude. It is botanizing in human nature. I have often, too,
the satisfaction of receiving thanks from parents for the reformation they perceive in their children. . . .

"With regard to the rules adopted, I only require that they
may come to the school on Sunday as clean as possible. Many
were at first deterred because they wanted decent clothing, but
I could not undertake to supply this defect; I argue, therefore,
'If you can loiter about without shoes and in a ragged coat, you
may as well come to school and learn what may tend to your
good in that garb. I reject none on that footing. All that I
require are clean hands, clean face, and your hair combed. If
you have no clean shirt, come in that you have on.' The want
of decent apparel at first kept great numbers at a distance; but
they now begin to grow wiser, and all press in to learn. I have
the good luck to procure places for some that were deserving,
which has been of great use. You will understand that these

children are from six years old to twelve or fourteen. Boys and girls above this age, who have been totally undisciplined, are generally too refractory for this government."

To a Mrs. Harris he writes:—

"In answer to your queries, I shall, as concisely as possible, state—that I endeavour to assemble the children as early as is consistent with their perfect cleanliness—an indispensable rule; the hour prescribed in our rules is eight o'clock, but it is usually half-after eight before our flock is collected. Twenty is the number allotted to each teacher; the sexes kept separate. The twenty are divided into four classes.

"The children who show any superiority in their attainments are placed as leaders of the several classes, and are employed in teaching the others their letters, or in hearing them read in a low whisper, which may be done without interrupting the master or mistress in their business, and will keep the attention of the children engaged, that they do not play or make a noise. Their attending the service of the church once a day has, to me, seemed sufficient; for their time may be spent more profitably, perhaps, in receiving instruction than in being present at a long discourse, which their minds are not yet able to comprehend; but people may think differently on this point. . . .

"To those children who distinguish themselves as examples of diligence, quietness of behaviour, observance of order, kindness to their companions, etc., etc., I give some little tokens of my regard, as a pair of shoes if they are barefooted, and some who are very bare of apparel I clothe. Besides, I frequently go round to their habitations, to inquire into their behaviour at home, and into the conduct of the parents, to whom I give some little hints now and then, as well as to the children."

Many interesting anecdotes, bearing on the relations which existed between Mr. Raikes and his scholars, have been preserved; we can spare room for only one or two. The following was related by Raikes himself.

One day, as he was churchward bound, he overtook a soldier, as he was about to enter the church door, and remarked that it gave him much pleasure to see him attending a place of worship. "Ah, sir," was the reply, "I may thank you for that." "Me?" said Mr. Raikes, "why, I don't know that I ever saw you before."

"Sir," answered the soldier, "when I was a little boy, I was indebted to you for my first instruction in my duty. I used to meet you at the morning service in this Cathedral, and was one of your Sunday scholars. My father, when he left this city, took me into Berkshire, and put me apprentice to a shoemaker. I used often to think of you. At length I went to London, and was there drawn to serve as a militiaman in the Westminster militia. I came to Gloucester last night with a deserter, and took the opportunity of coming this morning to visit the old spot, and in hope of once more seeing you." He then told Mr. Raikes his name, and reminded him of a curious circumstance which had occurred while he was at school. His father was a journeyman currier, and a vicious and profligate character. After the boy had been for some time at school, he went to Mr. Raikes one day, to tell him that his father was wonderfully changed, and that he had left off going to the alehouse on a Sunday. It happened soon afterwards that Mr. Raikes met the man in the street, and said to him: "My friend, it gives me great pleasure to hear that you have left off going to the alehouse on the Sunday; your son tells me that you now stay at home, and never get tipsy." He immediately replied that the change had been wrought by Mr. Raikes: not, indeed, that Mr. Raikes had ever spoken to him before, but that the good instruction afforded to his son at the Sunday-school the boy had carefully repeated to him; and that in this way he had been so convinced of the error of his former mode of life as to have determined on a reformation.

A striking story of one of Raikes's scholars, published originally in a pamphlet entitled "The Sea Boy's Grave," is repeated by Mr. Gregory.

The writer states that he once sailed home from the West Indies in a ship, which included among her crew a notoriously wicked sailor, and a cabin boy who had been trained in one of Raikes's Gloucester schools. The boy's name was Pelham, but he was known among the crew, perhaps from his frequent references to his philanthropic patron, as "Jack Raikes." In the course of the voyage the sailor was smitten with fever, and as he grew rapidly worse it was apprehended that he would die in his impenitence. Jack Raikes, however, obtained leave to nurse him. He watched over him with assiduous care, told him of the Saviour of whom he had learned at school, and prayed with him strenuously and earnestly for salvation in the Saviour's name. After awhile the hard heart yielded, and the sins of a misspent life were lamented with sincere contrition; the poor creature learned the sweet consciousness of his Master's loving forgiveness, and rested in the hope of eternal happiness with the Father. A few days afterwards the ship was overtaken by a violent storm, which cast her on a rock off the northern coast of Scotland, and shattered her into a hopeless wreck. As a last chance, the sailors took to the boats; but the one on board of which Jack Raikes found a place was capsized by the breakers, and next morning his body was thrown up on the neighbouring shore. The writer of the narrative, who got safely to land with a spar to which he had lashed himself, describes with touching simplicity the appearance of poor Jack as he saw him lying, with the other victims of the wreck, on the floor of the alehouse:—

"His countenance wore a sweet and heavenly expression, and, stooping down, I robbed his bare head of a little lock of auburn hair that lay upon his temple. His effects—alas! how poor, and yet how rich—were spread upon the table in the room, and consisted of a little leather purse in which were a well-kept half-crown and a solitary sixpence. His Bible, which he had ever counted his chief riches, and from which he had derived treasures of wisdom, was placed by his side. I took it up, and observed engraved on its clasps of brass these words: 'The gift of Robert Raikes to J. R. Pelham.' 'Oh, Raikes,' thought I, 'this is one gem of purest light indeed; still, it is but one of the many thousand gems which shall encircle thy radiant head in that day when the Lord of Hosts shall make up His jewels.'"

One last illustration of Raikes's work shall be a set of rules which he printed in 1784, for use in the Stroud Sunday-schools. They will have an interest for Sunday-school managers and teachers in comparison with the rules and regulations now in vogue.

I. The master (or dame) appointed by the subscribers shall attend (at his or her own house) every Sunday morning during the summer from 8 till 10.30, and every Sunday evening during the summer (except the second in every month) from 5.30 till 8 o'clock, to teach reading, the Church Catechism, and some short prayers from a little collection by Dr. Stonehouse; and also to read (or have read by some of those who attend, if any can do it sufficiently) three or four chapters of the Bible in succession, that people may have connected ideas of the history and consistency of the Scriptures.

II. The persons to be taught are chiefly the young, who are past the usual age of admission to the weekly schools, and by being obliged to labour for their maintenance, cannot find time to attend them. But grown persons that cannot read, who are desirous of hearing God's Word, and wish to learn that excellent short account of the faith and practice of a Christian, the Church Catechism, are desired to attend, and endeavour to learn, by hearing the younger taught and instructed.

III. Some of the subscribers will in turn visit these schools to see that their design is duly pursued, and give some little reward to the first, second, and third most deserving in each school.

IV. The subscribers will keep a blank book, in which shall be entered the names of all those parents, and other persons, who having need of these helps, neglect to send their children, or to attend; and of those who behave improperly when they attend; with intent that they may be excluded from the alms and other charitable assistance of the benevolent. Those who will take no care of their own souls, deserve not that others should take care of their bodies.

V. All that attend these schools shall, as much as may be, attend the public worship both morning and afternoon on Sunday; and shall assemble at church on the second evening of every month at six o'clock, to be examined, and to hear a plain exposition of the Catechism, which the minister will endeavour to give them.

In explanation of these rules we have an account of the way in which they were worked at Stroud :—*

As an early habit of reverencing and rightly using the Sabbath must be laid in the rising generation, as one of the foundation

---

* Quoted by Mr. Gregory, pp. 137, 138. Our sketch is mainly founded on Mr. Gregory's interesting narrative (edit. 1880).

stones of that reformation devoutly wished for by all serious persons, the attendance on public worship is particularly insisted on. To promote which some of the rewards to be given are the most necessary articles of apparel; and through the failure of the clothing manufacture in this county, these are wanting to many who do, and to more that would, attend these schools. Some of the children who are brought up to other communions are enjoined to attend their respective places of worship constantly and devoutly, and required to give an account of the preacher's text. The other rewards are Bibles of different sizes, New Testaments, Dr. Stonehouse's " Prayers for Private Persons and Families " (see Rule I.); "Admonitions against Swearing, Sabbath-breaking, and Drunkenness"; Catechisms, and papers of Hymns. The time before Divine service in the morning is employed in learning to spell and read. The reading in the evening is performed by those who can read fluently, as it is intended for the edification of all. The rules are read every Sunday evening as soon as the children are assembled. After reading three, four, or five chapters of the Bible (more or less, as the connection of the passage may require), the prayers are repeated. The youngest are taught, first, Dr. Watts's Short Prayers, pages 42 and 43 of the above-mentioned collection; when they are perfect in these, they learn the additions to them; and persons of more advanced age learn the longer prayers of Bishop Wilson and Bishop Gibson. While one is speaking aloud the prayer, or answer of the Catechism, all the rest are required to repeat the same in a whisper; by which inattention and trifling are in a great measure prevented, and a rapid progress is made in fixing what is to be learned in the memory. The minister and some of the subscribers attend one of these schools every Sunday evening, and make such familiar observations on the Scripture and catechism as they think adapted to such young minds. The most deficient scholars attend one or two other evenings in the week, for about two hours, at the house of the master or dame. The teachers are sober, serious persons, whose conscientious assiduity may be depended on, and whose indigent circumstances make the moderate pay of one shilling per Sunday an acceptable recompense.

But we must pass on to the close of Mr. Raikes's useful and benevolent career. His closing years were crowned with many blessings: home happiness, a competency, and the respect and esteem of all good men. No person of mark visited Gloucester without paying a visit to the "Founder of Sunday-schools," and as he possessed a liberal and generous temper, he delighted in dispensing his hospitality. Miss Burney, who accompanied the King and Queen on their pilgrimage to Gloucester, in July 1788, speaks of him as "witty, benevolent, good-natured, and good-hearted;" and these admirable qualities may surely be accepted as more than a sufficient counterbalance for the volubility and egotism of which she accuses him. That he was not without grave faults may very well be believed; that he was not endowed with any special intellectual gifts is certain; but it is no less certain that he spent his life in doing good; so he may well be quoted as an example of what may be accomplished by a man of ordinary parts, if he be diligent, enthusiastic, and in earnest.

At the age of sixty-seven, Raikes retired from business, but he lived for about nine years to enjoy a well-earned leisure surrounded by his family and friends. For some time before his decease, his health declined rapidly, and he lost his wonted strength and elasticity; but his end was wholly unexpected when it came upon him suddenly, on the evening of April 5th, 1811. He was then in the seventy-sixth year of his age.

A great advance was made towards a scheme of national education, some ten or twelve years after the foundation of Sunday schools, by the introduction of what is variously known as the Madras, the Monitorial, or the Lancastrian System. A national policy of education must be founded on the two great principles of efficiency and economy, and these principles imply the existence of a large body of trained teachers, whose services shall be available at a very moderate rate of remuneration. If the labours of a master be limited to a few pupils, they will necessarily be expensive; if they be divided among a very large number, they will necessarily be ineffective. To meet this patent difficulty, which greatly impeded the progress of parochial and other cheap schools, it occurred to Dr. Bell, when superintendent of the Orphan Hospital at Madras, in 1793, to employ the elder and more advanced pupils in the school to instruct the younger. These youthful teachers were called monitors. In England a similar method was adopted by Joseph Lancaster, a young Quaker, who threw himself into educational reform with equal vigour and ability. It soon sprang into popularity, its advantages were so **obvious.** A single adult superintendent could undertake the direction of 300 or 400 pupils, when assisted by the older and cleverer boys; while at the same time these boys were being subjected to a very useful training, both intellectually and morally. Not that the monitors could "teach," in the higher and better sense of the word, but they could assist in the organization and government of the school, they could instruct in elementary subjects, and they could supervise the work of the junior classes under the master's direction. In this way boys naturally gifted for the scholastic profession receive the necessary discipline, and paid monitors and pupil teachers now form a regular and **recognised** part of the organization of our public schools.

Joseph Lancaster was a native of London, and born in 1778. He is generally spoken of as springing from a Quaker stock; but some authorities contend that his father was at one time in the Household Guards. When about nineteen years old, he began to take a lively interest in the education of the masses, and anxious to do what he could in his own small sphere, **he rented** a room from his father in the Borough Road, Southwark, fitted it up for the purposes of a school, and gradually collecting about 90 **or** 100 children, addressed himself to the task of teaching them. Whether **he** derived any hints from a pamphlet published by Dr. Bell, in 1797, or whether the necessity of his position evolved the idea, **does not** seem decided, and is of trivial importance. At **all events,** he applied the monitorial system, and by its aid was enabled to deal with constantly increasing numbers of pupils. The success of his plan soon drew the attention of the friends of education, and among others of the Duke of Bedford, through whose influence Lancaster was admitted to the presence of **George III., in 1805. The** King listened with interest to his exposition, and uttered the celebrated wish " that every poor child in his dominions might be able to read the Bible," a wish which at this day seems within measurable distance of fulfilment. The British and Foreign School Society, established about this time, adopted the Lancastrian system; in the Church, or " National " schools, Dr. Bell's, which differed in some of its details, was generally used. But the progress of popular education was retarded by many obstacles, and more particularly by the jealous ignorance of the higher orders; so that, in 1818, in spite of Lancaster's efforts, and the exertions of societies and private individuals, not more than 175,000 scholars were receiving gratuitous or partly gratuitous instruction.

But, as Henry Brougham said, "the schoolmaster was abroad;" and an impetus had been communicated to the great cause of National Education which it never afterwards lost.

As for Lancaster, like too many other reformers, he fell upon evil days. His zeal for the public weal devoured his private interests; and after several years of energetic educational work, which exhausted his pecuniary resources, he became insolvent in 1812. Six years later, he removed to the United States, and in 1829 crossed into Canada, always toiling unselfishly in the sacred cause to which he had devoted the energies of a life. His method was everywhere adopted,—but he himself was forgotten, and he died at New York in great poverty in 1838.

If too much importance were at first attached to the Lancastrian plan of mutual education, its influence was unquestionably favourable to the foundation of schools by societies and individuals; and in conjunction with the Sunday-school system, it helped to fix the attention of statesmen on the necessity of educating the masses. In 1807 Mr. Whitbread reminded the House of Commons that the education of the people is the best security of a popular government. What a desperate weapon, he exclaimed, was ignorance in the hand of craft! But how important did craft become before an instructed and enlightened people! "In the adoption of a national system of education," he said, "I foresee an enlightened peasantry, frugal, industrious, sober, orderly, and contented; because they are acquainted with the true value of frugality, sobriety, industry, and order. Crimes diminishing, because the enlightened understanding abhors crime. The practice of Christianity prevailing, because the mass of your population can read, comprehend, and feel its divine origin, and the beauties of the doctrines which it inculcates. Your kingdom safe from the insults of the enemy, because every man knows the worth of that which he is called upon to defend."

Nothing was done, however, in the direction indicated by these eloquent and sagacious utterances until, in 1816, Mr. Brougham, whose services in the cause of national education may well induce us to forget or forgive his political eccentricities, procured from the House of Commons the appointment of a Select Committee to inquire into the educational condition of the poorer classes in London, Westminster, and Southwark. The inquiries of this committee disclosed the startling fact that a hundred and twenty thousand children in the metropolis were without the means of education. In 1818, the committee was re-appointed with power to extend its investigations over a wider area. But its labours met with the most uncompromising opposition; and Mr. Brougham and his colleagues, because they sought to raise the poor out of the slough of ignorance and vice into which the neglect of the rich had allowed them to fall, were accused of undermining the foundations of social order. Referring to this controversy, in 1835, when men's thoughts and feelings had undergone a salutary change, Brougham rejoiced very naturally in the great progress that had been made. "That bitter controversy," he said, "is at an end—the heats which it kindled are extinguished—the matter that engendered those heats finds equal acceptance with all parties. . . . Those who once held that the Education Committee was pulling down the Church by pulling down the universities and the great schools—that my only design could be to raise some strange edifice of power upon the ruins of all our institutions, ecclesiastical and civil—have long ceased to utter even a whisper against whatever was then accomplished, and have become my active coadjutors ever since. Nay, the very history of that fierce contention is forgotten. There are few now aware of a controversy having ever existed which, a few years back, agitated all men all over the country; and the measures I then propounded among revilings and execrations, have long since become the law of the land. I doubt whether, at this moment, there are above some half-dozen of your lordships who recollect anything about a warfare which for months raged with unabated fury—which seemed to absorb all men's attention, and to make one class apprehend the utter destruction of our political system, while it filled others with alarm lest a stop should be put to the advancement of the human mind. That all those violent animosities should have passed away, and that all those alarms be now sunk in oblivion, affords a memorable instance of the strange aberrations—I will not say of public opinion, but—of party feeling, in which the history of controversy so largely abounds."

For twenty years, however, the cause of national education made but small progress in the legislature. The reports of the Education Committee show that a large proportion of the children of the country were being allowed to grow up in ignorance. In 18,500 schools, 644,000 children were supposed to put in an attendance: of this number 166,000 were educated at endowed schools, and 478,000 at unendowed schools, on the week days. There were 452,000 children at 5,000 Sunday-schools; but we must not forget that a considerable proportion of these children were included in the returns of the secular schools.

The first practical scheme of national education was brought before Parliament and the people by Henry Brougham, on the 29th of June, 1820. In introducing it, he stated that the children requiring means of education were about one-tenth of the whole population in England, whereas the facilities provided were sufficient for only one-sixteenth; while if the number were deducted of those who received merely a decent training in regard to habits, such as the dame-schools and other inferior schools afforded, the amount of effectual teaching would be deplorably reduced. Large districts were destitute of all means of instruction whatever; in others, the sole reliance was the Sunday-schools of the Nonconformists. In the plan which he submitted, Brougham provided that all schoolmasters should be members of the Established Church; that they should be elected on the recommendation of clergymen, together with that of resident householders; and that they should qualify for office by taking the sacrament within a month of their appointment. These restrictions were immediately fatal to the measure, which was vehemently opposed by Nonconformists on the ground that it placed the education of the poor entirely in the hands of the Church of England. A similar difficulty overthrew every scheme of national education proposed during succeeding years; the members of the Established Church insisting upon direct religious instruction, and the Dissenters refusing either to place the religious instruction of their children in the hands of the Church, or to pay for a system from which their children were necessarily excluded. Brougham's measure was dropped, after the first reading of the Bill; but it accomplished a good work by awakening the mind of the nation to a subject of the highest importance, and it should always be respectfully remembered as the first express move in the direction of national education on a uniform system.

In 1823 was founded the London Mechanics' Institute, the parent of a large and flourishing progeny which have done much for the enlightenment of artisans and operatives, and the middle classes generally. It is obvious that the members of these institutions, which are now to be found in every town and suburban village, must be taught to appreciate to some extent the value of intellectual culture, and thus be led to desire the advantages of education for their children. When originally established, they were designed simply to supply facilities for obtaining knowledge to working-men, but they achieved, indirectly, an even more important object by elevating the idea of education in the mind of the people. They taught the masses to feel that knowledge was a thing to be loved and desired. They inculcated a sense of the value of refinement, and did much to exalt the popular standard of social morality. In their different districts they constituted so many centres, whence radiated a wave of intellectual life.

To Dr. Birkbeck belongs the honour of having originated these institutions. He had been preparing the way by bringing together classes and audiences of working-men for instruction by lectures, direct tuition, and mutual communication. His leading motive, and that of his coadjutors, was, to rouse the people to educate themselves, and not to depend upon the patronage of the wealthy or the assistance of the State. The response was immediate and enthusiastic, for his plan came just in time to meet an urgent need. Leaders were found in men of influence, character, and ability; mechanics, operatives, tradesmen, presented themselves as followers. In a short time, many large towns, such as Manchester, Sheffield, Birmingham, Liverpool, opened Mechanics' Institutes, and gradually they spread into the central settlements of the rural districts, everywhere awakening a new spirit, and clearing the ground for the future establishment of a comprehensive national system of education.

Mr. Constable, the Edinburgh publisher, meditated, in 1826, "nothing less than a total revolution in the art and traffic of bookselling." He proposed to issue "a three shilling or half-crown volume every month, which must and should sell, not by thousands or tens of thousands, but by hundreds of thousands—ay, by millions." But the sale of his "Miscellany," a very superior collection, was numbered only by hundreds, and the enterprising publisher was ruined by his speculation. In 1827, the "Society for the Diffusion of Useful Knowledge,"* founded by the energy of Brougham, Tooke, Charles Knight, and others, began the publication of their sixpenny treatises, ridiculed by the wits of the day as the "Sixpenny Sciences,"—a series of really excellent manuals, but still far from realizing the wants of the masses in the combination of cheapness and goodness. In 1828 was opened the "London University," though it did not succeed in obtaining a charter of incorporation until 1835. It differed from the old universities in not requiring a residential qualification from its members, and in excluding religious subjects from its curriculum. In truth, it is simply a great examining corporation, which grants its degrees and honours to all students who pass its examinations under the prescribed conditions. As such, its influence has been immense, and it has forced the older universities

---

* "The institution of this society was an important feature of its times, and one of the honours belonging to the reign of George IV. It did not succeed in all its professed objects; it did not give to the operative classes of Great Britain a library of the elements of all sciences; it omitted some of the most important of the sciences, and with regard to some others presented anything rather than the elements. It did not fully penetrate the masses that most needed aid. But it established the principle and precedent of cheap publication—cheapness including goodness—stimulated the demand for sound information, and the power and inclination to supply that demand, and marked a great era in the history of popular enlightenment. Bodies of men are never so wise and so good as their aggregate of individual wisdom and goodness pledges them to be; and this society disappointed the expectations of the public and of their own friends, in many ways; but this was because the conception and its earliest aspirations were so noble as they were; and it is with the conception and original aspiration, that, in reviewing the spirit of the period, we have to do. Any work suggested is sure to find doers,—one set, if not another; it is the suggestion that is all-important in the history of the time."—HARRIET MARTINEAU, *History of the Peace,* iii., 347, 348.

into the adoption of a more liberal and comprehensive policy, while it has promoted the adoption of the principle of competitive examinations in all our educational institutions.

In 1832, the issue of the *Penny Magazine* and of *Chambers's Journal* inaugurated—to use an objectionable yet convenient word—that movement of cheap literature which, in our own time, has attained such extensive proportions. The *Penny Magazine* rose at once to a circulation of nearly 200,000 copies per week, and drove out of the field the vulgar and immoral trash which had previously degraded the mind of the people.

The first parliamentary grant in aid of education was voted in 1834. It was only for £20,000; but it was a beginning, and through subsequent years the same amount was contributed until, in 1839, it was raised to £30,000. The grant was distributed in different proportions through the National School Association, which was in strict connection with the Church of England; and the British and Foreign School Society, which admitted children of all denominations, but imposed upon them no sectarian instruction. The principle adopted—an erroneous one, because it gave aid where aid was least needed—was, to assist applicants in proportion to the sums those applicants themselves could raise for the building of school-houses. Experience proving the futility of this method of procedure, the Educational Committee of the Privy Council resolved that it should not be insisted upon, if applications for help came from very poor and populous districts, where no adequate amount of subscriptions was forthcoming. But still no thought was given to the desolate districts which lay in the two-fold gloom of utter poverty and ignorance.

A beneficent work, accomplished at this time, was the establishment and organization of a Normal School, from which might descend "long generations of schools" for the training of teachers. Parliament, in 1835, voted a special sum of £10,000 for this object.

In 1839, by an Order in Council, the management of the education fund was vested in a Committee of the Privy Council. Thus unpretentiously was established the Education Department of the Government, which now administers the control and supervision of the national system of education. To what an extent its work gradually increased we may judge from the rapid growth of the funds voted by Parliament: in 1852, the annual grant was £150,000; in 1856-7, it had risen to £451,213; in 1864, to £705,404. In 1872, the grant for education, science, and art was £1,551,560. For some years the clergy, with exceptions, refused to allow their schools to participate in these annual benefactions; and a long quarrel was maintained between the Church and the State in regard to the principles on which they were distributed. One good result of a controversy, unfortunate in itself, was the strong and successful effort made by the clergy to extend and improve the National Schools, which thenceforth played an important part in the education of the poor.

The larger measure of attention which this great subject, a subject immediately affecting the most vital interests of the nation, was every day receiving, was shown by the introduction, in 1843, of a ministerial scheme. As explained by Sir James Graham, it proposed that factory children between the ages of eight and thirteen should not work for more than six hours and a half daily; that they should be compelled to attend schools provided for the purpose; the children of Churchmen, Catholics, and Dissenters being committed, for certain prescribed hours in every week, to the charge of their respective pastors, to be instructed according to the religious belief of their neighbours. The scheme was enlarged so as to include all pauper children in the towns, and all other children whose parents consented to their entering the schools. In this way the larger proportion of children then uneducated would have been provided for; while the Government held out a distinct promise of an early extension of the system, with the view of including the neglected part of the agricultural population. But a feature of the Government measure was the appointment of seven trustees to each school: four of whom were to be elective, but the other three were required to be the clergyman of the district and two church-wardens. As it was apprehended that this would yield a majority of Church trustees over Dissenters, the Nonconforming bodies initiated a strenuous resistance to the measure, and eventually succeeded in forcing the Government to withdraw it. The nation, through this inopportune display of bigotry, was compelled to wait seven-and-twenty years for a liberal system of national education.

Writing in 1846, Miss Harriet Martineau, a dispassionate and intelligent observer, presents us with her view of the educational "situation" at that date. "We have witnessed," she remarks, "the rise and progress of Mechanics' Institutes. We have seen a small beginning made of a State education of children. A very small beginning it was—the whole sum of parliamentary grants not yet reaching half a million. There has been a great amount of virtuous voluntary effort among Churchmen, Dissenters, employers of labour, and a multitude who were ready to aid; but there are bounds to the ability of individuals; and it cannot, in the nature of things, go on expanding in proportion to that ever-growing need. Again, the quality of the education given by private efforts is a very uncertain matter. It can rarely be so good as that which is planned from the united wisdom of a people, and it is apt to be of a very low order. The sectarian spirit which is the curse of English Society has therefore condemned the children of the nation to a defective education, or to total ignorance. While in no department of benevolent action has there been more energy and good-will than in extending education, in none are we more behind the needs of the time. We shall not be safe, morally, politically, or economically, till we join in agreeing that, as each Church cannot have its own way, nor any one, even though it be the Established Church, we must avert the evil of ignorance in the largest class of the people, by throwing open to all means, of sound moral and intellectual education, leaving the religious instruction and training to the pastors or guardians of the people."

We quote these words for two reasons: first, in order that the reader may see what cause there is for thankfulness in the vast educational progress that has taken place since they were written; and, second, because our national system is based upon the too narrow principle enunciated in the last sentence. All that the State professes to do is to encourage the moral and intellectual culture of its children; their religious training it puts aside as a matter for private effort. It makes no attempt to bring them up as Episcopalians, Baptists, Congregationalists, Catholics, but as honest and efficient members of the commonwealth, capable of contributing by their exertions to the national wealth, and of securing their own livelihoods. Farther than this the

State does not go; though perhaps it might go farther without offence to the law of religious liberty.

A movement on the part of the State which has exercised a far-reaching influence took place in 1861-2, when, acting upon the report of an educational commission, appointed in 1858, the Committee of the Privy Council on Education issued a "Revised Code" of regulations, providing, in all schools assisted by Government grants, for regular examinations of the pupils, payment by results, evening schools for adults, and other technical improvements. In the following year another step was made; a "conscience clause" being added to the Code, which allowed for the admission of children of Dissenters into the aid-supported schools, by exempting them from religious teaching and attendance at public worship.

In 1867, Earl Russell introduced into the House of Lords a resolution which asserted the plain truth that every child has a right to education, and recommended the appointment of a Minister of Education, with a seat in the Cabinet. The resolution was withdrawn; but the discussion which it excited was satisfactory, from the testimony it bore to the advanced views on the subject that were rapidly finding acceptance. It began to be felt that the time had come when the State must act with energy and courage; that the safety, prosperity, and honour of England demanded the establishment of a national system of education. This fact was so apparent that in March 1868 the Duke of Marlborough brought before the House of Lords a Public Elementary Education Bill; but it was framed on too narrow a scale to win for it any general support, and its sponsor hastened to withdraw it. The movement received an additional impetus from the formation, in October 1869, of the National Education League, with the view of advocating compulsory secular education by the State. At length, in 1870, the problem was ripe for solution, and Mr. Gladstone's government undertook to solve it. Their "Elementary Education Bill" was introduced into the House of Common on the 17th of February. It provoked—as any Bill on such a subject was sure to do—a considerable amount of vehement opposition; the Church party not unnaturally objecting to a measure which contained no distinct provision for religious instruction, and the Nonconformists contending that it dealt too favourably with the Church schools. Moderate men, however, on both sides, acknowledged that it was a fair, a judicious, and an enlightened attempt to settle, upon broad and intelligible principles, a difficult subject. It passed through both Houses by large majorities, and received the royal assent on the 9th of August. It underwent some amendments in the direction of greater liberality of spirit, in the session of 1872, and has since been left, unchallenged, to do its great and good work. Briefly speaking, it provides for the formation of *rate supported schools* in every district where sufficient school accommodation is not furnished by voluntary effort, and places their management in the hands of a School Board, whose members are triennially elected by the ratepayers. These schools share in the annual State grants according to the proficiency of their pupils and the general excellence of their organization. The Boards are armed with powers to compel the attendance at school of any child whose parents or guardians fail to supply him with due educational facilities. Thus, a really national education is at length being supplied, and in another generation an absolutely ignorant man or woman will hardly exist upon English ground. The instruction given is sound and broad: is regulated in accordance with the Revised Code (which is constantly undergoing amendment) of the Education Committee of the Privy Council; it affords the industrious pupil abundant means of equipping himself with the weapons which in the battle of life ensure success. The State has now only to draw up and set in motion a scheme of Secondary Education, and in another quarter of a century the power and capacities of the nation will almost be doubled by the skilled labour of its trained and educated children. Meanwhile, what is also wanted is the infusion of a religious spirit into our educational methods. At present, they are adapted, no doubt, to communicate a considerable amount of exact information to inquiring minds; but they do not aim at producing Christian men, who will live pure and manly lives, and resolutely endeavour to accomplish their proper work in the economy of life. For the high object of all rightly-conceived education will be, to fit us for the performance of our duty, with all those faculties of intellect, soul, and body which we have received from the Creator. "Duty!" Ay; that, as George Wilson says, is "the biggest word in the world;" and should be uppermost in all our serious doings. Education is successful or unsuccessful just in proportion as it trains us to feel and appreciate the responsibilities of our manhood, and to apply ourselves to discharging them nobly.

> "A sacred burden is the life ye bear;
> Look on it, lift it, bear it solemnly;
> Stand up and walk beneath it stedfastly."

We turn now to another branch of our subject.

"Those," says Dean Stanley, "who look back upon the state of English education in the year 1827, must remember how the feeling of dissatisfaction with existing institutions which had begun in many quarters to display itself, had already directed considerable attention to the condition of public schools,"—that is, the great endowed schools and grammar schools which we owe to the liberal wisdom of our ancestors. "The range of classical learning, in itself confined, and with no admixture of other information, had been subject to vehement attacks from the liberal party generally, on the ground of its alleged narrowness and inutility. And the more undoubted evil of the absence of systematic attempts to give a more directly Christian character to what constituted the education of the sons of the whole English aristocracy, was becoming more and more a scandal in the eyes of religious men, who at the close of the last century and the beginning of this—Wilberforce, for example, and Bowdler—had lifted up their voices against it. A complete reformation, or a complete destruction of the whole system, seemed to many persons sooner or later to be inevitable. The difficulty, however, of making the first step, where the alleged objection to alteration was its impracticability, was not to be easily surmounted. The mere resistance to change which clings to old institutions, was in itself a considerable obstacle, and in the case of some of the public schools, from the nature of their constitution, in the first instance almost insuperable; and whether amongst those who were engaged in the existing system, or those who were most vehemently opposed to it, for opposite but obvious reasons, it must have been extremely difficult to find a man who would attempt, or if he attempted carry through, any extensive improvement."

That man, however, eventually made his appearance in the

person of Dr. Thomas Arnold, head master of Rugby; a man who stands foremost among the educational reformers of England, who has stamped the impress of his genius on the higher education of the age, and by his teaching and example raised up a succession of philosophical educationists,—a man who possessed all the most distinctive qualifications of statesmanship, and used them for the benefit of the boys of a public school. By not a few the apparent incongruity of a man fit to be a statesman being employed in teaching schoolboys was felt and denounced; but no such incongruity was felt by Arnold himself. He took a high and serious view of the responsibilities of tuition, and held the opinion that no intellectual gifts could be too fine or too abundant for the adequate fulfilment of the work of the schoolmaster, which, in his eyes, was almost too great a burden for humanity to bear. For that work, as Arnold understood it, included the development and elevation of the character, the discipline of the heart, the purification of the soul, as well as the cultivation of the mind. We cannot do better than leave him to describe in his own simple but forcible words the qualifications which he deemed essential to the due discharge of a master's solemn task: "They may," he says, "in brief be expressed as the spirit of a Christian and a gentleman,—that a man should enter upon his business not ἐξ παρέργου, but as a substantive and most important duty; that he should devote himself to it as the especial branch of the ministerial calling which he has chosen to follow—that belonging to a great public institution, and standing in a public and conspicuous situation, he should study 'things lovely and of good report;' that is, that he should be public-spirited, liberal, and entering heartily into the interest, honour, and general respectability and distinction of the society which he has joined; and that he should have sufficient vigour of mind and thirst for knowledge, to persist in adding to his own stores without neglecting the full improvement of those whom he is teaching."

A brief sketch of the life of this great educational reformer cannot fail, I think, to be of interest to the reader, whom it may lead on to the study of Dr. Arnold's noble biography.

Thomas Arnold was born at Slatwoods, near East Cowes, in the Isle of Wight, on the 13th of June, 1795, and named after

DR. ARNOLD.

EARNEST LIVES. [*Face p.* 66.

Thomas, Lord Bolton, then governor of the island. His father, who came of an old Suffolk family, was collector of customs for the port of Cowes. After being educated at Warminster and Winchester, he entered the University of Oxford in 1811. At the degree examination in 1814 he took a first-class; and in the following year was elected Fellow of Oriel College. Here he mixed on intimate terms of friendship and sympathy with many men who, in after years, exercised a large and permanent influence upon English thought,—with the late Sir John Coleridge, Keble, Whately, Hawkins, Hampden, and Copleston. These friends speak of him as distinguished by the frankness and simplicity of his manners; the vigour and activity of his mind; the zeal with which he accumulated knowledge, and his delight in dialectics, philosophy, and history. He is described as having been vehement and almost presumptuously bold in argument; as of a quick temper, easily roused to indignation, yet more easily appeased, and absolutely without bitterness; as angered rather by what he deemed unjust or ungenerous to others, than by any sense of personal wrong; as showing somewhat too little deference to authority, yet, without any real inconsistency, an ardent admirer of what was good and great in antiquity, partly because it was ancient; as in heart devout and pure, generous, sincere, affectionate, and faithful. Altogether a noble and lovable character, though not without its superficial flaws.

In 1819 Arnold settled at Laleham, near Staines, in Middlesex; took unto himself a wife, Mary, daughter of the Rev. John Penrose, a Nottinghamshire rector, and began to receive pupils to prepare for the Universities. Prior to his marriage he was admitted into the diaconate of the Church of England; but, owing to the conscientious scruples he entertained in reference to some portions of the Thirty-Nine Articles and the Athanasian Creed, he delayed taking priest's orders until 1828. He remained at Laleham for nine years, and six of his children were born there. They were years of great domestic happiness and of assiduous study. He loved his work, and he threw himself into it with all the energies of his nature. "I enjoyed," he afterwards wrote, "and do enjoy, the society of youths of seventeen or eighteen, for they are all alive in limbs and spirits, at least, if not in mind; while in older persons the body and spirits often become lazy and languid, without the mind gaining any vigour to compensate for it." One of his pupils, who in later life served under him at Rugby, has sketched with graphic reality Arnold's mode of dealing with his pupils, and we find in it the secret of his educational system. He remarks that on joining the Laleham circle he was struck at once by its wonderful healthiness of tone and feeling; a healthiness too often absent from our great schools, and even from those smaller educational establishments where the influence of the master can more easily make itself felt. Everything about the new-comer he found to be most real; it was obviously a place where a great and earnest work was going forward. Now, this is exactly what, in too many schools, the pupils do not seem to feel; apparently they regard their work as a sham, as something to be trifled and played with, and got rid of as lightly and quickly as possible. They throw into it no earnestness, no effort; take no serious view of it, or of its relation to their future life. But it was the special excellence of Arnold as a master that he raised the moral standard of his pupils; he taught them (in the words of Mr. Thomas Hughes) "that life is a whole, made up of actions and thoughts and longings, great and small, noble and ignoble;" that therefore our only true wisdom is "to bring the whole life into obedience to Him whose world we live in, and who has purchased us with His blood." After all, it is not what the master teaches from books, but what he teaches by his daily living, that really influences for good or ill the young minds around him. "We listened," says Hughes, "as all boys in their better moods will listen (ay, and men too, for the matter of that), to a man whom we felt to be, with all his heart, and soul, and strength, striving against whatever was mean and unmanly and unrighteous in our little world." They did not, could not, fully understand him; could not fully appreciate that generous heart and noble nature; but they knew he was loftier and purer than themselves, and by this consciousness they gained greatly. Just as the babe can feel, and enjoy, and be the better for the sunshine in which it stretches out its little limbs, and towards which it reaches forth its little hands, without having any knowledge of the constituent elements of the great orb and its photosphere whence it flows.

Dr. Arnold's great power as a private tutor rested in this, that he gave such an intense earnestness to life, whereas most young men are inclined to take life so lightly! "Every pupil was made to feel that there was a work for him to do—that his happiness as well as his duty lay in doing that work well. Hence, an indescribable zest was communicated to a young man's feeling about life; a strange joy came over him on discovering that he had the means of being useful, and thus of being happy; and a deep respect and ardent attachment sprang up towards him who had taught him thus to value life and his own self, and his work and mission in the world. All this was founded on the breadth and comprehensivenes of Arnold's character, as well as its striking truth and reality; on the unfeigned regard he had for work of all kinds, and the sense he had of its value both for the complex aggregate of society and the growth and perfection of the individual. Thus, pupils of the most different natures were keenly stimulated; none felt that he was left out, or that, because he was not endowed with large powers of mind, there was no sphere open to him in the honourable pursuit of usefulness. This wonderful power of making all his pupils respect themselves, and of awakening in them a consciousness of the duties that God had assigned to them personally, and of the consequent reward each should have of his labours, was one of Arnold's most characteristic features as a trainer of youth." There was something astonishing in his hold over all his pupils. Yet the "hold," the influence, was due to something in the *man*, not in the *teacher*. It was not so much their admiration of his genius, his learning, or his eloquence,; it was a "sympathetic thrill," caught from a spirit that was earnestly at work in the world; whose work was healthy, sustained, and done in the fear of God; a work founded on a deep sense of its duty and its value,—caught from a spirit that was always reverent, and humble, and sincere, so that others could not help being invigorated by it, and catching from it a glow of deep, and true, and lasting emotion.

Arnold's leisure at Laleham was devoted to his favourite studies of philology and history, and he employed himself on an edition of Thucydides, and on articles upon Roman history, written for the *Encyclopædia Metropolitana*, which prepared him for that elaborate "History of Rome," the work of maturer years, on which his literary reputation is chiefly based.

By degrees it had become known to the public that in the shades of Laleham lived a man with a special capacity for teaching and a wonderful power of controlling and training the young; a man who had new and lofty views on the work of tuition and the teacher's duties and responsibilities; a man who carried the method and spirit of a Christian philosopher into his system of education: and so it came to pass that when, in August 1827, the head-mastership of Rugby became vacant, he was unanimously elected to it. In June 1828 he received priest's orders from Dr. Howley, then Bishop of London; in April and November of the same year took his degree of B.D. and D.D.; and in August entered on his new office, in which he was destined to "change the face of education all through the public schools of England."

I think we may take it for granted that before his time the initial axiom in school management was, that boys were the natural enemies of their masters, and, therefore, to be watched, cowed, and tyrannised over. Now, it was Arnold's distinguishing merit that he made it the basis of all successful tuition that boys were to be treated as rational beings, in whom confidence begat confidence, and who could most easily be controlled by a formal appeal to their honour. But he went further; he introduced "a religious principle" into education; he made it part of his duty to discipline the moral and spiritual nature as well as the intellectual powers.

In the public schools, under the *régime* of the old race of schoolmasters, the "flogging-block" was constantly to the front; it was the *alpha* and *omega* of the old system of education. At Rugby, under Dr. Arnold, it was kept in the background. Arnold ruled by attracting, influencing, and cherishing the better feelings and aspirations of those with whom he had to deal. Flogging he retained as a *dernier ressort*, but only for moral offences, such as lying and drinking; while his aversion to inflicting it rendered it still less frequent in practice than it would have been if he had acted strictly on his own rules. His constant aim was to make the school govern itself by elevating its public opinion. He strove to make his pupils recognise the littleness and meanness of those irregularities of conduct which boys too often regard as signs of courage and resolution. He encouraged, he exhorted them to be brave in well-doing, to fear God and love the truth, and to look upon this present life as a preparation and a rehearsal, so to speak, for the life hereafter. But to raise their *morale* was not his only, though it was his chief object: he strove to raise also the general standard of knowledge and application. Prizes and scholarships, therefore, were founded as incentives to study, and examinations instituted that a pupil's acquirements might be regularly tested. He believed, as I think most persons who have had any lengthened experience of boys will and must believe, in the union, as a general rule, of moral and intellectual excellence. It is an absurd mistake to suppose that the stupid boys are necessarily the virtuous ones. Of course, a boy may be clever and bad; and then his cleverness will be injuriously affected by his badness,—just as a strong plant may grow in an unhealthy atmosphere, but, if it do, will assuredly deteriorate in leaf and blossom.

Once, when preaching at Rugby, Arnold said:—"I have now had some years' experience. I have known but too many of those who in their utter folly have said in their heart, There was no God; but the sad sight—for assuredly none can be more sad —of a powerful, an earnest, and an inquiring mind seeking truth, yet not finding it—the horrible sight of good deliberately rejected and evil deliberately chosen—the grievous wreck of earthly wisdom united with spiritual folly,—I believe that it has been, that it is, that it may be. Scripture speaks of it, the experience of others has witnessed it; but I thank God, that in my own experience I have never witnessed it yet. I have still found that folly and thoughtlessness have gone to evil; that thought and manliness have been united with faith and goodness." And as his knowledge of the young increased, he was led to put increased faith in this combination. Various reasons may be adduced in support of it. As, for instance, that ability brings a boy into sympathy with his teachers in the nature of his work, and in their delight in the works of great minds; whereas a dull boy sympathises with the uneducated, and with those to whom animal enjoyments are the *summum bonum, summa felicitas*.

It was characteristic of Arnold that he believed in diligence, in the power and success of steady application. He was not, like some masters, always on the watch for "smartness,"—impatient with the "slow and sure,"—contemptuous of the plodder, however earnest he may be in his efforts. I think that in the race between the hare and the tortoise, his heart and hopes went with the latter. He was wont to relate how, on one occasion, before he went to Rugby, he had fretted somewhat over the slowness of a pupil of this kind, and reprimanded him sharply; and how the boy had looked up in his face, and pleaded—"Why do you speak angrily, sir? Indeed I am doing the best I can." "I never felt so much ashamed in my life," he said; "that look and that speech I have never forgotten." He learned, in the course of his long experience, that the superficial cleverness in which unwise masters so much delight bears little fruit. "If there be one thing on earth," he would insist, "which is truly admirable, it is to see God's wisdom blessing an inferiority of natural powers, when they have been honestly, truly, and zealously cultivated."

In the classical languages and literature he placed the foundation of his intellectual teaching. He affirmed that the study of language seemed to him to have been given for the very purpose of forming the human mind in youth; and he regarded the Greek and Latin tongues as in themselves so perfect, and at the same time so free from the inseparable difficulty attending any attempt to teach boys through the medium of their own spoken language, as to be the very instruments for effecting such a work. In my humble opinion Arnold set *too* high a value on the study of Greek and Latin; yet their essential importance in any well-considered scheme of mental culture I am prepared to admit. It is to be remembered, moreover, that it was Arnold who first made the study of modern history, modern languages, and mathematics, a regular part of the curriculum of English schools. In this respect, as in so many other respects, his example has brought about a precious and much-needed reform.

Much of Arnold's success was, of course, a *personal* success; a success due to the influence of his life and character. And in this he presents a remarkable contrast to Keate of Eton and Busby of Westminster, who were never the guides and friends of their pupils, never moulded their minds or formed their habits, or left upon them any distinct impression of themselves. "With very little boys," says Dean Stanley, "his manner partook of that playful kindness and tenderness which always marked his intercourse with children. . . . In those above this early age, and yet below the **rank** in the school which brought them into closer contact with him, the sternness of his character was the first thing that impressed them. . . . This was mingled with an involuntary and, perhaps, an unconscious respect, inspired by the sense of the manliness and straightforwardness of his dealings, and still more by the sense of the general force of his moral character." The elder boys cherished for him, we are told, a deep admiration, partaking largely of the nature of awe ; and **this** softened into a kind of loyalty, which remained even in the closer and more affectionate sympathy of later years. When **they left** Rugby, they felt that they had been living in a sphere of action purer than that of the world about them; a better thought than ordinary often reminded them how he first led to **it** ; and in reading the Scriptures, or other works, they constantly traced back a line of reflection that came originally from him as from a great parent-mind.

Here is an extract from one of his letters to Sir J. T. Coleridge, which the reader will peruse with interest,—it is so characteristic of Arnold as the head-master of Rugby :—

"We are going on comfortably, **and, I** trust, thrivingly, **with** the school. We are above 200, and **still** looking upwards ; **but I** neither expect, and much less desire, **any** great addition **to** our numbers. The school cannot, **I think**, regularly expect more than 200 or 250 ; it may ascend higher with a strong flood, but there will be surely a corresponding **ebb** after it. You may imagine that I ponder over, often enough, the various discussions that I have had with **you** about education, and verse-making, and reading the poets. I **find** the natural leaning of a schoolmaster is so much to your view **of** the question, that my reason is more than ever **led** to think my own notions strongly required in the present state of classical education, if it were only on the principle of the bent **stick**. There **is** something so beautiful in good Latin verses, and in hearing fine poetry well construed, and something so attractive altogether in good scholarship, that I **do not** wonder at masters directing **an** undue portion of their attention **to a** crop so brilliant. I feel it growing in myself daily ; and, **if I feel it**, with prejudices all **on** the other side, I do not wonder **at** its being felt generally. But my deliberate conviction is stronger, and stronger, that all **this** system is wholly wrong for the greater number of boys. **Those** who have talents and natural taste and fondness for poetry, find the poetry lessons very useful; the mass do not feel one tittle about the matter, and, I speak advisedly, do not, in my belief, benefit from them one grain. I am not sure that other things would answer better, though I have very little doubt of it; but, at any rate, the present plan is so entire a failure, that nothing can be risked by changing it. . . .

"For your comfort, I think I am succeeding in making them write very fair Latin prose, and to observe and understand some of the differences between the Latin and English idioms. On the other hand, what our boys want in one way they get in another; from the very circumstance of their being the sons of quieter parents, they have far less υρβις and more ευηθεια than the boys of any other school I ever knew. Thus, to say the least, they have less of a most odious and unchristian quality, and are thus more open to instruction, and have less repugnance to be good, because their master wishes them to be so."

In 1841, Dr. Arnold was appointed by Lord Melbourne to the professorship of Modern History at Oxford. He delivered an inaugural course of lectures in the following year, which attracted a large and enthusiastic audience of students.

His contributions to historical literature were of a solid and important character. They include a valuable edition of Thucydides; and a "History of Rome, to the End of the Second Punic War," which has been deservedly approved for close reasoning, sagacious observations on men and events, and judicious and always dispassionate criticism. Among his miscellaneous works may be mentioned his "Sermons," which exhibit some of the highest qualities of the Christian preacher; his "Commentary on the New Testament" (unfinished), and the inaugural "Lectures on Modern History," the sobriety and moderation of which cannot fail to impress the reader. But it was as a man rather than as a writer that Dr. Arnold was great; posterity will know him, not so much as the historian of Rome as the reformer of the public school education of England.

It seems to us to have been his distinctive merit that he realized that lofty ideal of education which Milton set forth in his characteristically dignified and noble language:—"The end of learning," says Milton, "is to repair the ruins of our first parents by regaining to know God aright, and out of that knowledge to love

Him and to imitate Him, to be like Him, as we may the nearest, by possessing our souls of true virtue, which, being united to the heavenly grace of faith, makes up the highest perfection. But because our understanding cannot in this body found itself but on sensible things, we arrive so clearly to the knowledge of God and things invisible, as, by orderly covering over the visible and inferior creature, the same method is necessarily to be followed in all discreet teaching." Here the purpose and object of education, as Arnold understood it, are plainly set forth. It is not to teach reading or writing, or anything else, except as a means to an end; not to teach even the higher, the more abstruse branches of knowledge; but to inspire the young mind with an admiration of the beautiful, and the young heart with a deep love of whatsoever is pure and holy. Dr. Arnold taught that the motive of all wise culture must be, that a man may learn to walk humbly before his God and uprightly among his fellows; that he may sow the seed of a good example wherever he plants his feet; that he may subdue his rebellious passions, discipline his wild desires, think high thoughts, and glow with noble sympathies. The error we so frequently commit is in discussing the accessories as if they were the essentials. Children are not sent to school that they may be encouraged to possess their "souls of true virtue," but that they may acquire so much of linguistic and scientific learning as will assist them in "getting on in the world." How far they will be helped to prepare themselves for that *other* world which lies beyond the narrow limits of human speculation is, to few of us, a matter of lively concern. "The inquiry of truth," says Bacon, "which is the love-making or wooing of it; the knowledge of truth, which is the presence of it; and the belief of truth, which is the enjoying of it— is the sovereign good of human nature." It was this "sovereign good" which Arnold taught his pupils to pursue. Unfortunately it meets with scant recognition in our primary and secondary schools; in few of even our larger and more pretentious academic institutions. In these the "sovereign good" is to gain the highest number of marks in a competitive examination; or to leap, jump, and run almost as well as a professional athlete. The inquiry, the knowledge, and the belief of truth, for instance, are hardly permitted by those "public athletic games," in which, for the prize of an electro-plated cup or vase of vulgar design, our "young gentlemen" assume the attire of the acrobats of the circus, and in the presence of applauding but surely unthinking "friends," compete in the "high jump" or "hundred yards' race." To guide our children, as Arnold guided them, into the right path of a noble and virtuous education, is the great national enterprise which still, in spite of all that has been accomplished, awaits consummation; an enterprise infinitely worthier of a statesman's energies than the puny political objects on which they are too often wasted.

"Man," says Bishop Berkeley, in his "Siris," "is formidable, both from his passions and his reason; his passions often urging him to great evils, and his reason furnishing the means to achieve them." To train this creature of passion and reason; to make him amenable to Christian law; to accustom him to a sense of justice and virtue; to dissuade him from the pursuit of evil, and to encourage him in the pursuit of good; to impress upon him that this life is but the cradle and nursery of faculties which will be fully developed hereafter in proportion to their measure of cultivation, here,—the aptest method of attaining such ends as these, was Arnold's conception of a "liberal education." But what kind of contribution towards it is made by that section of educational reformers who seek to exclude from our schools that religious element which Arnold valued so highly? And why? Because the instruction given is, they say, "sectarian." Such an objection comes strangely enough from men who, in their own religious professions, are sectarian or denominational; who belong, that is, to one particular religious body, recognizing its form of government, and adopting its formularies. But let that pass. Supposing that the religious teaching in the Board Schools is, like the religious teaching in church or chapel, "sectarian," is it not better than none at all? The writer strongly doubts, however, whether children can ever be made to accept and retain the shibboleths of the sects. How much of the theological portion of any catechism sinks into the mind of a child? Is not the hard, cold, and abstruse doctrinal matter instinctively rejected, while only its lessons of moral duty are taken up and absorbed? Are such lessons worthless? Is not their impression carried far on into later life? And is it nothing that boy or girl learns the wickedness of falsehood, the terrible consequences of sin? Alas!

the cardinal defect of our educational system is that it is not religious enough. Yet, from the vivid pages of history, what lessons might not a judicious teacher draw in illustration of the workings of God's providence? How would a survey of the physical aspects of earth assist him in demonstrating the Divine wisdom, and, yet more, the Divine love! And how, in every branch of study, in every stage of intellectual progress, might not the pupil be brought to reverence the beauty of holiness, and to receive into his soul the sacred lights of honour, and truthfulness, and love! To do true and lofty deeds, to live the life of a true and noble spirit,—this is the great lesson which the teacher should inculcate hour by hour, and day by day. But how is it to be taught if we draw a broad line of demarcation in our every-day teaching between the "religious" and the "secular"?

But we have digressed from our subject.

On the 5th of June, at the end of the summer half-year, and before the final dispersion of the boys for the holidays, Dr. Arnold preached in Rugby Chapel what proved to be his farewell sermon. In the preceding fortnight he had suffered from a feverish attack, but he appeared to have recovered his usual health, and also his usual spirits and energy, and was eagerly looking forward to his accustomed holiday at Fox How, his pretty rural residence "among the lakes." On Saturday, the 11th, after examining some of his pupils in Ranke's "History of the Popes," he was engaged in finishing the business of the school, distributing the prizes, and taking leave of boys whose school course was closed. By his own form, or class, it was afterwards remembered, with pathetic interest, that the last subject he had set them for an exercise was "Domus Ultima": the last translation for Latin verses was from Spenser's lines on the death of Sir Philip Sydney, in his "Ruins of Time"; and the last words with which he closed his last lecture on the New Testament were uttered in comment on the passage of St. John: "It doth not yet appear what we shall be; but we know that when He shall appear we shall be like Him, for we shall see Him as He is." "So, too," he said, "in the Corinthians—'For now we see through a glass darkly, but then face to face!' Yes," he added, with fervour, "the mere contemplation of Christ shall transform us into His likeness."

At nine o'clock he gave a supper, according to custom, to the

Sixth Form boys of his own house. They were impressed by the vivacity and cheerfulness of his manner, as he spoke of the end of the half-year, and of the pleasure with which he looked forward to his visit to Fox How.

Before retiring to rest he made an entry in his diary, which, read by the light of what afterwards occurred, carries with it a solemn significance:—

"Saturday evening, June 11th.—The day after to-morrow is my birthday, if I am permitted to live to see it—my forty-seventh birthday since my birth. How large a portion of my life on earth is already passed! And then—what is to follow this life? How visibly my outward work seems contracting and softening away into the gentler employments of old age. In one sense, how nearly can I say, 'Vixi!' And I thank God that, as far as ambition is concerned, it is, I trust, fully mortified. I have no desire other than to step back from my present place in the world, and not to rise to a higher. Still there are works which, with God's permission, I would do before the night cometh; especially that great work, if I might be permitted to take part in it. But, above all, let me mind my own personal work, to keep myself pure and zealous and believing, labouring to do God's will, yet not anxious that it should be done by me rather than by others if God disapproves of my doing it."

Between five and six o'clock on Sunday morning he awoke with a sharp pain across his chest, which he mentioned to his wife, on her asking him how he felt, adding that he had experienced it slightly on the preceding day, both before and after bathing. "He then again composed himself to sleep; but her watchful care, always anxious, even to nervousness, at the least indication of illness, was at once awakened, and on finding from him that the pain increased, and that it seemed to pass from his chest to his left arm, her alarm was so much roused, from a remembrance of having heard of this in connection with *angina pectoris* and its fatal consequences, that, in spite of his remonstrances, she rose and called up an old servant, whom they usually consulted in cases of illness. Reassured by her confidence that there was no ground for fear, but still anxious, Mrs. Arnold returned to his room. She observed him, as she was dressing herself, lying still but with his hands clasped, his lips moving, and his eyes raised upwards as if engaged in prayer, when all at once he repeated firmly and earnestly, 'And Jesus said unto him, Thomas, because thou hast seen thou hast believed; blessed are they who have not seen, and yet have believed;' and soon afterwards, with a solemnity of manner and depth of utterance which spoke more than the words themselves, ' But if ye be without chastisement, whereof all are partakers, then are ye bastards and not sons.' "

But as the symptoms did not pass **away**, Mrs. Arnold at length despatched messengers for medical assistance. At a quarter to seven it arrived. To the physician's inquiries the sick man replied calmly and clearly, though evidently suffering very seriously. In the absence of Mrs. Arnold, who had gone to call up her son, he asked what his illness was; the physician answered, disease of the heart. In his peculiar manner of recognition he exclaimed, "Ha!" and then on being asked if he had ever in his life fainted, " No, never." " Had he **ever** had difficulty of breathing?" "No, never." "If he had ever had sharp pain in the chest?" "No, never." "If any of his family had ever had disease of the chest?" "Yes, my father had—he died of it." "What age was he?" "Fifty-three." "Was it suddenly fatal?" "Yes, suddenly fatal." He then asked, "If disease of the heart was a common disease?" "Not very common." "Where do we find it most?" "In large towns, I think." "Why?" Two or three causes were mentioned. "Is it generally fatal?" "Yes, I am afraid it is."

The physician quitted the house for medicines, leaving Mrs. Arnold, who by this time was fully aware of her husband's danger. Her son now entered the room, but without any serious apprehension. On his coming up to the bed, his father, with his usual gladness of expression towards him, asked, " How is your deaf**ness**, my boy?" (he had been suffering from it the night before), **and** then, in playful allusion to an old jest against him, "You must not stay here—you know you do not like a sick room." Presently his father said to him, **in a** low voice, "My son, thank God for me," and as his son did not at once catch his meaning, he went on saying, "Thank God, Tom, for giving me this pain: I have suffered so little pain in my life that I feel it is very good for me, now God has given it to me, and I do so thank Him for it." And again, after a pause, "How thankful I am that my head is untouched." His wife, turning to the Prayer-Book, began to read the exhortation in "the Visitation of the Sick," he listening with deep attention, and at the end of many of the sentences emphatically saying, "Yes."

"There should be no greater comfort to Christian persons than to be made like unto Christ." "*Yes.*"

"By suffering patiently troubles, adversities, and sickness." "*Yes.*"

"He entered not into His glory before He was crucified." "*Yes.*"

At the words "everlasting life" she stopped, and his son said, "I wish, dear papa, we had you at Fox How." Dr. Arnold did not answer, but the last conscious look which remained fixed in his wife's memory was the look of intense love and tenderness with which he smiled upon them both at that moment.

The physician returned with the usual remedies, which he proceeded to apply. The spasms recurred slightly; and Arnold remarked, "If the pain is again as severe as it was before you came, I do not know how I can bear it." He then, with his eyes fixed upon the physician, who rather felt than saw them upon him, so as to make it impossible not to answer the exact truth, repeated one or two of his former questions about the cause of the disease, and ended with asking "Is it likely to return?" and on being told that it was, "Is it generally suddenly fatal?" "Generally." On being asked whether he had any pain, he replied that he had none but from the mustard plaster on his chest, with a remark on the severity of the spasms in comparison with this outward pain; and then a few moments afterwards inquired what medicine was to be given, and on being told, answered, "Ah, very well." The physician, who was dropping the laudanum into a glass, turned round and saw him looking quite calm, but with his eyes shut. In another minute he heard a rattle in the throat and a convulsive struggle, flew to the bed, caught his head upon his shoulder, and called to one of the servants to fetch Mrs. Arnold. She had but just left the room before his last conversation with the physician, in order to acquaint her son with his father's danger, of which he was still unconscious, when she heard herself called from above. She rushed upstairs, told her son to bring the rest of the children, and with her own hands applied the remedies that were brought in the hope of reviving animation, though herself feeling, from the moment that she saw him, that he had already passed away. He was indeed no longer conscious. The sobs and cries of the children, as they entered and saw their father's state, made no impression upon him; the eyes were fixed, the countenance was unmoved, there was a heaving of the chest, deep gasps escaped at prolonged intervals, and just as the usual medical attendant arrived, and as the old school-house servant, in an agony of grief, rushed with the others into the room, in the hope of seeing his master once more, he breathed his last.

I cannot dwell here upon the painful impression produced by the sudden death of the great schoolmaster. He was buried on the following Friday in Rugby Chapel, where a memorial has since been erected to him; but the most fitting and enduring memorial is that new spirit in public-school education which he was the first to inspire and foster. In his stanzas entitled "Rugby Chapel," his poet-son, Mr. Matthew Arnold, has poured out a tribute of affectionate praise, which has become part and parcel of our literature. He says :—

> "But thou wouldst not *alone*
> Be saved, my father! *alone*
> Conquer and come to thy goal,
> Leaving the rest in the wild.
> We were weary, and we
> Fearful, and we, in our march,
> Fain to drop down and to die.
> Still thou turnedst, and still
> Beckonedst the trembler, and still
> Gavest the weary thy hand!
> If, in the paths of the world,
> Stones might have wounded thy feet,
> Toil or dejection have tried
> Thy spirit, of that we saw
> Nothing! to us thou wert still
> Cheerful, and helpful, and firm.
> Therefore to thee it was given
> Many to save with thyself;
> And, at the end of thy day,
> O faithful shepherd! to come,
> Bringing thy sheep in thy hand.'

As a pendant to the foregoing sketches of English educational reformers, we shall furnish a brief memoir of John Frederic Oberlin, who has some claim to be regarded as the inventor or creator of industrial schools.

Oberlin was born at Strasburg, on the 31st of August, 1740. He was one of nine children, whom his father, a man of respectable character and considerable attainments, though not in affluent circumstances, educated with great care. Some interesting anecdotes are told of the child's early years, which seem to confirm the old adage that "the boy makes the man." The elder Oberlin, limited as were his means, was accustomed to give each of his children a couple of *pfenninge* (rather less than $\frac{1}{2}d$. English) as weekly pocket-money. When the tailor's or shoemaker's bill was brought home on a Saturday night, Frederic, who knew his father's anxiety always to discharge a claim immediately, would watch his countenance, and if he judged from its downcast expression that he was in want of money, would haste to his savings' box, and return in triumph to empty into his parent's hands his little treasure of accumulated *pfenninge*.

It is also related that, one day, when he was crossing the market-place, he saw some rough boys knock off a basket of eggs from the head of a countrywoman. Frederic, observing the woman's distress, rebuked the boys sharply, ran home, and fetching his store, presented her with the whole of it. On another occasion, he was passing by the stall of a vendor of old clothes. A poor and infirm woman was endeavouring, but without success, to cheapen some article she was specially desirous of purchasing. To complete the sum demanded she wanted two sous; and she was on the point of leaving the stall, sorely disappointed, when Frederic slipped the two sous into the dealer's hands, whispered to him to complete the sale, and then ran away before the woman could pour her thanks into his ear.

Oberlin, like most men who have become known for their greatness or their goodness, owed a great deal to his mother's practice and precept. She was sincerely desirous of bringing up her children in the "nurture and admonition of the Lord"; and for this purpose assembled them every evening to read, and pray, and sing hymns. By way of relaxation, their father, every Thursday evening in the summer months, would accompany them to his old family estate at Schiltigheim. On arriving there, he would fasten an old drum to his waist, draw up his seven blooming boys in military array, and make them face to right and left, and go through other military evolutions, to the noisy music of his drum. It has been suggested that the zest with which Frederic joined in this exercise may have begotten his early partiality for the military profession. While quite a lad, he would mingle with the soldiers, and march by their side: and, having attracted the attention of the officers by his knowledge of sieges and battles, he obtained permission to join in their exercises. It was under a peaceful banner, however, that he was destined to enlist, and in an army which owns as its captain the Lord Jesus Christ. Frederic's father required him to give up this fancy "soldiering," and devote himself to serious study. He at once obeyed, and set to work with such diligence and good-will that he soon regained the time he had lost. What impelled him to take orders, however, is not known; it was, perhaps, with no very decided convictions that he became a student in the theological class at the University; but he was confirmed in his resolution, and encouraged to take up the cross of Christ, by the preaching of a Dr. Lorentz.

He was ordained in 1760. Seven years passed, however, before he obtained a pastoral charge, and from 1760 to 1767 he acted as private tutor in the family of an eminent surgeon, Ziegenhagen, in that capacity acquiring a knowledge of medicine which, in after life, proved of singular usefulness. In 1767 he accepted the chaplaincy to a French regiment, and in the same year was offered the curacy of the Ban de la Roche, a valley of the Vosges in the province of Alsace. It was not an attractive sphere of pastoral labour, for the emoluments were scanty, while the inhabitants were unpolished; but it seemed a field where much good work might be done, and with a blithe heart he entered upon it. He arrived at Waldbach, the principal village in the district, on the 30th of March, 1767, being then in his twenty-seventh year.

Of the flock over whom he was set as guide, teacher, and spiritual father, we have the following description:—

They were wholly destitute of the means of mental and social intercourse. They spoke a rude patois, resembling the Lorraine dialect, which was almost unintelligible to their neighbours.

From the surrounding districts they were shut off by the want of roads, which, owing to the ravages of war, and the decrease of population, had so completely disappeared, that the sole mode of communication between the larger part of the parish and the neighbouring towns was by stepping-stones across the river Bruche. The husbandmen lacked the most necessary agricultural implements, and had no means of procuring them. The produce of the soil was inadequate to the support of even a scanty population. And finally, the restraints of feudalism, more fatal than the sterile land and ungenial climate, threw the most serious obstacles in the way of successful industry.

Few less inviting fields of labour, from a worldly point of view, could easily be found. Oberlin, however, placing his hope and trust in God, determined to attempt its cultivation.

The most salutary reform cannot be effected without exciting antagonism,—an antagonism generally the more violent as the reform is the more obviously needful; and reformers even in the Bans de la Roche of the world must count upon meeting with enemies and persecutors. The *laudatores temporis acti*, the adherents of the "old ways," determined at the outset to resist their pastor's benevolent innovations, and concocted a plan for waylaying him and beating him into a proper spirit of conservatism. It happened, however, that the plot became known to Oberlin, who took a characteristic way of frustrating the designs of its authors. On the Sunday, the day they had chosen for carrying them out, he preached a discourse upon the beauty of Christian patience and the forgiving spirit, taking as his text those words of our Saviour, so loving in themselves, but so hard to understand,—"But I say unto you, that ye resist not evil, but whosoever shall smite thee on thy right cheek, turn to him the other also." After service he proceeded alone to the house where the conspirators had assembled, and entering stood in their midst: "Here am I, my friends," he said, as they gazed upon him with astonishment, "I am acquainted with your intention. You have wished to chastise me, because you consider me culpable. If I have violated the rules of conduct which I have enjoined upon yourselves, punish me for it. It is better that I should deliver myself into your hands, than that you should be guilty of the meanness of lying in ambush." These simple words, and this unswerving courage, moved the peasants to shame and contrition, and they implored their pastor's forgiveness, which, we need hardly say, was granted immediately.

Oberlin's sagacious eye perceived at the outset the necessity of repairing and restoring the roads, so as to bring the peasants of the Ban de la Roche into contact with the civilization of the neighbouring districts. The most important height was that which led, or ought to lead, to Strasburg; and, assembling his people, he proposed that they should blast the rocks, and with the shattered masses construct a wall to support a road, about a mile and a half in length, along the banks of the river Bruche, and a bridge across the river near Rothau. His project was at once pronounced impracticable. Oberlin continued:—"The produce of your fields will then find a ready market, and instead of being shut up in your villages nine months out of twelve, you will be enabled to keep up an intercourse all the year round with the inhabitants of the neighbouring districts. You will have the opportunity of procuring a number of articles of which you have long stood in need, without the possibility of obtaining them; and your happiness will be increased by the additional means thus afforded of providing comforts for your children and yourselves." And meeting with no response, he exclaimed:—"Let all who understand the importance of my proposition come and work with me."

With a pickaxe on his shoulder he sallied forth. The peasants, who had been inexorable to argument, yielded immediately to example, and hastily procuring their tools, they followed their pastor. To each individual he assigned a suitable position, reserving for himself and a faithful friend the most difficult and dangerous places; then, with great enthusiasm, all set lustily to work, and the air resounded with the din of hammer and pickaxe. The enthusiasm spread. Recruits poured in from every village, rendering necessary an increased number of implements. He procured them from Strasburg, and when his funds were exhausted applied to his friends. Walls were raised to support the earth at all points where landslips seemed probable; the torrents were diverted into more convenient courses, or retained within embankments; arches were thrown over ravines, and the whole work was pressed forward with such perseverance and skill that, in 1770, Strasburg was reached, and a neat wooden bridge, still known as the "Pont de Charité," thrown across the river. The benefits of this remarkable achievement were felt at once, and, as a consequence, Oberlin's influence over his parishioners was so confirmed and established that thenceforth he secured the ready adoption of his successive plans. Highways were soon constructed between the various villages of the "Stony Valley," which had hitherto been practically isolated. The energy of the workers surmounted every obstacle; and it was a pleasant and suggestive sight to see, every Monday morning, some two hundred stalwart men starting forth, with the earnest pastor at their head who, the day before, had been revealing to them the "oracles of God."

When their agricultural tools and implements broke or stood in need of repair, considerable delay and loss were caused by the necessity of sending them to Strasburg. To remedy this serious evil, the indefatigable Oberlin established a large depôt in Waldbach, where purchasers could easily supply themselves, credit being given under suitable conditions. He also founded a loan society for the assistance of the deserving poor, insisting, however, on the utmost punctuality of repayment. Discovering that there were neither masons nor blacksmiths nor cartwrights in the district, which was greatly inconvenienced by the want of these necessary trades, he selected some of the cleverest and steadiest of the elder boys, and sent them to Strasburg to be instructed in them. This plan provided a supply of good workmen, who, on their return, plied their various avocations with industry and success; and thus the money which had previously gone to Strasburg was circulated in the district, to the rapid increase of its prosperity. Money had previously been so scarce that the gift of a single *sou* would overwhelm a poor woman with gratitude, because it enabled her to purchase some salt to eat with her potatoes. And finally, he directed his efforts to improve the house-accommodation of his people. Their dwellings were miserable cabins, like those of the commoner peasants,—hewn out of the rocks, or sunk into the sides of the mountains; but under his energetic direction decent cottages arose, with a deep and ample cellar to each, where their potatoes, their staple article of food, could be preserved from the winter frost. In truth, Oberlin was

PASTOR OBERLIN.

not so much the priest and religious guide of a parish as the founder and patriarch of a community.

Solicitous to increase the resources of the district, as the best means of raising it out of its pauperism, he resolved on the introduction of orchard-planting. But knowing that an agricultural population would listen with suspicion, and, perhaps, contempt, to any teaching of his on a subject which they would regard as peculiarly their own, he proceeded with much ingenuity to influence them by example. The parsonage-grounds were crossed by public footpaths, and therefore lay open to constant inspection. With the aid of his servant, he trenched them carefully, and planted, four or five feet deep, such fruit-trees—apples, pears, plums, cherries, and walnuts—as he thought best fitted to the soil and climate. In due time these grew and flourished, and with their crops of mature fruit presented a striking contrast to the nakedness around. The peasants at once applied to him for advice and assistance; young plants were readily furnished, lessons in the art of grafting found eager listeners; and before long almost every cottage was surrounded by its smiling garden-ground, and the district, previously so bare and desolate, assumed an aspect of fertility and plenty.

The indigenous plants of the Ban de la Roche were not neglected, and Oberlin, who was a good botanist, took much trouble to make his people acquainted with their excellent properties. Here is a list of the most useful:—

Brassica oleracea	Stripe-flowered cabbage.
Stellaria media	Common chickweed.
Cerastium aquaticum	Water mouse-ear chickweed.
Chenopodium bonus-Henricus.	Common goose-foot.
Leontodon autumnale	Common dandelion.
Epilobium montanum	Mountain willow-herb.
Ranunculus ficaria	Buttercup.
Galeobdolon luteum	Yellow dead-nettle.
Lamium album	White dead-nettle.
Humulus lupulus	Common hop.
Anagallis arvensis	Red pimpernel.
Plantago major	Great plantain.
Ranunculus acris	Upright crowfoot.
Polygonum bistorta	Twisted snake-weed.
Rumex acetosa	Common sorrel.
Valeriana locusta	Lamb's lettuce.
Cucubalus behen	Bladder campion.
Sisymbrium nasturtium	Watercress.
Agrostemma githago	Corn cockle.

The usefulness of some of these is not well understood even in rural England.

Oberlin taught his pupils to mix the corn-cockle seeds with corn in making their black bread; to obtain bread from beech-nuts; and—a more doubtful good—to distil a kind of wine, called *piquette*, from the wild berry, the dog-rose, or the juniper. He also introduced the cultivation of flax and Dutch clover.

In 1778 he made a further step in advance by establishing an Agricultural Association, composed of the more intelligent farmers and the better-informed inhabitants. The pastors of the adjacent towns and some of his friends became members; and he then connected it with that of Strasburg, in order to secure the communication of periodical works, and assistance in the distribution of prizes. The Strasburg Society, with the view of encouraging its interesting auxiliary, placed at its disposal a sum of two hundred francs, to be divided among such peasants as should most distinguish themselves in the planting of nursery grounds and the grafting of fruit-trees.

While thus vigorously endeavouring to improve the material condition of his people, Oberlin did not neglect their spiritual; and the earnestness and zeal which he threw into the discharge of his pastoral duties may be seen from the following New Year's address to his parishioners, issued in 1779:—

"Through the grace of God we have entered upon a New Year. Oh that it may be new with respect to our sins, our sufferings, and the temptations with which we may have to combat!

"As to sins, may their number diminish daily, and may we be more constantly animated and governed by the spirit of our Lord Jesus Christ. As to sufferings and tribulations, may they produce the effect which God designs in sending them, namely, that of detaching our affections from this transitory world, and of rendering us attentive to His Will and Word. May they quicken us to prayer; and induce us to strive more earnestly to enter in at 'the strait gate,' and to 'press toward the mark for the prize of our high calling.' And as to the temptations which may be placed in our way, may we live entirely to Jesus Christ, and maintain constant communion with Him, in order that we may receive, from time to time, fresh supplies of grace and strength to resist them, and be enabled to bring forth fruits of righteousness, to the glory of God and to the honour of His holy gospel. O Lord, be Thou pleased, with the renewal of the year, to renew our strength! O Lord Jesus Christ, Thou hast said, 'I make all things new'—O make our faith new also!

"May this year be marked by a more lively, more deep, and more serious repentance; by greater fervour in supplicating the influences of God's Holy Spirit; by renewed earnestness in devoting ourselves to Him and to His service. May we look to Him, and employ all our mental and bodily powers, our time, and our property, to His glory, and to the purpose for which Jesus quitted His throne, namely, the conversion and happiness of mankind. O may we, this year, apply ourselves, with renewed faithfulness, to obey all His commandments and all His precepts.

"May this year be distinguished by an increase of the number of the children of God, and of the followers of Jesus Christ; by the weakening of the kingdom of Satan within us, and by the coming of the kingdom of God.

"May we, not only during the present, but, also, during each succeeding year which God shall grant us in this probationary world, become more and more prepared for a blessed eternity, abound more in prayers of intercession and supplication, shed more tears of penitence, contrition, love, and pity, and perform more good works, in order that we may reap an abundant harvest on that day when God, through Jesus Christ, shall 'make all things new.'"

Into no branch of his work did Oberlin throw himself with greater fervour than into the educational. The instruction of the young occupied his thoughts from the moment that he began his beneficial career in the Ban de la Roche. At that time the only regular school-house in the five villages which composed his charge was a hut belonging to his predecessor, which having been constructed of unseasoned wood, was in a ruinous and wretched condition. We are told, however, that his parishioners received very unfavourably his proposition to build a more commodious one. The better education of their children was as nothing compared with the increased expense which they found he intended to bring upon them. And he did not succeed in overcoming their opposition until he entered into a formal engagement with the overseers of the Commune, that neither the expense of building nor the cost of repairing the projected school-house should ever become chargeable on the parish funds.

To defray the unavoidable expenditure, he sought assistance from some friends in Strasburg. His applications were not unsuccessful, but their donations were inadequate to the object he had in view. Yet, placing his trust in God, he began his philanthropic enterprise, and as the work went on, additional help was forthcoming; his faith found an abundant reward; the school-house was finished; and, as good work has a habit of multiplying itself, in the course of a few years a school-house was erected in each of the other five villages. Such was the influence of a noble example, that the inhabitants voluntarily came forward and took upon themselves the labour and cost of their erection. Meantime, Oberlin assiduously trained a number of teachers for these schools; and observing with anxiety the neglect from which the younger children suffered while their elder brothers and sisters were carefully looked after, he conceived the idea of establishing *infant schools*—of which he was thus the creator and founder.

Observation and experience had taught him that, even from the very cradle, children can be accustomed to distinguish between right and wrong, and inured to habits of industry and obedience: and in conjunction with his wife, he engaged and trained *conductrices* for each commune, hired larger rooms for them, and salaried them at his own expense. The useful and the agreeable went hand in hand in the curriculum adopted; recreation alternated with instruction; and whilst sufficient discipline was insisted upon to preserve order and teach the habit of obedience, a considerable degree of freedom was allowed, and the infant's mind and body were both allowed room for expansion. During school hours the children were collected on forms in large rings or circles. Two women were employed, the one to direct the work, the other to teach and amuse the workers. While the children of two or three years of age were made at intervals to sit quietly by, those of five or six were taught to knit, spin, and sew; as soon as they showed signs of weariness, their governess placed before them scriptural pictures, coloured, or natural history subjects, making them repeat after her the explanations she gave. A similar plan was adopted with geographical maps of France,

Europe, and the Ban de la Roche. They were also taught to sing moral songs and hymns.

As soon as they were old enough, the children thus carefully trained were removed to the public schools, in which were taught reading, writing, arithmetic, geography, the elements of agriculture, astronomy, and sacred and profane history; the religious instruction Oberlin, notwithstanding his many labours, reserved to himself. Every Sunday the village children assembled at the church, to sing the hymns they had learned, to recite the religious lessons they had committed to memory during the week, and to listen to their pastor's exhortations. As a specimen of those hymns, the following may be interesting. It is distinguished by its simplicity:—

"Je ne saurois de l'année
Sans toi commencer le cours,
Auteur de ma destinée !
Sage Arbitre de mes jours !
Entre tes mains je remets
Ma personne et mes projets :
Je t'adore et ja te prie
De renouveller ma vie.

"Guide-moi par ta lumière,
Soutiens-moi par ton amour
Dans la nouvelle carrière,
Que je commence en ce jour :
Affranchis-moi de l'erreur ;
Excite et porte mon cœur
A ne vouloir, à ne faire
Que le bien, qui peut te plaire.

"J'ai dès ma plus tendre infance
Souvent transgressé ta loi ;
Il est temps que je commence
A me rapprocher de toi :
Pour assurer mon bouheur
Fais qu'une sainte frayeur
Me porte à la pénitence
Pour disarmer ta vengeance.

"Daigne augmenter cette année
En moi tes graces, Seigneur !
Que mon âme illuminée
Se dévoue à ton honneur ;
Et qu'un fidèle Chrétien,
M'attachant toujours au bien,

> Et fuyant l'hypocrisie,
> Je te consacre ma vie.
>
> "Dieu tout-bon! fais que je passe
> Cette année heureusement;
> Jésus! fais luire ta face
> Sur moi favorablement:
> Rends-moi ferme dans la foi,
> Pour vivre et mourir en toi,
> Et pour avoir en partage
> De tes élus l'héritage."

Once a week **Oberlin** gathered all the scholars in the village schools at Waldbach, and compared the progress they made under their different instructors, rewarding the diligent, and by a kindly word of counsel shaming the laggard.

His efforts, so sagaciously conceived, and so energetically carried out, met with such success that his Strasburg friends were induced to increase their subscriptions; and Oberlin was thus enabled to establish a public library, to print several school books for the use of his district; to make a collection of indigenous plants, and to procure a number of philosophical and mathematical instruments. Prizes were likewise awarded to both masters and scholars; and various works upon natural history and other branches of science, some of which he printed at his own expense, were put in circulation on the plan of a little book-society, being retained for three months at a time, first at one village and then at another, passing successively from house to house, in order that the younger members of the family might be supplied with a continual fund of useful and agreeable information.

The thoroughly practical character of Oberlin's mind, and his abundant "common sense"—no other phrase is so true or expressive—is strikingly illustrated in the plain and forcible remarks he appended to a little Almanack which he annually drew up for the use of his parishioners. Oberlin was an enthusiast and a reformer; and it is a kind of traditional belief that enthusiasts and reformers are very imaginative and visionary persons. Such a belief can hardly be maintained in the face of the calm reasonableness of the following:—

"*Advice to my Countrymen of the Ban de la Roche, upon this Almanack.*"

"I. The people of Germany have private almanacks, divided, by means of ruled lines, into numerous partitions. In each partition the names of the different individuals of the family are written, with a little blank space below them, in order that some notice may there be made of the manner in which the day has been passed, or any necessary memoranda inserted. I have now prepared a similar almanack for your use.

"II. The Strasburg children are accustomed to find their baptismal names in their almanack, and to celebrate the days on which they are recorded. You may also do the same with yours. They will all be found in this almanack.

"III. The parents of large and numerous families are often puzzled to find pretty baptismal names to distinguish their children from those who bear the same family name. Henceforth, if they only consult this new almanack, they will quickly be able to decide.

"IV. In your common almanacks you find and pay for a number of incomprehensible things, and for others which are absolutely useless; for others contrary to the commands of God, such as prognostics of the weather, nativities, predictions from the planets according to birthdays, lucky and unlucky days, or good and bad omens. This new almanack is divested of such nonsense.

"V. The changes of the moon, eclipses, and even some information respecting the courses of the planets; the names and figures of the twelve signs of the Zodiac; the time of the sun's rising and setting; and even the number of the months, and that of the weeks, are, nevertheless, inserted here.

"VI. I have frequently been asked the signification of names of a strange origin. By means of this almanack, I am enabled to give a reply to all my parishioners, for it contains the meaning of every name which can be obtained with certainty.

"VII. What a pity, perhaps you will say, that it has come so late. I say the same. It ought to have been completed before the end of December. But what good do you possess, the acquisition of which has not been retarded by various delays and obstacles? For my own part, I am so accustomed to expect this, in everything I do for you, that I am heartily glad it is accomplished, even at this late period.

"VIII. What does it cost? you will inquire. Dear friends, this Almanack is the fruit of my long-cherished desires to promote your good. Accept it as such. If it prove of any real benefit to you, or afford you a moment's gratification, look up to your Heavenly Father, and say: 'Thy goodness, O Lord, has crowned me with blessings. Permit me to thank Thee for them; and do Thou strengthen, by whatever means it may please Thee to employ, the feeble faith of Thy too feeble child.'"

In 1782, with the view of deepening and strengthening the spiritual life among his people, he established an association called "The Christian Society," which, in some respects, seems to have resembled the Church "Guilds" founded, in recent years, amongst English Churchmen. The following is a summary of the Rules, translated from the original in his own handwriting:—

I. Regeneration.
II. Sanctification.
III. "We are all one in Jesus."
IV. "Abide in me."
V. "Christ is all, and in all."
VI. "Bring forth much fruit."
VII. "Love not the world, neither the things that are in the world."
VIII. Nourish the inner man, by
    (1) The word of God.
    (2) Continual prayer.
    (3) The frequent use of the Holy Sacraments.
IX. The Superintendents are the overseers, whom the members choose from among themselves.
X. Not only the Superintendents, but also all the members, ought to watch over each other for good; to exhort and to warn each other.
XI. With sweetness, charity, humility, and patience.
XII. As to the incorrigible,—follow the example of Jesus Christ, Matthew xviii. 15, 16.
XIII. Meet for prayer on this subject.
XIV. Be submissive to your superiors. All the members are fellow-workers with their pastor.
XV. Good management.
XVI. Good education.
XVII. "Wives, be in subjection to your own husbands."
XVIII. "Search the Scriptures" diligently.
XIX. Diligence. Diligence, with application and energy—that is to say, industry.

XX. "Be careful for nothing."
XXI. Lose no time.
XXII. Allow of no idleness, or negligence on the part of those confided to your care.
XXIII. Honest and exact payment; no artfulness or cunning. See Romans xii. 17.
XXIV. "Be kindly affectioned one to another with brotherly love."
XXV. Endeavour to promote the happiness of all.
XXVI. "Provoke unto love and to good works."
XXVII. Appropriate part of your earnings, at stated intervals, to the public good.

This, however, was the only one of Oberlin's schemes that did not prove successful,—perhaps because the constitution of the Society tended to establish a kind of inquisition among its members, rendering each a spy and overseer over the others, and thus breeding a good deal of spiritual pride and Pharisaic intolerance. No doubt the value of Christian fellowship cannot be too highly estimated, but it is better that that fellowship should depend upon the golden maxim, "Love one another," than upon any code of arbitrary regulations. After a year and a half's existence Oberlin dissolved it. In addressing his parishioners on the subject, he gave as his reasons for doing so, first, that he had, in a great measure, obtained the end he had in view; second, that names and external forms are not essential, but are subject to vicissitude; and third, that, in the event of his death or removal, this external form would have been liable to change; and the members, overtaken by surprise, would have resembled, in some degree, sheep without a shepherd, and would not have known what to do. It was better that this should happen during his lifetime. And he argued that he had, in a great measure, attained his end: first, with respect to those who had been willing to become members; because they had had the opportunity of declaring themselves on the side of their Lord and Saviour Jesus Christ, and of acknowledging Him in the spirit of that passage (Matt. x. 32), "Whosoever, therefore, shall confess me before men, him will I confess also before my Father which is in heaven." They had learned to know more of their spiritual wants, and how necessary it was for them to be found in Christ Jesus, "without spot and blameless," "rooted and built up in Him, and established in the faith." They had felt, more than ever, the duty and necessity of prayer; whereas many, previous to the formation of the Society, had not even an idea of that continual prayer of the heart which our Lord recommends to His disciples. They had been led to feel that many souls were anxious for their salvation; and had learned to be "kind to one another, tender-hearted, forgiving one another, even as God, for Christ's sake, hath forgiven them." Again, with respect to those who had not been members, a number of souls had been roused from their lethargy, and though they had been unable to resolve to declare themselves members, they had been induced to pay more serious and prayerful attention to their spiritual necessities.

"Wherefore," he exclaimed in conclusion, "I cannot sufficiently thank God, the Father of our Lord Jesus Christ, for all the good that He has, through this agency, been pleased to effect in my dear parish; and for the evident blessing that has rested upon it. May He watch over it, and grant that the good fruits brought forth may be perfected and rendered permanent. May the kingdom of our Lord Jesus Christ be promoted and extended by any other means that He may see meet to appoint. May He sustain His Church according to His promise, Matthew xvi. 18, so that 'the gates of hell shall not prevail against it.' May He who said to His disciples, 'He that receiveth you, receiveth Me,' register all its members in His Book of Life. May He abundantly shed His Holy Spirit upon them, and 'grave them upon the palms of His hands,' so that no one may be able to draw them away, or turn them from Him. May He protect them, sanctify them, purify them, and prepare them for their heavenly inheritance."

On the 18th of January, 1784, Oberlin sustained an affliction which shook him to the very deeps of his being, in the death of his beloved wife, who had been the indefatigable partner of all his evangelistic and philanthropic labours. He bore it without a murmur, as became a Christian, seeking consolation and strength in prayer; but thenceforward his interest in life was perceptibly weakened, and he would often breathe a yearning wish that the world in which God would re-unite him to his beloved wife—that other **half of his soul; to use** the tender Latin expression, *dimidium animæ meæ*—**would soon** admit him across its threshold.

Years passed away, years of patience and Christian labour, and a subdued peace and religious calm prevailed in the household of the pastor of the Ban de la Roche. From the letter of a French clergyman who visited Waldbach in March 1793, we obtain a delightful glimpse of domestic happiness, so delightful that we do not think the reader will object to the length of our quotation.

"During the thirty **years** in which **M. Oberlin** has been pastor of this canton, he has completely changed the **face of** it. From an unintelligible *patois* the language has been reformed into pure French; **the** manners **of** the people have been civilized without any injury to their morals; and ignorance has been banished without injuring the simplicity **of** their character. Many of the women belonging to his parishes, having been trained for the purpose under his paternal care **and** instruction, assist **him in his** occupations. They teach reading, writing, and the **elements of** geography in the different villages **in** which they **reside; and** through their agency **the** children **are** instructed in many necessary things, but, above all, have the **seeds of** religion and morality been sown in their hearts. So **well** known and so highly appreciated are these schools, that girls **of** the middle **class are** sent to them from distant **parts, and the** title of 'a scholar of Pastor Oberlin' is accepted **as an** indisputable testimonial of piety, **talent,** and gentle manners.

"As for **the** pastor himself, he has **an** open and affectionate countenance, strongly impressed with benevolence. His conversation is easy, flowing, and full of vivacity, yet always adapted to the calibre of those to whom he is speaking. In the evening his visitor accompanied him a league on his way back to Waldbach. They **ascended a** beautifully-wooded hill, which the sunset invested with a wonderful **radiance.** Moved by the tranquil loveliness of the **scene, and** feeling that he had a congenial listener, Oberlin **related the** simple story of his industrious and useful life, speaking in the most touching language of his views and ideas, and **the** fear and love of God. Sometimes he and his **friend** paused **to** admire the beauties of nature; at others the impressiveness of his discourse induced his hearer to linger. One moment was particularly affecting, when, stopping about half-way up the hill, he said in the softest tones, 'Ja, ich bin glücklich' (Yes, I am happy).

"The moon rose in unclouded majesty, and night drew on with all her retinue of stars, suggesting to Oberlin the thought that if five years are necessary to bring a ray of light from Sirius to this world, though it travels at the rate of twelve millions of miles in a minute, how much swifter must the communication of spirits be! What is so swift as thought? And he then proceeded to describe the felicity with which, as he apprehended, we should approach one another in a future state.

"On the following morning the visitor paid him a second visit. The worthy pastor, in a plain, clean morning gown, was just on the point of concluding a lecture; his pupils wore on their faces an expression of contentment and gentleness just like their master's.

"The house was pleasantly situated, and from the garden side enjoyed quite a romantic view; in every part of it prevailed that kind of elegance, or rather refinement, which results from a combination of order, taste, and cleanliness. The furniture was simple, yet it suggested to the visitor that he was in the residence of no ordinary man; the walls were covered with maps, drawings, and vignettes; texts of Scripture were affixed above every door. As thus, above the dining-room door: 'Blessed are they which do hunger and thirst after righteousness, for they shall be filled.' The texts above the other doors enjoined love to God and our neighbour.

"When the visitors first entered, each as a welcome received a printed text, 'Abide in me, and I in you;' 'Seek those things which are above,' etc. His study, a peculiar room, contained a well-chosen rather than a numerous selection of books in French and German, chiefly for youth. The walls were covered with engravings, portraits of eminent characters, plates of insects and animals, and coloured drawings of minerals and precious stones; in a word, it was literally papered with useful pictures relative to natural history and other interesting subjects.

"The dinner began with a blessing. The pastor's children, two maids, and a girl who received her instruction there, were seated at the table; in all their countenances was the same remarkable expression of amiability.

"Oberlin had a singularly happy method of 'improving' occurrences, and, under the form of similes, drawing a moral from every incident. There was no mysticism about him or his teaching. 'The Gospel,' said he, 'is my standard—I should be afraid to trust myself alone without it.' He related to his guests many of the difficulties he had to encounter, and the sacrifices he had to make, when he began his career in the Ban de la Roche. 'But now,' continued he, checking himself, 'let me observe, it is as great a fault to talk of our own virtues as of the faults of others.'"

The narrative continues:—

"It is surprising to witness the sound sense, refinement, and superiority of mind evinced by these simple peasants. The very servants are well educated, and they are clothed with that child-like spirit which is one of the truest tests of real religion. One of them, a widow, made many excellent remarks to us on the duties of married life. 'In order to introduce and preserve domestic peace,' said she, 'let us turn to Him who is peace.'

"I am writing this at his table, while he is busy preparing leather gloves for his peasant children. His family are around him, engaged in their different avocations; his eldest son, Frederick, is giving a lesson to some of the little ones, in which amusement and instruction are judiciously blended; and the *cher papa*, without desisting from his employment, frequently puts in a word. He took me this morning into his workshop, where he has a turner's lathe, a press, a complete set of carpenter's tools; also a printing-press, and one for book-binding. I assisted him in colouring a quire of paper, which is intended for covers of school-books. He gives scarcely anything to his people but what has been, in some measure, prepared by his own or his children's hands.

"He will never quit this place. A more lucrative living was once offered him: 'No,' said he, 'I have been ten years learning every person in my parish, and obtaining an inventory of their moral, intellectual, and domestic wants; I have laid my plan. I must have ten years to carry it into execution, and the ten following to correct their faults and vices.'

"Pastor Oberlin is too modest and generous not to bear

testimony to the **worth of** his predecessors who had begun to clear this wilderness, **and to** raise the superstructure which he has so beautifully completed.

"Yesterday I found him encircled by four or five families who had been burnt out of their houses. **He was** dividing amongst them articles of clothing, meat, assignats, **books,** knives, thimbles, and coloured pictures for the children, whom **he** placed in **a** row according to their **ages,** and then left them to take what **they** preferred. Absolute equality reigns **in** his house; children, servants, boarders—all are treated alike; **their** places at table change, that each in turn may **sit** next to him, with the exception of Louisa, his housekeeper, who of course presides, and his **two maids,** who sit at the bottom **of** the table. As it is his **custom to salute every member** of his family, night and morning, **these** two little maids come very respectfully curtseying **to him, and** he always gives them his hand, and inquires after **their** health, or wishes them good **night.** All are happy, and appear to owe much of their happiness **to him.** They seem to be ready to sacrifice their lives to **save his.** The following reply was made by one of his servants, **on his** inquiring the cause of **her** downcast looks during some slight **indisposition:** 'I fear, dear papa, there will be no servants in heaven, and that I shall lose the happiness of waiting upon you.'

"Oberlin appears to be looking forward to his Eternal Home with holy confidence and joyful hope."

Late in the year 1793 Oberlin experienced his second domestic affliction; the loss of his eldest and well-beloved son, Frederick, who had entered the army as **a** volunteer, **and was** killed in battle, being then in his twenty-fourth **year.**

The idyllic life of Christian tranquillity which the good pastor had nurtured in the Ban de la Roche was undisturbed by the French Revolution. The storm which raged in every other part of France passed over the Happy Valley without leaving behind it a rifled blossom or a broken bough. Though the rulers of the town had interdicted Christian worship, Oberlin ministered to his people every Sunday according to wont, and none molested him. It was as if the Angel of God watched at the portals of the valley, and permitted no sound of discord to break in upon its peace.

He was deprived, however, of the income allowed by the State. His people made an effort to supply its place by voluntary contributions, and in 1789 raised a sum of 1,133 francs; but in the three succeeding years it sunk to 400 francs, owing to the general poverty of the district. Upon this small annual stipend, with such additions as he could derive from the labours of tuition, Oberlin contrived to maintain his household and exercise his usual charities. The tithes of all he possessed his devoted generosity yearly allotted to the service of God and the poor.

Continuing that work of organisation for which he had a special genius, Oberlin founded a Ladies' Bible Society, through the medium of which a large number of copies of the New Testament were circulated in France. The cause of Foreign Missions also found in him an active helper.

For the material benefit of his flock, which from eighty or a hundred families had increased to five or six hundred, he introduced cotton-spinning, and fostered it by offering prizes to the best spinners. He knew that agriculture could support but a limited number, and was continually devising new resources for the benefit of his augmenting population, such as straw-plaiting, knitting, and the silk-manufactory. The good achieved by his extraordinary efforts was recognised in 1818 by the presentation of a gold medal from the Royal Agricultural Society of Paris; and all over Europe his name was mentioned with well-deserved expressions of admiration. On a small scale, and in a confined area, he had displayed all the qualities of a great statesman and a leader of men; and he had been more successful, perhaps, than any statesman could ever be, because he was the priest as well as the teacher of his people, and laboured for their spiritual as eagerly as for their national welfare. From Louis XVIII. he received the ribbon of the Legion of Honour, and it is certain that it was never worn on a breast more nobly animated by the highest and purest motives. No thought of self ever crossed the mind of Oberlin. He lived for others; for others he gave up all his powers and opportunities and capabilities; the general happiness was his first and latest care. And his career carries with it a valuable lesson, in showing, as it does most strikingly, how great an influence for good may be exercised by each one of us in his own sphere, if he will but take up the work in an unselfish spirit.

It needs no extraordinary, no exceptional intellectual powers; it does not even demand the possession of extensive means; the desideratum is simply an earnest and intelligent mind, and a heart that, filled with the love of God, necessarily bleeds and glows with the love of man.

The reader will probably desire to obtain some idea of Oberlin as the priest of his flock. Well, of the pure simplicity and naturalness of his teaching, the following translation of a sermon preached in November, 1819, may be given as an illustration. He took for his text Luke xx. 34-36: "The children of this world marry and are given in marriage: but they which shall be accounted worthy to obtain that world, and the resurrection from the dead, neither marry nor are given in marriage; neither can they die any more: for they are equal unto the angels; and are the children of God, being the children of the resurrection."

"Our Lord here presents us with a delightful prospect, an extremely enchanting future for all who have no greater, no more pressing anxiety than to become true disciples of Jesus Christ, true members of His body.

"To understand fully this fine passage, I must explain some of its terms:

"I. What does our Lord mean by 'this world' and 'the world to come'?

"By 'this world' our Lord means the present condition of the human race, since it has fallen from its originally glorious state.

"And by the 'world to come' He means the marvellously glorious condition of those in whom God shall perfectly restore His image, and the original glorious state for which we were created.

"II. What does our Lord mean by 'the resurrection of the dead'? Not the general awakening of the dead at the Last Day, when all human creatures will be summoned to appear before the tribunal of the Supreme Judge, but the perfect deliverance of the soul from all the ills which sin has brought upon us, and the re-establishment of the primitive glory. This it is which our Lord calls the resurrection of the dead.

"III. Who are they who will be esteemed worthy of this glorious resurrection and of their perfect re-establishment in the image of God?

"Those who give themselves up in heart, and soul, and mind to our Lord Jesus Christ, and strive to enter in by the narrow gate, and for this purpose carefully study and observe all our Lord's commandments to His disciples; who by continual prayer from the depths of their heart, and by frequent attendance at the Holy Table, endeavour to be more and more closely united to their Saviour; who aspire to love God with all their heart, with all their soul, with all their strength, and all their thoughts, and to love their neighbours as themselves, and to be the faithful servants and labourers of God in His vineyard.

"Those who travail to obtain those graces, not only for themselves, but also for all their families, and their friends and acquaintances, so far as they can reach them by their prayers.

"When such servants of God as these, by their faithfulness, humility, ardour, and charity, shall have arrived at the perfect holiness and perfection of the saints, and shall be received into the class and rank of the inhabitants of the Mount of Zion or Heavenly Kingdom, then shall they receive the glorified body or resurrection of which our Lord speaks.

"IV. Then shall they no more die; as our Lord expresses it in Rev. xxi. 4,—'There shall be no more death, neither sorrow, nor crying, neither shall there be any more pain: for the former things are passed away.'

"You know, my dear friends, that all terrestrial nature is a representation of the spiritual. The caterpillars, and indeed all insects, pass through different stages which have no resemblance to one another. At first, on emerging from the egg, they are but tiny grubs, which from time to time strip off their outer integument and issue forth as in a new attire.

"But at length they receive a completely novel form, that of the chrysalis. This is quite a new animal, so to speak, differing from the first in figure and in its properties or powers.

"This, however, is not all. Under the form of this chrysalis, it prepares to become yet another animal, perfect in itself, and yet wholly distinct from what it was in its two former stages; this is the butterfly, adorned with beautiful colours, and endowed with new tastes and qualities.

"It now disdains the coarser nutriment of its first stage, and feeds on one purer and more perfect, that is, on the honeyed juices of the flowers.

"And so far as its motions are concerned, it has no longer any need of its feet to transport itself from one place to another; by means of its wings it rises lightly, and soars rapidly above walls and rivers and mountains.

"In like manner those who are in Jesus Christ, passing, in proportion as they advance in humility, charity, and saintliness, through the different changes of their inner selves, spiritual, visible to the angels, but concealed from us under the earthly body.

"And these changes proceed from brightness to brightness, from splendour to splendour, until their bodies have become conformed and like unto the glorious body of our Lord Jesus Christ.

"Ah, my dear friends, what an enchanting prospect, what a delightful and amazing hope!

"O let us always love to pursue in Jesus Christ our sanctification, and to knit closer our connexion with Him.

"It is through Him, our dear Lord, and it is only through Him, that we can attain to this consummation. For it is He whom God hath given us that we may find in Him wisdom, and justice, and sanctification, and glorious redemption, and deliverance."

One other specimen, from a sermon preached on the Day of Pentecost, 1822. Text, "I indeed baptize you with water unto repentance, but He that cometh after me is mightier than I, whose shoes I am not worthy to bear. He shall baptize you with the Holy Ghost and with fire" (Matt. iii. 11).

"Beloved friends! In Holy Baptism we have been received children of God, according to the original destination of the human race.

"But does not a child who disobeys his father lose his right of childhood? And have you accomplished the orders of God? His orders, not only those of the New Testament, but also of the Old, the Lord of which assures us that He will not allow us to transgress a single iota? Have you fulfilled them all, and fulfilled them perfectly? Have you loved God with all your heart and all your soul? and your neighbour,—do you love *him*, and have you always loved him, as yourself? Have you, in consequence of this twofold love, constantly executed the will of God, freely and fully in all things? Have you made every possible effort to enter through the strait gate?

"Alas, alas! will every rational man reply to me, 'Oh, if the Lord willed to enter into judgment with us, who could stand against Him?'"

"And now, what is the object, the aim, of the Pentecost? It is to warn us that the first Baptism does not suffice; that we must, by dint of instant prayer, lay hold on the second Baptism, the Baptism of the Holy Spirit and of fire—that force and marvellous virtue which vivifies in us the Word of God, which makes it throw its roots into our heart, and bear fruit.

"Tell me, beloved friends! when you sow your seeds, by what marvellous and magical secret do you prevent these germs, so delicate and tender, from rotting in the earth, so that instead of multiplying, they may reward your pains with liberal largess?

"Certainly no human power can work that miracle. No, it is God, that tender and compassionate Father of all His beloved creatures, through His goodness and His love for His children—for it is like Him that He loves everything which He has created—our beloved Heavenly Father, I say, communicates to the germs of vegetation as it were a kind of baptism of fire and of life; who not only protects them from corruption, but endows them with a marvellous virtue, almost creative and divine, the virtue of producing others of the same species, and of multiplying them.

"And oh, friends! it is this same divine and marvellous virtue, which, through our ardent and persistent but secret vows and sighs, we should seek to obtain for the seed of the Word of God, when we listen to it for our own good, or when we communicate it to our children and household, either in the morning, or at different times in the day, according to circumstances.

"And then He who multiplies the seeds which you entrust to the earth will baptize you also with fire and the Holy Ghost, and in you, and in your beloved ones, will bless the seeds of His Holy Word. And it will come to pass that you, and your families, in spite of all the corruption of your hearts, and the seductive examples of those who inhabit the earth, and in spite of the temptations and assaults of the hosts of Satan, will become the sacred plants of the Church, capable of being transferred into the paradise of God, without fear or risk of ever being cast down from your ineffable felicity."

In these brief discourses there is no special eloquence, it is true; no originality, no signs of rare intellectual power: but we recognise a force and a sincerity which doubtless appealed to the hearts of his simple-minded hearers. He spoke in faith, and in faith they listened, and the sympathy between the teacher and the taught ripened into precious fruit. A Bourdaloue or a Massillon would have done infinitely less good in the Ban de la Roche, with all his splendid gifts, than the unassuming Oberlin: so true it is that God's instruments are always adapted to God's work, and so true is it also that for the work which He sets us to do we shall always be provided with the power to do it, if we apply ourselves with earnestness and in hope. Men often shrink from the duty incumbent upon them in a timid apprehension that it is beyond their strength: let them attack it at once, and they will find themselves rising spontaneously, as it were, to the required height. We cannot fail to grow to the standard which God ordains for us.

Yet another side of Oberlin's character is shown in the practical catechism which he addressed to his people in writing, requiring a straightforward reply to each query. The relations between pastor and congregation were of course absolutely exceptional, which enabled the former to institute, and the latter to welcome, so minute and curious an investigation, or, as in England it would assuredly be called, inquisition.

1. Do you and your family regularly attend places of religious instruction?

2. Do you never pass a Sunday without employing yourself in some charitable work?

3. Do neither you nor your wife nor children ever wander in the woods on a Sunday, in search of wild raspberries, strawberries, whortle-berries, mulberries, or hazel nuts, instead of going to church? And if you have erred in this manner, will you solemnly promise to do so no more?

4. Are you careful to provide yourself with clean and suitable clothes to wear when you go to Church on the Sunday?

5. Do those who are provided with the necessary clothes employ a regular part of their income in procuring such for their destitute neighbours, or in the relief of their other necessities?

6. Have your civil and ecclesiastical overseers reason to be satisfied with your conduct, and with that of the other members of your family?

7. Do you so love and reverence our Lord and Saviour, Jesus Christ, as to feel united in the bonds of Christian fellowship with that flock of which He is the Pastor?

8. Do the animals which belong to you cause no injury or inconvenience to others?—[Guard against this, for it would be as fire in tow, and a source of mutual vexation.]

9. Do you give your creditors reason to be satisfied with your honesty and punctuality? Or can they say of you that you are more desirous of purchasing superfluous clothes than of discharging your debts?

10. Have you paid all that is due this quarter to the church-warden, schoolmaster, and shepherd?

11. Do you punctually contribute your share towards the maintenance of the roads?*

12. Have you, in order to contribute to the general good, planted upon the common at least twice as many trees as there are heads in your family?

13. Have you planted them properly, or only as idle and ignorant people would do, to save themselves trouble?

14. Do you, when the manager wishes to assemble the community, render him all the assistance that lies in your power? and, if it be impossible for you to attend yourself, are you careful to inform him of your absence, and to assign a proper reason for it?

15. Do you send your children regularly to school?

16. Do you watch over them as God requires you should do? And is your wife's and your own conduct towards them such as will ensure their affection, respect, and obedience."

17. Are you frugal in the use of wood? And do you contrive to make your fires in as economical a manner as possible?

---

* A very important matter, as we have seen, in the Ban de la Roche.

18. Do you keep a dog unless there be absolute necessity?

19. Have you proper drains to carry off the refuse water in your yard? [Observe: with Oberlin cleanliness was next to godliness. He anticipated Kingsley in combining the sanitary reformer * with the priest.]

20. Are you and your sons acquainted with some little handicraft work to employ your leisure moments, instead of wasting them in idleness?

Our sketch of Oberlin's career must draw to a close. Have we not said enough to enable the reader to realize to himself this extraordinary man, who, in a secluded corner of Europe, carried out into principle not a few of the social and moral theories that brighten the pages of Plato's "Republic" and Moore's "Utopia"? this man who was at once philanthropist, pastor, statesman, legislator, and educational reformer,—whose organizing capacity created everything, from a highway to an infants' school? Well, let us take a final look at the worker and his works as they appeared to a lady who visited them in 1820:—

"I wish," she writes, "I had power to convey to you an idea of our present interesting and serious situation. In the first place, I must introduce you to the room I am sitting in. It is perfectly unique—I should think the floor had never been really cleaned. It is filled with old boxes, and bottles, and pictures, and medicines, and books, but everything is in its place. Two little beds are stuck up in each corner, and there are a few old chairs. The

---

* He was also a sumptuary reformer. On one occasion he addressed to the mothers in his parish an animated remonstrance on the fashion they had adopted of putting cambric or muslin frills to their children's shirts. "Do not do so, dear friends. Unpick them, cut them off, and seek not to increase your children's vanity, which is already too great by nature. Cut off all the finery that does not correspond with your station in life, and employ yourselves in clothing the poor families of this extensive parish, many of whom are in an exceedingly miserable condition. Love your neighbours as yourselves. Renounce every superfluity, that you may be the better able to procure necessaries for those who are in want. Be their care-takers—their fathers and mothers—inasmuch as it is for this purpose that God has blessed you with more temporal wealth than He has given to them. Be merciful. The time may come when you yourselves will stand in need of the Divine mercy." Can the reader imagine many English clergymen addressing their flocks in this outspoken manner?

window looks upon the tops of the mountains, near which we are, —separated from the world." . .

After describing their journey to Waldbach, she continues :—

"We set off for Mr. Oberlin's, a mile and a half farther,—a romantic walk through the valley. On the way we met this most venerable and striking man—the perfect picture of what an old man and minister should be. He received us cordially, and we soon felt quite at ease with him. We all proceeded together towards his house, which stands on the top of a hill, surrounded by trees and cottages. Owing to the fatigue of our journey, I felt quite overdone on our first arrival. I could see nothing like a mistress in the house; but an old woman, called Louisa, dressed in a long woollen jacket and black cotton cap, came to welcome us, and we afterwards found that she is an important person at the Ban de la Roche : she is mistress, housekeeper, intimate friend, maid-of-all-work, schoolmistress, entertainer of guests, and, I should think, assistant minister, though we have not yet heard her in this capacity. Besides Louisa, the son-in-law and daughter and their six children live here, two young girls, *protégées*, and two more maids out of the parish. Mr. Graff, the son-in-law, is a minister, and a very excellent man. There is much religion and simplicity both in him and his wife; but the latter is so devoted to the children that we seldom see her. We were ushered into the *salle-à-manger*, where stood the table, spread for supper; a great bowl of pottage, with a pewter plate and spoon for everybody :— the luxuries of a common English cottage not being known in the Ban de la Roche. . .

"*Tuesday.*—We have become better acquainted with this extraordinary people, who are as interesting as they are uncommon. I much regret that I cannot speak the language more fluently; yet I get on as well as I can; I have had a good deal of pleasing communication with them.

"I never knew so well what the grace of courtesy was till I saw this remarkable man. He treats the poorest people, and even the children, with an affectionate respect. For instance, his courtesy, kindness, and hospitality to our postilion were quite amusing. He pulled off his hat when he met him, took him by the hand, and treated him with really tender consideration. He is, I think, more than eighty—one of the handsomest old men I ever remember to have seen—still vigorous in mind and spirit, delighting in his parish, full of fervent charity. . . . The meals are really amusing :—we all sit down to the same table, maids and all, one great dish of pottage or boiled spinach, and a quantity of salad and potatoes, upon which they chiefly live, being placed in the middle. He shakes hands with all the little children as he passes them in the street, speaking particularly to each of them. The effect which such treatment has had in polishing these people, uncivilized and uncultivated as they formerly were, is quite wonderful. They have been taught a variety of things which have enlarged and refined their minds, besides religion—music, geography, drawing, and botany. My sketching has been quite a source of amusement in the parish. . . .

"If you go into a parish cottage they quite expect you will eat and drink with them; a clean cloth is laid upon a table, washed almost as white as milk, and the new milk and the wine [*kirschen wasser*, distilled from the fruit of the wild cherry], and the great loaf of bread, are brought out; yet they are in reality exceedingly poor. Their beds also look so clean and good that they would astonish our poor people. In some respects I think they are decidedly cleaner than our own peasantry. Their dress is simple to the greatest degree. The women and girls all dress alike, even down to the very little children. They wear caps of dark cotton, with black ribbon, and the hair bound closely under. Everybody —maids, children, poor and rich, call Mr. Oberlin their 'cher papa,' and never was there a more complete father of a large family. We breakfast at seven; the family upon potatoes boiled with milk and water—a little coffee is provided for us. We dine at twelve, and sup at half-past seven. Everything is in the most primitive style. I never met with such a disinterested people. It is almost impossible to pay them for any service they do for you. In our visits to the poor we have been afraid of offering them money; but we feel anxious to throw in some assistance towards the many important objects which Mr. Oberlin is carrying on amongst them. It is almost past belief what he has done, and with *very limited* means. Three poor dear women are noted for their benevolence: one especially, who is a widow herself with several children, has undertaken to support and bring up three orphan children; and she has lately taken another, from no other principle than abounding Christian charity. One seldom meets with such shining characters. Mr. Oberlin said the other day that he did not know how to pay Louisa, for nothing hurt her so much as offering her money. No one could be more devoted to his service, and that in the most disinterested manner. Her character has impressed me very much. We had a delightful walk to a church about two miles distant, on Sunday morning; the numbers of poor, flocking from the distant villages, dressed in their simple and neat costume, formed a striking object in the scene. It happened to be the Sunday Mr. Oberlin goes to the next parish, where his son requires his assistance in giving prizes to the schoolchildren.

"*Wednesday evening.*—The poor charm me. I never met with any like them; so much spirituality, humility, and cultivation of mind, with manners that would do honour to a court; yet the homeliness and the simplicity of the peasant are not lost. The state of the schools, the children, and the poor in general, is quite extraordinary, and as much exceeds our parish as ours does the most neglected.

"We have spent our time in the following manner: since Sunday the mornings have been very wet; we have therefore been chiefly shut up in our own room, reading, writing, and drawing; the eldest of the Graffs (Marie), a sweet girl, is a good deal with me, to read and to talk to me. The children and young people in the house are becoming fond of me; our being here is quite a gaiety and an amusement to them. About three o'clock Mr. Legrand comes for us, to take us different excursions, etc. He seems to us one of the kindest persons we ever met with, full of conversation; nothing can exceed the torrent of words they all have. The old gentleman delights in talking to F——, and tells him everything about himself, his family, his parishes. Our room joins his library, and all the family are free to enter whenever they like. The whole system is most amusing, interesting, and useful. It is a capital example, and instructive for the minister of a parish. There is a spirit of good fellowship and kindness amongst all the people that is quite delightful. The longer we have been here, the more we have been struck with the uncommon degree of virtue which exists among them. On Monday evening, after sketching Legrand's house, we were taken to the cottage of Sophia Bernard, where we found the table spread in the most complete manner for our tea—a luxury we had not enjoyed since we left England. Here we passed some time, eating, talking, and reading the Bible; and it ended with prayer, by Sophia Bernard, in a sweet and feeling manner. We then had a charming walk through the valley home. Tuesday, in the afternoon, we ascended towards the very top of the mountains, to another of his villages, where we again found some delightful women, and a capital school.

"*Colmar, Friday evening.*—Our scene is again quite changed, we are returned to the common world; and I now find myself by a comfortable fire at a good hotel, which is quite a luxury after the primitive fare of the Ban de la Roche, where we found but little indulgence for the body, though we were treated with genuine hospitality. They live sadly in the clouds. The sun does not appear very often to shine upon them. I never was so struck with the difference of climate as I was to-day, in coming down into the plains. It poured with rain for the last day or two; and all yesterday, in the mountains, everything was soaked with wet; but on entering the plains the dust began to fly. Delightful and uncommon as is this retreat, I must acknowledge we have rather enjoyed the comforts of the town and the conveniences of this place. It would be a trial to me to live surrounded and buried by mountains. I could not help rather feeling for Marie Graff, who is sensible of her privations. However, they are happy and contented, and highly blessed, and it is a great privilege to have passed this time with them; an event which must always be valuable through life. We parted from the excellent old man with many kisses, in the full spirit of Christian love."

Old age, though it did not weaken Oberlin's Christian enthusiasm, broke down his physical strength; and he was at last compelled to delegate the charge of his flock to his son-in-law, Mr. Graff. He continued, however, instant in prayer on their behalf, and devoted all his thoughts to the advancement of their spiritual and material welfare. His last illness came upon him suddenly. On Sunday, the 28th of May, 1826, he was seized with shiverings and fainting fits, which prevailed until a late hour of the night. During the next two days he was alternately conscious and insensible; exclaiming frequently, as his strength permitted, "Lord Jesus, take me speedily! Nevertheless, *Thy* will be done!" He was much cheered and consoled, on Tuesday evening, by a visit from his friend Legrand, embracing him warmly, and saying, in a distinct voice, "The Lord bless you, and all who are dear to you! May He be with you day and night!" The day following, his weakness had so increased that he was unable to speak, and had recourse to signs to express his feelings. During the night between Wednesday and Thursday, the 1st of June, he uttered incessantly plaintive moans, as though in pain, though probably they were the almost unconscious effects of physical debility; but at times he would seize the hand of either of his children who happened to be nearest to him, and press it to his heart. When Legrand visited him at six in the morning, his arms and legs had become lifeless and cold; but he gathered up strength enough to take off his cap, join his palms, and lift his eyes towards heaven, with a light on his countenance which told of inward peace in the assurance of eternal life through a risen Saviour. Then his eyes closed, to be opened no more in this world; though it was a quarter past eleven before his spirit passed away, and the death bell, pealing slowly and sadly through the valley, announced to his sorrowing people that their pastor, teacher, philanthropist, and friend was no more.

His funeral took place on the 5th of June. Never before had such a sense of mourning been seen in the Ban de la Roche. The procession was nearly two miles long, and included the mayors, elders, and magistrates, all the people, young and old, with the most aged inhabitant leading the way, and bearing aloft a simple wooden cross to be planted on the grave of "Papa Oberlin." At the close of the ceremony an address was delivered by the Vice-President of the Consistory of Ban, from which, as an appropriate peroration to our biographical sketch, we translate the following passages:—

"My Christian brothers," he said, "we have just sustained a great and sensible loss; our good father Oberlin has quitted us; he has terminated in peace his earthly career. Around his grave I see the faithful of the two parishes of the Ban de la Roche, the faithful of Waldbach and Rothau, uniting their grief and their tears with those of the children and the many friends of the venerable deceased. If, moved with sentiments of love and admiration for the venerable pastor of Waldbach, I speak on this day of sorrow, I know well, my brethren, that it is impossible for me to describe to you worthily the lofty virtues and the fine qualities of the good and great man for whom we are now mourning.

"Our Consistorial Church loses in him one of her most zealous pastors, a man distinguished by his talents and his virtues; the parishes of Waldbach and the Ban de la Roche in general, a benefactor, a father, of the utmost tenderness of heart; his family and friends, their model, and the source of their happiness; humanity, one of its finest ornaments. What a pure and elevated soul—what simplicity—what affability—what gentle tolerance—what unswerving rectitude—what candour, have we not admired in that thrice-happy old man! More than an octogenarian, the venerable Oberlin made use of his failing energies for the glory of God, and with his latest sigh implored the Divine mercy upon that beloved parish in which he had centred all his affections.

"How tender the care he lavished on the cherished flock which was confided to his charge! A worthy servant of his Divine Master, a zealous successor of the Apostles, he devoted himself wholly to the welfare of his fellows. For nine-and-fifty years he gave up all his energies, physical and intellectual, all the hours of his laborious life, to the civilizing of this interesting country; and with the noblest disinterestedness, with unshaken firmness, with inexpugnable zeal, he voluntarily sacrificed all his fortune in order that security, and ease, and prosperity might inhabit your humble dwellings... It is Oberlin who trained your teachers; it is he who covered your dry and naked rocks with fertile soil; it is he who transformed all these hamlets into flourishing villages; it is he who, working by your side, succeeded in restoring and enlarging your roads; it is he who showed a noble compassion for your poor, and nourished them in seasons of scarcity; it is he who succoured the widow and the orphan, and protected the deserted; it is he—but let us pause; your grateful hearts can finish for themselves this feeble outline of what he accomplished for your welfare. Oberlin did not allow his humanity to be limited by any narrow views; he made no distinction of creed; he was persuaded that intolerance dishonours charity. . . .

"Oberlin rekindled the torch of the faith, and illustrated religion in these districts. More urgently even than your well-being in this world did he strive for the salvation of your immortal souls. The glory of all his efforts, the prize of all his anxieties, was your spiritual welfare, O ye faithful of the parish of Waldbach!

"With what fire and force, what simplicity and perseverance, he preached to you the gospel of the Christ, that precious gift of heaven, those truths of religion engraved upon his heart! He taught you to discover in the Holy Bible, in the precepts of Jesus Christ, the remedy for all your ills, the resource for all your miseries, the true fountain of the purest pleasures, of the happiness of this life and the life to come. It was he who, Gospel in hand, purified, enlightened, consoled, sanctified you. Was it not he who, by his speech and practice, fostered in your hearts the love of God and man? Was it not he who led you to the feet of that Redeemer who has suffered for you?—to that Christian virtue, that fervent faith which makes the happiness of the Christian; who presented to you our adorable Saviour in the heavenly abodes where He awaits you, whither He went to prepare a place for you? Was it not he who so frequently exhorted you to labour for the meat which endureth unto everlasting life?*

"It is to your worthy patriarch that you owe this word of grace; it is he who distributed among you the manna which sustains your souls; it was he who carried the Gospel into your houses and into the cottages of so many of the poor outside the borders of his parish. Oh, my brothers, draw ye upon that treasure which never diminishes, which enriches you in proportion as ye draw upon it! Bless the name of Oberlin, bless the memory of that just man who might say in truth with St. Paul, the great apostle: † 'Ye know ... after what manner I have been with you at all seasons, serving the Lord with all humility of mind, and with many tears and temptations ... and how I kept back nothing that was profitable unto you, but have showed you, and have taught you publicly, and from house to house, ... repentance toward God, and faith toward our Lord Jesus Christ.... None of those things move me, neither count I my life dear unto myself, so that I might finish my course with joy, and the

---

* John vi. 27.   † Acts xx. 18-33.

ministry, which I have received of the Lord Jesus, to testify the gospel of the grace of God ... I take you to record, that I am pure from the blood of all men, for I have not shunned to declare unto you all the counsel of God ... I have coveted no man's silver, or gold, or apparel.'

"Do you not retrace in these details the image of your venerable pastor Oberlin?

"And, my brothers, what did he accomplish for the propagation of the holy religion of Jesus Christ, for the propagation of the sacred writings? Speak, Biblical Societies of Strasburg, of Paris, of London! Speak, Missionary Institutions of Basel and Paris! What moneys he contrived to collect, what donations and gifts, for these pious Societies, in order that the Bible might be diffused everywhere, that the teaching of Christ might penetrate even into the most savage climes, among the most barbarous nations, that God and the Saviour might be adored by all the inhabitants of the earth. What a joy for him, when perusing the reports of the Bible and Missionary Societies, to see the blessing of God bestowed upon his work!

"His career, full of trials, privations, and dangers, his prolonged sufferings, revealed his soul in all its purity, and the sublime virtues of which it was the seat. A patience which nothing could overthrow, an eminently Christian resignation, rendered him always superior to all misfortunes. He confronted death with a steadfast eye, with the calmness and serenity of the just. In taking leave of earth he commended his soul to God, he prayed for his family, for his friends, for his parish; and in the midst of benedictions, his soul soared up to the heavens. Oberlin has left us; his death was the recompense of a life crowded with good works, with just and generous actions.

"What a concourse at his funeral, what lamentations, what tears! Two parishes, eight communes, that crowd of friends, of strangers, all say with one voice, it is to a good man we pay the last sad homage; it is Oberlin, our father, our benefactor, whom we weep; it is friendship, reverence, gratitude, which has led us to this grave!... His ashes will repose in your midst, ye good people of the Ban de la Roche; and that grave which enshrines his mortal remains will be for all of us a sacred spot. We shall show it to our children and say to them, 'Here lies

Oberlin our father.' He rendered us happy; his image is engraved in our hearts; love is stronger than death; Waldbach will be a permanent monument of his glory; the names of Oberlin and Waldbach will be for ever united in the memory of men.

"Let us adore the ways of Providence, my brothers! In the stead of the venerable father, the Lord has given you the worthy husband of Oberlin's daughter, the friend of his heart, and one who walks in God's ways. It was the good father himself who made the choice, and this choice is a new sign of heaven's protection vouchsafed to this flock. It is with perfect confidence that Oberlin has passed on to the hands of his successor the sacred deposit of which the Divine Master had given him charge.

"Yes, Christians, let us adore that Providence which unites and parts us, afflicts and consoles us; let us enter into its views, let us accomplish its designs upon us. Let us be united by the bonds of that charity which is the most perfect of all the virtues (*les biens*); let us love one another in this mortal life, that we may love one another in the world beyond. Let us love one another in God, in whose bosom we shall one day find ourselves to be united for ever, if here below we serve Him with fidelity. Let us vow to this God of all goodness an absolute resignation, an unshaken faith. May the Father of all Mercy be the consoler and supporter of the afflicted family and friends of the departed saint, of this parish now filled with mourning!

"Farewell, venerable Oberlin! in the heavenly region thou gatherest what thou hast sown, thy works follow thee. Delivered from all trials and sorrows, thy Lord shall say to thee: 'I know thy works, thy charity, thy faith, thy patience' (Rev. ii. 19). Farewell, noble friend! Farewell, venerated father! Never shall thy image vanish from our soul; always thou shalt be the object of our reverence: thy memory, the memory of the just, shall remain for ever as a benediction." *

---

* This sermon, in the original French, is given in the Appendix to "Memoirs of John Frederic Oberlin" (published in 1831), a little volume to which we have been much indebted. It contains information not accessible elsewhere. The principal authority for the good pastor's life is, however, the " Notice sur Jean Frederic Oberlin," by M. Lutteroth. See also the Rev. J. Conder's article in the *Eclectic Review* for October 1827.

We shall conclude this chapter with the life of a woman, who, in her sphere, did work as noble as any done by Oberlin in his Alsatian valley, labouring among a population not less ignorant and infinitely more vicious.

Mary Carpenter was born at Exeter on April 3rd, 1807. She was the daughter of Dr. Lant Carpenter, a Nonconformist divine, who came of an old Nonconformist stock. At an early age she showed herself keenly alive to the religious influences that surrounded her, and would turn from playing with her dolls to plunge into the metaphysical maze of necessity and freewill. Her father removed to Bristol in 1817, and before long Mary Carpenter was allowed to take charge of a class in the Sunday-school. Meanwhile, her education was of a very thorough and comprehensive character, including the study of Latin and Greek, of Mathematics, with some of the elements of Physical Science and Natural History. Wide as was the field over which her active intellect ranged, the knowledge she acquired was exact and profound. Her father discouraged superficial work; all she did she was required to do conscientiously, to plumb the bottom, not to skim the surface. A schoolfellow bears witness to the fulness of her acquirements:—" The Latin reading," says this authority, " which I seem to associate most with the 'Agricola' of Tacitus, was marked by the same conscientious care which she evinced in everything, securing accuracy but not escaping stiffness, unless, at the appeal of some prophetic passage which softened more than the outer voice, it assumed for the moment a higher character, and admitted a gleam of poetic light. . . . Every Monday morning we had a Greek Testament reading with Dr. Carpenter, intended not less as a religious lesson than as an exercise in the language and criticism of Scripture. . . . While translating her verses with precision, and prepared with answers to questions of history and analogy, she unconsciously betrayed, by voice, by eye, by the very mode of holding her book, that she treated the text as sacred, and in following its story felt a touch from which a divine virtue went out."

In 1827 she accepted the charge of some young girls in the Isle of Wight, where the love of natural scenery and her sympathy with the beautiful found ample food. Thence she went to

Odsey, near Royston, vigilantly keeping up her own mental culture, and losing no opportunity of adding to her stores of knowledge. In 1829, she returned to Bristol, and, in conjunction with Anna, opened a school for girls. Happy pupils who had Mary Carpenter for teacher! Her vivid fancy played upon the dry bones of facts, and made them live. She infused a new, fresh interest into every study by comparing it and correlating it with other studies. Her heart was in her work; she did not take it up as a dreary task that had to be accomplished and endured, but as a real and genuine pleasure which could not be too fully enjoyed. One of her pupils wrote:—" Miss Carpenter is quite delightful; she understands Greek, Latin, Italian, French, and every other language for anything I know to the contrary, for I only know of these, hearing her teach them. She is fond of poetry, geology, and conchology, which two latter she seems to understand very well. In short, she seems to be universal. She possesses the quality of great kindness, as do all the family."

But as yet she had not discovered the mission which God had sent her into the world to discharge, the great end for which her powers had been given and matured. It was not until 1831, when she became Superintendent of the Sunday-school, that her attention was directed to the wretched condition of the poor and ignorant in our large English towns. There, wealth and poverty seem almost to touch each other, and yet between them yawns a gulf not less wide than that between Lazarus and Dives in the parable. One half the world knows not how the other half suffers, because, unfortunately, it does not care to know. The Bristol riots, which fill so dark a chapter in the history of the time, shocked her into a conviction that beneath the surface of social life stormy currents raged uncontrolled, and she formed within her mind a deep resolve to save as many as possible of the waifs and strays which they tossed helplessly to and fro, to devote her life and her gifts to the cause of God's poor. She did not at first find the way, and she had the wisdom to wait until Heaven should make it clear to her. So much well-meant effort is lost by unwise haste! Some persons seem in a hurry to anticipate the counsels of God Himself! In 1833 the Rajah Raumshem Raj visited Bristol, and so did Dr. Joseph Tuckerman, of Boston, U.S.; and the first touched the springs of Mary Carpenter's sympathies by his visions of a regenerated India, the second aroused her to the sad lot of destitute children. These two influences determined and shaped out her career. The impression made upon her mind by the Brahman Theist we have in some verses which she wrote on hearing of his death :—

> "Thy nation sat in darkness, for the night
> Of pagan gloom was o'er it. Thou wast born
> 'Midst Superstition's ignorance forlorn,
> Yet in thy breast there glowed a heavenly light
> Of purest truth and love, and to thy sight
> Appeared the day-star of approaching Morn.
> What ardent zeal did then thy life adorn,
> From deep degrading guilt to lead aright
> Thy fallen people! to direct their view
> To that blessed Son of Righteousness, whence beams
> Guidance to all that seek it—faithful, true ;
> To call them to the Saviour's living streams.
> The cities of the East have heard thy voice,
> 'Nations, behold your God! Rejoice, rejoice !'"

Mary Carpenter was one day accompanying Dr. Tuckerman in his exploration of the poorer quarter of Bristol, when a ragged boy, rushing out of a dark entry, dashed recklessly across their path. "That child," remarked Dr. Tuckerman, "should be followed to his home and seen after." These few words were as seed that falls on a fertile soil. They sank deep into Mary Carpenter's mind, with a painful feeling that a duty was being neglected. They opened to her the "way"—they pointed out the "work" for which she had so long been waiting. With the co-operation of her sister she began to lay her plans for future action ; and at length, in 1835, they developed into the "Working and Visiting Society" for visiting the homes of the poor of the congregation, and of the Sunday-school. Mary Carpenter became its secretary, and took charge of the worst and poorest of the districts over which the Society extended its range of operations. The admirably thoughtful and prudent spirit in which she entered on her task shows itself plainly in the entry in her journal, dated Thursday, May 21st, 1835. "In the year 1832," she writes, "on occasion of the public fast, and also of the public thanksgiving, I made a solemn determination to devote myself in any way that lay in my power to the good of my fellow-creatures. A means appears to be now open to me to do this more efficiently than heretofore, and I feel much gratitude to my Father for it. I pray to Him to enable me to discharge these happy duties to His glory; never to allow them to interfere with my other duties, but only with my hours of relaxation; and to remember that, though I give my goods to feed the poor and have not charity towards all men, I am nothing."

She was under no delusion as to the character of the work she had undertaken. She contemplated none of that fancy charity so easily practised by young ladies, who, in trim attire, go from cottage to cottage in a quiet village, without risk, without labour, and flatter themselves that, while simply passing away an idle hour, they are realizing the highest dreams of benevolence. From the serene domesticities of a happy household, and the refined pleasures of self-culture, she was prepared to penetrate into the reeking courts and squalid alleys of a great commercial and seafaring town, and to experience the repulsion of the coarsest aspects of a foul and degraded life. Poverty in a woodbine-trellised cottage, reading its Bible, and supported by the alms of the "great houses," is not without a certain attractiveness; but how different is the poverty which struggles for a crust of bread in the byways of London or Bristol, Liverpool or Birmingham, and in filthy tenements crouches side by side with vice! Mary Carpenter, however, had chosen her work deliberately, and executed it patiently. Hers was no fugitive emotion of sham philanthropy, but a real deep love for her fellow-creatures, flowing from, and sustained by, her love for their Saviour. She soon discovered that many of her fellow-workers were not animated by so lofty a courage or so tenacious a purpose as herself; that they shrank from contact with the very lowest of the poor, and desired to base their charitable efforts on a principle of selection. To meet the difficulty she organised a new band of labourers, under the title of a Ministry to the Poor; and pressed forward on her path more resolutely than ever. Yet not without much mental conflict, over which she triumphed only through the severest self-discipline Weariness and dejection, a sense of personal unworthiness, a tendency to morbid analysis of every thought and feeling, constitutional irritability, against which she strove continually,—these were trials which she was compelled to bear alone, until she found rest and peace in her acceptance of the promises of God. The death of her father, who was drowned on his way from Leghorn to Marseilles, in 1840, was a shock beneath which her whole nature reeled. She summoned up all her energy and all her fortitude to bear it, and gradually recovered something of her brighter and happier self; but it was long before the shadow it had cast upon her life entirely disappeared.

The reader must not suppose that Mary Carpenter, amidst all the stress of her philanthropic work, neglected the multiform interests of daily life. She frequently indulged herself in the practice of poetical composition; her scientific studies were prosecuted with ardour; and her reading was large and various. She plunged into German literature with much zest, reading Schiller, Wieland, and Herder, and pouring forth her love, as any true German student must do, on the incomparable Jean Paul. Among the later English poets Wordsworth commanded her warmest sympathies; but in Tennyson's "Idylls" she learned to take a true delight. Her literary criticism, as I think is the case with most women, was qualified by her moral instincts; and she was apt to judge a work of art by its meaning and motive rather than by its purely technical merits. It was natural that a mind like hers would turn to history with peculiar pleasure; and we find her studying D'Aubigné's "History of the Reformation," Dr. Arnold's "Rome," and Lord Mahon's "Essai sur le Grand Condé," and similar works. Her love of art found abundant food in the galleries and studios of London, on the occasions of her metropolitan visits; and her skilful pencil was called into frequent requisition.

Of this side of her character the reader will find an interesting illustration in the following letter, which she addressed to a friend in February 1845. It will show that the highest and holiest duties abroad are by no means incompatible with that other high and holy duty, the duty of self-culture.

"Have you read," she writes, "'The Vestiges of Creation'? When it first came out people were very enthusiastic about it, and the first review mamma saw made her buy the book, which we thought a wonderful step on her part. But one soon began to feel that the author was very superficial, and every one found particular fault with the branch of science with which he or she was most acquainted. Altogether, it is an interesting book as the production of a mind aspiring after the grand, beautiful, and universal, but not sufficiently acquainted with the height and depth of nature to subject all her kingdoms to one great law. I have not much satisfaction in reading the book, not being able to repose with security on the accuracy of his facts. For instance, an important theory much depends for support on the fact that Mr. Crosse's creatures, which made a sensation at the British Association in 1836, appear in an infusion containing 'gelatinous silex,' which this author supposes to be silex transformed into gelatine, and thus exhibiting a transition from the mineral to the animal kingdom. Now Mr. Crosse, whom I had the great pleasure of meeting the other day at Mr. Estlin's, told me that this was a complete error, as gelatinous silex was a perfect mineral, deriving its name not from its nature but from its appearance. This was certainly a most careless assumption, which ought not to have been made on so important a question.

"I quite agree with you in feeling that *The Chimes* gives one a heartache, and do not wonder that you feel it often very painful to witness the mass of evil in the metropolis which you can do nothing to alleviate. I do not possess your gaiety of heart to help to remove the painfulness of the feeling; and I believe it was intended that we should suffer sympathetic pain, to stimulate us to make efforts for our fellow-creatures; but I feel the most supporting view to take to be a firm conviction of the parental character of the Deity, and of His infinite wisdom, love, and power. He would not permit all these evils but for His own benevolent purposes. . . .

"Last Saturday fortnight Anna and I breakfasted with Mrs. Schimmelpenninck, a most fascinating woman, full of genius and sentiment and religious feeling, and a keen sense of the ludicrous. She asked me about Dannecker's 'Christ,' and of the effect produced on us by it, and what Mrs. Jameson had said of Dannecker; and then she was quite satisfied because she had heard a corresponding account from Mrs. ——, a missionary's wife. When she saw this statue in a gallery, she remained for some time quite transfixed with absorbing feeling, looking at it; at last she perceived a gentleman attentively observing her; and struck with her admiration, he said, 'That statue converted to Christianity the artist who sculptured it—and I am he!' He told her that he had a **strong desire** to have something that should immortalise him, and after in vain attempting to satisfy himself, travelled in Italy, but none of the splendid works of art he saw there seemed to reach his ideal. Then he devoted himself to the study of the Gospels, but at first he could see nothing but beautiful and **sublime disjointed fragments**, until one text seemed a key-note to him, 'God manifested in the flesh.' He became a devout Christian, but the subject he had proposed to himself seemed too great for him: after a time, however, he reflected that as others could preach and write on Christianity, which he could not, he should do something, and consequently determined to make the statue.

"Mrs. Schimmelpenninck allowed me to come to her house and **draw** quietly (from her copy of David Roberts's 'Views in Egypt and Palestine') during the Easter week; and seldom have I **enjoyed any view** more than the view of Jerusalem from the road **to Bethany over** the Mount of Olives, where I could better imagine our Saviour walking than in almost any sketch I have ever seen. I made a tolerable copy in colours of that, and of the Desert of the Temptation, with the Dead Sea in the distance; but how often did I long for the privilege which I had at your house, of having Mr. Roberts's own touches on my drawing!"

The "Ministry to the Poor," or "Domestic Mission," which she had established, continued, meanwhile, to prosecute its unpretending but useful labours. Even this, however, failed to hit the mark at which Miss Carpenter aimed: it did not reach that latest stratum of the social mass which it was most important of all to penetrate. Another agency **was wanted, to bring** within its scope the **boys** and girls who filled **the streets and** roamed about the quays. She found that **agency in the** "Ragged School" system which John Pounds originated **in** Portsmouth. It had afterwards, **on a** larger scale, been adopted at London and Aberdeen, Dundee and Edinburgh and **Glasgow**; and eventually the Ragged School Union was formed. Miss Carpenter resolved on working it in Bristol, **and, with a** few friends to assist her, hired a room, engaged a master, and opened a "Ragged School" at Lewin's Mead, on the 1st of August, 1846. There were seven pupils at first; **and** on the following Tuesday nearly twenty assembled. Beginning to be tired in the afternoon, one of them said, " Now let us fight," and in an instant they were all fighting. Peace, however, was quickly restored; and each week brought increased numbers and improved order. It was literally a *Ragged* School: none of the boys had shoes or stockings; some had no shirt and no home, sleeping in casks on the quay, or on steps, and living, possibly, by petty depredations; but all better fed, apparently, than the children of the decent poor. The experiment proved so successful that a larger room was soon required; and one was accordingly secured in St. James's Back, to which the school was transferred early in December. It was the first of a series of Institutions which owed their origin to the zeal and far-sighted charity of Mary Jane Carpenter. Fixed in one of the lowest and most populous quarters of Bristol, it speedily taxed all the energies of its managers, and the opening of a Night School in connection with it brought in a swarm of young men and women, whose habits and character tested even the courage of the founder. Early in 1847, the attendance, one Sunday evening, rose to 200; the attempt to close the school with prayer was frustrated by disorder and shouts of mockery, and the court beneath resounded with yells and blows. The neighbours not unnaturally complained of the disturbance, and it became necessary to obtain aid from the police. Gradually, however, the master obtained a control which rendered official vigilance unnecessary; and the policeman who came to protect remained for another purpose,—he was one day reported to the magistrates by an unsympathetic inspector for " having been two hours in the Ragged School, setting copies to the boys."

The secret of the success which crowned this institution must be sought in the enthusiasm of the teachers,—an enthusiasm which they caught from Miss Carpenter. " Week by week," we are told, "and month by month, she was ever at hand to lighten the burden, not only by ready counsel and sympathy, but by taking a large share in the toil. The morning and evening of Sunday were consecrated to her Scripture-class in St. James's Back, —the afternoon being already pledged to the Sunday-school; two nights every week were regularly given, at no matter what social sacrifice, to the evening school; and day after day found her in the same haunt, ready to take a class, to preside over the midday distribution of the soup to the most needy, or even bear the sole charge of management if sickness kept the master away. By this constancy she soon acquired a complete familiarity with the ways of the scholars, and also with the habits of the neighbourhood. Strong in the power of a sacred purpose, she was perfectly devoid of fear, and would traverse alone and at night courts into which policemen only went by twos. The street quarrel was hushed at her approach, as a guilty lad slunk away to avoid her look of sorrowful reproof; and her approving word, with the gift of a flower, a picture, or a Testament, often made sad homes cheerful and renewed the courage of the wavering."

Her mode of teaching will best be understood from the following entries in her journal :—

"I showed them the orrery, which greatly delighted them, and they seemed quite to understand it, and to enter into the idea of the inclination of the earth's axis producing a change of seasons. . .

"This class had never seen a map, and had the greatest difficulty in realizing it. T—— was delighted to see Bristol, Keynsham, and Bath. I always begin with the 'known,' carrying them on afterwards to the 'unknown.' . . .

"I had taken to my class in the preceding week some specimens of ferns neatly gummed on white paper; they were much struck with their beauty, but none knew what they were, though W—— thought he had seen them growing; one thought they were palm-trees. They seemed interested in the account of their fructification I gave them. This time I took a piece of coal-shale, with impressions of ferns, to show them. I explained that this had once been in a liquid state, telling them that some things could be proved to be certain, while others were doubtful; that time did not permit me to explain the proofs to them, nor would they understand them if I did : but that I was careful to tell them nothing as certain which could not be fully proved. I then told each to examine the specimen and tell me what he thought it was. W—— gave so bright a smile that I saw he knew; none of the others could tell; he said they were ferns like those I showed them last week, but he thought they were chiselled on the stone. Their surprise and pleasure were great when I explained the matter to them. . .

"The history of Joseph : They all found a difficulty in realizing that this had actually occurred. One asked if Egypt existed now, and if people lived in it. When I told them that buildings now stood which had been erected about the time of Joseph, one said that it was impossible, as they must have fallen down ere this. I showed them the form of a pyramid, and they were satisfied. One asked if *all* books were true. . . .

"The story of Macbeth impressed them much. They knew the name of Shakespeare, having seen his head over a public-house."

While Miss Carpenter anxiously strove to minister to the mental improvement of her ragged scholars, she was even more solicitous for the development of their religious faculties. To teach them the great truths of Christ's religion, to accustom them to self-control and self-sacrifice, to nurture in them a love of purity and truth,—these were her great, her dominant aims. She knew that by an absolutely secular education she could not make them useful or trustworthy members of society; that only by inspiring them with the love and fear of God could she bring them to respect and observe our social laws. Every Sunday morning and evening, and often on the week nights besides, she drew around her a Bible-class, and told them that old, old story—which is ever new—of the sacrifice of Calvary. Her religious teaching was wonderfully effective, because it was so earnest. Speaking from her heart, she went straight to the hearts of her listeners. And, indeed, I think the wonderful narrative of the life and death and resurrection of Jesus Christ will never fail in its influence so long as it is told by one who believes in it. Only when it drops from the frigid lips of men who have never realized it in their own natures does it cease to fertilise and brighten and bless.

In 1849 she published an interesting little volume entitled "Ragged Schools, their Principles and Modes of Operation By a Worker," which may be accepted as the standard text-book or manual on the subject. It contains a vigorous and well-reasoned argument for Government aid, and some valuable particulars of the condition of the destitute children whom she sought to befriend. It is written by a worker who feels the value and responsibility of her work, is not ignorant of its anxieties, but loves it profoundly—loves it because she believes in it and in the good it does, and the warmth of human affection which it stimulates. "How I prize the love I receive in the school!" she exclaims in one of her letters; "I must confess that it is not so attractive to me from a mere sense of duty, for I might find duties elsewhere; but it is so delightful to me to gain so much love as I feel I have from these young beings, and to help to kindle their souls by mine." Thus it is that the work of the Good Samaritan is twice-blessed; blessing the worker, and those for whom he works.

It was not the nature of Mary Carpenter, however, to rest content with a certain measure of accomplishment; from the stage of one success she was always ready to mount up to another, —always, however, with a clear perception of what she wanted and how it might best be attained,—showing neither undue haste nor unwise hesitancy—*ohne hast, ohne rast*. Her experience of Ragged Schools convinced her that something additional, something complementary, was wanted, by which the juvenile offender might be separated from deteriorating influences and trained up in a wholesome atmosphere. She saw that to thrust him into prison, where he was exposed to the society of veteran criminals, was to seal and consummate his ruin, and effectually prevent him from retracing his misguided steps. We should not place a person, showing symptoms of illness, in a plague-smitten hospital, if we desired his recovery! Such being her convictions, she published, in 1851, a book entitled "Reformatory Schools for the Children of the Perishing and Dangerous Classes, and for Juvenile Offenders." In this she indicated three kinds of schools as necessary for the different grades of destitution, vagrancy, and criminality;—good Free Day Schools; Feeding Industrial Schools, aided by the rates, at which attendance should be compulsory; and, thirdly, Reformatory Schools,* in lieu of the existing prison system. She brought together a great number of facts to illustrate the total failure of the gaols to reform juvenile criminals, and she put before the public four general propositions:—

First, That, as a general rule, all children, however apparently vicious and degraded, are capable of being made useful members of society, and beings acting on a religious principle, if placed under right influences and subjected to judicious control and training.

Second, That the existing system adopted towards offending children renders them almost certainly members for life of the

---

* These were originally tried at Mettrai.

criminal class, for it neither deters nor reforms them; while, by checking the development of their powers and branding them with ignominy, it prevents them from gaining an honest livelihood.

Third, That good Penal Reformatory Schools, conducted on Christian principles, with a wise union of kindness and restraint, have been successful in converting the most corrupt and degraded into useful members of society; but that to secure their permanency and efficiency it was essential they should be under the authority and supported by the State.

And fourth, That the parents being in reality the guilty parties, rather than the children, inasmuch as parental neglect is usually the source of juvenile delinquency, every parent should be chargeable for the maintenance of a child thrown by crime on the care of the State, as much as if the child were under his own roof; and should be held responsible for the maintenance of his child in a Reformatory School, or in some other way made to suffer for the non-discharge of his duty.

Miss Carpenter went on to say that if these four propositions were accepted—as, indeed, they had been, by a Committee of the Lords in 1847, and a Committee of the Commons in 1850—legislative enactments would be needed to carry them out. A sufficient number of Reformatory Schools, under Government inspection and supported by Government aid, must be established; and magistrates and judges empowered to send all convicted children to such schools, instead of committing them to prison.

The next step, while these propositions were slowly sinking into the public mind, always slow to receive any idea which conflicts with old traditions and prejudices, was to bring together a conference of workers, so that some means might be adopted of carrying them into action. The arrangements were laboriously completed in the course of 1851; and on the 9th of December the Conference held its first meeting, under the presidency of Lord Lyttelton. Mr. M. D. Hill took a foremost part in its organisation, and delivered a very important and solid address. A Committee was appointed to "agitate" in the cause, and a memorial submitted to the Government. But Governments are in no hurry to move in new paths; and Mary Carpenter determined to show the practicability of her scheme, in the meantime, by establishing a Reformatory School at Bristol. There is nothing the Englishman so quickly understands as a fact; there is nothing from which he so instinctively shrinks as a theory. Premises at Kingswood formerly occupied as a Wesleyan School, and containing accommodation for upwards of a hundred children, were purchased by a Mr. Russell Scott. Liberal contributions flowed in from generous friends, and the Kingswood Reformatory School was opened on the 11th of September.

Following up the good work, Miss Carpenter published in 1853 her "Juvenile Delinquents, their Condition and Treatment," which supplied an interesting *aperçu* of the treatment of juvenile delinquents in France, Wurtemberg, Prussia, Bavaria, Belgium, and Switzerland. The moral of the book, which was also the burden of her teaching, she stated thus:—

"The child must be placed where he will be **gradually restored to the** true position of childhood. He must be brought **to a sense of dependence** by reawakening in him new and healthy **desires, which he cannot** himself gratify, and by finding that there is a power far **greater** than his **own** to which he is indebted for the gratification **of these desires.** He must perceive, by manifestations which he cannot mistake, **that this power, while** controlling him, is guided by wisdom **and love; he must** have his affections called forth by the obvious personal interest felt in his own individual well-being by those around him; he must, **in** short, be placed in *a family*. Faith in those around him being once thoroughly established, he will soon yield his own *will* in ready submission to **those** who are working for his good; it will thus be gradually **subdued** and trained, and he will work with them in effecting his reformation, trusting, where he cannot perceive the reason of the **measures** they adopt to correct or eradicate the **evil** in him. This, **it is** apprehended, is the fundamental principle of all **true reformatory action with** the young; **and** in every case where striking **success has** followed such efforts, it **will be** traceable to **the greater development of** this principle, to a more **true and powerful action on the soul of the** child by those who have assumed towards it the holy duties of a parent."

A second Conference on the subject of reformatory schools was held at Birmingham in December 1853; and public opinion now pronounced itself so decidedly in favour of the movement that, in the following session, the Government introduced and carried through Parliament what was known as the "Youthful Offenders' Act." It authorised the establishment of Reformatory Schools by voluntary managers, and placed them under the control of the Home Secretary.

Experience had proved to Miss Carpenter the undesirability of including, as at Kingswood, boys and girls under the same roof; and she now sought very anxiously for some means of separating the girls, so that her supervision over them might become more direct. Assisted by Lady Byron and other friends, she succeeded in purchasing a fine old Elizabethan building in Park Row, Bristol, known as the Red Lodge, which was opened as a Reformatory School for girls on the 10th of October, 1854. It was entirely under her own control, and she threw herself into its management with all the energy of her ardent nature, until overwrought nature gave way beneath the strain, and in the following spring she was prostrated by a severe attack of rheumatic fever. On her recovery, which for some time was doubtful, she was sent by her physicians to the south coast of Devon, and in the mild air of Torquay she gradually recruited her physical powers. Then she resumed the threads of her many philanthropic labours, and entered once more upon that life of practical enthusiasm which was fraught with so many blessings for her fellow-creatures. For it is not only in the work, but in the example of such a woman that there lies a perpetual benediction for humanity.

In the opening pages of this chapter we have insisted on the absolute necessity of making religion the basis of all education: we have argued that the religious spirit ought to permeate and inspire our educational systems, and that the proper discipline of the soul is at least as essential as the adequate culture of the intellect. At the Red Lodge this fact was fully recognised by Miss Carpenter. She did not conceive it possible that the work of reformation could be accomplished without any appeal to those higher aspirations and purer feelings which lie dormant in our nature, until the springs are opened by the divining rod of God's holy word. The following extracts from her journal show how assiduously she sought to foster among the inmates of the Red Lodge a deep and genuine love of religious feeling:—

"February, 1856. I have continued to give my lessons as usual, and have increasing satisfaction in them, perceiving that they really take root in the girls, who show great capability of intellectual culture. The Scripture lessons especially give me most pleasure. At the interval of a week they can answer accurately every fact of the previous lesson, with evident understanding and recollection of my explanations. The blank looks of the new girls fully prove to me how much work has been already done in preparing the soil to receive the good seed. My regular lesson times are these:—

"*Sunday afternoon* from 2.30 to 4, generally longer. Review of hymns, with remarks, which have been learnt during the week. Gospel of Luke, with explanations and comments, after examination on the last Sunday's lesson. If there is time, I permit each girl who can read to choose a text for herself, which much pleases them, and fixes the attention on particular passages. When there is time, I show them Scripture pictures.

"*Monday evenings* from 6 o'clock to bedtime, when I visit them when in bed, which gives an opportunity for private communication with individuals. Hitherto I have read a story to the younger ones while the older ones were writing, and then heard the older ones read. I mean to vary this. Afterwards I read the old Testament to them, being now engaged on the history of Abraham, which rises in grand antique beauty before me every time I realize it to present to these children. Indeed, the study of these ancient records gives me something of the same feeling that seeing the disinterred Assyrian remains would do. When the girls are in bed I visit each, and find an interchange of affection and occasional private word very useful in strengthening the bond which I wish to exist between my children and me."

Into this happy and useful life a great sorrow came in the summer of 1856,—as great sorrows *will* come into the lives of all of us,—the death of a beloved mother, who had shared her thoughts and hopes and cares with broad and helpful sympathies. It was some time before her mind recovered its elasticity, but the healing influences of work gradually had their way, and in the following year she was once more immersed in the activities of a sagacious and comprehensive benevolence. The institution at the Red Lodge was expanded through the liberality of Lady Byron, and a home fitted up for eight or nine girls, under a matron, who were there trained for domestic service. The experiment was entirely successful.

It was natural enough that from Reformatory Schools for the benefit of juvenile delinquents she should be led on to the consideration of agencies for the benefit of adult offenders. A visit to Dublin, in 1861, to attend the annual congress of the Social Science Association, introduced to her notice the admirable system of prison management devised and carried out by Sir Walter Crofton; and she convinced herself that a very large percentage of criminals could, by a system of reformatory training, adopted towards the close of their terms of imprisonment, be restored to society as industrious and useful members. With characteristic energy she took up this new subject, side by side, as it were, with her favourite topics of Reformatories and Ragged and Industrial Schools. The results of incessant inquiry and investigation were brought together in a book which she published in 1864, under the title of "Our Convicts." It was a forcible and exhaustive indictment of the English convict system.*

---

* Of the general character of its contents we shall quote the following description :—

"Borrowing from the records of prison officials, and the police narratives of the daily papers, the author first described the actual moral condition of the convict class, and then proceeded to inquire what were the influences which produced the fearful moral degradation thus revealed, special stress being laid upon the facilities afforded by imprisonment for corruption and training in crime. The third chapter was devoted to an exposition of the principles of convict treatment, the chief of which was stated to be the necessity that 'the will of the individual should be brought into such a condition as to wish to reform, and to exert itself to that end, in co-operation with the persons who are set over him.' This, it was urged, can never be done by mere force, or by any mechanical appliance. But that reformation, even of the most hardened offenders, was possible, was proved by the remarkable results attained by Colonel Montesinos of Valencia, by Herr von Obermaier at Munich, and by Captain Maconochie in Norfolk Island. How far, then, did the English convict system fulfil the conditions of true reformatory discipline? The answer was given in an elaborate inquiry, occupying the rest of the first volume, into the arrangements of various prisons, the disposal of criminals, tickets-of-leave, and, finally, transportation.

"From the English convict system the reader was carried to Ireland, where the treatment of prisoners was founded on the same Acts, but had been carried out to very different results. Intermediate establishments were instituted between the prisons and the world. The freedom of agency of the

True charity is many-sided; it does not confine itself to one branch of Christian work, but readily responds to every demand made upon it by suffering or sorrowing or sinning humanity. We have seen that Mary Carpenter's large heart could find room for the amelioration of the condition of the poor, the reformation of juvenile offenders, the discipline and training of adult criminals. She sympathized keenly with missionary effort abroad, and every movement against slavery commanded her hearty assistance. And it is to be noted that, enthusiast as she was, she was no visionary theorist, no fanatic stricken with blind reverence for impossible ideals; her mind was eminently practical, and she undertook nothing which could not be defended by sober and rational arguments. Hence it is that her name is so happily associated with achievement, instead, as has been the case with many would-be reformers, with *intention* only. At various times

---

inmates was gradually enlarged as they showed themselves deserving of trust, and strict supervision was exercised over those who went out on licence. The details of this method were exhibited with convincing wealth of illustration. The history of the system was set forth; and to the evidence of personal observation, and the witness of official reports, there was added the testimony of other critics from England, from the Continent, and from Canada, in its support. Was the Irish system applicable to women as well as to men? The question was discussed in a chapter on Female Convicts, and after a contrast between the prison experiences on both sides of the Channel, it was unhesitatingly answered in the affirmative. In conclusion, various suggestions for improvement were laid down, including strict registration of criminals, greater certainty and uniformity of judicial sentences, cumulative sentences, and changes in the county gaols in the direction of the principles of the Irish system, such as were already being carried out at Winchester and Wakefield. The next chapter, headed Prevention, afforded opportunity for a survey of the principal agencies available for the diminution of the causes of crime; such as temperance, the diffusion of pure literature, the improvements of the dwellings of the labouring classes. The most important, however, was education; which gave occasion for a review of the progress of Reformatory and Industrial Schools since the Conference of 1851, a plea for the separation of pauper children from workhouse management, and a renewed appeal on behalf of Ragged Schools. Finally, in brief but earnest words, the co-operation of society was invoked, and different channels for voluntary effort were marked out. 'Thus may all labour together, government and people, for the regeneration of the misguided and neglected in our country, and for the restoration to society of "Our Convicts."'—*The Life and Work of Mary Carpenter*, by S. ESTLIN CARPENTER, M.A., pp. 304-306. Upon this very valuable and interesting book of Mr. Carpenter's our sketch is founded.

in her life the vast field of philanthropic effort afforded by British India had arrested her imagination; but, true to her principle of doing the work which lay nearest at hand, she did not allow herself to be involved in radiant dreams of which she could not then anticipate the realization. But as the years passed by, and her various undertakings grew in consolidation and security, she allowed herself to consider the subject more seriously, and in 1864 her interest in it was re-kindled by conversations which she had with a couple of native Hindu gentlemen. Into what channel should she direct her energies? At first she thought of receiving Indian ladies into her house; but further inquiry and reflection convinced her that the work to be done must be done in India. So, on the 12th of January, she registered a solemn resolution :—

"I here record," she writes, "my solemn resolve that henceforth I devote my heart and soul and strength to the elevation of the women of India. In doing this I shall not suddenly abandon my work here, which has long and deep claims on me, nor will I give it up until I have put it, so far as in me lies, on a firm and settled basis. I believe that it is come to a point at which this can be done. But I shall obey the remarkable call which has been given me so unexpectedly, which is in accordance with former days' feelings and resolves. Without any present and apparent change of plan, I shall watch openings, devote myself to perfecting my present work, and bearing my testimony in my proposed book, gain information, and prepare in every way for my great object—going to India to promote the Christian work for the women."

On the 14th of February she wrote :—

"A month has passed since I made the foregoing entry. I have closely questioned myself,—suspected myself of enthusiasm, of weariness of work, etc., etc.; but nothing has changed, but only confirmed, my strong and settled conviction that a new field is now about to open to me, one in which I shall seem especially to be working with my beloved Father, and in which the gifts which He gave me of mental culture will be especially useful; one in which my natural powers will have free scope. 'Other sheep I have, which are not of this fold.' Now that my poor little forsaken ones are cared for here, I may go to the 'others' and help them . . . Should I never return, heaven will be as near to me from that region as from here."*

It was not until 1866, however, that she could carry out her resolve. Her friends had at first embarrassed her with warnings and discouragements, but with her usual calm persistency she set them aside, and as soon as she saw the way clear before her she went. She felt it to be her duty; and though in her sixtieth year,—with her constitution strained by severe illnesses,—never dreamed of shrinking from it. To have neglected such an opening for good would have been to have sinned against her conscience and inner light. Her last work in England was to plan the establishment of a Girls' Industrial School; and then, commending herself to God, she set out for India on the 1st of September. Six weeks later she was at Ahmedabad, and studying its different Government institutions, prisons, hospitals, lunatic asylums, schools, normal training institutions, and embracing every opportunity of becoming closely acquainted with the native character and wants. From the varieties of Oriental life, her imagination, with its keen sense of the picturesque, derived inexhaustible delight; but she allowed nothing to displace the one thought, the one idea, which had possession of her mind. The lamentable condition of the Hindu women,—fettered by the restrictions of a narrow creed, cabined and confined by traditional prejudices,—was always before her; and she studied deeply and anxiously the best method of attacking a problem which was complicated by both social and religious customs. Her conviction was, that it could be solved only through the development of female education; and the first step in this direction she perceived to be the introduction of trained female teachers into the girls' schools. Her views, as soon as she had distinctly formulated them, she laid before the Indian Government. At

---

* Miss Carpenter refers to the touching story of the Elizabethan navigator, Sir Humphrey Gilbert, who, when his little pioneer was almost overwhelmed by the storm-tossed waters of the Arctic Sea, called out to his men, " Courage, my lads, we are as near to heaven by sea as by land"—

"He sat upon the deck,
The Book was in his hand :
' Do not fear : heaven is as near,
He said, ' by water as by land.' "

Calcutta she was welcomed by Keshub Chunder Sen, the well-known leader of the Brahmo Somaj, or new Hindu Theistic school, and from him and the native gentlemen associated with him she obtained a hearty and sympathetic support. The then Viceroy, Sir John (afterwards Lord) Lawrence, was well disposed to afford her every facility in maturing and carrying out her plans. Writing from Government House, on the 23rd of December, she says:—

"Here I have been located for a fortnight. The Governor-General most kindly sent and appointed an interview with me immediately after his return from Simla, and after introducing me to Lady Lawrence, she wrote and invited me to take up my abode here while in Calcutta. . . .

"I have beautiful large rooms here in one wing of the palace, all to myself, where I am perfectly independent, and may receive what visitors I please. At first I felt very like a state prisoner, but soon got to understand the ways of things. A red-liveried man keeps guard in the passage before my door, or rather spends his days in calm repose, lying on the matting, unless I send him on an errand, which I think very good for his health. He cannot, or will not, speak a word of English, except 'Tea,' which he gets for me whenever I wish. The household is beautifully ordered, and the servants most attentive. You would be rather frightened at first to meet to many red-liveried soldiers and servants wherever you go, but I get used to it and do not mind it. I have had numerous visitors, and often have been in a constant state of *levée* when in the house. I have been getting such an insight into native homes and ways of thinking, as few people have an opportunity of doing. The very bigoted ones keep out of my way. I have no sympathy with them, for it is not from any religious prejudice, but from the selfish wish to keep their wives perfectly in thraldom, that they object to education for them. But there are many good enlightened men who deserve every sympathy. . . .

"The ladies I visit all receive me with the greatest enthusiasm. They think it so wonderful that I should have taken such a journey on their account. One greeted me with: 'I am very glad you spent your own money to come and see us,'—of course in Bengalee. The husband of another said that he could hardly make his wife realize that I had come from such a distance to see them, and when he did make her understand, she said that 'I ought to be adored.' The effect of my coming is far greater than I ever anticipated, and I feel inexpressibly thankful to have had such a reward.

"You will perceive from the accompanying newspaper extracts that I have had some valuable opportunities of stating principles, and I am glad, in this case, of the disagreeable habit they have of putting everything into the newspapers. I had another opportunity on Friday, at Judge Phear's. He kindly invited me to dinner with Mr. and Mrs. Tagore and Mr. Ghose, and afterwards about a dozen or more of first-rate grand legal Hindus assembled. In the drawing-room, Mr. Phear asked me to say something to them, and I addressed them on the duty of society to criminals, and particularly juveniles. I am glad to find that I can quite trust myself to develop any subject logically and clearly with only a few minutes' thought. To-morrow evening I have promised to join native Christians at tea at Bhavasierpore, and then give an address on Female Education to Hindus in general."

Under her auspices a free school for "the lowest of the low" was started at Calcutta. She originated the Bengal Social Science Association, on the plan of the English Society. She prepared for the Viceroy a statement on the condition of female education in the Metropolitan district. The organisation of a female normal training school sprang from her active brain. And after six weeks of incessant labour at Calcutta, the indefatigable worker proceeded to Madras on a similar mission of philanthropy. Thence she went on to Bombay, everywhere making the mark of her well-directed energy and singular tenacity of purpose. She returned to England in April 1867, believing that she had sown much good seed in a favourable soil, which, under the blessing of Heaven, would one day ripen into an ample harvest. "India is a great country," said Lord Dufferin, "and the history of a great country deals only with important events; but I am certain that when the history of that country is being written during the present century, the visit of Miss Carpenter to the shores of India will not remain unrecorded." The progress which female education has made of recent years in India is unquestionably due to the impulse communicated by the wise and vigorous philanthropy of Miss Carpenter.

In 1868 she returned to India, to superintend the progress of the work she had so happily begun. She took with her several lady assistants, besides such books, pictures, and apparatus as might be of use for general purposes of culture, as well as the specific needs of school education; and on her arrival was gratified to find that the Government, in order to promote the establishment of Female Normal Schools, had granted £1,200 per annum, for five years, to each of the three presidency towns, Calcutta, Madras, and Bombay. Arriving at Bombay in November, she at once undertook the organisation of a Normal School in that city, and prospered greatly; while giving her support and advice to every other institution that aimed at promoting the education of the Hindu women. The direct instruction of native teachers in their own schools was begun. Scholarships were offered by the Countess of Mayo, the Rani of Jumkhundi, and other native ladies and gentlemen. A class of married ladies was formed for studying English; and requests for trained teachers came flowing in from various parts of the Presidency.

A dangerous illness, however, abruptly snapped the thread of her work, and compelled her return to England. There she recruited her strength, and conferred with her friends, and examined into the progress of the many institutions which owed their existence to her combined zeal and prudence. When her health was re-established, she made a third journey to India, and was rewarded for all her toils and pains by finding that the good cause was steadily making its way. So that when she left Bombay, in the early spring of 1870, she was able to write:—" I know and feel that while the worldly may scoff and disbelieve, there are many spirits here which have felt its power and rejoiced in it; and I believe that they will kindle others. The work *will* go on. In faith and hope I can say, 'India, Farewell.'"

Having resumed her customary avocations at Bristol, Miss Carpenter undertook the formation of a National Indian Association with the following objects: "She wished," says her biographer, "to enable native visitors to England to study its institutions, and enter into its society, to the best advantage. She sought to extend a knowledge of India and its special social wants, the education of the masses of the people, the education of women, the improvement of prison discipline, and the establishment of juvenile reformatories. And she desired to find some common ground whereon the scattered endeavours put forth in India itself should be brought into friendly relation, and gather strength by feeling sympathy and support around them instead of isolation or hostility." The association was "inaugurated" at Bristol in September 1870.

In telling the story of Mary Carpenter's life we have no reference to make to those sweet episodes of love and marriage and motherhood which fill so conspicuous a place in the lives of most women. And this, not because she was wanting in the capacity of deep and trusting affection, for upon her parents and her brothers and her sisters she lavished a wonderful wealth of tenderness, but because she voluntarily and consciously devoted herself, her means, and her opportunities, her talents and her time, to the welfare of humanity. She lived not for herself, but others. At the age of sixty-five we find her, with all the vigour of youth and wisdom of age, promoting the establishment of Day Industrial Schools for the benefit of a class of children to whom access to the Board Schools was virtually denied. The International Prison Congress engaged her attention in July. Later in the year she visited Germany. In 1873 she accomplished a visit to the United States, where she addressed many large and influential assemblies on the subjects dearest to her heart. She passed on into Canada, to receive a hearty welcome from her old friend, Lord Dufferin, then Governor-General of Canada.

In 1874 Miss Carpenter lent her powerful help to the movement in favour of the Higher Education of Women; of which, indeed, she was herself an example and a type. "The systematic study of language, of literature, of science, of philosophy, had given her a variety of culture which had proved of the utmost value to her in unexpected ways; and every effort to supply a loftier guidance to capacities which had too long remained undeveloped, seemed to put in a positive claim upon her aid. Rarely could she be induced to speak on any subject in which she was not an active worker. But on this topic she possessed a large store of observation and experience; and these were always at the service of the leaders who were striving to carry out on a larger scale principles of education with which she had been familiar since her earliest years." The temperance cause and the movement for the repeal of the Contagious Diseases Act also enlisted her sympathies. The "nihil humani alienum" principle was the guiding motive and purpose of her nobly useful life.

In September 1875 she paid another and a final visit to India, partly to further the work of female education, and partly to fetch two children of a Hindu family, whose parents had consented that they should share her lonely home and enjoy the advantage of her loving care. She saw much to encourage her at Bombay, at Madras, and at Calcutta; the bread which she had cast upon the waters had come home again, and in fewer days than she could have hoped or anticipated. "In due time ye shall reap, if ye faint not." To Mary Carpenter the promise was abundantly fulfilled. Writing to the Marquis of Salisbury, on her return home, she said: "The general impression I have formed from my present visit to India on the subject of female education is a hopeful one. The idea of education seems increasingly to permeate the masses from high to low. Native chiefs are thinking of the education of their ladies, and a single instance in which they carry this into effect is more valuable than any mere professions of interest. Native gentlemen of position are in many cases anxious to obtain for their ladies instruction from English ladies. The class of women requiring to obtain a maintenance, find that they can do so better by being educated. I have formed a much higher idea than before of the capabilities of native ladies, both in acquiring knowledge and in becoming teachers. There is not the great dread of female education which formerly existed, and altogether the way appears open to rapid progress, if only the conditions necessary to this are provided. These conditions are, in the first place, a good teaching power, with suitable premises and appliances. These cannot be supplied by the natives, and without these the schools for girls will continue as they have done, without any sensible improvement."

In the spring of 1876 this noble woman once more took up her abode in Bristol. Her solitary home, no longer solitary, was cheered by the presence of her Hindu boys and of an adopted daughter; and though she was close upon threescore years and ten, her affections had not diminished in their strength, nor was there any apparent diminution of her natural energy. She still continued to give her best thoughts to the engrossing occupations of her useful life, and had the felicity of seeing her Day-Feeding Industrial Schools recognized by the legislature and incorporated into the educational system of the country. From the first she had steadfastly held the sound opinion that there were three classes to be dealt with: a class of habitual young criminals, who could be treated only in reformatory schools; a class of lesser criminals and vagrants, for whom certified industrial schools were required; and beneath these, and swelling their ranks by a constant influx, a third class of truant and neglected children, haunting the streets of every considerable town, and living in an atmosphere of juvenile crime and vagrancy. For these she recommended a separate class of schools, more of an educational than of a penal character. We have seen that Reformatory Schools were established; Certified Industrial Schools followed; and, lastly, in 1876, a Parliamentary enactment was obtained for the provision of Day-Feeding Industrial Schools. Thus her whole programme was carried out after years of patient and enlightened labour,—marked by a singular tenacity of purpose and an unusual breadth of view,—and she could say, "*Opus consummatum est.*"

We get an idea of her indomitable energy from the group of institutions which she originated at Bristol, and over which she maintained to the last an active supervision. We have, first, the Boys' Reformatory School at Kingswood; second, the Girls Reformatory in the Red Lodge; third, the Certified Industrial School for Boys in Park Row; fourth, the Girls' Certified Industrial School in the Fort; fifth, the Day-Feeding Industrial School in St. James's Back, which was also the centre of the Children's Agency; and, sixth, the Boys' Home. These various lines of work she followed up with undiminished interest; so that, as Miss Nightingale said, one forgot her age in the eternal freshness of her youthful activity. It is worth recording that in the spring of 1877 she delivered a course of six lectures at the Philosophical Institution, speaking fluently on each occasion for an hour and a quarter.

The 3rd of April, 1877, witnessed the completion of her seventieth year. To a member of her family she wrote on this interesting occasion with pathetic simplicity:—

"This day seems to mark a distinct era in my life, when the great battles are over, and I have only to carry on the work to its completion, always, however, watching and working quietly to amend and perfect where required.

"I do not look back with sorrow on the past. There have been many painful woundings, and sad bereavements, and great struggles, and dark perplexities, but they have all blended together to make a calm whole of the past, very wonderfully calm when I think of parts alone. As you say, there has been one deep moving spirit running through all. I used often to desire to have

> "'A soul by force of sorrows high
> Uplifted to the purest sky
> Of undisturbed humanity.'

Now, I do not seek that, or anything, but thankfully take whatever is given. 'She hath done what she could,' I can truly say of myself, whatever errors I have fallen into; so I look very serenely back from this boundary, and hopefully to what remains of life, the brightest and best of all, and most full of blessings."

A few weeks later she received the distressing intelligence of the death of her youngest brother, Dr. Philip Carpenter, at Montreal. "This is a great blow to me," she wrote, "but there is no bitterness; it comes from the Father's hand." On the 6th of June, she delivered an address of more than an hour's length, in a chapel at Kingswood, on the "Religious Aspects of India." On the 14th, she wrote to her brother, Dr. W. B. Carpenter, of London, proposing a visit in reference to her Indian work; and on the same day she completed the revision of a volume of poetry, "Spirit Voices." In the evening she met with one of the Parliamentary friends who cordially assisted her benevolent efforts, though separated from her by religious and political views. The conversed upon public topics, and she expressed herself with her usual earnestness of feeling and clearness of thought. Retiring to her quiet study, she wrote until a later hour than usual. "The nightly greetings were exchanged with her adopted daughter, and when she was last seen it was with a smile upon her face. She lay down to rest and slept; before the dawn she had passed quietly away."

To her memory a monument has been erected in the north transept of Bristol Cathedral. The inscription upon it was written by Dr. Martineau, and we quote it in full as an emphatic summary of her noble work, and a significant tribute to her noble life:—

SACRED TO THE MEMORY OF

MARY CARPENTER,

FOREMOST AMONG THE FOUNDERS
OF REFORMATORY AND INDUSTRIAL SCHOOLS
IN THIS CITY AND REALM.
NEITHER THE CLAIMS OF PRIVATE DUTY
NOR THE TASTES OF A CULTURED MIND
COULD WITHDRAW HER COMPASSIONATE EYE
FROM THE UNCARED-FOR CHILDREN OF THE STREETS.
LOVING THEM WHILE YET UNLOVELY,
SHE SO FORMED THEM TO THE FAIR AND GOOD
AS TO INSPIRE OTHERS WITH HER FAITH AND HOPE,
AND THUS LED THE WAY TO A NATIONAL SYSTEM
OF MORAL RESCUE AND PREVENTIVE DISCIPLINE.
TAKING ALSO TO HEART THE GRIEVOUS LOT
OF ORIENTAL WOMEN,
IN THE LAST DECADE OF HER LIFE
SHE FOUR TIMES WENT TO INDIA,
AND AWAKENED AN ACTIVE INTEREST
IN THEIR EDUCATION AND TRAINING FOR SERIOUS DUTIES.
NO HUMAN ILL ESCAPED HER PITY, OR CAST DOWN HER TRUST:
WITH TRUE SELF-SACRIFICE SHE FOLLOWED IN THE
TRAIN OF CHRIST,
TO SEEK AND TO SAVE THAT WHICH WAS LOST,
AND BRING IT HOME TO THE FATHER IN HEAVEN.
DESIRING TO EXTEND HER WORK OF PIETY AND LOVE,
MANY WHO HONOURED HER HAVE INSTITUTED IN HER NAME
SOME HOMES FOR THE HOUSELESS YOUNG,
AND NOW COMPLETE THEIR TRIBUTE OF AFFECTION
BY ERECTING THIS MEMORIAL.

———

BORN AT EXETER, APRIL 3rd, 1807;
DIED AT BRISTOL, JUNE 15th, 1877.

BOOK II.

WORK ON BEHALF OF THE SLAVE.

ABOLITION OF THE SLAVE TRADE.
WILLIAM WILBERFORCE.
EMANCIPATION OF THE SLAVE.
SIR THOMAS FOWELL BUXTON.

WORK ON BEHALF OF THE SLAVE.

WILLIAM WILBERFORCE, only son of Robert Wilberforce, the descendant and representative of an old Yorkshire family, and his wife Elizabeth, was born at Hull, on the 24th of August, 1759.

His childhood was not distinguished by any remarkable incidents in prophecy or promise of future greatness. His frame was feeble, his stature small, his eyes were weak; but with these physical defects were united a clear strong intellect, and a sweet temper. At the age of seven he was sent to the Hull Grammar School, then under the charge of Dr. Milner. Here he was remarkable for his elocutionary gifts, so that his master would set him upon a table, and make him read aloud as an example to the other boys. The death of his father in 1768 transferred him to the care of his uncle, with whom he lived at Wimbledon, and in St. James's Place. His education at this time does not seem to have made much progress; but from his aunt, who was a Methodist, he received strong religious impressions. These were not of a kind to please his mother, who was a moderate (or, as her son called her, an Archbishop Tillotson) churchwoman. She recalled him to Hull, and surrounded him with the pleasures of fashionable society, which, after awhile, produced their natural effect upon a clever boy, and he plunged into a life of idleness and amusement. His social talents and his musical skill rendered him everywhere a welcome guest; and there seemed little prospect or promise of his entering upon any work of notable usefulness. But he cultivated a taste for literature, and graced his leisure with reading and original composition. It was observed, too, that he evinced a deep detestation of the slave trade, of the enormities of which, it is probable, he would hear many stories in a seaport like Hull; and he addressed, when not more than fourteen, a letter to a York newspaper, in sharp condemnation of the hateful traffic in human flesh.

Endowed with very considerable abilities, of which he had made but little use, and with a great charm of manner, springing from his geniality of disposition, he entered St. John's College, Cambridge, in October 1778. At the age of seventeen, master of an independent fortune, he was necessarily exposed to grave temptation, and at first fell among "as licentious a set of men as can well be conceived." But he was too sound at heart to be drawn into profligate excess; fond as he was of amusement, he shook off these dangerous companions, and became the centre of a cultivated and agreeable circle. "There was no one at all like him," writes a friend, "for powers of entertainment. Always fond of repartee and discussion, he seemed entirely free from conceit and vanity." He lived much at this time amongst the Fellows of the College. "But those with whom I was intimate," he says, "did not act towards me the part of Christians, or even of honest men. Their object seemed to be, to make and keep me idle. If ever I appeared studious, they would say to me, 'Why in the world should a man of your fortune trouble himself with fagging.' I was a good classic, and acquitted myself well in the college examinations; but mathematics, which my mind greatly needed, I almost entirely neglected, and was told that I was too clever to require them. Whilst my companions were reading hard and attending lectures, card-parties and idle amusements consumed my time. The tutors would often say within my hearing, that 'they were mere saps, but that I did all by talent.' This was poison to a mind constituted like mine." His biographers remark that it was surely by God's especial goodness that in such a course he was preserved from profligate excess. For though he would say in after life, that upon the habits thus formed by evil influence and unbounded licence "he could not look back without unfeigned remorse," yet he had rather to deplore neglected opportunities of moral and intellectual profit, than vicious practice or abandoned principles. Still, such a life was no fitting preparation for a great or useful career; and it will be interesting to observe how Wilberforce gradually rose to a higher moral standard, and to a loftier sense of the duties and responsibilities which his social advantages imposed upon him.

Probably it was his election as Member of Parliament for Hull, in 1780, which rescued him from the life of a fashionable idler and "ornament of society." Not that it immediately broke the spell of bad habits with which his self-indulgence or levity had enthralled him. On his first entering into the London world he ran no small risk of degenerating into a confirmed gamester. He was weaned from the Faro-table in a characteristic manner. One night he "kept the bank," and rose the winner of £600. Most of this was lost by young men who were only heirs to future fortunes, and who could not meet such a call without inconvenience. The pain he felt at their annoyance cured him of his dangerous taste.

He had already made the acquaintance of William Pitt, the great son of a great father, and, while preserving his political independence, became his friend and general supporter. They spent much of their time together; and Pitt was a constant visitor at Wilberforce's Wimbledon residence. The political integrity of the austere young statesman probably exercised a strengthening and elevating influence on Wilberforce's character; and he took each year a deeper and more intelligent interest in public affairs. In the House of Commons he spoke frequently and always with effect. This, in the opinion of his filial biographers, was the most critical period of his career. He had entered in his earliest manhood upon the dissipated scenes of fashionable life, with a large fortune and most acceptable manners. His ready wit, his conversation continually sparkling with polished raillery and courteous repartee, his chastened liveliness, his generous and kindly feelings,—all secured him that hazardous applause with which society rewards its ornaments and victims. His rare accomplishment in singing tended to increase his danger. "Wilberforce, we must have you again,—the Prince says he will come at any time to hear you sing," was the flattery which he received after his first meeting with the Prince of Wales, in 1782, at the luxurious soirees of Devonshire House.

On the 18th of December, 1783, Pitt, then only twenty-four years of age, became Prime Minister, on the fall of the Coalition cabinet of Fox and Lord North. He entered office with a great majority against him in the House of Commons, but strong in the confidence of the King, and believing that he could secure the support of the country. **For several** weeks he bravely maintained in Parliament an unequal struggle, warmly assisted by the counsels and eloquence of Wilberforce. Gradually the majority declined, and at length, in March 1784, Pitt seized an opportune moment to appeal to the country. Few general elections have called forth angrier feelings: and none, if we except that which occurred in 1880, have had a more decisive result. The Opposition was beaten all along the line. Horace Walpole, writing on the 11th of April, remarks that the scene had wofully changed for the Whig party, though not half the new Parliament was then chosen. "Though they still," he says, "contest a very few counties and some boroughs, they own themselves totally defeated. They reckoned themselves sure of two hundred and forty members; they probably will not have one hundred and fifty. In short, between the industry of the Court and the India Company, and that momentary frenzy that sometimes seizes a whole nation, as if it were a vast animal, such aversion to the Coalition, and such a detestation of Mr. Fox, have seized the country, that, even when omnipotent gold retains its influence, the elected pass through an ordeal of the most violent abuse."

Mr. Wilberforce, in spite of the vast influence of the Whig aristocracy, was returned for Yorkshire. This was the turning-point of his career. It placed him in a position of exceptional power and responsibility, as the chosen representative of the middle classes; and he *rose* to his position, as a man of strong mind and sound principles will always do. But something more was needed to fit him for the discharge of the great "mission" which Providence devolved upon him,—the deepening and strengthening of that spiritual life which in the world of fashion had almost faded into nothingness. While travelling on the Continent with his friend, Isaac Milner, afterwards Dean of Carlisle, his attention was often turned upon religious topics, and by slow degrees he was led to feel that the life he was leading, however blameless it might appear in the eyes of society, was unworthy of a being endowed with an immortal soul. His feelings did not immediately affect his conduct, but they were at work beneath the light and gay exterior. His conscience spoke to him, and would not be denied.

"I laughed," he writes, "I sang, I was apparently gay and happy, but the thought *would* steal across me, 'What madness is all this! to continue easy in a state in which a sudden call out of the world would consign me to everlasting misery, and that when eternal happiness is within my grasp!' For I had received into my understanding the great truths of the Gospel, and believed that its offers were free and universal; and that God had promised to give His Holy Spirit to them that asked for it. At length such thoughts as these, completely occupied my mind, and *I began to pray earnestly*." The victory was won. With a new purpose in his life, and a new spirit animating his conduct, he returned to England in November, resolute to persevere in paths of truth and righteousness.

We have said the victory was won; but prayer and meditation were needed to confirm it. Many of us climb the Hill of Difficulty, but take no heed to make good our footing on the summit; then we slip and stumble and are hurried headlong down the treacherous descent; and of such the last stage is worse than the first. In what manner and at what cost Wilberforce secured his faith and hope in Christ and Christ's religion may be seen in the following extracts from his private journal:—

"November 24th.—Heard the Bible read two hours, Pascal an hour and a quarter, meditation one hour and a quarter, business the same. If ever I take myself from the immediate consideration of serious things, I entirely lose sight of them; this must be a lesson to me to keep them constantly in view. Pitt called, and commended Butler's 'Analogy'—resolved to write to him, and discover to him what I am occupied about: this will save me much embarrassment, and I hope give me more command both of my time and conduct."

"Sunday, 27th.—Up at six, devotions half-an-hour, Pascal three-quarters, Butler three-quarters, church, read the Bible, too ramblingly, for an hour; heard Butler, but not attentively, two hours; meditated twenty minutes; hope I was more attentive at church than usual, but serious thoughts vanished the moment I went out of it, and very insensible and cold in the evening service; some very strong feelings when I went to bed; God turn them to account, and in any way bring me to Himself! I have been thinking I have been doing well by living alone and reading generally on religious subjects; I must awake to my dangerous state, and never be at rest till I have made my peace with God.

My heart is so hard, my blindness so great, that I cannot get a due hatred of sin, though I see I am all corrupt and blinded to the perception of spiritual things."

"November 28th.—I hope as long as I live to be the better for the meditation of this evening; it was on the sinfulness of my own heart, and its blindness and weakness. True, Lord, I am wretched, and miserable, and blind, and naked. What infinite love that Christ should die to save such a sinner, and how necessary is it He should save us altogether, that we may appear before God with nothing of our own! God grant I may not deceive myself in thinking I feel the beginnings of Gospel comfort. Began this night constant family prayer, and resolved to have it every morning and evening, and to read a chapter when time."

"November 30th.—Was very fervent in prayer this morning, and thought these warm impressions would never go off. Yet in vain endeavoured in the evening to rouse myself. God grant it may not all prove vain; oh, if it does, how will my punishment be deservedly increased! The only way I find of moving myself, is by thinking of my great transgressions, weakness, blindness; and of God's having promised to supply these defects. But though I firmly believe them, yet I read of future judgment, and think of God's wrath against sinners, with no great emotions. What can so strongly show the stony heart? O God, give me a heart of flesh! Nothing so convinces me of the dreadful state of my own mind as the possibility, which, if I did not know it from experience, I should believe impossible, of my being ashamed of Christ. Ashamed of the Creator of all things One who has received infinite pardon and mercy ashamed of the Dispenser of it, and that in a country where His name is professed! Oh, what should I have done in persecuting times?"

Though all of us must be the better for occasional intervals of self-communion and meditation, we should not care to recommend the habit of introspection and anxious mental inquiry revealed in the preceding passages. It seems to us that, at all events to many minds, it would prove dangerous by encouraging morbid ideas of dissatisfaction and despondency. Wilberforce, however, was of too firm and healthy a nature to linger long in such a condition, and he gradually struggled out of it into a state of tranquil faith and hope. He derived much help from the ministrations of Newton and Romaine, both of them leaders of the evangelical school; and the friendly counsels of Mr. Thornton. To his old associates he frankly made known his change of views; withdrew his name from the clubs of which he was a member; sought the friendship of men of earnest religious views; and spent several hours daily in study of the Scriptures. But he had no intention of withdrawing from his position in public life. He felt that he had sacred duties to fulfil, and that their faithful discharge would be more pleasing in the eyes of Heaven than any ascetic seclusion in selfish solitariness. "If I were to fly,' he wrote, "from the post where Providence has placed me, I know not how I could look for the blessing of God upon my retirement: and without this heavenly assistance, either in the world or in solitude, our own endeavours will be equally ineffectual. When I consider the particulars of my duty I blush at the review; but my shame is not occasioned by my thinking that I am too studiously diligent in the business of life; on the contrary, I then feel that I am serving God best when from proper motives I am most actively engaged in it."

Wilberforce's spiritual discipline and education were now complete, and he was fitted to take up the work which God had designed as the special work of his life. Like all work, it purified, strengthened, and ennobled his character. The work which each of us has to do is, in itself and its results, intended to train us to take higher views of our responsibilities and lift us out of self-indulgence and apathy; it benefits the worker no less than those for whom he works. It may be trivial enough in the eyes of the world, and perhaps in our own eyes; or it may be like that of Wilberforce, true Samaritan-work—"work of noble note"—work involving the happiness of millions; but whatever it is, or great or little, if done in a faithful and devout spirit, if done thoroughly and conscientiously, it brings with it a Divine benediction.

In the spring of 1786, Wilberforce, "an altered man," resumed his attendance in the House of Commons, and attempted some practical reforms. In the following year he took part in the debates on Pitt's treaties with France and Portugal, and on the impeachment of Warren Hastings. But at this time his labours outside Parliament were of greater value and importance, for he aimed at a reformation of the nation's morals, and the purification of the social atmosphere. Beginning with his friends, he sought to inspire them with a resolution to resist the growing vices of the times; and, extending his operations, he then sought to obtain a Royal Proclamation against vice and immorality, and to form an influential association for carrying it into effect. It may be, and is, true that nations are not made virtuous by royal proclamations or by associations; but yet such agencies are by no means without a salutary influence. It is a positive gain when, in the face of the nation, an open stand is made on behalf of the right. Through his unceasing efforts the society was established, with the Duke of Montagu as its first president, and many of the bishops as members; and during its existence it obtained several very useful Acts of Parliament, and greatly checked the spread of indecent and blasphemous publications. Was this no good? Was not the result worth the effort? Why, God and His angels rejoice when any one brand is plucked from the burning, one soul saved from pollution and death; and many brands must have been rescued, many souls delivered, through the charity of Wilberforce and his friends.

It was at this time that Wilberforce began to feel his way, as it were, towards what all the world will never cease to regard as his special mission—the abolition of the slave-trade. We have seen that the subject had occupied his thoughts when he was a school-boy. After his religious change, he naturally took it up as one that would be acceptable to the Saviour of mankind; and there seems no reason to believe that he was in any way guided by the example or counsel of Lady Middleton or the venerable Clarkson, though the friends of each have sought for them the merit of having summoned the appointed champion to the lists. He himself remarks that as early as the year 1780 he had been strongly interested for the West Indian slaves, and in a letter, asking a faiend who was going to Antigua to collect information for him, he expressed his determination, or at least his hope, that some time or other he should redress the wrongs of those wretched and degraded beings. It was not until the end of 1783 that Mr. Ramsay published a book on the condition of the negroes, which was the first trumpet-note of the coming battle. In 1786 Thomas Clarkson published his pamphlet against the slave-trade, and thenceforward the fight raged strenuously until the victory was won.

Wilberforce possessed all the qualifications which could grace the champion of such a cause,—glowing and persuasive eloquence, simple and earnest piety, high political influence, enthusiasm, courage, and profound conviction. "God Almighty," he exclaimed, "has set before me two great objects, the suppression of the slave-trade and the reformation of manners." This conviction enabled him to endure discouragements and delays with patience, and to labour on, in calm assurance of eventual success. He began by collecting the fullest possible information respecting the African slave-trade and the condition of the slaves in the West Indies. Then he discussed the all-important theme with William Pitt and George Grenville. Pitt recommended him to undertake the conduct of it in Parliament as one suited to his character and talents. "At length," he writes, "I well remember, after a conversation in the open air at the root of an old tree at Holwood, just above the steep descent into the vale of Keston, I resolved to give notice on a fit occasion in the House of Commons of my intention to bring the subject forward." At Holwood* this "old tree" is still preserved, and an inscription on a stone beneath it records the association that invests it with an enduring interest.

At first everything seemed to promise a speedy success. But great movements, like the tidal waters of a river, have their ebb and flow, and it soon became apparent that the abolition of the slave trade would be carried only in the face of a determined opposition. A long delay was caused by Wilberforce's dangerous illness (1788). Then came the King's first attack of insanity, and the parliamentary contests which the Regency Bill provoked. In 1789 Wilberforce renewed his philanthropic efforts, assisted by Granville Sharp, James Stephen, Thomas Clarkson, and other "good men and true," whose hearts had been touched to the quick by the miseries of the wretched negroes, torn from their homes and families, and handed over to the overseer's brutal lash. His opponents were not less active; and by meetings and pamphlets and newspaper articles endeavoured to convince the public that slavery lay at the very root of our colonial prosperity and commercial existence. If Wilberforce and his friends were moved

---

* Holwood is about four miles from Bromley, in Kent.

in their hearts, the slave-trade advocates were moved in their pockets; and the reader needs not to be told how powerful a motive to action is the fear of pecuniary loss. On the 12th of May the question came before the House of Commons, and a motion for the abolition of the slave-trade was made by Wilberforce in a speech of great power and eloquence, which lasted three hours and a half. Close and logical reasoning and clear statements of facts were skilfully interwoven with fervent appeals to the feelings; and we can even yet perceive the graphic force which describes the horrors of the sea-passage:—"So much misery crowded into so little room, where the aggregate of suffering must be multiplied by every individual tale of woe;" and the impressive character of the peroration, in which, after disproving the alleged comforts of the helpless victims, he summoned death as his last witness, "whose infallible testimony to their unutterable wrongs could neither be purchased nor repelled."

The effect of his speech was considerable, and it drew a compliment from Mr. Burke, who declared that "the House, the nation, and Europe were under great and serious obligations to the honourable gentleman for having brought forward the subject in a manner the most masterly, impressive, and eloquent. The principles," he said, "were so well laid down, and supported with so much force and order, that it equalled anything he had heard in modern times, and was not perhaps to be surpassed in the remains of Grecian eloquence."

Wilberforce's opponents, however, availed themselves of the forms of the House to prevent anything from being done that session. He again renewed the attack, and obtained a special committee to examine witnesses in reference to the whole subject. In 1790 he was re-elected for Yorkshire. Passing over successive phases of the gallant struggle, we come to April 1792, when he moved for a committee of the whole House to consider the African slave-trade, with a view to its immediate abolition. On this occasion he was supported by Pitt in one of his finest speeches. In a very effective passage Pitt compared the early condition of the Britons as slaves exported to the Roman market with that of the African negroes exported to the West Indies:— "Why might not some Roman senator," he said, "reasoning on the principles of some honourable gentleman, and pointing to

British barbarians, have predicted with equal boldness, 'There is a people that will never rise to civilisation; there is a people destined never to be free; a people without the understanding necessary for the attainment of useful arts; depressed by the hand of nature below the level of the human species; and created to form a supply of slaves for the rest of the world?' Might not this have been said, in all respects, as fairly and as truly of Britain herself, at that period of her history, as it can now be said by us of the inhabitants of Africa?"

It was decided that night, by a large majority—238 to 85—that the slave-trade should be *gradually* abolished. "I am congratulated on all hands," writes Wilberforce, "yet I cannot but feel hurt and humiliated. We must endeavour to force the gradual Abolitionists in *their* Bill (for I will never myself bring forward a parliamentary license to rob and murder) to allow as short a time as possible, and under as many limitations."

Mr. Dundas brought forward his resolutions for a gradual abolition on the 23rd. "After a hard struggle," writes Wilberforce, "we were last night defeated in our attempt to fix the period of the Abolition for the 1st of January, 1795: the numbers being 161 to 121. But we carried the 1st of January, 1796 (Mr. Dundas had proposed 1800), by a majority of 151 against 132. On the whole, this is more than I expected two months ago, and I have much cause for thankfulness. We are to contend about the number of slaves to be imported; and *then for the House of Lords.*" The resolutions passed the Commons, but unhappily the Peers rejected them; and again the battle had to be renewed. And renewed it was, in the following year, but not with the success that had formerly attended the Abolitionists. By a majority of eight votes the House of Commons refused to endorse its own decision of the preceding year. In 1796 Wilberforce was more fortunate. Then came a long interval of delay and discouragement, marked by the stirring events of the war with Republican France, and the fierce political struggle at home between the Government and its adherents and the advocates of peace under Charles James Fox. Notwithstanding his strong attachment to Pitt, and general confidence in his policy, Wilberforce contemplated the continuance of the war with anxiety, and used all his influence with the Prime Minister to incline him towards a pacific settlement.

The year 1797 is memorable in Wilberforce's personal history as that of the publication of his "Practical View of Christianity"; a plain and earnest exposition of religious duty which was eagerly welcomed by the public. In six months it ran through five editions (7500 copies). It was reprinted immediately in America, and was soon translated into the French, Italian, Spanish, Dutch, and German languages. To this day it retains something of its original popularity. "Its influence was proportionate to its diffusion. It may be affirmed, beyond all question, that it gave the first general impulse to that warmer and more earnest spring of piety, which amongst all its many evils has happily distinguished the last half-century." From a literary point of view, it is undoubtedly open to criticism; but as a manual of practical devotion its merits are very considerable, and the evangelical churchman will always find in it a welcome substitute for Thomas à Kempis.

On the 30th of May in the same year, Wilberforce was married to Barbara Ann, eldest daughter of Isaac Spooner, Esq., of Elmden Hall, Warwickshire.

The annual efforts made by our heroic Samaritan to induce the House of Commons to put a stop to the iniquities of the slave-trade, bear witness to his perseverance and to the moral apathy of Parliament. Re-elected for Yorkshire in 1802, he seemed to gain fresh energy from this proof of the continued confidence of his countrymen; and energy almost inexhaustible was needed to maintain the struggle in the face of constant vicissitudes. Thus, in 1804, he carried his Abolition Bill through the Commons by large majorities at each stage; but it was lost in the Lords. In the following year it was lost in the Commons. Then, in 1806, under the ministry of Lord Grenville and Mr. Fox, a Bill, introduced in the Peers to prohibit British subjects from engaging in the slave-trade for supplying foreign settlements or the conquered colonies, was successful. This encouraged Mr. Fox to move a resolution in the Commons, "that this House, conceiving the African slave-trade to be contrary to the principles of justice, humanity, and sound policy, will, with all practical expedition, proceed to take effectual measures for abolishing the said trade, in such manner, and at such period, as may be deemed advisable;" and the resolution was carried by 114 against 15. This was

Fox's last effort in the House which had so often been charmed by his eloquence. In the following September he was dead.

In 1807, the Abolition Bill was introduced in the House of Lords, and carried through it with triumphant rapidity. On the 10th of February it was sent down to the Lower Chamber, which, on the 23rd, decided, by the vast majority of 283 to 16—so great had been the change in public opinion—to go into committee upon it. Sir Samuel Romilly, then Solicitor-General, broke out into a burst of fervent oratory, contrasting the feelings with which Wilberforce would that night lay his head on his pillow, as the preserver of millions of his fellow-creatures, with those of the French Emperor, who had waded to a throne through slaughter and oppression. Surprised from its usual reserve, the House rang with repeated acclamations: and Wilberforce might well feel himself repaid for the tenacity and patient labour and unwearied effort of twenty years.

The debate proceeded, with slight show of opposition, except from one West Indian planter, who gave him an opportunity of replying in a speech distinguished for splendour of eloquence and force of argument; and on the 18th of March the Bill was read a third time by 283 to 16. On the 25th of March it received the royal assent.

"To speak," wrote Sir James Mackintosh, "of fame and glory to Mr. Wilberforce, would be to use a language far beneath him; but he will surely consider the effect of his triumph on the fruitfulness of his example. Who knows whether the greater part of the benefit that he has conferred on the world, the greatest that any individual has had the means of conferring, may not be the encouraging example that the exertions of virtue may be crowned by such splendid success? We are apt petulantly to express our wonder that so much exertion should be necessary to suppress such flagrant injustice. The more just reflection will be, that a short period of the short life of one man is, well and wisely directed, sufficient to remedy the miseries of millions for ages. Benevolence has hitherto been too often disheartened by frequent failures; hundreds and thousands will be animated by Mr. Wilberforce's example, by his success, and—let me use the word only in the moral sense of preserving his example—by a renown that can only perish with the world, to attack all the forms of corruption and cruelty that scourge mankind. Oh, what twenty years in the life of one man those were which abolished the slave-trade! How precious is time! How valuable and dignified is human life, which in general appears so base and miserable! How noble and sacred is human nature, made capable of achieving such truly great exploits!"

As for Wilberforce himself, all sense of personal triumph was absent from his mind. The cause was too great; he dared not measure his individual satisfaction against the thousands of lives which its success had rescued. His heart overflowed with gratitude: "I have indeed," he wrote, "inexpressible reasons for thankfulness in the glorious result of that struggle which, with so many eminent fellow-labourers, I have so long maintained. I really cannot account for the fervour which, happily, has taken the place of that fastidious, well-bred lukewarmness which used to display itself on this subject; except by supposing it to be produced by that Almighty power which can influence at will the judgments and affections of men."

Parliament was dissolved shortly after the completion of this noble work; and Wilberforce again became a candidate for the representation of his native county. He was confronted, on this occasion, by a formidable opposition in the person of Lord Milton, eldest son of Earl Fitzwilliam, who was prepared to expend a fortune on the contest. His colleague, Mr. Lascelles, son of Lord Harewood, was in a position to be similarly lavish; but Wilberforce's means, though not inconsiderable, were by no means adequate to such a struggle. His supporters, however, came forward immediately with a subscription of £18,000, and abundant promises of voluntary help; and the battle began and was fought out with extraordinary enthusiasm. On the first and second days of the polling, his chances seemed desperate; but on the third, a vast number of freeholders from the North Riding entered York, and polled for their old representative. Another large body, chiefly of the middle class, from Winsley Dale, was met on their road by one of his committee—"For what parties, gentlemen, do you come?" "Wilberforce, to a man," was their leader's reply. "During the early stage of the poll, such parties arrived at York at every given hour of time, both by day and by night, by land and by water; such was the loyalty and independence of this class of the Yorkshire freeholders, and such was their determination to support their old and favourite member, who had faithfully served them and their country during three-and-twenty years."

The poll was kept open for fifteen days, with the following result:—Wilberforce, 11,806 votes; Lord Milton, 11,177; and Mr. Lascelles, 10,989. The fund subscribed for Wilberforce's expenses reached the large total of £64,455,—a striking proof of his popularity; but only £28,600 were expended, while the election cost his two opponents no less than £200,000. Writing in his private diary after this signal triumph, the humble-minded Christian philanthropist says:—"Surely it calls for deep humiliation, and warm acknowledgment, that God has given me favour with man; that after guiding me by His providence to that great cause, He crowned my efforts with success, and obtained for me so much good-will and credit. Alas! Thou knowest, Lord, all my failings, errors, infirmities, and negligences in relation to this great cause; but Thou art all goodness and forbearance towards me. If I do not feel grateful to Thee, oh how guilty must I be brought in by my own judgment! But, O Lord, I have found too fatally my own stupidity; do Thou take charge of me, and tune my heart to sing Thy praises, and make me wholly Thine."

His daily life at this time followed a tolerably regular routine. The first hours of the morning, which were all so busy a man could really call his own, were spent in devotional exercises. "In the calmness of the morning," he was wont to say, "before the mind is heated and wearied by the toil of the day, you have a season of unusual importance for communing with God and with yourself." After this secret intercourse with his Divine Master, he joined his assembled household for morning prayer, which he always conducted himself, and with peculiar interest. With breakfast came his first batch of visitors, not a few of whom were admitted as guests to the breakfast-table; and his biographers tell us that his great social powers were never seen to more advantage than in drawing out and harmonizing all the shades of character and feeling which were here brought suddenly together. Thus while, on one occasion, he was seeking to relax the rigidity of "a starched little fellow," whom he did not wish to disgust, Andrew Fuller was announced; a man of considerable mental gifts, but bearing about him very plainly the *vestigia curis*. Not a moment was to be lost, "So before he came in I said to my little friend, 'You know Andrew Fuller?' 'No, I never heard his name.' 'Oh, then, you must know him; he is an extraordinary man, whose talents have raised him from a very low situation.' This prepared the way, and Andrew Fuller did no harm, although he walked in looking the very picture of a blacksmith."

When he had got rid of his visitors, his correspondence demanded his attention, and this being cleared away, he took such exercise as his scanty leisure enabled him to enjoy. At dinner he again met his family and friends, and when the House was not sitting, the evening was devoted to music, reading, and conversation. Some days were set apart, when in the country, for more entire devotion to prayer and meditation. His Sundays he invariably gave up to religious exercises, wholly putting aside all secular subjects. His children, after meeting him at prayers, accompanied him to church, repeating to him in the carriage hymns or verses, or passages from his favourite Cowper. Then they rambled with him in the garden, and each had the inestimable pleasure of bringing him a Sunday nosegay, for which they had hoarded the flowers of their own little plots all the week. At an early hour the family dined together, in the midst of cheerful yet suitable talk. "'Better,'" was one of his Sunday commonplaces, "'better is a dinner of herbs where love is, than a stalled ox and hatred therewith;' but, my children, how good is God to us! He gives us the stalled ox and love too."

But with Sunday ended, at least in London, the sweet enjoyments of domestic life. "While the House is sitting," he said, "I become almost a bachelor." The session at an end, and Wilberforce again in his rural seclusion, it became his delight "to live amongst his children;" to take his meals with them so far as possible; to carry them out with him on agreeable little excursions; to share in their amusements. Every day, too, he read aloud with them, allotting a certain portion of the afternoon to light and entertaining literature, then selecting one of them to read more serious works to him while he dressed. "Happy was the young performer who was chosen for this office. The early and quiet intercourse which his dressing-room afforded, drew forth all a father's tenderness, whilst the reading was continually changed into the most instructive conversation.—— read to me

Robertson's 'America' whilst dressing, and we talked over it." All his efforts were aimed at opening the mind, creating a spirit of inquiry, and strengthening the powers; while he was jealous of such acquirements as yielded an immediate return, and so afforded opportunities for gratifying vanity. . . . The practical character of his personal piety was of the utmost moment in his treatment of his children. He was always on his guard against forcing their religious feelings, and shielded them carefully from the poison of Antinomian teaching. After receiving a very promising account of one amongst his children, he says, "I am afraid of ——'s making him artificial by telling him it is God's work on the heart. I fear above all his being led to affect more than he really feels." Yet with all this careful watchfulness, tenderness was the distinctive feature of his domestic character. Though he never weakly withheld any necessary punishment, he did not attempt to dissemble the pain which its infliction cost him. "Alas!" he says at such a time, "—— grieved me much to-day, discovering the same utter want of self-government or self-denial when disappointed of anything on which he had set his heart, as he had done before. He behaved very ill. I talked with him plainly, and set him a punishment. Poor fellow! it made my heart heavy all the evening, and indeed ever since. But I hope he will mend. God will grant much to prayer; and I humbly trust it is our object to train him up in the nurture and admonition of the Lord."

The later history of Wilberforce is necessarily less interesting than the earlier, because the special object of his life having been achieved, his efforts, thenceforth, though still animated by a wise and genial spirit of benevolence, were diffused over various channels, and lacked that definiteness and prominency which are given by singleness of aim. His activity in the House of Commons continued without abatement; and though in strictly political questions his views were sometimes less broad and sympathetic than could be desired, on all moral points his clearness and fineness of judgment were invariably conspicuous. But on reaching middle age he began to feel the onerousness of county representation, and to desire a seat for some small borough which would not involve him in the incessant consideration of local interest. His consciousness of failing memory impelled him to adopt this course. He felt, too, that the education of his children called for more attention than he had been able to give to it, while his delicate health was a reason that could not be overlooked. In October 1812 he carried out his intention, and after twenty-eight years' honourable service retired from the representation of Yorkshire. He was almost immediately afterwards elected for the "close borough" of Braintree, in Essex.

On two subjects that now came before Parliament, his opinions were very distinctly expressed and energetically maintained. He spoke and voted in favour of the admission of Roman Catholics to the House of Commons, and with greater fervour and enthusiasm in support of Christian missions in India. When the renewal of the last India Charter took place, he contended strenuously for the insertion in it of clauses for the protection of our missionaries. He rightly felt that our civilization without our Christianity was but a sorry gift, and, indeed, time has shown that if ever the East accept our civilization it will be for the sake of our Christianity. With all his characteristic vigour and pertinacity he pushed forward his motion; gradually converted Lord Liverpool's Cabinet to his views, and, on the 22nd of June, 1813, defeated his opponents by 89 to 36.

But the main object and work of his life was not forgotten. He had struck down the slave-trade, but slavery still survived, and in the West Indian colonies assumed some of its most odious forms. To check these evils he proposed that there should be a complete Registration of the slaves. The Bill for this purpose, however, made but slow progress, and was eventually dropped. Other points connected with the welfare of the negro race incessantly occupied his attention, and to the last moment of his public life he eloquently expounded their wrongs and defended their rights, though, as years went on, he entrusted the leadership of the campaign to Thomas Fowell Buxton, a man fully worthy of the sacred charge.

His influence in the House and with the country was, during all these years, unparalleled on the part of a man who held no high official position, and had displayed no great qualities of statesmanship. It was an influence of which, if pride could have found a place in his gentle nature, he might well have been proud, for it was an influence due to character, to spotless integrity, to high-toned conscientiousness, and to the closest harmony between the practice and profession of religion; it was an influence due to a life unselfishly devoted to the welfare of humanity. Not only the condition of the negro race and the political questions of the day received his attention; but also such subjects as the Bible Society, the building of new churches, the education and more generous treatment of the poor, and the propagation of Christianity by missionary effort. His real position, as Sir James Stephen said, was that of "a minister of public charity, holding his office by popular acclamation."

In 1825, his bodily strength being visibly impaired, he withdrew from Parliament, and took up his residence at Highwood Hill, about ten miles to the north of London. There he remained, enjoying a tranquil and dignified old age, until 1831, when a heavy pecuniary loss compelled him to give up his establishment. He bore his misfortune with noble resignation. "I am bound," he writes, "to recognise in this dispensation the gracious mitigation of the severity of the stroke. It was not suffered to take place till all my children were educated, and nearly all of them placed out in one way or another; and by the delay Mrs. Wilberforce and I are supplied with a delightful asylum under the roofs of two of our own children. And what better could we desire? A kind Providence has enabled me with truth to adopt the declaration of David, that goodness and mercy have followed me all my days. And now, when the cup presented to me has some bitter ingredients, yet surely no draught can be deemed distasteful which comes from such a hand, and contains such grateful infusions as those of social intercourse and the sweet endearments of filial gratitude and affection. What I shall most miss will be my books and my garden, though I own I do feel a little the not being able to ask my friends to take a dinner or a bed with me, under my own roof. And as even the great Apostle did not think the 'having no certain dwelling-place,' associated with his other far greater sufferings, unworthy of mention, so I may feel this also to be some, though I grant not a great evil, to one who has so many kind friends who will be happy to receive him."

Thenceforward he spent his time either with his son Samuel (afterwards Bishop of Winchester), at his pleasant rectory-house in the sunny village of Brightstone Isle of Wight, or with his son Robert (Archdeacon of the East Riding) at East Farleigh, near Maidstone. At both places some relics of the venerable philanthropist are still shown—his favourite walk, the hedge he planted. His last appearance in public was at Maidstone, on the 12th of April, 1833, when at a large meeting he proposed a petition against slavery. Thus his "ruling passion"—a glorious one—prevailed with him in his declining days. And, indeed, the sun was now sinking rapidly beneath the horizon; the shadows were lengthening fast; night was at hand with its silence and its solitude, and its promise of a new dawn in a brighter world. He went to Bath on the 17th of May to drink the waters, from which he had often derived much benefit; but his pain and languor increased, and there was no sign of rallying energies. On Saturday, the 6th of July, while at dinner, he was taken ill quite suddenly. He was conveyed to bed, and medical aid was summoned. To his physician, "Thank God," he said, "I am not losing my faculties." "Yes, but you could not easily go through a problem in arithmetic or geometry." "I think," he replied, "I could go through the Asses' Bridge. Let me see," and he began the fifth problem of Euclid's first book, correcting himself if he omitted anything.

To his youngest son, who was in constant attendance upon him, he spoke frequently on such religious subjects as his condition suggested, and of the delight he had in the affection and care of his wife and children.

A friend who visited him on the 11th thus describes the interview:—

"I was introduced to an apartment upstairs, where I found the veteran Christian reclining on a sofa, with his feet wrapped in flannel, and his countenance bespeaking increased age since I had last seen him, as well as much delicacy. He received me with the warmest marks of affection, and seemed to be delighted by the unexpected arrival of an old friend. I had scarcely taken my seat beside him before . . . it seemed given me to remind him of the words of the Psalmist—'Although ye have lain among the pots, yet shall ye be as the wings of a dove covered with silver, and her feathers with yellow gold;' and I freely spoke to him of the good and glorious things which, as I believed, assuredly awaited him in the kingdom of rest and peace. In the meantime the illuminated expression of his furrowed countenance, with his clasped and uplifted hands, were indicative of profound devotion and holy joy."

The severity of this attack having been to some extent mitigated, Wilberforce was removed to London, that he might consult the eminent physician, Dr. Chambers. On the 19th of July, he arrived in Cadogan Place, Sloane Street. Parliament was still sitting, and many of his old friends flocked around him, bringing him the welcome intelligence (on the 26th) that the Bill for the Abolition of Slavery in the West Indian Colonies had passed its second reading in the House of Commons. After a persistent struggle of fifty years, this great curse and shame was finally removed from the conscience of England, and Wilberforce lived to see the day of triumph. On the evening of the 27th he was evidently weaker, and next day he experienced a succession of fainting fits, which for a time suspended his power of recollection. During an interval in the evening of Sunday, "I am in a very distressed state," he said, alluding apparently to his physical condition. "Yes," it was answered, "but you have your feet on the Rock." "I do not venture," he replied, "to speak so positively; but I hope I have." After this utterance of humble faith, with not a single groan, he passed away into the rest of his Lord,—dying at three o'clock on the morning of Monday, July 29th, aged seventy-three years and eleven months.

He was buried in Westminster Abbey on the 5th of August, his funeral being attended by the Members of both Houses of Parliament, by the Bishops of the Church, the Duke of Wellington, and most of England's ablest and greatest sons.

We have spoken of Thomas Fowell Buxton as the Elisha of the anti-slavery movement, upon whom the veteran Wilberforce devolved his mantle. The biography of this thorough English gentleman is worth studying, for it tells of a good and great life, inspired by a really lofty sense of duty and by a wise and generous philanthropy.

Thomas Fowell Buxton was the son of a respectable country squire, of Castle Hedingham, in Essex, where he was born on the 1st of April, 1786. At the time of his father's death he was but six years old; a vigorous boy, however, with a singularly bold and determined character. As an illustration, it may be mentioned that on one occasion, while walking with his uncle, he was requested to give a message to a pig-driver who had passed along the road. He immediately started in pursuit; and although one of his shoes was soon lost in the mud, he plodded on through lonely and intricate lanes, tracking him by the foot-marks of his pigs, for nearly three miles, into the town of Coggeshall; nor was he contented until he had overtaken the man and delivered his message.

He was educated by Dr. Charles Burney, of Greenwich, a schoolmaster who turned out several useful and remarkable men. His holidays he spent at home, where he derived great advantages from the wise, affectionate, but energetic rule of his mother. In his studies, however, his progress was not satisfactory; he is described as leading a desultory and aimless life,—sporting, riding, fishing, reading amusing books, but incapable, as it seemed, of systematic and continuous application. It was, indeed, a critical time for his character. He stood in need of the guidance of some kindly and noble nature, some man of "light and leading;" and happily such he found in John, the oldest son of the Quaker banker, Mr. Gurney of Earlham Hall, near Norwich, whose acquaintance he formed in the autumn of 1801.

"I know no blessing," he said in after years, "of a temporal nature (and it is not only temporal) for which I ought to render so many thanks as my connection with the Earlham family. It has given a colour to my life. Its influence was most positive and pregnant with good, at that critical period between school and manhood. They were eager for improvement—I caught the infection. I was resolved to please them; and in the college of Dublin, at a distance from all my friends, and all control, their influence, and the desire to please them, kept me hard at my books, and sweetened the toil they gave. The distinctions I gained at college (little valuable as distinctions, but valuable because habits of industry, perseverance, and reflection were necessary to obtain them), these boyish distinctions were exclusively the result of the animating passion in my mind, to carry back to them the prizes which they prompted and enabled me to win."

In October 1803, Buxton entered Trinity College, Dublin, as

a fellow-commoner. His career there was eminently successful, and surprised those who from the apathy and negligence of his childhood had formed a poor opinion of his capacity. He carried off the highest distinctions. His vacations were spent at Earlham; and thus it came to pass that an attachment, which he dated from the first day they met, gradually ripened between him and Mr. Gurney's fifth daughter, Hannah, until, in March 1805, the seal of a formal engagement was set upon it.

In the following year he made a tour through some of the romantic scenery of Scotland, which the genius of Scott had just revealed to Englishmen in all its picturesque beauty of mountain and loch, and glen and waterfall. During this holiday ramble his attention was directed with a good deal of earnestness to religious subjects. He mentions in one of his letters that a great change had been worked in his mind with respect to reading the Holy Scriptures. "Formerly," he says, "I read generally rather as a duty than as a pleasure, but now I read them with great interest, and, I may say, happiness. I never before felt so assured that the only means of being happy is from seeking the assistance of a Superior Being, or so inclined to endeavour to submit myself to the direction of principle." The impression was not a fugitive one, but strengthened and deepened with every year; and the light and glow of an unaffected but earnest piety ennobled and glorified his whole life.

The gold medal, the highest honour bestowed by his Alma Mater, fell to his lot in April 1807, and marked the close of his collegiate career. A flattering distinction awaited him: he was pressed by his fellow-graduates to come forward as a candidate for the representation of the University. A greater proof of their esteem and confidence could not well be afforded, as Buxton was without wealth or Irish connections; in truth, without the slightest claim upon the consideration of the University other than his personal character and conduct afforded. But he was on the point of marriage; and against those prospects of parliamentary renown and influence which colour so brightly the dreams of young politicians, he balanced the duties and responsibilities his domestic life would soon involve; and finally, though not without some natural reluctance, declined the honour of entering the House of Commons under such favourable circumstances.

Buxton was married on the 13th of May, 1807. A serious pecuniary loss compelled him to devote himself to a business career; and in 1808 he entered the well-known establishment of Hanbury and Truman's brewery, with the prospect of becoming a partner in the firm after a probation of three years. With intense energy and ardour and singleness of purpose he applied himself to the discharge of his new duties, occupying a house close to the brewery that he might do his work the more thoroughly and promptly. Meanwhile, he devoted his leisure to the study of English literature, and especially of political economy; and keeping before his mind the possibility of entering Parliament at some convenient time, he practised the art of public speaking in a debating club of which he was a member. He laboured also with philanthropic zeal for the improvement of the distressed district in which the brewery was situated. He was no dilettante philanthropist, flinging down his alms with lavish indifference, or taking credit for charity by proxy: like the Good Samaritan, when he saw the sufferer bleeding by the wayside, he crossed over to him, and with his own hands bound up his wounds. His benevolence was active and discriminating; and thus it developed into a true and genial beneficence.

In 1811 he was admitted into the brewery as a partner; and during the next seven years the management of so extensive a concern monopolised almost all his energies. His senior partners, recognizing his force of character and strength of mind, devolved upon him the difficult task of reorganizing the establishment; a task he performed with so much tact and judgment as largely to increase the income of the firm, while, after a time, he was able to leave the minor details to proper subordinates.

A dangerous illness with which he was afflicted in 1813 deepened the seriousness of his religious views. "It was then," he said at a later period, "that some clouds in my mind were dispersed; and from that day to this, whatever reason I may have had to mistrust my own salvation, I have never been harassed by a doubt respecting our revealed religion." As his health improved, and he recovered his strength, he gave an increased and a more active support to the principal benevolent societies of the metropolis, and especially to the Bible Society,* over the opera-

---

* The British and Foreign Bible Society was founded in 1803, and in the

tions of which he watched with enlightened interest to the very day of his death.

A remarkable example of his courage, decision, and presence of mind occurred in July 1816. As a valuable illustration of the distinctive features of his character, we record it here, making use of his own simple and unaffected narrative:—

"As you must hear"—he is writing to his wife—"the story of our dog Prince, I may as well tell it you. On Thursday morning, when I got on my horse at Mr. Hoare's, David told me that there was something the matter with Prince" (a favourite mastiff)—"that he had killed the cat, and almost killed the new dog, and had bit at him and Elizabeth. I ordered him to be tied up and taken care of, and then rode off to town. When I got into Hampstead, I saw Prince, covered with mud, and running furiously, and biting at everything. I saw him bite at least a dozen dogs, two boys, and a man.

"Of course I was exceedingly alarmed, being persuaded he was mad. I tried every effort to stop him or kill him, or to drive him into some out-house, but in vain. At last he sprang up at a boy, and seized him by the breast; happily I was near him, and knocked him off with my whip. He then set off towards London, and I rode by his side, waiting for some opportunity of stopping him. I continually spoke to him, but he paid no regard to coaxing or scolding. You may suppose I was seriously alarmed, dreading the immense mischief he might do, having seen him do so much in the few preceding minutes. I was terrified at the idea of his getting into Camden Town and London; and, at length, considering if ever there was an occasion that justified a risk of life this was it, I determined to catch him myself. Happily he ran up to Pryor's gate, and I threw myself from my horse upon him, and caught him by the neck. He bit at me, and struggled, but without effect, and I succeeded in securing him, without his biting me.

"When I seized the dog his struggles were so desperate that it seemed at first almost impossible to hold him, till I lifted him up in the air, when he was more easily managed, and I contrived to

---

following year completely organised. Wilberforce, Hughes, Reyun, Grant, Bishops Porteus and Barrington, and others, were the promoters. It rests on an undenominational basis.

ring the bell. I was afraid that the foam, which was pouring from his mouth in his furious efforts to bite me, might get into some scratch and do me injury; so with great difficulty I held him with one hand, while I put the other into my pocket and forced on my glove; then I did the same with my other hand, and at last the gardener opened the door, saying, 'What do you want?' 'I've brought you a mad dog,' replied I; and telling him to get a strong chain, I walked into the yard, carrying the dog by his neck. I was determined not to kill him, as I thought if he should prove not to be mad, it would be such a satisfaction to the three persons whom he had bitten. I made the gardener (who was in a terrible fright) secure the collar round his neck, and fix the other end of the chain to a tree, and then, walking to its furthest range, with all my force, which was nearly exhausted by his frantic struggles, I flung him away from me, and sprang back. He made a desperate bound after me, but finding himself foiled, he uttered the most fearful yell I ever heard. All that day he did nothing but rush to and fro, champing the foam which gushed from his jaws. We threw him meat, and he snatched at it with fury, but instantly dropped it again.

"The next day, when I went to see him, I thought the chain seemed worn, so I pinned him to the ground, between the prongs of a pitchfork, and then fixed a much larger chain round his neck. When I pulled off the fork, he sprang up and made a dash at me, which snapped the old chain in two! He died in forty-eight hours from the time he went mad."

Mr. Buxton entered upon his parliamentary career in 1818, when he was elected member for Weymouth. In his public as in his private life he relied for success not upon great mental endowments—which he can hardly be said to have possessed—but upon his lofty sense of duty and his tenacity of purpose. It was Buxton's belief that the race is always to the swift and the battle to the strong. He maintained that nothing was impossible to extraordinary perseverance and ordinary capacity. In working out his noble Samaritan-like schemes, he employed this extraordinary perseverance with a successful result. What indeed but success could result from labours undertaken with Buxton's solemn feeling of responsibility? "Surely," he writes, "it is in the power of all to do something in the service of their Master; and surely I among the rest, if I were now to begin and endeavour to the best of my capacity to serve Him, might be the means of good to some of my fellow-creatures."

It is interesting to see in what spirit he entered upon the cares and responsibilities of public life. "Now that I am a Member of Parliament," he writes, "I feel earnest for the honest, diligent, and conscientious discharge of the duty I have undertaken. My prayer is for the guidance of God's Holy Spirit, that, free from views of gain or popularity, that careless of all things but fidelity to my trust, I may be enabled to do some good to my country, and something for mankind, especially in their most important concerns. I feel the responsibility of the situation, and its many temptations. On the other hand, I see the vast good which one individual may do. May God preserve me from the snares which may surround me; keep me from the power of personal motives, from interest, or passion, or prejudice, or ambition, and so enlarge my heart to feel the sorrows of the wretched, the miserable condition of the guilty and the ignorant, that I may 'never turn my face from any poor man'; and so enlighten my understanding, that I may be a capable and resolute champion for those who want and deserve a friend."

One of the first subjects taken up by Buxton in public life was the condition of our prisons, which, since the reforms of Howard, had sunk again into disorder and anarchy, ill controlled by tyrannical oppression. Buxton felt that though a man may be a rogue and deserve punishment, it is neither wise nor just to convert punishment into cruelty. He was led to doubt the wisdom of a penal code which inflicted on the poor wretch who sought to appease his hunger with a stolen loaf the same terrible sentence of death it allotted to the murderer red with his victim's blood. On the 2nd of March, 1819, a motion for the appointment of a committee on the criminal laws was made by Sir James Mackintosh, and seconded by Mr. Buxton, whose speech was both lucid and forcible. "There are persons living," he said, "at whose wish the criminal code contained less than sixty offences, and who have seen that number quadrupled, who have seen an Act passed making offences capital by the dozen and by the score; and, what is worse, bundling up together offences trivial and atrocious,—some nothing short of murder in malignity of intention, and others nothing beyond a civil trespass,—I say, bundling together this ill-sorted and incongruous package, and stamping upon it ' **Death** without benefit of clergy.' " He added that the law, by declaring that "certain crimes should be punished with death, had declared that they should not be punished at all. The bow had been bent till it snapped asunder. The Acts which were intended to prevent evil had proved Acts of indemnity and free pardon to the fraudulent and the thief, and Acts of ruin and destruction to many a fair trader."

By his speeches in Parliament Buxton speedily secured a considerable reputation. He was not an orator; but he was a good and steady debater, and his strong logical reasoning was always set forth in a clear style and with appropriate illustration. He was not one of those speakers who, in Bacon's phrase, " hunt more after words than matter, and more after the choiceness of the phrase, the sweet falling of the clauses, and the varying illustration of their words, with tropes and figures, than after the weight of matter, worth of subject, or soundness of argument." He usually prepared his speeches with great care, not for the sake of artifices of style, but to collect supplies of fact, and enforce the different points of his statement. Speaking as he did from eager conviction, and because he had something to say,—on subjects which appealed to the feelings no less than to the judgment,—he frequently rose above the general level of his manly and vigorous style into passages of passionate declamation: these, however, sprang from the rush and tumult of his emotions, and never smelt of the midnight oil.

In 1820, Mr. Buxton's labours for the amendment of prison discipline bore some good fruit, and he had the satisfaction of seeing the solution of a difficult problem begun—how to reform our criminals while we punish them. It must be admitted that the solution even yet is not complete, but a great deal of satisfactory progress has been made, and for this progress we are indebted to the efforts of Buxton and his fellow-workers.

Hitherto his life had been one unbroken flow of happiness, so that, like the ancient monarch, he began to be afraid of so much prosperity. A heavy domestic affliction, however, came to remind him that life must have its shadows as well as its sunshine. An inflammatory disorder carried off his eldest son, a boy of great promise, "the peculiar object of our anxious care; a boy of great life and animation; of a most beautiful countenance; of a most sweet disposition;" and shortly afterwards his then infant daughter died of measles. The blow was terrible; but he bore it with the fortitude of a Christian, though the keenness of his suffering is shown by the brief but pregnant inscription he placed upon the four-fold grave—*Eheu! eheu!* (Alas! alas!) "Thus, in little more than a month," he writes, "have we lost the darlings and delights of our life; but they are in peace: and, for ourselves, we know that this affliction may redound to our eternal benefit, if we receive it aright. . . . How are all our most choice and comely blossoms cut off; how naked do we appear, how stripped of our treasures! Oh, my God! my God! Be Thou our consoler, and comfort us, not with the joys of this world, but with faith, love, obedience, patience, and resignation."

In the autumn of 1820, Mr. Buxton permanently took up his residence, when Parliament was not sitting, at Cromer Hall, near Cromer, in Norfolk. "It was situated," says his son, "about a quarter of a mile from the sea, but sheltered from the north winds by closely surrounding hills and woods; and, with its old buttresses and porches, its clustering jessamine and its formal lawn, where the pheasants came down to feed, it had a peculiar character of picturesque simplicity. The interior corresponded with its external appearance, and had little of the regularity of modern buildings; one room was walled up, with no entrance save through the window; and, at different times, large pits were discovered under the floor, or in the thickness of the walls, used, it was supposed, in old times, by the smugglers of the coast."

Here, in the enjoyment of domestic tranquillity and cultured ease, Buxton spent his leisure hours. The happiness of his home was so great that it strongly moved the mind of Wilberforce, himself the head of a loving Christian household:—"I love to muse about you all," he wrote; "and form suitable wishes for the comfort and good of each member of your happy circle: for a happy circle it is; and surely there is nothing in the world half so delightful as mutual confidence, affection, and sympathy; to feel esteem as well as good-will towards every human being around you, not only in your own house, but in the social circle that surrounds your dwelling; and to be conscious that every other being is turning with the same esteem and love toward you."

Happy is it for the world that in every good cause, every movement for the welfare of humanity, an Elijah's mantle always falls upon an Elisha. The torch, once kindled, is passed from hand to hand—passed through a long series of willing workers, until its light is no longer needed; so that in philanthropical efforts, at least, we may well believe in the existence of a species of Apostolical succession. We have seen how, for upwards of thirty years, William Wilberforce lifted up his voice against the iniquities of slavery and the horrors of the slave-trade, until he succeeded in stirring up the popular indignation against the foul crime that tarnished the name and fame of England. We have seen what great things he accomplished in the face of a powerful and unscrupulous opposition, by dint of lofty eloquence, the influence of a noble life, and the force of a strong character. Now (May, 1821), the warrior was spent and worn with his prolonged struggle, and looked around for some brave young knight, worthy to carry his shield, and wear his sword. It was necessary that his successor should be gifted with some at least of the qualities which he himself possessed: with the same equanimity, the same dauntless perseverance, the same indifference to calumny, and the same earnest belief in the righteousness of his cause. All this was found in Buxton, and Wilberforce recognized in him also a weight of moral influence, a power of lucid exposition, and a capacity for hard work which well fitted him for the task of advocating the claims of the slave.

It was thus that the veteran wrote to the young soldier:—

"For many, many years, I have been longing to bring forward that great subject, the condition of the negro slaves in our Trans-Atlantic colonies, and the best means of providing for their moral and social improvement, and ultimately for their advancement to the rank of a free peasantry; a cause thus recommended to me, or rather enforced on me, by every consideration of religion, justice, and humanity.

"Under this impression I have been waiting, with no little solicitude, for a proper time and suitable circumstances of the country, for introducing this great business; and, latterly, for some Member of Parliament, who, if I were to retire or to be laid by, would be an eligible leader in this holy enterprise.

"I have for some time been viewing you in this connection; and after what passed last night, I can no longer forbear resorting to you, as I formerly did to Pitt, and earnestly conjuring you to take most seriously into consideration the expediency of your devoting yourself to this *blessed service*, so far as will be consistent with the due discharge of the obligations you have already contracted, and in part so admirably fulfilled, to war against the abuses of our criminal law, both in its structure and its administration. Let me then entreat you to form an alliance with me, that may truly be termed holy, and if I should be unable to commence the war—and still more, if, when commenced, I should (as certainly would, I fear, be the case) be unable to finish it, do I entreat that you would continue to prosecute it. Your assurance to this effect would give me the greatest pleasure—pleasure is a bad term—let me rather say peace and consolation; for alas! my friend, I feel but too deeply how little I have been duly assiduous and faithful in employing the talents committed to my stewardship; and in forming a partnership of this sort with you, I cannot doubt that I should be doing an act highly pleasing to God, and beneficial to my fellow-creatures."

It is difficult for us, in these days of general enlightenment, when slavery is without a supporter, or, at least, an open advocate, to understand the reckless abuse, the foul aspersion, the shameful misrepresentation which were hurled at the friends of the negro. The West India planters, whose enormous fortunes had been gained with slave-labour, were active and powerful; their party in the House of Commons was numerous, strong, and unscrupulous; while among the outside public were thousands of the credulous who really believed that the abolition of slavery would be followed by the downfall of our Colonial Empire. And here let the reader remember the distinction between slavery and the slave-trade. We have seen that, after a twenty years' struggle on the part of Wilberforce, Clarkson, and their coadjutors, the importation of negroes from Africa to our Colonies was declared illegal in 1807. And no sooner had England thus rid herself of the shame, than, with her usual chivalry, she endeavoured, by purchase or persuasion, to obtain a similar measure from the other European powers. But though the British slave-trade had been abolished, British slavery remained. It was true that no more negroes could be imported into our Colonies, but those who had already been imported were still in bondage, and their children and their children's children were doomed to the same unhappy fate.

The hostility with which Buxton contended for many long and anxious years was as determined as it was venomous; and to persevere in the face of the storm that raged around him, in spite of obloquy and misrepresentation, demanded all the highest qualities of the Christian character. Powerfully supported, however, by Lord Brougham and Sir Francis Burdett, Sir James Mackintosh and Dr. Lushington, he pressed upon the House of Commons, year after year, the iniquity of the institution of slavery. The facts which he brought forward gradually moved the conscience of the nation. Thus, he told his hearers that in Jamaica, for example, the amount of field labour allotted by law was *nineteen hours* a day during crop time, and *fourteen and a half* during the remainder of the year, with intervals of rest amounting to two hours and a half per diem. This work, be it remembered, had to be done under an almost vertical sun, and in the following manner:—" The slaves were divided into gangs of from thirty to fifty men, generally selected of a nearly equal degree of strength, but many were often weak or diseased. They were placed in a line in the field, with drivers armed with the whip at equal distances; and were obliged to maintain that line throughout the day, so that those who were not so strong as the others were literally flogged up by the drivers. The motion of the line was rapid and constant." The effect of this atrocious cruelty, and of the severe punishments constantly inflicted, was seen in the rapid diminution of the slave population. In 1807, there were 800,000 slaves in the West Indies; in 1830, only 700,000. So that in twenty-three years, in spite of births, the slave population had diminished by 100,000.

Such facts as these told their own tale, and Buxton had the satisfaction of seeing the number of his followers increase every year. Year after year the truths he proclaimed secured a larger audience. It was inevitable that success should crown his unselfish efforts in so noble a cause; efforts made in a spirit of the purest and sincerest devotion. It is well that the reader should understand in what way he sustained and prepared himself for the burden of his great task. From one of his private papers, dated New Year's Day, 1832, we take the following extracts:—

"Grant, O Lord, that I may begin the next year under the guidance and influence of that blessed Spirit, which, if I grieve it not, if I follow it implicitly, if I listen to its still small voice, if I love it as my friend, and consult it as my counsellor, will surely lead me in this life in the pleasant paths of peace and holiness, and as surely conduct me hereafter to the habitations of unutterable joy.

"Now am I sufficiently assiduous in the discharge of my duties? My great duty is the deliverance of my brethren in the West Indies from slavery both of body and soul. In the early part of the year I did in some measure faithfully discharge this. I gave my whole mind to it. I remember that I prayed for firmness and resolution to persevere, and that in spite of some formidable obstructions I was enabled to go on; but, latterly, where has my heart been? Has the bondage of my brethren engrossed my whole mind? The plain and the painful truth is that it has not. Pardon, O Lord, the neglect of this honourable service to which Thou hast called me.

"Give me wisdom to devise, and ability to execute, and zeal and perseverance and dedication of heart, for the task with which Thou hast been pleased to honour me. 2 Chron. xx. 12-17.

"And now, Lord, hear and answer my prayer for myself; my first desire is, that this next year may not be thrown away upon anything less than those hopes and interests which are greater and better than any that this world can contain. May no subordinate cares or earthly interests interrupt my progress. May I act as one whose aim is heaven; may my loins be girded, and my lights burning, and myself like unto men who wait for their Lord. Conscious of my own weakness, of my absolute inability to do anything by my own strength, anything tending to my own salvation, I earnestly pray for the light and the impulse of Thy Holy Spirit, and that Christ may dwell in my heart by faith.

"Bless, O Lord God, my efforts for the extinction of that cruel slavery; or, rather, take the work into Thine own hands."

Those efforts *were* blessed. Some of Buxton's political friends were in favour of *gradual* emancipation; but he himself rightly insisted that the only cure for the evil was *immediate* and *total* abolition; and he called upon England to declare that at one blow the fetters should be struck off the mangled limbs of the unhappy slave. "Deeply versed in the state of the West Indies, it was to him a thing plain and undoubted that no policy could be so pernicious as that of hesitation and delay. He thought that the dangers of rapid emancipation were not nearly so great as they were held to be. He believed that a good police and kind treatment would suffice to prevent those 'frightful calamities' (the result of such an act) which Sir Robert Peel 'shuddered to contemplate.' He boldly stated his belief that the negroes would go to work for wages as soon as they were released from the terrors of the whip. And that at any rate the legislature would find it the most hopeless task in the world to do what Lord Althorp called 'employing itself most usefully in bringing the slaves to such a state of moral feeling as would be suitable to the proposed alteration in their condition.'"

His disinterested labours finally prevailed. The country was thoroughly roused at last to a full sense of the wrongs under which the unfortunate negroes groaned, and made abundantly clear its resolve that they should cease. It was proposed with splendid generosity to compensate the slave-owners for the loss of their "property"—their human property—their supposed ownership of the thews and muscles of their fellow-men. Crowded public meetings were held all over the kingdom; and in 1833 the Government found themselves compelled to take up the question, and introduce a Bill providing for the immediate abolition of slavery on payment of £20,000,000 to the planters. It passed the Lower House on the 7th of August; was read a third time in the House of Lords on the 20th; and received the royal assent on the 28th. In the West Indies the new Act was received in a way which satisfactorily confuted the prognostications of evil in which its opponents had indulged. The planters showed no signs of irritation, the negroes neither excitement nor insubordination; and the Colonial Legislatures immediately prepared to carry it into effect on the following 1st of August, when 770,280 slaves received that freedom which, according to one of the commonplaces of moralists, is "man's inalienable birthright."

The following data in reference to the slave-trade may prove convenient to the reader.

1. So far as England is concerned, the slave-trade was begun by Sir John Hawkins, in October 1562.

2. It had grown to such terrible proportions in course of time that, towards the close of the eighteenth century, no fewer than one hundred thousand African negroes were annually thrown into slavery. In 1786 the English slave-trade employed 160 ships.

3. The first debate upon the proposed abolition of the trade took place in the House of Commons in April 1791.

4. In April 1798, Mr. Wilberforce's motion was defeated by 88 to 83.

5. The English slave-trade was abolished March 25th, 1807.

6. Treaties for its suppression were concluded with Spain in 1817; the Netherlands, 1818; Brazil, 1828; the United States, 1862; Zanzibar, 1873.

7. The Emancipation Act received the royal assent August 28th, 1833.

8. Death of Wilberforce, 1833; of Thomas Clarkson, September 1846; of Sir Thomas Fowell Buxton, February, 1845.

9. In the United States, the total abolition of slavery took place in 1862.

Though this noble crusade against slavery was the chief labour of Buxton's life, he found time and means to support every project which was destined to promote the welfare of humanity; and the numerous charitable associations of the metropolis could always calculate on his generous help and counsel. We have not space, however, nor would it interest the reader, to record, month by month and year by year, his exertions as a Good Samaritan. We have said enough to show that the motive which animated his life, the ruling passion which informed and guided his career, was a devotion to duty which no discouragement, no difficulty, no temporary failure could weaken. He took up the cause of the enslaved and oppressed negro as a duty, in the discharge of which he brought to bear all the best qualities of a manly character. Calm, resolute, self-controlled, he repelled with dignity the attacks of unscrupulous adversaries. Prudent and moderate, he indulged in none of those exaggerations by which over-zealous advocates too often diminish the force of their own assertions. He made no statements which were not capable of incontrovertible proof; and his opponents soon discovered that if he was earnest and direct in the attack, he was always ready and prompt in the defence. Their utmost ingenuity failed to discover a weak point in his armour. His character may be described as formed of a " durable material;" so that an impression once effectually made seemed never to be effaced.

A letter which Buxton addressed to one of his sons on entering Trinity College, Cambridge, will show the reader what manner of man he was. It is the letter of a man who, in the highest sense, knew how to make "the best of both worlds":—

"It is always a disappointment to me to be absent, when my boys are at home; but I particularly regretted being away last week, as I think I might have done something for your shooting before you went to College. I need not, I hope, tell you of the extreme interest I take in the launch of your little skiff on the ocean of life, and how ardently I desire that 'soft airs and gentle heavings of the wave' may accompany your voyage; and that you may be safely piloted into the serene and lovely harbour prepared by the love of God. It is not often that I trouble my children with advice, and never, I believe, unless I have something particular to say. At the present time, I think I have that to say which is deeply important to your success in the business of life; nay, its effects may extend beyond the grave. You are now a man, and I am persuaded that you must be prepared to hold a very inferior station in life to that which you might fill, unless you resolve, with God's help, that whatever you do, you will do it *well*; unless you make up your mind, that it is better to accomplish perfectly a very small amount of work than to half-do ten times as much. What you do know, know thoroughly. There are few instances in modern times of a rise equal to that of Sir Edward Sugden.* After one of the Weymouth elections, I was shut up with him in a carriage for twenty-four hours. I ventured to ask him what was the secret of his success; his answer was, 'I resolved

---

* Afterwards Lord St. Leonards, and Lord Chancellor; died Jan. 29, 1875.

when beginning to read law, to make everything I acquired perfectly my own, and never to go to a second thing till I had entirely accomplished the first. Many of my competitors read as much in a day as I read in a week; but, at the end of twelve months, my knowledge was as fresh as on the day it was acquired, while theirs had glided away from their recollection.'

"Let the same masculine determination to act to some purpose go through your life. Do the day's work to-day. At college I was extremely intimate with two young men, both of extraordinary talents. The one was always ahead of his tutor; he was doing this year the work of next year, and although, upon many parts of the subject, he knew more than his examiner, yet he contrived to answer what was actually proposed to him most scandalously;— while the other, by knowing perfectly what it was his business to know (though not confining himself to that), never, to the best of my recollection, failed to answer any question that was put to him.

"Again, be punctual. I do not mean the merely being in time for lectures, etc., but I mean that spirit out of which punctuality grows, that love of accuracy, precision, and vigour which makes the efficient man; the determination that what you have to do, *shall be done*, in spite of all petty obstacles, and finished off, at once, and finally. I believe I have told you the story of Nelson and his coachmaker, but you must hear it once more. When he was on the eve of departure for one of his great expeditions, the coachmaker said to him, 'The carriage shall be at the door punctually at six o'clock.' 'A quarter before,' said Nelson,—' I have always been a quarter of an hour before my time, and it has made a man of me.'

"How often have I seen persons who would have done well, if they would but have acted up to their own sense of duty! Thankful I am to believe that conscience is the established rule over your actions; but I want to enlarge its province, and to make it condescend to these, which may appear to you minor matters. Have *a conscience* to be fitting yourself for life, in whatever you do, and in the management of your mind and powers. In Scripture phrase, 'Gird up the loins of your mind.' Sheridan was an example of the want of this quality. In early life he got into a grand quarrel and duel, the circumstances of which were to his credit (always excepting fighting the duel), but they were misrepresented: he came to town, resolved to set the British public right, and as Perry, the editor of the *Morning Chronicle*, was his friend, he resolved to do so through the channel of that paper. It was agreed between them that Sheridan, under a fictitious name, should write a history of the affair, as it had been misrepresented, and that he should subsequently reply to it in his own name, giving the facts of the case. The first part he accomplished, and there appeared in the *Chronicle* a bitter article against him, written, in fact, by himself; but he could never find time to write the answer, and it never was written: 'The slothful man roasteth not that which he took in hunting.'

"All the men who have done things well in life have been remarkable for decision of character. Tacitus describes Julius Cæsar as 'monstrum incredibilis celeritatis atque audaciæ'; and Bonaparte, having published to all the world the day on which he should leave Paris to meet Wellington at Waterloo, did actually start on that day; but he had so arranged matters, and travelled with such expedition, that he took the British army by surprise.

"The punctuality which I desire for you involves and comprehends the exact arrangement of your time. It is a matter on which much depends; fix how much time you will spend upon each object, and adhere, all but obstinately, to your plan. 'Method,' says Cecil, 'is like packing things in a box; a good packer will get in half as much again as a bad one.' . . . Ponder well what I have said, and call on God to help you in arraying yourself in the qualities which I desire. If you mean to be the effective man, you must set about it earnestly and at once. No man ever yet 'yawned it into being with a wish;' you must make arrangements for it; you must watch it; you must notice where you fail, and you must keep some kind of journal of your failures.

"But, whatever negligence may creep into your studies, or into your pursuits of pleasure or of business, let there be one point, at least, on which you are always watchful, always alive: I mean in the performance of your religious duties. Let nothing induce you, even for a day, to neglect the perusal of Scripture. You know the value of prayer; it is precious beyond all price. Never, never neglect it."

The well-known lines of Sir William Jones touching the distribution of one's time, Mr. Buxton adapted to himself as follows:—

> "Secure six hours for thought, and one for prayer,
> Four in the fields for exercise and air,
> The rest let converse, sleep, and business share."

Such a division, of course, was impossible in London, and during the parliamentary season; but he seems to have kept to it with some closeness in his rural retirement at Northrepps. He spent his mornings in his study or with his gun; his afternoons in meditation or correspondence; and after dinner, when no guests were present, he would lie upon the sofa while someone read aloud to him from the passing literature of the day. He had a strong liking for biography, perhaps even stronger for works of humour; but especially an insatiable thirst for military adventure. His love of poetry was keen, and he endeavoured to cultivate a similar taste in his family. Every Sunday evening his children were expected to repeat a passage of poetry, and he always insisted on the utmost fluency and accuracy in the repetition. When tea was finished, he usually withdrew to his study; returning after a time with any letters or papers connected with his work which he might have received or written in the course of the day, and the reading of these, with the discussions upon them, which he encouraged, usually occupied the remainder of the evening.

In 1840, Buxton, in acknowledgment of his philanthropic labours, was created a baronet.

A man of almost gigantic stature, with a powerful frame, he was nevertheless not endowed with robust health; and the severity of his labours broke him down before his time. He had scarcely passed his fiftieth year when he began to suffer frequently from serious attacks of illness, inducing a strange and excessive prostration. The decline was gradual; but, towards the close of 1843, when he was still but fifty-seven years of age, his condition became such as to excite the alarm and anxiety of his friends. His bodily weakness was pitiful to see; oppression on the brain existed; and he suffered from a partial loss of memory. Early in the following year he was blessed with a temporary recovery, which lasted for a few happy months, and gave great hopes to his friends. Then, in the sunny summer mornings, he would often rise at four or five o'clock and go into his dressing-room, where his voice could be heard for an hour or two in earnest devotion. When he was warned of the risk to his health, he would reply: "I have not time enough for prayer; I must have longer time for prayer." One night, his voice being audible after he was in bed, he was asked what he was saying. "Praying hard," was his reply; and he added,—"I have been praying *vehemently* for myself, that I may receive faith, that I may receive the grace of God in my heart; that I may have a clear vision of Christ, that I may perfectly obey Him, that I may have the supporting arm of the Lord in every trial, and be admitted finally into His glorious kingdom."

After a long illness, endured with Christian patience, Sir Thomas Fowell Buxton expired on February 19th, 1845, aged fifty-eight. His remains were interred in the ruined chancel of the little church at Overstrand. The old ivy-mantled walls, the antique fane itself, with its near view of the sea, and the aspect of the surrounding scenery, form an impressive picture.

One of Buxton's friends has said of him:—"I have seldom known a mind of such determined industry, patience, and undaunted resolution in the pursuit of any object which it might present to itself." In his vocabulary, as in Napoleon's, there existed no such word as "impossible." What had to be done, could and must be done; obstacles vanished before his determined will. "The race is not always to the swift," he would say, "nor the battle to the strong, and there are some *very few* occasions in which labour fails; but labour unactuated by selfish considerations, and solely fixing its eye on the goal of duty, and steadfastly determined to reach it, is, I believe, *never* defeated.

> 'His way once clear, he forward shot outright,
> Not turned aside by danger or delight.'"

It would be folly to speak of Buxton as a man of genius. He was an admirable specimen of the English gentleman; a man of cultivated mind and refined taste, with a good deal of that mild wisdom which comes of patient observation and reflection. The thing that gave dignity and interest to his life was the perseverance with which he maintained a great and sacred cause. The cause raised the man; it elevated his thoughts,—it broadened the horizon of his vision,—it lifted him **out of the** atmosphere of commonplace.

It must be owned that his judgment was sound and clear, and that he knew how to express himself in terse and vigorous language. There is much excellent sense, pithily conveyed, in the following "Hints for Maxims for the Young":—

"Mankind in general mistake difficulties for impossibilities. That is the difference between those who effect, and those who do not.

"People of weak judgment are the **most timid, as horses** half-blind are **most apt to start.**

"Burke **in a letter to Miss Shacklteon** says:—'Thus much in favour of activity and occupation, **that** the more one has to do, the more one is capable of doing, even beyond our direct task.'

"Plato, 'better to err in acts than principles.'

"Idleness the greatest prodigality.

"Two kinds of idleness,—a listless, **and an** active.

"If industrious, we should direct our efforts to right ends.

"Possibly it may require as much (industry) to be best billiard player as to be senior wrangler.

"The endowments of **nature we cannot command, but we can** cultivate those given.

"My experience, that **men of great talents are** apt to do nothing for want of **vigour.**

"Vigour,—energy,—resolution,—firmness **of** purpose,—these carry the day.

"Is there **one** whom difficulties dishearten,—who bends to the storm?—He **will do** little. Is there one who *will* conquer?—That **kind of man never** fails.

"Let it be your first study to teach the world that you **are not** wood and straw—*some iron in you.*

"Let men know that what you say you will do; that your decision made is final,—no wavering; that, **once resolved, you are** not to be allured **or** intimidated.

"Acquire and maintain that character."

     *   *   *   *   *   *   *

"*Eloquence*—the most useful talent; one to be acquired, or improved; all the great speakers bad at first.—How to be acquired.

"Write your speeches,—no inspiration.

"Labour to put your thoughts in the clearest view.

"A bold, decided outline.

"Read 'multum, non multa,—homo unius libri.'

"Learn by heart everything which strikes you.

"Thus ends my lecture; nineteen out of twenty become good or bad as they choose to make themselves.

"The most important part of your education is that which you **now** give yourselves."

BOOK III.

WORK AND WORKERS IN THE MISSION-FIELD.

JOHN ELIOT: A MISSIONARY AND A LEADER **OF MEN**.
DAVID BRAINERD.
HENRY MARTYN: TYPE OF THE MODERN MISSIONARY.
JOHN WILLIAMS, THE "MARTYR OF ERROMANGA."

WORK AND WORKERS IN THE MISSION-FIELD.

JOHN ELIOT was born at Nasing, in Essex, in 1604. He came of a good stock, and being bred up by pious parents, who sympathized with the phase of Christian life and practice already known as Puritanism, he was educated so that he might do no dishonour to his ancestry. At Cambridge he won distinction by his earnest application to his studies, and showed much linguistic ability. He gave an eager attention to the languages in which the Scriptures were written, and became a fair scholar in Greek and Hebrew. While still a young man, he obtained employment as an assistant to Mr. John Hooker, master of the Grammar School at Little Baddow, and under this godly man the religious impressions he had derived from his parents were deepened and confirmed. His zeal in the cause of Christ was so ardent that he would fain have devoted himself to the ministry; but the laws then prohibited an unordained person from praying or preaching in public, and conscientious scruples prevented him from accepting orders in the Church of England. Except with a licence from the Bishop of the diocese, even the instruction of youth was declared illegal, and as Hooker, a Puritan of the strictest type, would not obey the prescribed conditions, his school was suppressed, and he himself, as his personal liberty was endangered, compelled to take refuge in Holland.

Perceiving that freedom of thought was no longer possible in England, John Eliot, in 1631, determined on following in the path of the Pilgrim Fathers, and seeking a home in that New England across the seas where no royal or episcopal tyranny interfered with a man's liberty of conscience. He embarked on the 3rd of November, in the ship *Lyon*, with some sixty others, driven from their native land by the same hateful cause, and before the close of the year landed at the newly-planted but already prosperous city of Boston. The congregation of "the faithful" which assembled there immediately sought his services, as their pastor had been temporarily summoned to England to arrange his affairs; and he laboured among them with so much earnestness and so much acceptance that, on their pastor's return, they were anxious to retain him as assistant-minister. He declined the engagement, however, as he knew that many friends in England were preparing to form a new settlement; and in the course of the following year, a goodly company of East Anglians arrived, and in the fresh forest-land near Boston founded the town of Roxbury. They brought with them a young Puritan maiden, named Anne, to whom Eliot was betrothed. Thereupon Eliot was married, elected pastor of the new congregation, and ordained by the laying-on of the hands of his brother-presbyters.

Eliot's great capacities as a leader of men were soon developed. He became the priest, patriarch, ruler, and teacher of the little community at Roxbury. In preaching and catechizing he was assiduous, but he taught, perhaps, scarcely less effectually by his example, his life being so ordered as to convey to all men a lesson, and set before them an ideal. He walked in constant and intimate communion with God, an atmosphere of devout calm seemed to surround him always. He prayed often and fasted often, keeping the body in subjection as well as the desires and passions. Not that he found it an easy task; he was far removed from the Pharisaism felt and proclaimed by many of "the elect." Life was to him a field of constant effort; the human soul was for ever waging war against foes within and without. One day, as he toiled up the hill on the summit of which stood his church, he remarked that this was very like the way to heaven. "'Tis up hill!" he said. "The Lord in His grace fetch us up. And surely there are thorns and briars in the way also." He was a great enemy to all contention, and would ring a loud "Curfew Bell" whenever he saw the fires of animosity. When pastors complained in his hearing of troubles among their flocks, he would say, "Brother, compress them;" and, "Brother, learn the meaning of those three little words, bear, forbear, forgive!" At an assembly of ministers, a bundle papers relating to a dispute between two of them was laid on the table; Eliot suddenly rose and committed them to the flames. "Brethren," he said, "wonder not at that which I have done; I did it on my knees this morning before I came among you." His Samaritanism was a very real and practical virtue. His wife, who was an adept in medicine and in healing wounds, bestowed her advice freely upon all who solicited it. It chanced that a man who had taken offence at one of Eliot's sermons, and had reviled him publicly, wounded himself severely. Eliot immediately sent his wife to attend to him. On his recovery, the man had the grace to offer his thanks and a gift; Eliot would take nothing, but detained him to a friendly meal, and by this gentle dealing "mollified and conquered the stomach of his reviler."

At this time the English and others were scattered along the coast, and had made scarcely any attempt to occupy the great plains inland. The country was inhabited by a branch of the Iroquois nation, the Pequots, an athletic and active tribe, whose men occupied themselves in hunting when they were not at war, and imposed on their squaws, not only the duties of the household, but the labour of the fields. There was a touch of nobleness in this manly people, however, and as yet they had not been contaminated by the vices of civilization, except in a few individual cases. For some years a good feeling had existed between the natives and the colonists, but as the latter began to encroach on the wilderness, trust gave way to suspicion, and an angry temper was awakened on both sides. In 1634, two English settlers, with their boat's crew, were killed on Connecticut River, and the feud was on the point of blazing out into open hostilities, when the Pequots, who were at war with the Dutch, and the Narragansetts, or River Indians, despatched a deputation to conclude, if possible, an alliance, offensive and defensive, with the English. After due deliberation, a treaty was signed, on condition that the murderers of the Englishmen were delivered up, and a fine paid down of forty beaver and thirty otter skins, besides 400 fathoms of wampum, that is, strings of the small whelks and Venus-shells which passed as current coin, a fathom being worth about five shillings.

The treaty, however, was not long observed by the Pequots,

and at length their acts of aggression broke down the forbearance of the colonists. Allying themselves with some friendly tribes, and with the Mohicans and River Indians, a force of seventy-five Englishmen invaded the country of the Pequots and drove them from it. In 1637 a battle known as "the Great Swamp Fight" was fought between the English, Dutch, and their Indian auxiliaries, on the one hand, and the Pequots on the other, in which the latter lost thirteen chiefs and seven hundred men. A great number were taken prisoners and sent to the West India islands as slaves; while the survivors were hunted down by the Mohicans and Narragansetts, until the once-powerful tribe was reduced to 200 "braves," who, suing for peace on any terms, were deprived of their territories, and distributed among the Mohicans and Narragansetts.

It was about this time, apparently, that Eliot resolved upon undertaking the conversion of the Red Men, incited thereto by the noble example of the Romish missionaries, who were labouring with much success among the Indians of Louisiana. He began by collecting the necessary funds among the colonists, and by mastering the Indian language, of which he afterwards published a grammar. Cotton Mather, the biographer of Eliot, refers with much contempt to the length of many of the Indian words. "I am sure," he says, "the words it contains are long enough to tire the patience of any scholar in the world; they are *sesquipedalia verba*, of which their lingua is composed. For instance, if I were to translate our 'loves' it must be nothing shorter than *Noowomuntamoonkammonush*. Or, to give my reader a longer word, *Krunmogokodonattootummootiteaonganunnonash* is, in English, our "question."

In 1646, being then in his forty-second year, John Eliot entered on his campaign of evangelization. On the 28th of October, an assembly of Indians took place in the forest, under the presidency of their chief, Waban, or the Wind, who was a friend of the English, and had a son at the English school. Eliot attended, with three companions—

> "Came the Black-robe chief, the Prophet,
> He the Priest of Prayer, the Pale Face ..
> And he ..
> Stammered in his speech a little,

> Speaking words yet unfamiliar...
> Then the generous Hiawatha,
> Led the stranger to his wigwam...
> All the old men of the village,
> All the warriors of the nation,
> All the Jossakeeds, the prophets,
> The magicians, the Wabonos,
> And the medicine-men, the Medas,
> Came to bid the strangers welcome:
> 'It is well,' they said, 'O brothers,
> That you come so far to see us!'
> In a circle round the doorway,
> With their pipes they sat in silence.

Mr. Eliot offered up a prayer in English, and then preached in the Indian tongue, taking as his text the ninth and tenth verses of the thirty-seventh chapter of Ezekiel, in which the prophet is ordered to call the breath of God from the four winds of heaven to give life to the dry bones around. The Indian word for "breath" or "wind" was Waban, and this coincidence much impressed the hearers, and was afterwards regarded as an omen.

> "Then the Black-robe chief, the Prophet,
> Told his message to the people,
> Told the purport of his mission,
> Told them of the Virgin Mary,
> And her blessed Son, the Saviour,
> How in distant lands and ages
> He had lived on earth as we do;
> How He fasted, prayed, and laboured;
> How the Jews, the tribe accursèd,
> Mocked Him, scourged Him, crucified Him;
> How He rose from where they laid Him,
> Walked again with His disciples,
> And ascended into heaven."
>   And the chiefs made answer, saying:
> 'We have listened to your message,
> We have heard your words of wisdom,
> We will think on what you tell us:
> It is well for us, O brother,
> That you come so far to see us!'"

About once a fortnight Eliot repeated his visits, and had the satisfaction of seeing that many were much interested in his teaching. There was not wanting opposition on the part of the

Powaws, or priests; but Eliot had a potent ally in Waban, who went from one to the other, repeating the instruction he had received, and teaching them how to pray; for at first it had been the belief of many that to the English God prayers must be addressed in English. When it seemed to Eliot that the Indians were ready for a settled life, he obtained for his congregation, the "praying Indians," as they were called, a grant of the site of his first instructions. He named it "Rejoicing"—a word which the Indians soon corrupted into Nonantum,—and set his people to work to plant it, and cultivate it, and enclose it in various allotments. Wigwams of an altogether better kind were built. The women learned to spin. A manufacture of eel pots, baskets, and brushes was vigorously carried on: these were sold to the English settlers, together with fruit, vegetables, venison, fish, and turkeys.

Before many months had passed by, a second settlement of praying Indians was established at Neponset, the head of which was a chief named Cutshamakin, in rank and influence superior to Waban. He, too, was well disposed towards the English, and had undertaken to observe the ten commandments. Unfortunately he had learned to love the "fire-water," that most fatal gift of civilization, which has desolated the savage world. While Mr. Eliot was teaching the rudiments of Christianity to his family, one of his sons, a boy of fifteen, on coming to the fifth commandment, refused to say more than "honour thy mother," alleging that his father had given him fire-water and made him ill, and moreover had treated him harshly. The boy had always been rude and disobedient; and Mr. Eliot, in speaking of his faults to the Sachem, pointed out that the best way to induce him to reform would be for himself to acknowledge his sins, and amend his ways. The chief felt the force of Eliot's remarks; stood up, and made open confession of his trespasses; whereat the boy was so moved that he in turn repented openly, and entreated his father's forgiveness. All shed tears. For the time Cutshamakin was wounded to the quick, but he knew well the weakness of his character, and mistrusted the reality of his penitence. "My heart," he said, "is but very little better than it was, and I am afraid it will be as bad again as it was before. I sometimes wish I might die before I be so bad again!"

The teaching of the Puritans was, in some respects, not well adapted to the Indian character. It laid too much stress upon trifles; took too close an account of anise and cummin, of the letter rather than the spirit. The Indian preacher Mabaulia once reproved Cutshamakin's squaw in public because she fetched water on a Sunday. She replied, very pertinently, that he had done more harm by exciting an angry debate than she by fetching the water. The Scotch Presbyterians were never more rigid in their views of Sabbath observance than the New England Puritans. At Nonantum a man who, when his fire was nearly out, had split a piece of dry wood with his axe, was publicly lectured; and a reprimand was addressed to Waban, because he killed a capon to entertain two unexpected guests.

But it is only fair to admit that with weightier offences against the law, the Christian missionaries contended in a spirit of equal severity. They waged unceasing war against drunkenness, and against the old Indian habit of ill-treating women, and the superstitious belief in the power of the priests and sorcerers. Here is a story told by Cotton Mather :—

"While Mr. Eliot was preaching of Christ unto the other Indians, a demon appeared unto a Prince of the Eastern Indians in a shape that had some resemblance of Mr. Eliot, or of an English minister, pretending to be the Englishman's God. The spectre commanded him 'to forbear the drinking of rum, and to observe the Sabbath-day, and to deal justly with his neighbours;' all which things had been inculcated in Mr. Eliot's ministry, promising therewithal unto him that, if he did so, at his death his soul should ascend into a happy place, otherwise descend unto miseries; but the apparition all the while never said one word about Christ, which was the main subject of Mr. Eliot's ministry. The Sachem received such an impression from the apparition that he dealt justly with all men except in the bloody tragedies and cruelties he afterwards committed on the English in our wars. He kept the Sabbath-day like a fast, frequently attending in our congregations; he would not meddle with any rum, though usually his countrymen had rather die than undergo such a piece of self-denial. That liquor has merely enchanted them. At last, and not long since, this demon appeared again unto this pagan, requiring him to kill himself, and assuring him that he should revive in a day or two, never to die any more. He thereupon divers times attempted it, but his friends very carefully prevented it; however, at length he found a *fair* opportunity for this *foul* business, and hanged himself,—you may be sure without his expected resurrection."

Eliot's great object was to realize the ideal he had formed of an Indian city, which should be governed wholly on Scriptural principles; which should possess all the advantages of civilization without its drawbacks; which should be wholly independent of English rule, and secured from the contagion of English vices; a city, in fact, after the pattern so earnestly meditated by the zealous Puritans, the government to be in the hands of devout men, and based upon a rigid interpretation of the Mosaic Law. He was prevented, however, from carrying out his scheme by want of funds; and the same cause prevented him from printing and publishing his translation of the Bible into the Indian language. It is surprising how much, in spite of his poverty, he *did* succeed in accomplishing: but his heart was in his work, and under his zealous auspices, Christian order and industry began to prevail in the wilderness. Acres of forest land were cleared, and converted into smiling corn-fields; happy villages sprang up in quiet nooks and corners; schools were established for the instruction of the Indian children; and the Word of God was preached with faithfulness and power, if in a somewhat austere and narrow spirit.

In 1649 the cost of printing Eliot's Indian Bible was undertaken by the Society for the Propagation of the Gospel in New England, which had just been founded, with the direct sanction of Parliament; and this society also supplied him with the necessary funds for engaging and paying teachers, and furnishing the converts with the tools and implements necessary for their industrial enterprises. Eliot's work thenceforward progressed more rapidly; but every reformer raises up opposition as the primary condition of reform, and Eliot found himself impeded by the contempt with which the English settlers regarded the red men,—by the hostility of the Powaws or "medicine-men," who strained every nerve to retain or recover their influence over their dupes,—and even by the jealousy of the Sachems, who discovered that the spirit of Christianity was inimical to every from of tyranny, and that men in becoming Christians ceased to be slaves. The calm courageous soul of the great missionary was wholly unmoved by these demonstrations; he felt that God had laid a mission upon him from which he durst not allow the hostility of man to turn him aside. He had in him much of the temper of Luther, who, when his friends would have dissuaded him from going to Worms lest he should lose his life, answered, that "he would repair thither, though he should find there thrice as many devils as there are tiles upon the housetops!"

Even Cutshamakin turned round upon his benefactor. The scheme for the erection of an independent Indian city so enraged him that he broke out into furious howls, like those of a wild beast; but Eliot, subduing him with his calm grave eye, told him that the work was of God, and no fear of him would frustrate it. Afterwards the Sachem professed that his only objection to Eliot's labours was that the praying Indians did not pay him his proper dues. To render under Cæsar the things that are Cæsar's was a Scriptural principle fully recognized by the missionary, and he preached a sermon strongly enforcing it upon the members of his congregation. To his great surprise they came to him after his discourse, and expressing their mortification at the charge brought against them, showed that they had fully discharged their obligations both by way of gifts and service; each having paid the Sachem twenty bushels of corn, six bushels of rye, fifteen deer, and a certain number of days spent in hunting, in reclaiming land, and in building a wigwam. Eliot, justly indignant at Cutshamakin's conduct, preached, on the following lecture-day, on the Saviour's rejection of the kingdoms of the world, and applied the text to the avaricious chief, whom he reproached with his greed and lust of power, and warned against the consequences of backsliding. Cutshamakin was moved to repentance, and his loud professions of sorrow obtained for him Eliot's forgiveness; but to the last he remained a man who could not be trusted.

In 1651 the missionary's plans came into actual fulfilment. The Council of Government granted him a site for his Indian town on the banks of Charles River, about eighteen miles southwest of Boston. They called it "Natich," or the place among the hills, and Eliot believed it had been specially pointed out in answer to prayer. Thither he removed his people from Nonantum, and the work of construction began. A bridge was thrown across the river, 80 feet long and 9 feet wide: three broad straight streets were laid out, two on one side of the river, and one on the other; to each Indian family a suitable allotment was made; houses were built, gardens planted, cornfields sown. A few of the houses were built in the English fashion; but most of them were bark wigwams on an improved pattern. In the centre of the town stood a circular fort, palisaded with trees; and adjoining it a large house of two storeys: the upper of which was used as a wardrobe and storehouse, with a room for Mr. Eliot known as "the prophet's chamber," while the lower served as a schoolroom on week-days and a place of worship on Sundays.

Eliot next proceeded to institute a form of government, of which the Bible was to furnish the model and act as the foundation. Taking up Jethro's advice to Moses, he divided his Indians into hundreds and tens, with a ruler for each division, each tithing man being responsible for the ten under him, and each chief of a hundred for the ten tithings. "This was done on the 6th of August, 1651; and Eliot declared that it seemed to him as if he beheld the scattered bones he had spoken of in his first sermon to the Indians come bone to bone, and a civil political life begin. His hundreds and tithings were as much suggested by the traditional arrangements of King Alfred as by those of Moses in the wilderness; and his next step was, in like manner, partly founded on Scripture, partly on English history,—namely, the binding his Indians by a solemn covenant to serve the Lord, and ratifying it on a fast day. His converts had often asked him why he held none of the great fast days with them that they saw the English held, and he had always replied that there was not a sufficient occasion, but he regarded this as truly important enough. Moreover a ship containing some supplies, sent by the Society, in England, had been wrecked, and the goods, though saved, were damaged. This he regarded as a frown of Providence and a fruit of sin. Poor Cutshamakin also was in trouble again, having been drawn into a great revel, where much spirits had been drunk, and his warm though unstable temper always made him ready to serve as a public example of confession and humiliation. So when, on the 24th of September, 1651, Mr. Eliot had conducted the fast day service, it began with Cutshamakin's confession; then three

Indians preached and prayed in turn, and Mr. Eliot finally preached on Ezra's great fast. There was a pause for rest; then the assembly came together again, and before them Mr. Eliot solemnly recited the terms of the Covenant, by which all were to bind themselves to the service of the Lord, and which included all their principal laws. He asked them whether they stood to the Covenant. All the chiefs first bound themselves, then the remainder of the people; a collection was made for the poor; and so ended that 'blessed day,' as the happy apostle of the Indians called it."

The prudent watchfulness with which Eliot carried out his work of organisation is shown by the fact that he did not receive a single Indian to baptism until 1660, or nine years after he had first begun to preach,—a striking contrast to the impetuosity of some present-day evangelists, who admit their converts without even an hour's probation, requiring from them only some semi-hysterical declarations of repentance and faith. From the first, it was his design to train up for the ministry some of his more promising native scholars, rightly believing that native pastors would be more successful in their labours than men alien to their flocks in race and language, and unable to make a direct appeal to their sympathies. One of the earliest of these red-skinned messengers was a John Hiacoomes, who transfigured, as it were, the natural bravery of the Indian people into a high force of moral courage. On one occasion, while praying, he was rudely assaulted by a Sachem, and but for the interposition of some English who were present, would certainly have been killed. Yet his only answer was, "I have two hands, one for injuries, and the other for God. While I received wrong with the one, with the other I laid hold more earnestly upon God." Two other converts, Joel and Caleb, were sent to Harvard College, Cambridge, where they earned distinction by their abilities and perseverance.

It is considered that Eliot's greatest success as an apostle was during the years 1660 to 1675, and towards the close of that period the Christian Indian community numbered about eleven hundred, with six regularly constituted "Churches," and fourteen towns, of which seven were called old, and seven new. They were exposed to frequent attacks from the hostile Redskins, and in 1676 they undertook a regular campaign against their enemies, in which they proved victorious, but after such severe suffering and heavy loss of life, that Eliot's mission received a fatal blow. The aged Apostle, however, did not desist from his labours, and preached and prayed with unabated fervour, while exercising all his influence to put down the cruel custom of selling captive Indians into slavery. The burden of years did not depress his mental or physical energies. The immediate results of his Christian toil were not wholly encouraging; but he knew that the spark he had kindled would one day expand into a glowing fire of Gospel love, that the seed he had sown would one day ripen into a glorious and an abundant harvest.

Eliot survived four of his children, and his loving and noble wife, who died, full of years, in 1684. By this time his strength had largely failed him, and when any questions were put to him respecting his condition, he would humbly reply, "Alas! I have lost everything: my understanding leaves me, my memory fails me, my utterance fails me, but, I thank God, my charity holds out still; I find that rather grows than decreases." Daily approaching nearer to the boundless ocean of God's love, its music and its light more and more penetrated into his soul. To the last he retained a profound interest in the great work of his life, the evangelization of the Indians; to the last he continued his brave opposition to the cruel traffic in negro slaves; to the last, this Good Samaritan was engaged in binding up the wounds of the distressed wayfarer, and directing his feet to the throne of the Eternal Father.

Of old age, rather than of any definite disease, the great Apostle of the Red Indians died in 1690. He was then in the eighty-seventh year of his age. To few men has been granted so long a life of such noble Christian work. His good deeds lived after him; and to this day their memory is green.*

David Brainerd was born on the 20th of April, 1718, at Haddam, in the county of Hartford, in Connecticut. His father, a

---

* Jabez Sparks, "Life of John Eliot," pub. 1836.

member of the Colonial Council, died when he was only nine years old; his mother, Dorothy, a daughter of the Rev. Samuel Whiting, minister of the Gospel, first at Boston in Lincolnshire, and afterwards at Lynn in Massachusetts, was cut off when he was about fourteen. The death of the parents did not plunge the family into poverty; but it was a heavy loss, for while they were both of them self-denying earnest Christians, of the Calvinistic school, they were gifted with sufficiently healthy and practical minds to have kept under control, during his earlier years, the mental and spiritual precocity of their son David.

David was, by birth, of a delicate temperament, and it was probably a presentiment of premature death, as well as the effect of the influences surrounding him, that led him, at seven or eight years of age, to withdraw from play, and devote himself to prayer and meditation as a preparation for the great change. It must not be thought, however, that we would recommend Brainerd's example as one to be followed entirely by my younger readers. They are to live, indeed, as knowing that life is not everything; but they are to live so as to be fitted for the discharge of life's daily duties. The best work is work lightened and invigorated by intervals of wholesome recreation; and Heaven does not desire of us that we should, except under special circumstances, den ourselves the enjoyment of pleasures which are innocent and rational.

But here is Brainerd's own account of his early years:—

"I was, I think, from my youth," he says, "something sober, and inclined rather to melancholy than the contrary extreme; but do not remember anything of conviction of sin, worthy of remark, till I was, I believe, about seven or eight years of age; when I became something concerned for my soul, and terrified at the thoughts of death, and was driven to the performance of duties: but it appeared a melancholy business, and destroyed my eagerness for play. And, alas! this religious concern was but short-lived. However, I sometimes attended secret prayer; and thus lived at 'ease in Zion, without God in the world,' and without much concern, as I remember, till I was above thirteen years of age. But some time in the winter of 1732, I was something roused out of carnal security by I scarce know what means at first; but was much excited by the prevailing of a mortal sickness in

Haddam. I was frequent, constant, and something fervent in duties, and took great delight in the performance of them; and I sometimes hoped that I was converted; or at least in a good and hopeful way for heaven and happiness, not knowing what conversion was. The Spirit of God at this time proceeded far with me; I was remarkably dead to the world, and my thoughts were almost wholly employed about my soul's concerns; and I may indeed say, 'Almost I was persuaded to be a Christian.' I was also exceedingly distressed and melancholy at the death of my mother, in March 1732. But afterwards my religious concern began to decline, and I by degrees fell back into a considerable degree of security, though I still attended secret prayer frequently."

At nineteen, young Brainerd felt a great desire to become a preacher of the Gospel, and engaged in a laborious course of theological reading; and, in the following year, to carry out his design, he went to reside with a Mr. Fiske, the minister of Haddam (April 1738). In him he found, for the first time, a friend to whom he could reveal the secret depths of his heart, all his humility and self-distrust and anxiety. Fiske advised him to withdraw entirely from "young company," and associate with "grave elderly people." "Whether this were good advice," says Miss Yonge," we do not know; but a period of terrible agony had to be struggled through." For our own part, we have not a shadow of doubt that the advice was foolish and dangerous; that it tended to foster in Brainerd an unhealthy condition of religious feeling, from which he did not escape until he found relief in constant and active work. "It seems plain," remarks Miss Yonge, "from comparison of different lives, that in the forms of religion which make everything depend upon the individual person's own consciousness of the state of his heart and feelings, instead of supporting this by any outward tokens for faith to rest upon, the more humble and scrupulous spirits often undergo fearful misery before they can attain to such security of their own faith as they believe essential. Indeed, this state of wretchedness is almost deemed a necessary stage in the Christian life, like the Slough of Despond in the 'Pilgrim's Progress;' and with such a temperament as David Brainerd's, the horrors of the struggle for hope were dreadful, and lasted for months, before an almost physical perception of light, glory, and grace shone out upon him; although, even to the end of his life, hope and fear, spiritual joy and depression, alternated,—no doubt, greatly in consequence of his constant ill-health."

With some minds such a struggle may be necessary; it is only with the sweat of their brow, as it were, that they can wrestle their way into a state of hope and faith. Like Bunyan, they must pass through the Valley of the Shadow of Death before they can aspire to the tablelands lighted up by the Sun of Righteousness. But happily, most young souls are not called upon to undergo so terrible a probation, which, indeed, they might prove unable to bear.

Brainerd's description of the circumstances under which he was reconciled to God will interest the reader:—

"On the Sabbath evening, July 12, 1739, I was walking again in a solitary place where I was formerly brought to see myself lost and helpless, and here, in a mournful, melancholy state, was attempting to pray; but found no heart to engage in that or any other duty; my former concern and exercise and religious affections were now gone. I thought the Spirit of God had quite left me, but still was not distressed: yet disconsolate, as if there was nothing in heaven or earth could make me happy. And having been thus endeavouring to pray, through being, as I thought, very stupid and senseless, for even half-an-hour, and by this time the sun was about half-an-hour high, as I remember, then, as I was walking in a dark thick grove, *unspeakable glory* seemed to open to the view and apprehension of my soul: I do not mean any external brightness, for I saw no such thing; nor do I intend any imagination of a body of light, somewhere away in the third heavens, or anything of that nature; but it was a new inward apprehension or view that I had of God, such as I never had before, nor anything which had the least resemblance of it. I stood still and wondered and admired! I knew that I never had seen before anything comparable to it for excellency and beauty; it was widely different from all the conceptions that ever I had had of God or things divine. I had no particular apprehension of any one Person in the Trinity, either the Father, the Son, or the Holy Ghost; but it appeared to be *divine glory* that I then beheld; and my soul *rejoiced with joy unspeakable* to see such a God, such a glorious Divine Being; and I was inwardly pleased and satisfied that He should be *God over all*, for ever and ever. My soul was so captivated and delighted with the excellency, loveliness, greatness, and other perfections of God, that I was even swallowed up in Him; at least to that degree, that I had no thought, as I remember, at first, about my own salvation, and scarce reflected there was such a creature as myself."

In 1742, at the age of twenty-five, David Brainerd was examined by a council or committee of ministers of Danbury, and licensed to preach the Gospel. His zeal and self-devotion soon attracted the notice of a Scottish Society for the Propagation of Christian Knowledge; and its delegates invited him to undertake a mission to the Indians then settled at Kanaumeek, between Albany and Stockbridge. The work was laborious and difficult: it would have been a burthen for a man of strong constitution and vigorous health: for Brainerd's weakly frame and nervous temperament it would have proved intolerable, had he not been supported by his devout enthusiasm, his zeal for the saving of souls, and his trust in God. Devoting the whole of his little patrimony to the maintenance of a scholar at the University, he took up his Master's cross and went forth into the wilderness.

With a young Indian to act as interpreter, for as yet he knew nothing of the language of the people to whom he was appointed to preach, he arrived at Kanaumeek. The first night he slept on a heap of straw. Kanaumeek was a lonely, melancholy spot where the Indians were herded together, jealously watched by adventurers, who were always seeking to gain possession of their lands, and sadly degenerated from the grave, free, and high-minded race to whom Eliot, the great "Apostle of the Indians," had so successfully ministered. He lodged at first in the log-house of a poor Scotchman, who lived among the Indians; a single room, without so much as a floor, where he shared the hard fare of his host. The family spoke Gaelic, only the master of the house knowing any English; and *his* English being more imperfect than even that of the Indian interpreter. Brainerd's lines had certainly not fallen upon pleasant places.

In his diary, on the 18th of May, he writes with simple pathos: "My circumstances are such that I have no comfort of any kind, but what I have in God. I live in the most lonesome wilderness; have but one single person to converse with, that can speak English. Most of the talk I hear is either Highland Scotch or Indian. I have no fellow-Christian to whom I might unbosom myself, and lay open my spiritual sorrows; or with whom I might take sweet counsel in conversation about heavenly things and join in social prayer. I live poorly with regard to the comforts of life: most of my diet consists of boiled corn, hasty pudding, etc. I lodge on a bundle of straw, and my labour is hard and extremely difficult; and I have little appearance of success to comfort me. The Indians' affairs are very difficult; having no land to live on but what the Dutch people lay claim to, and threaten to drive them off from; they have no regard to the souls of the poor Indians; and, by what I can learn, they hate me, because I come to preach to them."

On the 15th of August he writes:—"Spent most of the day in labour, to procure something to keep my house on in the winter. Enjoyed not much sweetness in the morning: was very weak in body through the day, and thought this frail tabernacle would soon drop into the dust; had some realizing apprehensions of a speedy entrance into another world. In this weak state of body I was not a little distressed for want of suitable food. I had no bread, nor could I get any. I am forced to go or send ten or fifteen miles for the bread I eat; and sometimes it is mouldy and sour before I eat it, if I get any considerable quantity. Then, again, I have none for some days together, for want of an opportunity to send for it, and cannot find my horse in the woods to go myself. This was my case now; but through Divine goodness I had some Indian meal, of which I made little cakes, and fried them. Yet I felt contented with my circumstances, and sweetly resigned to God. In prayer I enjoyed great freedom, and blessed God as usual for my present circumstances, as if I had been a king, and thought I found a disposition to be contented in any circumstances. Blessed be the Lord!"

The Indians, after awhile, seem to have been pleased and even affected by his earnest, simple addresses; and much good might have been done but for that serious obstacle which faces the missionary in almost every quarter,—the animal habits and blasphemous language of the whites. How were the Indians to be assured of the merits of a religion which, apparently, produced such disgraceful interpreters? These men called themselves Christians: their pastor also called himself a Christian. The contrast between the two was so great, so surprising, that we can well believe the Indians were unable to comprehend it.

One of his earliest efforts was to establish a school, of which his interpreter was to act as master. To raise the necessary funds, he was compelled to make a journey on horseback to New Jersey. It proved successful, yet it cost him dear; for, as he was riding home, he was seized with acute pain in the face, and violent shiverings in the limbs, which forced him to halt at the first place of refuge he could find. God tempers the wind to the shorn lamb! Brainerd fell in with kind and Christian friends, who nursed him tenderly for a fortnight, until he could resume his journey. He believed that, had his illness attacked him in his log-house at Kanaumeek, he would certainly have died for want of proper care and skilful attendance.

Even for a robust and vigorous man, with nerves like steel and a frame like iron, this life in the wilderness would have been exceptionally severe, but for Brainerd it was a prolonged martyrdom, under which he was sustained only by his deep sense of the worthiness of his work. It was work done in Christ's name, that souls might be brought to Christ; and this knowledge supported his failing limbs, and infused vitality into his enfeebled constitution. When weak and sick for lack of sufficient food, he was compelled with his own hands to gather a winter supply of fodder for his horse. To get bread, he had to ride fourteen or fifteen miles. If he returned with a stock beyond his immediate wants, it turned sour and mouldy before he could eat it. If the quantity proved insufficient, he could go for no more until he had caught his horse, which was turned out to graze in the woods. Thus he frequently found himself without any better food than cakes of Indian meal, roasted in the ashes. But these physical hardships caused him no annoyance, no sinking of the heart, or mental depression: he wrote in his journal: "I have a house, and many of the comforts of life to support me," and he blessed God as if he had been a king.

The war between England and France, which raged in America, necessitated, at last, the removal of Brainerd's small congregation of Indians to the town of Stockbridge (April 1744). There he made up his mind to leave them; and though suffering from bleeding at the lungs, and in a consumptive condition, he resolved to penetrate farther into the wilderness, and visit the less civilized tribes. For this purpose he accepted a mission to the Delaware Indians, and on the 10th of May arrived at a place called Minniosinks, about one hundred and forty miles from Kanaumeek. Here he fell in with a number of Indians, whose "king," or chief, he proceeded to address with his usual directness. "After some discourse, and attempts to contract a friendship with him, I told him," says Brainerd, "I had a desire, for his benefit and happiness, to instruct them in Christianity. He laughed at it, turned his back upon me, and went away. I then addressed another principal man in the same manner, who said he was willing to hear me. After some time I followed the king into his house, and renewed my discourse to him; but he declined talking, and left the affair to another, who appeared to be a rational man. He began and talked very warmly near a quarter of an hour. He inquired why I desired the Indians to become Christians, seeing the Christians were so much worse than the Indians. The Christians, he said, would lie, steal, and drink, worse than the Indians. It was they who first taught the Indians to be drunk; and they stole from one another to that degree that their rulers were obliged to hang them for it; and yet it was not sufficient to deter others from the like practice. But the Indians, he added, were none of them ever hanged for stealing, and yet they did not steal half so much; and he supposed that if the Indians should become Christians, they would then be as bad as these. They would live as their fathers lived, and go where their fathers were when they died. I then freely owned, lamented, and joined with him in condemning the ill conduct of some who are called Christians; told him these were not Christians in heart; that I hated such wicked practices, and did not desire the Indians to become such as these. When he appeared calmer, I asked him if he was willing that I should come and see them again: he replied, he should be willing to see me again as a friend, if I would not desire them to become Christians. I then bid them farewell, and prosecuted my journey towards Delaware. On May 13th I arrived at a place called, by the Indians, Sakhauwotung, within the Forks of Delaware, in Pennsylvania.

"Here, also, when I came to the Indians, I saluted their king and others in a manner I thought most engaging, and soon after informed the king of my desire to instruct them in the Christian religion. After he had consulted a few minutes with two or three old men, he told me he was willing to hear. I then preached to the few that were present: they appeared very attentive, and well disposed. The king in particular seemed both to wonder, and, at the same time, to be well pleased with what I taught them, respecting the Divine Being, etc. Since that time he has ever shown himself friendly, giving me free liberty to preach in his house, whenever I think fit. Here therefore I have spent the greater part of the summer past, preaching usually in the king's house.

"The number of Indians in this place is but small; most of those that formerly dwelt here are dispersed, and removed to places farther back in the country. There are not more than ten houses that continue to be inhabited; and some of them are several miles distant from others, which makes it difficult for the Indians to meet together so frequently as could be wished.

"When I first began to preach here, the number of hearers was very small; often not exceeding twenty or twenty-five; but towards the latter part of the summer their number increased, so that I have frequently had forty persons or more at once. The effects of God's Word upon some of the Indians in this place are somewhat encouraging. Several of them are brought to renounce idolatry, and to decline partaking of those feasts which they used to offer in sacrifice to certain unknown powers. Some few among them have for a considerable time manifested a serious concern about their eternal welfare, and still continue to 'inquire the way to Zion' with such diligence, affection, and becoming solicitude, as gives me reason to hope that 'God who (I trust) has begun this work in them' will carry it on until it shall issue in their conversion to Himself. They not only detest their old idolatrous notions, but strive also to bring their friends off from them; and as they are seeking salvation for their own souls, so they seem desirous that others might be excited to do the same.

"In July last I heard of a number of Indians residing at a place called Kauksesauchung, more than thirty miles westward from the place where I usually preach. I visited them, found about thirty persons, and proposed to preach to them. They readily complied, and I preached to them only twice, they being just then removing from this place, where they only lived for the present, to Susquehannah River, where they belonged.

"While I was preaching they appeared sober and attentive, and were somewhat surprised, having never before heard of those things. Two or three, who suspected that I had some ill design upon them, urged that the white people had abused them, and taken their lands from them, and therefore they had no reason to think that they were now concerned for their happiness; but, on the contrary, that they designed to make them slaves, or get them on board their vessels, and make them fight with the people over the water, as they expressed it, meaning the French and Spaniards. However, most of them appeared very friendly, and told me they were then going directly home to Susquehannah. They desired I would make them a visit there, and manifested a considerable desire of further instruction. This invitation gave me some encouragement in my great work, and made me hope that God designed to open an effectual door for spreading the Gospel among the poor heathen farther westward."

It is a remarkable circumstance that Brainerd never learned the Indian language, and all his earnest appeals, therefore, were filtered through a medium, more or less unsympathetic, before they reached those for whom they were intended. That a man of so much enthusiasm and such vast energy made no attempt to remove this obstacle we cannot but regard as surprising. Perhaps he felt that his days were numbered, and that he had barely time before him in which to accomplish his special work.

This ignorance of the Indian language, moreover, seems to have been less of a difficulty than one might reasonably have expected. We are told of a band of Indians at Crossweeksung, who were so impressed by his teaching that, day after day, they followed him, and from village to village, hardly caring to provide for their physical wants. The description of their conduct reminds one of the narratives of the revivals effected by Wesley among the Cornish miners—"They threw themselves on the ground, wept bitterly, and prayed aloud, with the general enthusiasm of excitement, though he expressly says, without fainting or convulsions; and even the white men around, who came to scoff, were deeply impressed."

After accomplishing much admirable work at Crossweeksung, and gathering together a considerable congregation, Brainerd again resumed the pilgrim's staff and wallet, and departed, in September 1746, on a missionary expedition to the Indians of the Susquehannah. Unfortunately, it was without result, or at least result direct and visible. Brainerd writes in his journal: "September 8th.—Had proposed to tarry a considerable time longer among the Indians upon Susquehannah; but was hindered from pursuing my purpose by the sickness that prevailed there, the weakly circumstances of my own people that were with me, and especially my own extraordinary weakness, having been exercised with great nocturnal sweats, and a coughing up of blood, in almost the whole of the journey. Great part of the time I was so feeble and faint that it seemed as though I never should be able to reach home; and at the same time destitute of the comforts and even necessaries of life; at least, what was necessary for one in so weak a state. In this journey I was sometimes enabled to speak the Word of God with power, and Divine truth made some impression on divers that heard me. Several men and women, both old and young, seemed to 'cleave to us,' and to be well disposed towards Christianity; but others mocked and shouted, which damped some of those who before seemed friendly. Yet God at times was evidently present, assisting me and my interpreter, and other dear friends who were with me. I sometimes had a good degree of freedom in prayer for the ingathering of souls there, and could not but entertain a strong hope that the journey would not be wholly fruitless. Whether it will issue in the setting up Christ's Kingdom *there*, or only the drawing of some few persons down to my congregation in New Jersey, or whether they were now only preparing for some further attempts that might be made among them, I did not determine; but I was persuaded the journey would not be lost. Blessed be God that I had any encouragement and hope!"

A vivid and pathetic picture of his condition he draws in his journal of the 27th:—

"Spent this day, as well as the whole week past, under a great degree of bodily weakness, attended with a violent cough and fever. Had no appetite to any kind of food, and frequently brought up what I ate, as soon as it was down; and oftentimes had little rest in my bed, by reason of pains in my breast and back. I was able, however, to ride over to my people, about two miles, every day, and take some care of those who were then at work upon a small house for me to reside in amongst the Indians. I was sometimes hardly able to walk, and never able to sit up the whole day, through the week. Was calm and composed, and but little exercised with melancholy, as in former seasons of weakness. Whether I should ever recover or no, seemed very doubtful; but this was many times a comfort to me —that *life* and *death* did not depend upon *my* choice. I was pleased to think that He who is infinitely wise had the determination of this matter, and that I had no trouble to consider and weigh things upon all sides, in order to make the choice whether I would live or die. Thus my time was consumed. I had little strength to pray, none to write or read, and scarcely any to meditate; but, through Divine goodness, I could with great composure look *death* in the face, and frequently with sensible joy. Oh how blessed it is to be habitually prepared for death! The Lord grant that I may be actually ready also!"

Brainerd's health was now very seriously affected; he suffered from nocturnal perspirations, bleeding from the lungs, cough, fever, and general pain. Yet, whenever he could mount his horse, he rode fifteen miles to his flock at Cranberry, or preached to them sitting in a chair before his tent, when they assembled round him at Crossweeksung.

In the following year his strength utterly failed him, and he was compelled to seek the civilized districts, where medical aid might be forthcoming. At Northampton he consulted Dr. Mather, who informed him that his lungs were incurably affected. Thence he proceeded to Boston to see his fellow-ministers, and many Christian friends; but a week after his arrival, his illness suddenly came to a crisis, so that he was for some time delirious, and apparently on the point of death. Summer came; its genial airs revived for awhile his declining energies; the flame shot up in the socket, like that of a taper just before expiring, and he resolved to avail himself of this partial restoration to return to Northampton, where he found a home in the family of the celebrated Calvinist divine, Jonathan Edwards, afterwards President of the College of New Jersey.

Edwards bears a high tribute to his many excellences:—" I found him," he says, "remarkably sociable, pleasant, and entertaining in his conversation, yet solid, savoury, spiritual, and very profitable; appearing meek, modest, and humble, far from any stiffness, moroseness, superstitious demureness, or affected singularity in speech or behaviour, and seeming to nauseate all such things. We enjoyed not only the benefit of his conversation, but had the comfort and advantage of hearing him pray in the family from time to time. His manner of praying was very agreeable, most becoming a worm of the dust, and a disciple of Christ; addressing an infinitely great and holy God and the Father of Mercies, not with florid expressions or a studied eloquence, not with any intemperate vehemence or indecent boldness, at the greatest distance from any appearance of ostentation, and from everything that might look as though he meant to recommend himself to those who were about him, or set himself off to their acceptance; free too from vain repetitions, without impertinent excursions, or needless multiplying of words. He expressed himself with the strictest propriety, with weight and pungency, and yet what his lips uttered seemed to flow from the fulness of his heart, as deeply impressed with a great and solemn sense of our necessities, unworthiness, and dependence, and of God's infinite greatness, excellency, and sufficiency, rather than merely from a warm and fruitful brain, pouring out good expressions. And I know not that ever I heard him so much as ask a blessing or return thanks at table but there was something remarkable to be observed both in the matter and manner of the performance. In his prayers he dwelt much on the prosperity of Zion, the advancement of Christ's kingdom in the world, and the propagation of religion among the Indians. He generally made it one condition in his prayer, that 'we might not outlive our usefulness.'"

For some time after his domestication with the family of Jonathan Edwards, he was able to ride out twice or thrice daily, and sat much with his kind and attentive friends, writing or conversing cheerfully when not engaged in prayer. His brother John came from Crossweeksung to visit him, and cheered him with a most hopeful account of his Indian flock. Learning that another school was greatly needed, he wrote to his friends and coadjutors at Boston, and was gratified with an immediate contribution of £200 for the purpose, besides a sum of £75 for the establishment of a mission to the Indian Six Nations. To their kindly communications he replied with his own hand; but he had become so much weaker that he felt it would be his last task. He had been one who, in his short life, had sown in tears to reap in joy.

As the chill winds of autumn began to blow, he sank more rapidly. The 20th of August was the last day on which he was able to ride out. In the same week he was removed to a room on the ground floor, as his increasing debility prevented him from going up and down stairs. The following Wednesday was the day of the public lecture; and he seemed to derive much pleasure from seeing the neighbouring ministers who came to attend it. He expressed a great desire to repair to the house of God on that day, and accordingly attended divine service, for, as it proved, the last time.

At times his sufferings were hard to bear, and he would cry,—"Why is His chariot so long in coming? why tarry the wheels of His chariot?" But, immediately recovering himself, he would ask pardon for his impatient words. Being asked, one morning, how he did, he answered,—"I am almost in eternity: I long to be there. My work is done. I have done with all my friends: all the world is nothing to me. I long to be in heaven, praising and glorifying God with the holy angels: all my desire is to glorify God."

During the last two weeks of his life, he continued in this tranquil state of mind, loose from all the world, as having completed his work on earth; having nothing to do but to die, and resting meanwhile in earnest desire and expectation of the manifestation of the things of God. He had a smile for Jerusha—Mr. Edwards's second daughter, and his devoted attendant—as she came into his room on Sunday morning, October 4th. "Dear Jerusha," he said, "are you willing to part with me? I am quite willing to part with you—I am willing to part with all my friends: I am willing to part with my dear brother John, although I love him the best of any creature living. I have committed him and all my friends to God, and can leave them with Him. Though, if I thought I should not see you, and be happy with you in another world, I could not bear to part with you. But we shall spend a happy eternity together."

In the evening, as she entered the room with a Bible in her hand, he exclaimed : " Oh, that dear Book ! that lovely Book ! I shall soon see it opened : the mysteries that are in it, and the mysteries of God's providence, will be all unfolded."

He lingered in great agony at times, and on the 8th, the body for awhile overcame the mind, and his reason was affected. In the evening, however, he grew more composed, and recovered the use of his faculties. The physical pain continued and increased, and he told Mr. Edwards it was impossible for any one to conceive of the distress he felt in his breast. His anxiety was great lest he should dishonour God by impatience under his extreme sufferings, which were such, he said, that the thought of enduring them one minute longer was almost insupportable. He expressed his belief that he should die that night, but seemed to fear a longer delay. Notwithstanding the pains that racked him, he showed a lively concern for the "interest of Zion," and held a considerable discourse that evening with one of the neighbouring ministers on the great importance of the work of the ministry. Afterwards, as the night advanced, he had much profitable conversation with his brother John concerning his congregation in New Jersey, and the progress of Christ's religion among the Indians. In the latter part of the night his physical distress was severe; and to those about him he remarked that "it was another thing to die than people imagined," explaining himself to mean that they were not aware what "bodily" pain and anguish are undergone before death. Happily, however, this is not always the case. Towards day there came a cessation of pain, and in the interval he passed away,—Friday, October 9, 1747, wanting then six months of his thirtieth birthday.*

" David Brainerd's career," says Miss Yonge, " ended at an age when Eliot's had not begun. It was a very wonderful struggle between the frail suffering body and the devoted, resolute spirit, both weighed down by the natural morbid temper, further depressed by the peculiar tenets of the form of doctrine in which he had been bred. The prudent, well-weighed measures of the ripe

---

* The foregoing sketch is taken from the " Life of the Rev. David Brainerd," by Jonathan Edwards (edit. 1824).

scholar, studious theologian, and conscientious politician, formed by forty-two years' experience of an old and a new country, could not be looked for in the sickly, self-educated, enthusiastic youth who had been debarred from the due amount of study, and started with little system but that of 'proclaiming the gospel,' even though ignorant of the language of those to whom he preached. And yet that heart-whole piety and patience was blessed with a full measure of present success; and David Brainerd's story, though that of a short life, overclouded by mental distress, hardship, and sickness, fills us with the joyful sense that there is One that giveth the victory."

It teaches us something more,—the sacred power and potency of enthusiasm; what may be accomplished by an enthusiast, in a holy cause, though without genius, health, or fortune. It may be said that Brainerd did not accomplish *much;* and this would be true if we judged his work only by its *visible* results. But who can estimate the good effected by his example? How many a young heart, touched by the simple pathetic narrative of his unselfish perseverance, has endeavoured to do likewise; not, perhaps, as a missionary among the heathen, but as a missionary in his own home, his own household, his family circle, or his neighbourhood! Seldom has the title of a "Good Samaritan" been better deserved than by David Brainerd. He did not pass by "on the other side," but went down among the heathen, and gave them of the manna of God's Word, and the balm of Christ's benediction, at the cost of his own life.

I have always felt that for young readers, or, indeed, for old readers on whom the canker of worldliness has taken hold, the study of the records of missionary effort may strongly be commended, as specially adapted to feed in them that holy fire of enthusiasm which will warm and brighten and make glorious their lives. Each of us, it is well to remember, can and should work as a missionary in his own circle; not as a preacher or priest, but as a living example of the truths which it is the office of the priest or preacher to proclaim. Yes, each of us can be a missionary in his own circle; living purely, devoutly, charitably; honourable and just in all his dealings; generous, where generosity is possible and likely to be fruitful; tender towards the errors and weaknesses of his fellows, but severe upon his own; not sparing, on proper occasion, the word of counsel, reproof, or encouragement, but teaching rather by his actions, and the daily pattern of his character, than by verbal profession and formal exposition. What a Brainerd and a Martyn, a Heber and a Williams, have done, at the cost of their very lives, in far-off lands and islands, and among the savage races, we may do in our little households, our immediate neighbourhoods, at no sacrifice whatever except that of selfishness, pride, idleness, and indifference.

But is not the life of such a man as Henry Martyn worth *living?* It had its flaws, but as a whole how pure, how bright it was! How intense in its devotion! How sublime in its enthusiasm! How eager in its endeavour to do something in Christ's name for the good of human souls! He was no cold apathetic philosopher, no languid man of the world, no busy seeker after wealth, passing by "on the other side": he saw when humanity lay bleeding and ailing in the darkness, and he went down to it like the Good Samaritan, and bound up its wounds and bid it live!

Martyn's father was a miner and a self-educated man, who lived as if he feared God; lived, like one who apprehends that he may at any time entertain angels unawares, and, therefore, keeps his soul pure and bright that he may be fit for such companionship. By integrity, patient self-culture, and holy living, the common miner raised himself to the position of head clerk in a merchant's office; and he held that post when his son Henry was born to him, on the 15th of February, 1781. A Wesleyan, he kept his house in order, desiring that all about him should enjoy the happiness which springs from a Christian life. The domestic influences, therefore, that surrounded Henry Martyn's childhood were of the very highest and purest. And he seems to have needed such a training; for a delicate frame, a susceptible temperament, and a precocious brain, rendered him liable to sudden accesses of violent irritability, though at most times he displayed a tenderness of feeling and a softness of manner exceptional in one of such early years. He received the rudiments of education at the Truro Grammar School, where his great talents recommended him to his masters, while his almost girlish gentleness made him the butt of most of his rough companions. Happily, he found, after awhile, a protector in one of the older lads, who was of firm, manly, and honourable character. And it is pleasant to record that their school intimacy duly ripened into a lifelong friendship.

In 1795, when only fourteen, Martyn had made such progress in "the humanities" that he was sent up to compete for a scholarship at Corpus Christi College, Oxford. It is true he did not gain the election, but he passed a surprisingly excellent examination. He returned to school for another two years' work, and in 1797 was entered a member of St. John's College, Cambridge; a college illustrious for the number of missionaries it has produced. It was here that the full extent of his intellectual gifts was first understood: here, too, his thoughts were first determined towards the things of God by the influence of a devout friend, confirmed and strengthened by his intercourse with his sister, a woman of gentle spirit and earnest piety. The sudden death of his father helped to stay his feet in the path of righteousness, and he learned to regard his Bible with a new interest, as a book which not less closely concerned him in the next world than in this. "I attended more diligently," he says, "to the words of our Saviour, and devoured them with delight: where the offers of mercy and forgiveness were made so freely, I supplicated to be made partaker of the covenant of grace with eagerness and hope; and thanks be to the ever-blessed Trinity for not leaving me without comfort."

In Martyn's day the spiritual life of Cambridge chiefly radiated, so to speak, from the pulpit and rooms—that is, from the teaching and example—of the Rev. Charles Simeon, the light and leader of what is known as the "Evangelical party" in the Church of England. Martyn became one of his most earnest disciples, and profited greatly by the new and higher views of religious duty which he opened up to him. A fire of enthusiasm burned within his heart; and he longed to devote himself to the service of the Saviour. His original intention had been to enter the legal profession; but his newly-awakened repugnance to the things of the world induced him to listen eagerly to Mr. Simeon when he spoke of the lofty character and great opportunities of the Christian ministry; and he resolved to dedicate himself to it. He was led to choose the most arduous, but certainly not the least noble, branch of this vocation by hearing Mr. Simeon discourse on Dr. Carey's signal success as a labourer in the Indian mission field; and reading, at the same time, the Life of David Brainerd, "the spark of missionary zeal was kindled in his ardent nature." Accordingly, he offered himself to the "Society for Missions to Africa and the East" (now known as the Church Missionary Society), which, in 1800, had been established by some members of the Church whose religious views prevented them from co-operating with the older "Society for the Propagation of the Gospel." But as he was only twenty-one, and too young to take Holy Orders, he had to put a curb upon his zeal, and to learn the great lesson of patience, while prosecuting his studies in divinity, and acting as a tutor at Cambridge.

At this time, and to the day of his death, he kept a journal of his daily work and spiritual experience. Every page contains striking evidence of the depth of his piety and the sincerity of his character; but also, as it seems to me, of an excessive self-consciousness and unhealthy delight in self-introspection, which would probably have developed into morbidness, had not God mercifully arrested the tendency by calling him to a life of Christian action. Of the slowness with which he passed judgment upon himself, an example or two may be given :—" Pride shows itself every hour of the day; what long and undisturbed possession does self-complacency hold of my heart! what plans and dreams and visions of futurity fill my imagination, in which self is the prominent object. . . In my intercourse with some of my dear friends, the workings of pride were but too plainly marked in my outward demeanour; in looking up to God for pardon for it, and deliverance from it, I felt overwhelmed with guilt. . . . Mr. Simeon's sermon this morning, on 2 Chron. xxxii. 36, discovered to me my corruption and vileness more than any sermon I had ever heard. . . Oh that I had a more piercing sense of the Divine presence! How much sin in the purest services! If I were sitting in heavenly places with Christ, or rather with my thoughts habitually there, how would every duty, but especially this of social prayer, become easy :—' Memoriæ tua sancta, et dulcedo tua beatissima, possideat animam meam, atque in invisibilium amorem capiat illam.' "

On the 23rd of October, 1803, when still within five months of the full canonical age, he was admitted to deacon's orders, became Mr. Simeon's curate, and, at the same time, took charge of the neighbouring parish of Lutworth. His diary now affords more and more frequent illustrations of the extent to which a habit of excessive self-examination cramped his powers and narrowed his views. He was attracted too strongly by the emotional side of Evangelicalism, and suffered himself to believe that it was a sin to cultivate, even in a healthy and legitimate manner, the faculties which God Himself had bestowed. "I read Mitford's History of Greece," he writes, "as I am to be classical examiner. To keep my thoughts from wandering away to take pleasure in those studies, required more watchfulness and earnestness in prayer than I can account for. . . . Did I delight in reading the Retreat of the Ten Thousand Greeks, and shall not my soul glory in the knowledge of God, who created the Greeks, and the vast countries over which they passed? I examined in Butler and in Xenophon; how much pride and ostentatious display of learning was visible in my conduct; how that detestable spirit follows me whatever I do!" Happily, the force of events opened out to him a wider sphere of thought and action, which brought with it wiser judgments and soberer opinions. A warm attachment which he formed to a young Cornish lady, named Lydia Grenfell, awakened and fostered a broader sympathy; and the serene light of their mutual affection dissipated the mental gloom in which he was beginning to be involved.

His design of leaving England in the service of the Church Missionary Society was frustrated by a pecuniary disaster, which involved the loss not only of his own patrimony, but of that of his younger sister, whom, to a great extent, it rendered dependent upon his support. It became necessary for him to seek some appointment to which a salary was attached. Application therefore was made for a chaplaincy under the East India Company, as offering a double advantage,—a sufficient maintenance for his sister, and an opportunity of missionary work for himself. The application was successful; he was promised the first vacancy. He then went down to Cornwall to spend the long vacation, and take leave of those he loved before setting out on his long and lonely voyage. "The trial was severe; especially in parting from his sister and the young lady in whom his hopes of earthly happiness were fixed. For many days after the farewell had been said the mental suffering was extreme,—scarcely inferior to that which the poet Keats suffered in parting from Miss Fanny Brown;

but then, unlike Keats, he could turn to God and find in His Word a strength and consolation. He could speak to God as to one who knew the great conflict within him : he was convinced that, as God willed his happiness, he was providing for it eventually by that bitter separation : he resolved through grace to be His, though it should be through much tribulation ; he experienced sweetly and solemnly the excellence of serving Him faithfully, and of following Christ and His Apostles ; he meditated with great joy on the end of this world, and enjoyed the thought of walking hereafter with her, from whom he was removed, in the realms of glory."

On the 27th of August, 1804, he wrote in his journal :— "Walked to Marazion, with my heart more delivered from its idolatry, and enabled to look steadily and peacefully to God. Reading in the afternoon to Lydia alone, from Dr. Watts, there happened to be among other things a prayer on entire preference of God to the creatures. Now, thought I, here am I in the presence of God and my idol. So I used the prayer for myself, and addressed it to God, who answered it, I think, for my love was kindled to God and divine things, and I felt cheerfully resigned to the will of God, to forego the earthly joy which I had just been desiring with my whole heart. I continued conversing with her, generally with my heart in heaven, but every now and then resting on her. Parted with Lydia, perhaps for ever in this life, with a sort of uncertain pain, which I knew would increase to greater violence afterwards, on reflection. Walked to St. Hilary, determining in great tumult and inward pain to be the servant of God. All the rest of the evening in company, or alone, I could think of nothing but her excellences. My efforts were, however, through mercy, not in vain, to feel the vanity of this attachment to the creature. Read in Thomas à Kempis many chapters, directly to the purpose ; the shortness of time, the awfulness of death, and its consequences, rather settled my mind to prayer. I devoted myself unreservedly to the cause of the Lord, as to one who knew the great conflict within, and my firm resolve through His grace of being His, though it should be with much tribulation."

Returning to Cambridge, he continued to work there until he received his appointment in January 1805. In the following March he was admitted to Priest's Orders at St. James's Chapel, London ; after which the degree of B.D. was conferred upon him by mandate from the University. While preparing for the voyage to India, he applied himself to the study of Hindustani, in which he made considerable progress; and attended several lectures on elocution, in order to correct some defects in his speech. On the 17th of July he sailed from Portsmouth in the *Union*, which carried, besides her crew and passengers, the 59th Regiment, some other soldiers, and a number of cadets. An accident which befell a sister-vessel—for the *Union* was one of a large fleet of merchantmen—led to their putting into Falmouth Harbour, where they remained for three weeks; thus affording Martyn an opportunity for a brief visit to his friends, which comforted him greatly. He found his sister engaged to a man of much worth, and was encouraged to form a hope that after he was settled in India Miss Grenfell would join him.

On the 18th of August, the *Union* put to sea; but for two or three days continued near the coast, where the sight of each well-known scene and familiar landmark awoke in Martyn's heart a tumult of conflicting emotions. Under the influence of continual prayer and devout meditation the storm subsided; and as soon as he had overcome the physical discomfort attending his first experience of the sea, he zealously applied himself to his work on board. While continuing his study of Hebrew and Hindustani he acted as chaplain, though permitted only to hold one service every Sunday; and he toiled most anxiously to improve the spiritual condition of those around him by private exhortation and Scriptural reading. Scarcely a day passed but he went between decks; where, to all who chose to attend, he read and commented upon some suitable religious book. Describing his congregation, he writes:—"Some attend fixedly,—others are looking another way, some women are employed about their children, attending for a little while, and then heedless; some rising up and going away—others taking their place, and numbers, especially of those who have been on watch, strewed all along upon the deck fast asleep—one or two from the upper decks looking down and listening." Nor did he find more encouragement among the officers and better class of passengers, who resented the stern and uncompromising character of his teaching, and marked their sense of it by drinking and smoking and jesting while he held his Sunday service. His ignorance of mankind was proved by his supposing that persons so obdurate or apathetic could be brought to repent by terror; could be converted by discourses which resounded with the thunderbolts of Sinai. On the 22nd of September he writes: —"Was more tried by the fear of man than I have ever been since God has called me to the ministry. The threats and opposition of these men made me unwilling to set before them the truths which they hated; yet I had no species of hesitation about doing it. They had let me know that if I would preach a sermon like one of Blair's, they would be glad to hear it, but they would not attend if so much of hell was preached. This morning again Captain —— said, 'Mr. Martyn must not damn us to-day, or none will come again.' I was a little disturbed; but Luke x. 1, —above all, our Lord's last address to His disciples, John xiv. 16, strengthened me. I took for my text Psalm cx. 17, 'The wicked shall be turned into hell, and all the nations that forget God.' The officers were all behind my back, in order to have an opportunity of retiring in case of dislike. B—— attended the whole time. H——, as soon as he heard the text, went back, and said he would hear no more about hell; so he employed himself in feeding the geese. —— said I had shut him up in hell, and the universal cry was, 'We are all to be damned.' However, God, I trust, blessed the sermon to the good of many. Some of the cadets, and many of the soldiers, were in tears. I felt an ardour and a vehemence in some parts which are unusual with me." We may admire this uncompromising Puritan-like sternness, while at the same time feeling that Martyn would have been more likely to have succeeded in his object if he had exercised more tact and shown more geniality,—if, like St. Paul, he had been all things to all men.

Putting in at the Cape, the *Union* disembarked the 59th Regiment to assist Sir David Baird's in the campaign against the Dutch, and it shared in the great victory which placed South Africa in the hands of the English (January 8, 1806). Martyn went on shore next day to minister to the wounded, and accompanied a body of Indian troops to the battle-field. "Mournful as the scene was," he writes, "I yet thanked God that He had brought me to see a specimen, though a terrible one, of what men by nature are. May the remembrance of this day ever excite me to pray and labour more for the propagation of the Gospel of

Peace. Then shall men love one another. Nation shall not lift up sword against nation, neither shall they learn war any more. The Blue Mountains, at a distance to the eastward, which formed the boundary of the prospect, were a cheering counterpart to what was immediately before me; for there I conceived my beloved and honoured fellow-servants, companions in the kingdom and patience of Jesus Christ, to be passing the days of their pilgrimage free from the world, imparting the truths of the precious Gospel to benighted souls. May I receive grace to be a follower of their faith and patience."

After a voyage of nearly ten months' duration, Martyn arrived, ill and exhausted, at Calcutta. Almost immediately on landing, he was seized with a violent attack of fever, through which he was nursed with unselfish assiduity by a brother-missionary, the Rev. David Brown. On his recovery, his friends—and his fine character had already procured him many—would fain have kept him among them at Calcutta; but his enthusiastic spirit burned for labour among the heathen, and was constantly excited and renewed by the sights and sounds of a hideous idolatry which met him in every direction. In a sacred grove near Serampore, he heard the clash of drums and cymbals summoning the poor natives to the worship of monstrous images; and before a black figure, enthroned in a pagoda, with scores of lights blazing around it, he saw the worshippers prostrate, prone, with foreheads touching the ground; a spectacle which filled his soul with large and liberal compassion, and made him shiver as if he stood "in the neighbourhood of hell." In conjunction with Mr. Brown, Dr. Carey, and other missionaries, he purchased a heathen pagoda, and appropriated it for the purposes of Divine service. He still continued his Hebrew and Hindustani studies, and began to work at Sanscrit, while neglecting no opportunity of advancing the great cause he had at heart. His stipend as chaplain was liberal enough to justify him in inviting Miss Grenfell to come out to him that they might be married. In those days communication between India and England occupied a period of sixteen or eighteen months; a period during which he lived in a state of happy expectation, allowing himself to enjoy some innocent dreams of domestic sympathy and peace.

The station to which he was appointed chaplain was Dinapore;

and on the 15th of October he began his journey inland. So slow was then the rate of travelling in India that he did not reach his destination until the 26th of November. He then set before himself three points of attainment,—the opening of native schools, the acquisition of such fluency in Hindustani as would enable him to preach the truths of God in that language, and the preparation of translations of the Bible and religious tracts for distribution among the people. With the assistance of his moonshee, or munshie, he undertook to render the Parables into Hindustani; a task of no small difficulty, as each district had its peculiar dialect.

At Dinapore the arrangements for public worship were very inadequate; and Martyn had to read prayers to the soldiers with a long drum for his desk, and to omit the sermon because no seats were available. Through his energetic remonstrances a room was afterwards provided and decently fitted up; and the families of the English residents began to attend, though as they manifested a dislike to the innovation of an extempore sermon, he found it prudent to conciliate them by recurring to the old practice. It must be owned that with all his wonderful ardour and energetic Samaritanism he lacked "sweetness and light," that discretion and reasonable consideration for the small prejudices and partialities of others which is included in the Pauline precept of being all things to all men; and he was unquestionably better fitted to succeed as a missionary among the heathen than as a priest and pastor among his own people. He had been bred up in a narrow school, and he never emancipated himself from its narrowness. Thus he held strictly to the Judaic interpretation of the Fourth Commandment; and, one Sunday, having translated the Prayer Book into Hindustani as far as the end of the "Te Deum," he abruptly terminated his labours from a fear "that they were not in perfect harmony with the solemnity of the day." But these minor deficiencies count for nothing when compared with the transparent clearness of his character, his generous self-devotion, his fervent piety. His courageous sympathy with the natives, for whom he frequently interfered to protect from gross cruelty and oppression, also calls for our admiration.

While at Dinapore, he became acquainted with an admirable woman and an excellent writer, Mrs. Sherwood, to whom the reading public are indebted for many graceful tales, as well as for a touching memoir of her friend the missionary enthusiast. She thus describes him as he appeared at their first interview :—

"He was dressed in white, and looked very pale, which, however, was nothing singular in India; his hair, a light-brown, was raised from his forehead, which was a remarkably fine one. His features were not regular; but the expression was so luminous, so intellectual, so affectionate, so beaming with divine charity, that no one could have looked at his features and thought of their shape or form; the out-beaming of his soul would absorb the attention of every observer. There was a very decided air, too, of the gentleman about Mr. Martyn, and a perfection of manners, which, from his extreme attention to all minute civilities, might seem almost inconsistent with the general bent of his thoughts to the most serious subjects. He was as remarkable for ease as for cheerfulness. He did not appear like one who felt the necessity of contending with the world and denying himself its delights, but rather as one who was unconscious of the existence of any attractions in the world, or of any delights which were worthy of his notice. When he relaxed from his labours in the presence of his friends, it was to play and laugh like an innocent child, more especially if children were present to play and laugh with him."

Is not this a charming protrait? the portrait of a man who lived in and for Christ, but felt that Christian zeal was not incompatible with Christian courtesy; while his love for children, was it not a very sweet and pleasing aspect of character?

For rest or relaxation, however, he allowed himself but little time, much as he needed both. His labours were continuous and continuously heavy; and his strong sense of duty allowed no suspension of them, no imperfect or half-hearted performance. For baptisms, marriages, and burials he had often to travel great distances; he attended on the sick in the hospitals; he taught in the schools which he had established for the children both of natives and the English; he preached frequently; he conversed with Hindu and Mohammedan, with all who sought instruction or counsel; and he toiled at his versions of the Prayer Book into Persian and Hindustani. Yet at this time he was experiencing intense agony in having to abandon all hope of an union with Miss Grenfell, who, for family reasons, had finally refused to join

him in India. In his journal, November 23rd, 1807, he writes:—
"I am filled with grief. I cannot bear to part with Lydia, and she seems more necessary to me than my life; yet her letter was to bid me a last farewell. Oh, how little have I been crossed from childhood, and yet how little benefit have I received from the chastisements of my God? The Lord now sanctify this, that since the last desire of my heart also is withheld, I may with resignation turn away for ever from the world, and henceforth live forgetful of all but God."

The year had also been overshadowed by the death of his eldest sister, so that it passed away in a thick cloud and amid sore tribulation; brightened only by that faith in God, that love of Christ, that resignation to the Divine Will, in which the young missionary never failed. On the 1st of January, 1808, he writes:—
"The events which have taken place in the past year most nearly interesting to myself are, my sister's death, and my disappointment about Lydia; in both these afflictions I have seen love inscribed, and that is enough. What I think I want, it is still better to want; but I am often wearied with this world of woe. I set my affections on the creature, and am thus torn from it; and from various other causes, particularly the prevalence of sin in my heart, I am often so full of melancholy that I hardly know what to do for relief. Sometimes I say, 'Oh that I had wings like a dove: then would I flee away and be at rest!' at other times, in my sorrow about the creature, I have no wish left for any heavenly rest. It is the grace and favour of God that have saved me hitherto; my ignorance, waywardness, and wickedness would long since have plunged me into misery; but there seems to be a mighty exertion of mercy and grace upon my sinful nature every day, to keep me from perishing at last. My attainments, in the Divine life, in the last year, seem to be none at all; I appear, on the contrary, to be more self-willed and perverse, and more like many of my countrymen, in arrogance and a domineering spirit over the natives. The Lord save me from my wickedness! Henceforth let my soul, humbly depending on the grace of Christ, perfect holiness in the fear of God, and show towards all Europeans and natives the mind that was in Christ Jesus!"

The year 1808 was a year of quiet industry. Martyn continued his ministrations at the hospital; and, daily, when his feeble health permitted, received the more religious members of his flock at his own house. He revised the sheets of his completed Hindustani version of the New Testament, and carefully supervised the Persian translation, which he had entrusted to Sabat. And he undertook the study of Arabic, that he might fit himself to prepare another rendering of the Testament into that tongue.

In the following year Martyn was removed to the station at Cawnpore, where he again came in contact with the Sherwood family. Forced to travel thither at a hot season of the year, when the wind, blowing over the hot breadths of sandy plain, burns like the breath of a furnace, he found himself growing weaker every day, and when he arrived at his destination, fainted before he could be led into his bungalow. Describing this terrible experience, he says :—" Two days and two nights" [from Allahabad to Cawnpore] " was I travelling without intermission. Expecting to arrive early on Saturday morning, I took no provision for that day. Thus I lay in my palanquin, faint, with a headache, neither awake nor asleep, between dead and alive— the wind blowing flames. The bearers were so unable to bear up, that we were six hours coming the last six *kos* [twelve miles], . . . even now the motion of the palanquin is not out of my brain, nor the heat out of my blood."

His acquaintance with the Sherwoods lent a certain brightness to his life at Cawnpore. They conversed together and they sang together; and he delighted in petting and fondling Mrs. Sherwood's baby-daughter. A welcome was always ready for him in his moods of weariness and despondency—moods inseparable from his physical condition; and in his attacks of illness kind hands supplied him with all needful comforts. Otherwise he lived at Cawnpore as he had lived at Dinapore, studying laboriously, and discharging his pastoral duties with a solemn sense of their sacredness and of the responsibilities they involved. A glimpse of the moral courage which distinguished this Good Samaritan is afforded in the following extract from a letter dated September 1st, 1809 :—

" To-morrow the Commander-in-Chief is to be here, and I must let you know whether I can get the promise of a church from him. His family are all at General S.'s, where I breakfasted with them this morning, and baptized a child of Mrs. C., his daughter. Mrs. H. and her three daughters joined with exemplary piety in the baptismal and churching services; and they read the responses aloud, and knelt as if they were accustomed to kneel in secret, from the manner in which they bow their knees in public prayer. The Miss ——s are remarkably modest and correct; a great deal of pains seems to have been taken with them by their mother. General —— has never been very cordial, and now he is likely to be less so; for while we were walking up and down together, I reproved him for swearing; though it was done in the gentlest way, he did not seem to like it. It was the first time he had been called to order for some years, I suppose. 'So you are giving me a private lecture,' said he. He then went on in a very angry and confused manner defending the practice of swearing—'God judges of the heart, and sees there is no bad intention,' etc. Against all this I urged Scripture."

Mrs. Sherwood records some interesting anecdotes in illustration of Martyn's simple-mindedness, and his ignorance of the details of household management. One evening he observed, "The coolie" [a native porter and messenger] "does not come with my money. I was thinking this morning how rich I should be, and now I should not wonder in the least if he has run off and taken my treasure with him." Upon inquiry, the Sherwoods found that, not having drawn his stipend for some time, he had sent a note to the collector requesting him to forward it by bearer. It was sent accordingly, in silver coin, tied up in bags; but no one expected Martyn would ever see it. However, before the evening was over, the coolie arrived with it in safety. Another time, when both he and the Sherwoods had ordered a pine apple cheese, it was remarked that "the cuts" in the two cheeses were curiously similar—and no wonder! For it appeared that the servants made one cheese do duty for both tables, and this the more easily because Martyn supped always on limes and other fruits, and produced his cheese only when the Sherwoods came to supper.

It was in the winter of 1809 that he made his first attempt at preaching in the native language. Every Sunday evening he threw open the gate of his garden, and admitted the devotees and fakeers who thronged the neighbourhood, promising them a pice per head. The appearance of the congregation thus brought together was very striking. We are told that no dreams suggested by the delirium of a raging fever could surpass the reality. There they stood, or crouched, clothed in abominable rags, or nearly without clothes, or plastered with mud and cow-dung, or with long matted locks streaming down to their heels; every countenance foul and frightful with evil passions; the lips black with tobacco or reeking with henna. One man, who arrived in a cart drawn by a bullock, was so bloated as to resemble an enormous frog; another had kept his arm above his head with hand clenched until the nails had penetrated through the palm; and one very tall man had all his bones marked on his dark skin in white chalk, so that he resembled a skeleton figure of ghastly Death. To this strange and motley audience Martyn addressed himself. After requesting their attention, he told them that he gave with pleasure such alms as he could afford, but that he wished to give them something better, namely, eternal riches, or the Word of God, which revealed God to His creatures; and then, producing a Hindustani version of Genesis, he read the first verse, and explained it word by word:—" In the beginning there was nothing, no heaven, no earth, but only God. He created, without help, for His own pleasure. But who is God? One so great, so good, so wise, so mighty, that none can know Him as he ought to know, but yet we must know that He knows us. When we rise up, or sit down, or go out, He is always with us. He created heaven and earth; therefore, everything in heaven, sun, moon, and stars. Therefore how should the sun or the moon be God? Everything on earth, and therefore the Ganges also: how then should Ganga be a god?" In this strain he continued, and his hearers listened always with interest, if not always with approval."

With burning enthusiasm he carried on these Sunday addresses, *conciones ad populum*,—in spite of the anxiety and alarm of the British authorities, and the howls and threats of a large section of the natives,—until the number of his congregation increased to nine hundred. But symptoms of pulmonary disease at length developed themselves, and proved so serious that his physicians ordered him to give up work, take a sea-voyage, and visit England. His soul was in his work; and to accept and act upon such advice as this was very hard. But hearing from critical authorities that a translation he had made of the Gospels into Persian was scarcely simple enough in style for popular use, and too full of Arabic idioms, he resolved to spend his leave of absence in travelling through Arabia and Persia, in order to collect the opinions of learned natives, and improve himself in the languages of those countries.

On the last day of September, 1810, he took leave of his congregation at Cawnpore, after preaching for the first time in the church which had been raised by his energetic efforts. "He began," says Mrs. Sherwood, "in a weak and faint voice, being at that time in a very bad state of health; but gathering strength as he proceeded, he seemed as one inspired from on high. Never was audience more affected." After the morning service was over, he returned home, nearly fainting, and was laid upon a couch in the hall of his bungalow. As soon as he revived he begged his friends to sing to him. The hymn they selected roused him like the sound of a trumpet:—

> "O God, our help in ages past,
> Our hope for years to come,
> Our shelter from the stormy blast,
> And our eternal home."

After an early dinner, and an afternoon's rest, he preached again in the evening, and this time to his wild, strange Hindu congregation. He preached with a sad heart, however, for of all the seed he had flung abroad he found that not one grain had ripened. Nothing is so discouraging to the earnest worker as the prospect of no result from his work. But then he should remember that all progress is slow and silent, and that the blossom may burst from its enveloping sheath when he is not there to see it. Moreover, he is but one of a great army of workers, who are moving, though unknown to themselves, on certain definite lines and towards an appointed goal, and that the extent of the field they cover prevents him from discovering the full reach of their mighty march. Let him be assured that if his work be honest it will not fail.

On the 1st of October, 1810, Mr. Martyn embarked on the Ganges, and on the last day of the month arrived at the house of his friend, Mr. Brown, at Aldun. He was still in a very feeble condition: yet, so great was his devotion to his ministerial office, that he preached every Sunday but one at Calcutta until the 7th of January, 1811. He then took final leave of his friends, and departed alone on his adventurous journey to lands almost entirely strange (at that time) even to his countrymen, in the hope of rendering God's Word available for the study of the numerous Hindus and Mohammedans who understood Persian better than any other literary language.

He went by sea to Bombay, and there obtained a passage on board an English ship intended to cruise in the Persian Gulf against Arab pirates. On the 22nd of May he landed at Bushire. As a protection against insult on his road to Shiraz, where the British Ambassador, Sir Gore Ouseley, resided, he was advised to assume an Oriental dress; and accordingly attired himself in very wide Zouave-like blue trousers, a chintz coat, and long red boots, with a tall conical cap of black Tartar lambskin. He also allowed his beard and moustache to grow, and learned how to eat rice dexterously by handfuls from the common dish.

Accompanied by an English officer, he set out for Shiraz—a terrible journey, under a glaring brazen sun, and up steep rugged mountain paths; no clouds softly tempering the fierce heat of heaven, no verdure refreshing the parched barrenness of earth. They travelled only by night, and encamped by day, sometimes without even the shelter of a tree, wrapping the head in a wet cloth, and the body in all the heavy clothing he had, to prevent the waste of moisture; but even thus, his condition, says Martyn, "was a fire within my head, my skin like a cinder, the pulse violent. At morn the thermometer rose as high as 126°; even at close of day it did not sink lower than 100°."

On the 9th of June Martyn arrived at Shiraz, where he was cordially received by the British Ambassador, and presented to Prince Abbas Mirza, the heir to the throne. He thus describes the ceremony —

"Early this morning I went with the Ambassador and his suite to Court, wearing, agreeable to custom, a pair of red cloth stockings, with green high-heeled shoes. When we entered the great court of the palace, a hundred fountains began to play. The Prince appeared at the opposite side, in his talar, or hall of audience, seated on the ground. Here our first bow was made. When we came in sight of him, we bowed a second time, and entered the room. He did not rise, nor take notice of any but the Ambassador, with whom he conversed at the distance of the breadth of the room. Two of his ministers stood in front of the hall, outside; the Ambassador's Mehmandar, and the Master of the Ceremonies, within, at the door. We sat down in order, in a line with the Ambassador, with our hats on. I never saw a more sweet and engaging countenance than the Prince's; there was such an appearance of good nature and humility in all his demeanour, that I could scarcely bring myself to believe that he would be guilty of anything cruel or tyrannical."

With the energy and ardour of his nature, Martyn worked at his Persian translation, deriving valuable assistance from the services of an accomplished Sufite. It was completed by the 24th of February, 1812, and in six weeks more he had translated the Psalms. On the 14th of May, one year after entering Persia, he set out, with another English clergyman, to lay his translation before the Shah; but finding that, without a letter of introduction from the British Ambassador, he could not gain admission to the royal presence, he determined to proceed to Tabriz, whither Sir Gore Ouseley had removed. The journey occupied nearly two months, including a six days' halt at Ispahan, and another delay at the Shah's camp; and the latter portion involved considerable suffering and not a little danger. Both Martyn and his companion were attacked with fever, and reduced almost to the extremities of famine. On the 28th of June he writes:—" We have now eaten nothing for two days. My mind is much disordered from headache and giddiness, from which I am seldom free; but my heart, I trust, is with Christ and His saints. To live much longer in this world of sickness and pain seems no way desirable; the most favourite prospects of my heart seem very poor and childish, and cheerfully would I exchange them for the unfading inheritance."

He was in a wretched condition of health when he arrived at Tabriz; and an illness of nearly two months' duration baffled his intention of presenting in person his translation to the Shah. During his illness he received great kindness from Sir Gore Ouseley, who, together with his wife, nursed the sick scholar with assiduous attention; and that nothing might be wanting to gain the Shah's favourable acceptance of the result of his persevering labours, undertook himself to present it at Court.

On recovering from the fever, Martyn resolved to make his way to Constantinople, and thence to England, where he hoped to regain his health and strength, so that, accompanied, perhaps, by his beloved Lydia, he might resume in the East his missionary labours. To Miss Grenfell his last letter was written from Tabriz on the 28th of August, and he refers in it to the possibility of their meeting :—" Do I dream," he says, "that I venture to think and write of such an event as that? Is it possible that we shall ever meet again below? Though it is possible, I dare not indulge such a pleasing hope yet. I am still at a tremendous distance ; and the countries I have to pass through are many of them dangerous to the traveller from the hordes of banditti, whom a feeble government cannot chastise." He set out from Tabriz on the 2nd of September ; on the 10th he arrived at Erivan ; on the 25th, at Erzeroum. This last-named Armenian city he left on the afternoon of the 29th, but immediately after he was attacked by his old complaint of fever and ague, which he was in too feeble a state to resist. He still pressed forward, however, though warned that the plague prevailed in the country into which he was advancing. In his journal he writes :—" Thus I am passing inevitably into imminent danger. O Lord, Thy will be done ! living or dying, remember me !" He experienced much annoyance and discomfort from the insolence of Hasan Aga, a Tartar who had been engaged to act as his escort; and he felt it the more as his weakness hourly increased. The last entries in his journal bear date the 5th and 6th of October, and are very pathetic :—

"*October* 5th.—Preserving mercy made me see the light of another morning. The sleep had refreshed me, but I was feeble and shaken. . . . The manzil, however, being not far distant, I reached it without much difficulty. I expected to have found it another strong fort at the end of the pass, but it is a poor little village, within the jaws of the mountains. I was pretty well lodged, and tolerably well till a little after sunset, when the ague came on with a violence I never before experienced. I felt as if in a palsy, my teeth chattering, and my whole frame violently shaken. Aga Storzn and another Persian, on their way here from Constantinople, going to Abbas Mirza, whom I had just before been visiting, came hastily to render me assistance if they could. These Persians appear quite brotherly, after the Turks. While they pitied,

Hasan sat with perfect indifference, ruminating on the further delay this was likely to occasion. The cold fit, after continuing two or three hours, was followed by a fever, which lasted the whole night, and prevented sleep.

"*October* 6th. No horses being to be had, I had an unexpected repose. I sat in the orchard, and thought, with secret comfort and peace, of my God—in solitude my company, my friend, my comforter. O, when shall Time give place to Eternity? When shall appear that new heaven and new earth wherein dwelleth righteousness? There—there shall in no wise enter in anything that defileth; none of that wickedness that has made men worse than wild beasts—none of those corruptions, that add still more to the miseries of mortality, shall be seen or heard of any more."

Ten days later, Henry Martyn was dead. On the 16th of October, at Tocat, the struggle was ended; but whether the final stroke was death by fever, plague, or exhaustion, cannot be determined. He lies in an unknown grave, with no memorial to record his enthusiasm in well-doing.

Does the reader ask what Henry Martyn accomplished? Let him consider a moment. Was his life misspent? Did he nothing for Christ's sake, and for the sake of his fellow-men? To me it seems that such a life, even with such an end, was infinitely better worth living than is the life of the drawing-room idler, immersed in frivolities; or of the man of business, steeped to his lips in the love of lucre. It was a life spent in high endeavour, in Christian effort; and to me it seems that such a life, even with such an end, can be no real failure. It might seem so to the world, but the world's selfishness is never right in its judgments. For myself, I would rather die as Martyn did, a soldier of the Cross, in the throb and stress of his labours for men's eternal good, than like the warrior on a victorious battle-field, purchased by the expenditure of human suffering and human blood!

In Holme Lee's "Title of Honour," which is founded on this beautiful story of Martyn's devotion and self-sacrifice, two characters are introduced as conversing thus :—

"No man," says one, "ever more literally fulfilled the Divine command to forsake all, take up the cross, and follow Christ."

"If self-renunciation," says another, "be the first of Christian virtues, he practised it, and also he imposed it upon others. He was holy, just, and true—but what profit was there in his life? You call him *missionary*—where are his witnesses? He held disputations with several learned Eastern doctors—did he convert any? With the help of native scholars he made translations from Holy Writ. I believe he baptized one poor old Hindu woman. I know he bore with much ridicule, scoffing, mockery; I know he suffered a martyrdom of sorrows; I know he died—in a strange land—alone. If God accepted his sacrifice, where is his witness?"

"His witness," says the first interlocutor, "is the loving admiration of all good men. His noble example has drawn many after him. The seed he sowed is springing up an hundredfold. His name will be a light to the world for many generations."

"Well, take them, take his journals—let the world know how he laboured and sorrowed, and saw no fruits of his labours."

"It is not true," says the first, "that success makes the hero. Some day you will be satisfied that what Henry Martyn did was well done; you will not call his journals only a pathetic record of a disappointed life. He was happier than you or I, for he fulfilled more perfectly the will of his heavenly Father."

"The sweet peace in his Saviour that he felt when dying, worn out in His service, is, I suppose, the moral of his story?"

"It is a beautiful story," is the answer, "a noble story, look at it as you will. Yes—take that for the moral of it. So God giveth His beloved sleep."

In the annals of Missionary enterprise we know of few, if any, names worthier of honour than that of John Williams, the "Martyr of Erromanga." As Eliot has been called the "Apostle of the North American Indians," and Boniface the "Apostle of Germany," so may Williams be distinguished as the "Apostle of Polynesia." It may be said, without exaggeration, that he was the founder of a new system of missionary effort. He combined "civilization" with "conversion." He taught the savage races among whom he laboured the arts of peace as well as the truths of Christianity. He made them Christians, and he also made them *men*. Not only was there this distinction in his *work*, but his *character* marked him out for enduring honour and respect.

His sublime unselfishness, his deep piety, his devotion to his Master's service, have been equalled by others; but with them he combined a rare energy, a remarkable fertility of resource, a rich fund of invention, and a singular quality of influencing and attracting his fellow-men. In truth, his gifts were very many. He was not a scholar or a profound theologian; but scholars and theologians were not wanted in Polynesia. Yet was he by no means deficient in intellectual power; in any sphere of life he would have been a remarkable man; but circumstances directed his mind towards practical and utilitarian objects. He was a born administrator; had a *faculty of governing* which kings might have envied; and an almost intuitive grasp of the means by which certain ends could best be attained,—a prompt and comprehensive perception of what was fittest and most necessary in the circumstances by which he chanced to be surrounded or for the purposes he desired to accomplish. The soundness and clearness of his judgment cannot be disputed. Quick as he was in decision, he rarely made a mistake; and, as one of his biographers remarks, he seldom found himself obliged to abandon his opinion or retrace his steps, except on subjects which he had imperfectly considered or which lay out of his usual range of thought and action. "It may very safely be asserted that there was no leading principle, nor design, nor plan of operations, which he ever found it requisite to relinquish or revise. His judgments upon all points of personal and practical importance had been thought out with too much care, and tested by too long experience, to be open to serious correction." Such was John Williams, the Martyr of Erromanga.

John Williams was born at Tottenham High Cross, on the 29th of June, 1796. There he passed his childhood, and there he was educated: though the tuition he received was imperfect and unsatisfactory; of the classics he learned but little, and of mathematics less. His religious training was undertaken by his mother, a devout and loving woman, like Monica of old, who belonged to one of the stricter Nonconformist denominations. Every morning and evening her children assembled in her chamber for instruction and prayer; and if no strong religious impression was produced on her son's mind, he learned at least a scrupulous regard for truth. In his eleventh year the boy was apprenticed to a London ironmonger, a man esteemed, we are

JOHN WILLIAMS.

EARNEST LIVES.]   Face p. 238.

told, for his consistent piety. Young Williams was to learn the commercial part of the business only, but it soon appeared that the workshop had a stronger attraction for him, and that he studied with attention its tools and processes. When the men left the place at the accustomed hour for meals, he would resort to the forge or the bench in order to put his previous observations to a practical test. We shall see to what good he afterwards turned the knowledge and skill he thus obtained.

At this time John Williams, like too many lads, had grown indifferent to Christ and His religion, and had forgotten or neglected his mother's early teaching. He was an estimable youth, faithful, industrious, and honest, against whose moral character no imputation could be made; but he was not fervent in spirit, serving the Lord. The world was too much with him; he lived only for this life, and the things of this life. And as time went on, for want of a noble aim and a fixed purpose, he rapidly deteriorated. Not that he became what society would call "a bad young man;" but he grew more and more indifferent to his religious duties, and his favourite companions were young men even more indifferent and thoughtless than himself. The prospect was that he would sink into that slough of "respectability" which avoids immorality simply because it has a bad name and does not pay; but that of any really good or useful work for the elevation of himself or his fellow-men he would prove incapable. But at this critical epoch he was induced, one Sunday evening, to accompany his employer's wife to a dissenting place of worship, the Tabernacle. A well-known Nonconformist pastor, the Rev. Timothy East, chanced to preach that evening. He was a man of some talent and eloquence, and his sermon in its power and faithfulness went home to the heart and conscience of young Williams. It was the "word in season" which gave the key-note to his future career. Henceforth he studied the Scriptures with fervent assiduity, and became a regular attendant at the house of God. He daily grew more serious and earnest, and his mind expanded as his sense of religious truth quickened. He learned to think, to take new and higher views of life, to form a new and higher conception of its duties.

In the Sunday-school connected with the Tabernacle he was an industrious and a capable teacher. The addresses he delivered to his pupils accustomed him to public speaking, and he acquired the habit of expressing himself with fluency, accuracy, and directness. A branch of the London Missionary Society was worked from the Tabernacle, and thus it came to pass that John Williams's attention was gradually directed to the wide rich field of missionary work. A conviction grew up in his mind that it was a field in which he might do some service, and he made known his feelings and wishes to the pastor of the Tabernacle. Under his care he devoted what leisure he could command to the task of preparation, and did his best to supply the deficiencies of his early education. His improvement was so rapid that, in July 1816, he was able to pass the examination ordained by the Directors of the London Missionary Society, and was unanimously received as a missionary.

His biographer justly observes that Williams's immature age and imperfect education, at the time of his reception, clearly indicated the propriety of additional instruction before he was entrusted with the responsible charge of a missionary station. But the directors were in urgent want of men, and in that early period of missionary work the great importance of carefully-trained and well-educated missionaries was scarcely recognized; so that they determined to send him forth at the earliest possible moment. The subsequent success of John Williams must not be taken, however, as any argument in favour of such a conclusion. His case was entirely exceptional: an unusual activity of mind and fertility of resource compensated for the absence of educational advantages; and it so happened that he was sent to a part of the mission-field where that absence was of less serious import than it might have been elsewhere.

Meanwhile, he continued the work of self-preparation, reading and writing with great diligence, and accumulating such literary and theological knowledge as lay within his reach. Moreover, he devoted a portion of his time to a careful inspection of manufactories and manufactures, of mechanical appliances and processes; for he had already formed for himself an ideal of what a missionary should be and should do, and it was his fixed purpose not only to teach the great truths of Christ's religion to the Polynesian races amongst whom he was to labour, but to introduce as extensively as possible the arts and comforts of civilized society.

On the 29th of October, he was married to Miss Mary Channer, a woman in every way worthy of him; in Christian heroism his equal, in patient endurance his superior. On the 17th of November, the young couple embarked for Sydney on board the *Harriet*, after taking an affectionate farewell of their families and friends. At Rio de Janeiro they were joined by Mr. and Mrs. Threlkeld, who were destined to be their fellow-labourers. They reached Sydney in May 1817, and through various causes were detained there until the following September. It was not until the 17th of November, exactly a year after their embarkation, that they landed at Eimeo, in Tahiti, which was at that time the centre of missionary effort in Polynesia. Its beautiful scenery, so rich in colour and so graceful in outline, its lofty hills clothed with luxuriant palm groves, its coral strands washed by a sea as blue as the heaven above it, did not fail to produce a strong impression on our missionary's mind, notwithstanding its eminently practical and sober cast. He was more interested, however, in the appearance and manners of the natives. Attending the mission-chapel, he contemplated, with much emotion, the spectacle of "seven or eight hundred people who, not five years ago, were worshipping idols and wallowing in the most dreadful wickedness, now praying to and praising our Lord and God. It was pleasing," he adds, "to see so many fine-looking females, dressed in white native cloth, and their heads decorated with white flowers, and cocoa-nut leaves plaited in the shape of a cottage bonnet, surrounding the preacher who occupied the centre of the place."

Soon after his arrival at Eimeo, the missionaries resolved on building a small ship as a means of communication with the neighbouring islands and with New South Wales. "We set to work immediately, every man to his post. My department was the iron work. The others did the wood, and in eight or ten days she was ready to be launched. A great concourse of natives was gathered to see this extraordinary spectacle. Pomare (the king) was requested to name the vessel as she went off. To effect this we passed ropes across her stern, which were pulled by from two to three hundred natives on either side. No sooner was the signal given, than the men at the ropes began to pull most furiously; and at the same moment, Pomare, who stood on the left-hand side of the vessel, threw the bottle of wine against her bow. This so startled those who held the ropes on the side of the ship where the king stood, that they lost their hold; and as those on the opposite side continued to pull, she gave a lurch and fell upon her side. The natives immediately raised the lamentation, *Aue te pahi e!* (O! the poor ship!) and were dreadfully discouraged. Pomare had always maintained that she could never be launched, but must be broken in pieces when we should attempt it; and now he went away exclaiming that his word had come true. But not discouraged, we set to work again, and by the afternoon had raised her upon the stocks, and prepared everything for a second attempt on the Monday, as it was Saturday when she fell. Monday arrived. We drove in the wedges, placed a cable round her stern, stationed the natives as before, and had the satisfaction to see her go off beautifully, amidst the shouts of the people. While this was passing, there was an old warrior, called by the natives a *taata faa ito ito (i.e.,* a man who puts life and energy into them during a battle), who stood on a little eminence, exerting himself to animate the men at the ropes. I was near him, and he did in reality 'put life into them.' His action was most inspiring. There seemed not a fibre of his frame which he did not exert; and from merely looking at the old man, I felt as though I was in the very act of pulling."

During a residence of some months at Eimeo, Mr. Williams made himself master of the Tahitian language. On the 7th of January, 1818, a son was born to him; six months later he started, with two colleagues and their wives, Mr. and Mrs. Ellis and Mr. and Mrs. Orsmond, with a Mr. Davies as interpreter, and accompanied by several chiefs, to establish a mission at Huahine, the most windward of the Society Islands. Their welcome from the natives was all that could be desired. Mr. and Mrs. Williams were at once provided with a commodious hut, of which they had scarcely taken possession when a hot baked pig and a large bowl of yams were supplied to them. "We then made some tea," writes Mrs. Williams, "and ate a very hearty meal. Our next business was to fit up a lodging for the night, which was done by putting a piece of native cloth across one end of a very large house. Here we slept as soundly as if we had been in a palace. The next day we removed to a neat little oval house, and fitted it up with native cloth as comfortably as we could. As usual, my dear John made lime, and plastered the floors. In a few days, the principal chief of the island sent each of us nine pigs, with a roll of native cloth, and all kinds of their fruit. I wish you could taste some of our breadfruit and arrowroot cakes. I daresay you frequently talk of us, and wonder what we have to eat. I will tell you as nearly as I can. There are plenty of fowls here, and we dress them in a variety of ways. Sometimes we have fresh pork, and occasionally we kill a sucking pig, and get it cooked as well as you can in England, who have large kitchen fires. Our method is to run a long stick through it, and to let the ends rest on two forked sticks, and, having kindled a fire behind, a native sits to turn and baste it until it is well done. We have also had some roast and boiled beef. I only wish we had a cow; I should then be able to make butter, but we get plenty of milk for our tea, as we have five goats."

Visitors from the other islands flocked to see these wonderful white men; among whom the most important was Tamatoa, "King" of Raiatea, and the *Ulitea* of Captain Cook,—which is the central and the largest island of the Society group. As this became Mr. Williams's chief sphere of action for some years, a brief description may prove acceptable. It measures nearly fifty miles in circumference, and lies enclosed, along with Tahaa, a smaller island, six miles to the north, within a noble reef of coral, which forms a spacious and sheltered lagoon communicating with the outer ocean by numerous wide deep channels. It is not only the largest but the loftiest of the archipelago. With the exception of a rich littoral belt of culturable soil, it consists of huge mountain-masses, rising abruptly to a height of 1500 and even 2000 feet, and intersected by some fertile glens and valleys; the scenery is described as bolder and gloomier than that of its sister isles, and to the voyager, until he approaches near enough to discern the wild luxuriance that crowns its lowlands, its aspect is one of "frowning majesty." But when he lands upon its shores, he sees beauty and verdure everywhere around him. Like Prospero's isle, it is full of music, the harmonious noises of streams falling from rocky heights in shining waterfalls, and of murmuring waves flinging their crests of foam against the coral reef. The valleys bloom with the foliage of innumerable trees, the plantain, the feathery palm, the banana, and the precious bread-fruit tree, which, in shady groves and clusters, descend to the very margin of the encompassing ocean.

Not only the size and fertility of Raiatea recommended it as a prominent mission-station, but the fact that it enjoyed a kind of traditional supremacy over the other islands of the Society and Georgian groups. Indeed, up to the date of the introduction of Christianity, its principal chiefs, and among them Tamatoa, received not only civil allegiance but divine honours, and were worshipped as gods. There was yet another reason, as Mr. Prout points out, in its influence upon the long-prevailing and wide-spread superstitions of Polynesia. From time immemorial it had been the focus and source of the abominable idolatries which had darkened, demoralised, and destroyed the inhabitants of its own and the surrounding shores. "Here were to be found the types of the manifold usages, even the most debasing and cruel, which had become the customs of the race; here were the archives of their religious legends; the temple and altar of Oro, the Mars and Moloch of the South Seas; and this had been the theatre of more sanguinary deeds than were to be found in the dark records of all the other islands around it. Hither hecatombs of human victims had been brought from near and distant shores to be offered in the blood-stained marai of Apoa. What Christian soldier would not have felt the spirit-stirring prospect of assaulting such a citadel of his own and of his great Captain's foe, and preferred a post in these high places of the field beyond all other positions?"

Tamatoa had gathered some knowledge of the blessings of Christian civilization from a missionary named Wilson, who had formerly visited Raiatea, and he had come to Huahine on purpose to obtain the services of a teacher. Mr. Williams, with his colleague, Mr. Threlkeld, eagerly responded to the invitation, and with their families arrived at Raiatea on the 11th of September, 1818. They met with a gratifying reception. "As soon as we landed," writes Mr. Williams, "they made a feast for us, consisting of five large hogs for myself, five for Mrs. Williams, and one for our little Johnny. The same provision was made for Mr. Threlkeld. Besides the 'feeding,' they brought us a roll of cloth, and about twenty crates of yams, taro, cocoa-nuts, mountain plantains and bananas. Those crates were a foot deep and three feet square. Several persons of consequence were with us, and the place was a complete market. Visitors are considered strangers until they are fed, when they become *taata tabre*, 'neighbours.'

"While getting our things on shore, I passed a house in which they were eating, when my man slipped in, and having snatched some food out of the hand of a person who was eating it, came out again without saying a word. I asked him why he did so, and whether the man from whom he had taken the food was not angry? He said, 'No, it was a custom among them.' And we now see it frequently. A man is eating his food, and another comes up, wrenches it out of his hand, and walks away without exchanging a syllable. When any of them come from other islands, or from distant parts of the same island, they walk into any house they like, look about them, and, without consulting the owner, say to one another, 'This is good, we'll stay here.'

"It is very delightful to see them on Sabbath morning, dressed very neatly, and going to the house of prayer. After the service, they return to their homes, and eat what had been prepared on the previous day. After the meal they again go to chapel. assure you that you would be delighted to observe the attention of many to the Word of God. They there inquired who sent me, and how I came to think of visiting them. I told them that the thought grew in my mind, and I hoped God put it there. They wished to know whether I should ever go home again. I told them I should very much like to do so, and if it was as near as Tahiti, I could go and return to them; but if I went to England, I should perhaps never get back again."

On examining into the moral condition of the natives, the missionaries found much to discourage them. Their customs, or at least many of them, were loathsome; their idleness was inveterate. They made a profession of Christianity without a single effort to live up to that profession. And again, the scattered state of the population was a serious hindrance to their missionary work. Williams remedied the latter evil with singular boldness; he induced the chiefs and their peoples to assemble together and build a new settlement at Vairaaia, so that they might live near their teachers. A temporary chapel and schoolhouse were quickly erected, and then Williams prepared to build a house for himself and his family in the English style, so that it might become a model for future native residences. He laid his plans with forethought, and carried them out with resolution. Necessarily, the bulk of the labour devolved upon himself; the natives assisted him in procuring and placing the materials, but the *work* had to be done by his own diligent and ingenious hands. When finished, the house measured sixty feet by thirty, and consisted of three front and four back rooms. The sitting-rooms, which commanded a fine view of the harbour, were adorned with French sashes, and shaded with a green verandah and Venetian blinds. The framework of the building was of wood, but the walls, both outside and inside, were wattled and plastered with coral lime. From this time Mr. Williams made not only a whitewash, but a grey and an orange colouring, with which he decorated the interior. On either side, and in front, he laid out a spacious garden in grass-plots, gravel-paths, and pastures,—in which bloomed a variety of ornamental shrubs and plants, some of them indigenous, and others exotics introduced by himself and his brethren. A poultry-yard was well-stocked with turkeys, fowls, and English and Muscovy **ducks**; while a large kitchen-garden supplied them with several **British** roots and vegetables, including cabbages, beans, peas, cucumbers, pumpkins, onions, and pot-herbs.

The furniture, like the house, was the missionary's handiwork. Tables, chairs, sofas, and bedsteads, with turned and polished legs and pillars, and carpeted floors, gave to the interior all the comfort and convenience of an English home. The wonder of the natives was excessive. Their imitative faculties were soon stimulated into exercise, and the settlement, which had formerly been as lethargic as if inhabited by lotus-eaters, rang from end to end with the din of activity. Writing in September 1819, Mr. Williams thus describes the progress that had been made:—" When we came to this place," he says, " there were only two native habitations, and it was difficult to walk along the beach for bushes. But **the** former wilderness is now an open, clear, and pleasant place, with a range **of** houses extending nearly two miles along the **sea-**beach, in **which** reside about a thousand of the natives. We earnestly desire to see the moral wilderness present the same improved appearance. The king, who, we are happy to say, is one of the most consistent characters, resides very near to us.

He is a very constant attendant both at the chapel and the schools. He will probably be one of the first whom we shall baptize in the islands. We are happy in being able to state that his behaviour is circumspect, and that he is very active in suppressing crime.

"We are glad to be able to inform you that many have built themselves very neat little houses, and are now living in them with their wives and children. The king, through seeing ours, and by our advice, has had a house erected near to us. It contains four rooms, wattled, and plastered inside and out, and floored. He is the first native on these islands that ever had such a house; but many others are now following his example. Thus, while teaching them the things which belong to their eternal peace, we do not forget their temporal improvement, and desire to remember the connexion between being fervent in spirit and diligent in business.

"We have been constantly exhorting the people to abandon their pernicious custom of living several families together in one dwelling, and have advised their separation. Several have complied with our request, and before six months more have elapsed, it is probable that there will not be less than twenty houses, wattled, plastered, with boarded floors, and divided into separate rooms for meals and sleeping. Thus you see that, although our station was the last formed, it is the first in these things. We think it a great object gained, that many of the natives, with their wives and children, are now living separately, in neat habitations of their own, and that the people have been induced to engage in preparing such habitations. . . .

"Upon the whole, our prospects are indeed very encouraging, and we doubt not, if blessed with faith, patience, and perseverance, we shall be made very useful. We shall give every possible attention to the instruction of the natives in useful arts, and shall urge them to works of industry, to which we ourselves devote as much time as we can spare; and perhaps the advocates of *civilization* would not be less pleased than the friends of *evangelization*, could they look upon these remote shores, and upon a portion of the natives diligently employed in various useful arts; some sawing, some carpentering, some boat-building, some as blacksmiths, some as plasterers, etc. They have lately constructed two long bridges, which would do credit to any country village in England. But we cannot, we dare not, devote our time to temporal concerns, when it is at the expense of the eternal interests of those whom we came to instruct."

Into the various social reforms introduced by Williams, and the gradual advance of the islanders in the path of law and order, our limits will not permit us to enter. Sufficient be it to say that on the basis of Christianity he raised the goodly structure of civilization; and that he did on a small scale much the same kind of work, in addition to his spiritual labours, as Charlemagne of old did on a large scale, to the immortal glory of his name. He created an orderly and peaceable society, bound together by the ties of justice and goodwill. Schools were established for the education of the people, and copies of the Gospel of St. Luke, besides elementary books, were freely distributed. It is difficult to conceive of any nobler or more interesting achievement than that which was wrought by the devoted missionary in the island of Raiatea. He not only sowed the seed, but was permitted to gather in the earliest harvest, as well as to see the fields brightening with the promise of far more abundant harvests in the happy future.

During his second year's residence Mr. Williams built a chapel and court-house, capable of holding between 2000 and 3000 persons; drew up a code of laws; obtained the appointment of a chief judge; and still further instructed the natives in the processes of mechanical industry. "The natives have learned to work very well indeed, and some of them can saw, and adze, and plane better than I can; but any part that requires particular care, or in which great exactness is necessary, such as turning spindles, rollers, etc., I am obliged to do myself. Perhaps you will wonder how we can do such things, having never before seen anything of the kind. I think that a person, having tolerably good mechanical genius, and a book that will give him general outlines, will be able to accomplish almost anything (not extraordinarily complicated) that he sets his mind to. We are going to attempt a large clock and wooden smith's bellows almost immediately. Our various little works of this kind, our boats and our houses, have given the natives many new and important ideas. These they readily receive and act upon, and it is with delight I observe them engaged in the different branches of carpentering, some box-making, some bedstead-making, some making very neat sofas (which we have lately taught them), with turned legs, and looking very respectable indeed; some, again, lime-burning, some sawing, some boat-building; some working at the forge, and some sugar-boiling; while the women are equally busy in making gowns, plaiting bark, and working neat bonnets—all the effect of the Gospel."

It is evident enough that the administrative or organizing faculty was one of Mr. Williams's special gifts. He exercised an influence over all with whom he came in contact, which marked him out as a born ruler. Chiefs and natives yielded to him immediately as a natural and proper and necessary thing to do; they recognised in him a man fitted to lead, and followed him with implicit confidence. It may be observed that his brother-missionaries just as readily and spontaneously gave to him the first place. A mind so active and masterful, however, animated by the impulses of religious zeal and faith, was sure to weary of any single and limited field of operation. Mr. Williams began to long for a fresh theatre of labour, and had applied to the Directors of the London Missionary Society to remove him to another station, when his thoughts were turned in another direction by an accidental, or, rather, a providential circumstance. This was the arrival of Auura, a chief of Rurutu, with thirty of his people, driven from their own island by a desolating epidemic. What they saw at Raiatea filled them with surprise and delight. They were never weary of gazing at the wonders which had been wrought by the Gospel and civilization. After a residence of three months, actively employed in the acquisition of knowledge, Auura returned to his island home, accompanied by his people, some Raiateans, and two native teachers, the "light in his hand," without which he refused to depart. From this circumstance Mr. Williams conceived the idea of making Raiatea a missionary centre, in order that the Gospel radiance might be diffused over all the islands of the South Pacific. But for this purpose he saw that a missionary ship would be required, "a schooner of about twenty or twenty-five tons," with which to keep up a frequent intercourse with the adjacent islands.

While his enthusiasm was kindling at the contemplation of the great evangelizing work that lay before him, he was seized with a severe and dangerous malady, which baffled all the skill of his fellow-missionary, Mr. Threlkeld, and apparently rendered necessary a speedy return to England. But his earnest prayers, and those of his attached followers and disciples, were heard; the disease diminished in severity, and his work of usefulness went on its happy course. The death of his mother, of which, at this critical time, he received the intelligence, proved a heavy blow. He had no leisure, however, for other than silent sorrow. A new project engaged his attention: he would pay a visit to Sydney, partly to obtain medical advice, but chiefly with a view, by the appointment of an agent and the purchase of a ship, to open up a regular communication between the colony and the Society Islands. On the way he proposed to leave teachers at the island of Aitutaki. Accompanied by Mrs. Williams, he sailed from Raiatea, left two teachers at Aitutaki, and reached Sydney in safety. The agent of the London Missionary Society at first declined to entertain his scheme of the purchase of a ship; but eventually advanced one half the sum required, on Mr. Williams agreeing to advance the other half from some property bequeathed to him by his mother. The purchase was completed; a new schooner of between eighty and ninety tons, called the *Endeavour*, a name for which the natives substituted the more appropriate one of *Te Matamua*, "The Beginning." Mr. Williams returned to Raiatea on the 6th of June, 1822.

In conversation with an aged priest, the missionary had gained much information relative to a large island called Rarotonga, the longest and most fertile of the Hervey Islands, the group to which Aitutaki belongs. When the illustrious navigator, Captain Cook, discovered this beautiful archipelago, which he named after Captain Hervey, one of the Lords of the Admiralty, and afterwards Earl of Bristol, he visited Atiu, Hervey's Island, Aitutaki, and Mangaia, but failed to meet with Rarotonga. The honour of discovering this important island was reserved for Williams, who, with a Mr. Bourne, left Raiatea in July 1823, and after touching at Aitutaki, Mangaia, and Mauke, succeeded, after a long search, in finding it, under circumstances which he thus describes:—

"After leaving Atiu, we were baffled and perplexed for several days by contrary winds. Our provisions were nearly expended, and our patience all but exhausted, when, early in the morning of the day on which we discovered the island, the captain came to me, and said, 'We must, sir, give up the search, or we shall all be starved.' I replied, that we would continue our course till eight o'clock, and if we did not succeed by that time, we would return home. This was an hour of great anxiety; hope and fear agitated my mind. I had sent a native to the top of the mast four times, and he was now ascending for the fifth; and when we were within half-an-hour of relinquishing our object, the clouds which enveloped its towering heights having been chased away by the heat of the ascending sun, he relieved us from our anxiety by shouting, *Teie, teie, taua, fenua nei!* (Here, here is the land we have been seeking). The transition of feeling was so instantaneous and so great, that, although a number of years have intervened, I have not forgotten the sensations which that announcement occasioned. The brightened countenances, the joyous expressions, and the lively congratulations of all on board showed that they shared in the same emotions; nor did we fail to raise our voices in grateful acknowledgment to Him who had graciously led us by a right way."

Rarotonga, situated in lat. 21° 20′ S., and 160° W. long., is a mass of rocky heights, green to the summit, and intersected by leafy and luxuriant valleys. It measures about thirty miles in circumference, and is surrounded by a ring of coral.

The missionaries were received here with a cordial welcome from the king, but this flattering prospect was swiftly dissipated, and it seemed at first as if their enterprise were doomed to failure among a people false, debased, and cannibal. But an heroic native teacher, Papeiha, offered to remain and brave every peril, provided Mr. Williams sent him a coadjutor from Raiatea. His offer was accepted, and the two men laboured with so much earnestness and success that, a twelvemonth afterwards, the whole population had renounced idolatry, and undertaken the erection of a Christian place of worship, 600 feet in length. Thus it is that God "gives the increase" when the husbandmen put their hands to the plough, and scatter the seed in a spirit of loving faith.

After his return to Raiatea, the indefatigable missionary visited the stations at Rurutu and Rimatara, but a sudden and unanticipated check was given to his evangelizing labours by the prohibitory duties levied upon Polynesian produce by the government of New South Wales. These duties almost annihilated the trade which had grown up between the islands and Sydney, and involved Mr. Williams in such serious pecuniary responsibilities that he was obliged to dispose of his little mission-ship. This was an affliction which he felt very deeply. "Satan knows well," he exclaimed, "that this ship was the most fatal weapon ever formed against his interests in the great South Sea; and, therefore, as soon as he felt the effects of its first blow, he has wrested it out of our hands." But he continued to labour on at his twofold work of evangelization and civilization, perfecting the organisation which he had established, and confirming the islanders in the ways of peace and order. On the 8th of February, 1826, a new and spacious church was opened for Divine service. It measured 145 feet by 40, was thoroughly substantial, and finished in every detail with anxious care, and the façade presented to the natives the novel and imposing features of two handsome folding-doors, and nine windows arched and glazed.

On the 26th of April, 1827, leaving the work at Raiatea in charge of Tuahine, a native deacon, Mr. and Mrs. Williams, accompanied by Mr. and Mrs. Pitman, proceeded to Rarotonga on board a vessel engaged for the purpose. They landed on the island on the 6th of May, and were immediately surrounded by a multitude of converts, eager to welcome and embrace the Apostle of Polynesia. His first care was to erect a church, and acquire the Rarotongan dialect. He then began to organise the settlement on the same plan as that of Raiatea. Translating the Raiatean code of laws, he contrived, with his usual success, to secure its adoption by the chiefs, and the work of social reconstruction and renovation went on apace. I suppose the secret of this man's extraordinary influence lay in the conviction of his sincerity which he never failed to produce. Certain it is that at Rarotonga as at Raiatea he was "lawgiver, priest, and king." But in due time the question pressed itself upon his mind. How was he to return to Raiatea? Month followed month, and no vessel approached the island-shores. As each morning dawned he swept the horizon for a sail with as eager an eye as ever did the Solitary of Juan Fernandez, and always in vain. Rarotonga lay out of the track of commerce, was scarcely known and seldom visited. At length he resolved on what must justly be called one of the most remarkable achievements of his wonderful career; he resolved, as no ships came to the island, to *build a ship*.

To appreciate the boldness of this idea the reader must remember that Mr. Williams had no knowledge of the ship-building craft, no tools, no workmen, and we might almost say no materials. To carry out his purpose, he had to invent some things and create others, and to teach his artificers before he could employ them. The fertility of resource which he displayed was not less surprising than his patience and perseverance. Some of my readers may be familiar with Mr. Longfellow's picturesque poem, "The Building of the Ship"; side by side should be placed Mr. Williams's simple narrative.

> "Day by day the vessel grew,
> With timbers fashioned strong and true,
> Stemson and keelson and sternson-kneel,
> Till, framed with perfect symmetry,
> A skeleton ship rose up to view!
> And around the bows and along the side
> The heavy hammers and mallets plied,
> Till after many a week, at length,
> Wonderful for form and strength,
> Sublime in its enormous bulk,
> Loomed aloft the shadowy hulk!"

So sings the poet. Let us now follow the missionary's plain and unadorned tale in all its graphic truthfulness: "Although," he says, "I knew little of ship-building, and had scarcely any tools to work with, I succeeded, in about three months, in completing a vessel between seventy and eighty tons burden, with no other assistance than that which natives could render, who were wholly unacquainted with any mechanical art."

His first step was to make a pair of smith's bellows, as little could be done towards building a ship without a forge. There were four goats on the island, but of these, only three could be killed, as one was required for milk. With their skins, as a substitute for leather, the bellows were manufactured after three or four days' labour. These, however, did not prove efficient: "indeed," he says, "I found bellows-making to be a more difficult task than I had imagined, for I could not get the upper box to fill properly; in addition to which my bellows drew in the fire. I took my old English bellows to pieces; not, as the tale goes, to look for the wind, but to ascertain the reason why mine did not blow as well as others. I had not proceeded far when the mystery was explained, and I stood amazed at my own ignorance; for, instead of making the pipe communicate only with the upper chamber, I had inserted it into the under as well, by which the wind escaped, and the flame was drawn in." This mattered little, however; as, during the night, the rats penetrated into the workshop, and, on the following morning, he discovered nothing left of his bellows but the bare boards.

Mr. Williams was forced to draw again upon his inventive powers. He could not construct another pair of bellows, for he had no leather, but it occurred to him that if a pump could throw water, a machine constructed on the same principles could throw wind. He therefore made a box, about eighteen or twenty inches square, and four feet high; at the bottom he put a valve, and he fitted in a damper, similar to the piston in the cylinder of a steam engine. To force it down with sufficient velocity it was loaded with stones, and a long lever was attached to it, by which it was again raised. "Before placing it near the fire we tried it, and were delighted with our success; but, on bringing it in contact with that devouring element, its deficiencies were soon developed. In the first place, we found that there was too great an interval between the blasts, and, secondly, that, like its predecessor, it sucked in the fire so fast that in a few minutes it was in a blaze. We soon extinguished the flames, and remedied the evil by making a valve at the back of the pipe which communicated with the fire, and opened to let out the wind, and shut when the machine was filling. To overcome the other inconvenience, we concluded that, if one box would give us one blast, two would double it, and we therefore made another of the same dimensions and worked them alternately; thus keeping up a continual blast, or, rather, a succession of blasts. Eight or ten men were required to blow them; but labour was cheap, and the natives were delighted with the employment."

With this ingenious machine Williams wrought all his iron work, using a perforated stone for a fireiron, an anvil of the same material, and a pair of carpenter's pincers for tongs. Charcoal made from the cocoa-nut, *tamanu*, and other trees, formed a substitute for coals. Great was the wonder of the natives at seeing the first iron wrought, and especially the welding of two pieces together! Old and young, men and women, chief and peasant, hastened to see the miracle, and when they saw with what facility the heated iron could be manipulated, they exclaimed, "Why did not *we* think of heating the hard stuff instead of beating it with stones? What a reign of dark hearts Satan's is!" Perhaps they were not altogether wrong in regarding ignorance as an invention of Satan!

The pumps gave profound delight to every spectator; and as for the king, he would cause his stool to be carried on board the ship, and amuse himself for hours by pumping out the bilge-water.

Having no saw, Mr. Williams split the trees in twain with wedges; after which the natives adzed them down with small hatchets, which they tied to a crooked piece of wood as a handle, and used as a substitute for the adze. When a bent or twisted plank was required, they bent a piece of bamboo into the needed shape, and despatched the natives into the woods to search out a crooked tree, which was afterwards split in halves. The supply of iron was small, and Mr. Williams was compelled to economize it; accordingly, he bored large auger holes through the timbers, and also the outer and inner planking of the vessel, and drove in wooden pins (or binails), instead of iron, by which the structure was held together with sufficient firmness. As a substitute for oakum, he used cocoa-nut husk, native cloth, or dried banana stumps. A rope machine was constructed by the ingenious shipwright, and excellent cordage manufactured out of the bark of the *hibiscus*. Mats served instead of sails; the sheaves of blocks were wrought out of the *aito*, or iron-wood. Thus the work went on to a successful consummation; and after fifteen weeks of incessant and anxious labour, the vessel, which measured 60 feet long by 18 feet broad, was safely launched. She was named, with obvious appropriateness, *The Messenger of Peace*.

His first experience with her was not very fortunate. Thinking it prudent to go on a trial-trip before he ventured to Tahiti, which lay 700 or 800 miles distant, he resolved on a visit to Aitutaki, which was only about 170 miles, and set out, accompanied by the king, Makea, and several natives. When some six miles from the shore, the natives, in shifting the sails, not observing their orders, let the foresail go, and as the wind was very strong, it broke the foremast. Providentially, however, about twelve or fifteen feet above the deck were left standing; and having cleared the wreck, and hoisted a portion of the sail on the wreck of the mast, Mr. Williams turned back, and rejoiced to find that he could reach the land, although several miles to leeward of the harbour. By sunset he was safe in port. A new mast was shipped; damages were repaired; and in a few days the undaunted missionary sailed again. This time the voyage was prosperous. He reached Aitutaki, remained there for eight or ten days, and then returned to Rarotonga with a cargo of pigs, cocoa-nuts, and cats, —a curious cargo, but one of great value and acceptability to the Rarotongans.

In February 1828, Mr. and Mrs. Buzacott arrived at Rarotonga, and Mr. Williams was able to place them in charge of that interesting settlement. He then set sail for Tahiti, where he made arrangements for the extension of mission-work to the west, and afterwards returned to Raiatea,—to receive a welcome such as a king might have envied. There he remained until the end of the following year. In the autumn of 1829 the island was visited by the U. S. man-of-war *Vincennes*, whose chaplain has left on record his impressions of the work effected by our great religious and social reformer. He writes:—

"We are in the midst of another varied and beautiful panorama. The ship lies within a short distance of the shore, which is richly edged with groves and single trees, and a fine undergrowth of the banana, sugar-cane, and various shrubbery, surrounding and overhanging the white cottages of the inhabitants. These stand thickly, in regular lines, along a single street two miles or more in length.

"The landing is on a substantially-laid quay of coral, where we met an intelligent lad of twelve years, the son of the Rev. Mr. Williams, the missionary of the station. He informed us that his father was at the chapel, delivering a customary weekly lecture; and, on directing our walk up the street, we met and returned with him to the mission-house, and were introduced to Mrs. Williams and her family. Their establishment is more neat and rural, and more comfortable in its whole arrangement, than any we have before seen.

"The house is large and convenient, having three pleasant rooms in front, opening by large folding-doors on a verandah extending the entire length of the building, and commands, across an enclosure filled with shrubbery, fruit, and flowers, a fine prospect of the ocean. Everything around looked neat and prosperous; and on taking a walk through the village, we found the same features marked, in a greater or less degree, on the habitations and appearance of the people everywhere.

"September 5.—To-day has been the Sabbath on shore. The chapel here, like all we saw at the Windward-group, is large, well-built, and a noble edifice for such a people. The number assembled to-day amounted to about eleven hundred; all well and neatly clad, and exhibiting in their whole appearance and manner of attending the service, every characteristic of civilization, respectability, and piety, found in any common congregation in the United States. But for the colour of the audience, indeed, it would have been difficult for any one to believe himself worshipping with those who, till within a few years, had been lost in all the gross vice, licentiousness, and wildness of paganism. The sight was at once delightful and affecting.

"Captain Finch and a dozen of the officers attended the chapel in the morning. Arrangements had been made to take the band ashore, to play a few pieces of sacred music at intervals in the service. The exercises began, as on shipboard, with the Portuguese hymn. I was fearful that the novelty might occasion some confusion; but it did not in the least. There was not the slightest unbecoming excitement; not even among the children, who took their seats together, as they entered in long procession from the Sabbath-school.

"It was the day of Communion; and after the general congregation had been dismissed, about three hundred of both sexes, and of a variety of ages, with solemnity, and seemingly deep interest, partook of the emblems of the broken body and shed blood of Him who gave His life a ransom for many. Much as the sincerity and piety of the Church members in the islands have been doubted by the calumniators of missions, from all I have observed and known, and from all passing before me on this occasion, I was led to the fervent prayer that I might myself, at last, be equally worthy, with many of these, of a seat at the marriage supper of the Lamb.

"Mr. Hiebling and myself spent the evening with Mr. and Mrs. Williams. This we invariably do; and never without being deeply impressed by hearing, in the stillness of the night, the melody of the native hymn falling on the ear in various directions, from the little cottages of the islanders, as they engage in their evening devotions. Family worship, consisting of the reading of a portion of Scripture, of a hymn, and of prayer, is generally practised."

On the 24th of May, 1830, the *Messenger of Peace* weighed anchor, carrying Mr. Williams as an "ambassador of mercy" to the Navigator Islands. On the way she touched at Mangaia, at Atui, and at Rarotonga, to find that at each island the good work was prospering bravely. Savage Island and Tongatabu were also included in this missionary circuit. After visiting Lefuga, the mission-ship stood direct for the Samoan group, and in the month of August sighted the cloud-capped mountains of the largest and most imposing of the islands, the beautiful Savaii. She was quickly surrounded by a multitude of canoes, and her deck crowded with natives, who were so agile that they climbed like monkeys over the boarding nettings, though these were ten feet deep. When Mr. Williams and his companions landed, a remarkable scene occurred. The natives had kindled a large beacon-fire, and supplied themselves with torches of dry cocoa-nut and other leaves to conduct their visitors to the chief's dwelling. A passage was maintained by a kind of native police, armed with spears and clubs, and stationed all along the route; while some of the natives were busily employed in feeding the fire, some in conveying articles from the ship's boat, and others in conveying them to the lodgings set apart for the use of the missionaries. The majority, however, had enough to do to gaze upon the wonderful strangers, and for this purpose they clustered on the stems and branches of the palms and other trees, peeping with glistening eyes from amongst the rich dark foliage which surrounded them.

As Mr. Williams walked along, he chanced to mention to a young chief that he was exceedingly fatigued from labouring the whole of the day in the boat. Immediately he spoke to his people, and behold, a number of stalwart fellows seized the missionary, some by his legs, and others by his arms; one placing his hand under his body, and another, unable to find so large a space, poking a finger against him; and thus, sprawling at full length upon their extended arms and hands, he was carried a distance of half a mile, and deposited safely and carefully in the presence of the chief and his principal wife, who, seated on a fine mat, received their strange visitors with all the etiquette of heathen royalty.

A beautiful mat having been spread for them, they squatted down upon it, and explained to the chief that they had not come to transact business with him, but simply to pay their respects before they retired to rest. He expressed himself well pleased to to see them; welcomed them cordially to the shores of Savaii; and requested them to take up their abode at his house, a request, however, which they put aside with all due courtesy. On their way from the chief's house to that allotted for the accommodation of the teachers, they passed a dancing-saloon, in which a number of performers were entertaining a large gathering of spectators. Two persons drummed away on an instrument formed of a mat wound tightly round a framework of reeds; and six young men and two young women jumped about with great violence, making motions with their hands and feet in time with the musicians, while others swelled the rude harmony with a song in honour of the arrival of "the two great English chiefs." In their performance there was no indecency, but a good deal of exertion, and the bodies of both the males and females were bathed in perspiration.

Such was Mr. Williams's introduction to Savaii. On further acquaintance with it, he formed a very favourable opinion of its natural resources and of its inhabitants, whom he describes as Polynesian Asiatics. Not so tall or robust as the Tahitians, they were infinitely more agile and graceful; in truth, of all the island races, they bore away the palm for physical as well as intellectual qualities. Mr. Williams was present at a marriage ceremony, in which the two principal performers were a chief named Malietoa, and a handsome young woman, whom he had purchased from her father for some axes and other useful articles. A group of women, *sub tegmine fagi*, under the shade of a wide-spreading tree, which raised its crown of verdure near Malietoa's house, chanted, to a lively air, a song commemorative of the great deeds of the chief and his ancestors; and opposite to them, shaded by the foliage of a bread-fruit tree, sat the bride, a tall and beautiful young woman, about eighteen years of age. Her dress was a fine silky mat, hanging from her waist to her ankles, while a graceful wreath of leaves and blossoms garlanded her head. The upper part of her person was anointed with sweet-scented cocoa-nut oil, and tinged partially with a red preparation of the turmeric root; two rows of large beads were twined around her neck. Her demeanour was modest in the extreme.

"While listening to the chanters," says Mr. Williams, "and looking upon the novel scene before us, our attention was attracted by another company of women, who were following each other in single file, and chanting as they came the praises of their chief. Sitting down with the company who had preceded them, they united in one general chorus, which appeared to be a recital of the valorous deeds of Malietoa and his progenitors. This ended, a dance in honour of the marriage was commenced, which was considered one of their grandest exhibitions, and held in high estimation by the people. The performers were four young women, the daughters of chiefs of the highest rank, who took their stations at right angles on the fine mats with which the dancing-house was spread for the occasion, and then interchanged positions with slow and graceful movements both of their hands and feet, while the bride recited some of the mighty doings of *her* forefathers. To the motions of the dancers, and to the recital of the bride, three or four elderly women were beating time upon the mat with short sticks, and occasionally joining in chorus with the recitative. We saw nothing in the performance worthy of admiration, except the absence of everything indelicate—a rare omission in heathen amusements."

Mr. Williams succeeded in obtaining permission to settle Christian teachers in the Samoas, and the mission started under favourable and encouraging auspices. When he re-visited the islands in 1836, he found that a most satisfactory progress had been made; the Word of God had had free course, and been glorified. The settlement at Sapapalii had proved a centre of spiritual warmth and light, from which the blessed influences of the truth of Christ had radiated over the whole of Savaii and Upolu, and had extended even to the remoter islands of Mamea and Tutuila. In his second visit Mr. Williams did much to confirm and strengthen the good work that had made so prosperous a beginning. And here we must again allude to the characteristics of his *missionary genius*. As Mr. Prout justly observes, his influence, like that of St. Paul, was personal rather than official. He was loved more for his own than for his work's sake; because, as a Christian, he illustrated in himself the gifts and graces of the religion he taught. Long before the natives appreciated his labours as a minister of Christ, they rejoiced in him as their benefactor and friend. He was fond of the proverb, and frequently quoted it, " Kindness is the key to the human heart." And it was the key which he persistently and successfully applied. In his sweet and loving nature was a charm which the savages of Polynesia instinctively felt, and to which they at once responded. A very striking proof of the reality of his personal influence, of the sway he exercised over their hearts, is to be found in the songs, rude enough and simple enough, which the Samoans composed in his honour, and would chant unweariedly for hours:—

"Let us talk of Viriamu.
Let cocoa-nuts grow for him in peace for months.
When strong the east wind blows, our thoughts forget him not.
Let us greatly love the Christian land of the great white chief.
All *malo* [conquerors] are we now, for we have all one God.
No food is sacred now. All kinds of fish we catch and eat:
Even the sting-ray.
          The birds are crying for Viriamu,
          His ship has sailed another way,
          The birds are crying for Viriamu,
          Long time is he in coming.
          Will he ever come again?
          Will he ever come again?
Tired are we of the taunts of the insolent Samoans.
'Who knows,' say they, 'that white chief's land?'
Now our land is sacred made, and evil practices have ceased.
How we feel for the *Cotea!* Come! let us sleep and dream of Viriamu,
Fistaulau [a star] has risen. *Taulua* [another star] has also risen,
But the war-star has ceased to rise,
For Suluclede [the king's daughter] and the king have embraced the sacred word,
And war has become an evil thing."

Early in January 1833 Mr. Williams was back at Rarotonga, where for some months he busied himself in many useful labours, preaching and teaching, and bringing to a happy close the translation of the New Testament into the native tongue. During this period of comparative tranquillity the chapels at Arorangi and Avaru were rebuilt, and new and noble mission premises erected; the *Messenger of Peace* was also refitted thoroughly. In July he sailed for Tahiti, where he took much interest in the establishment of Temperance Societies, to counteract the mischief done by the wholesale importation from Europe of ardent liquors. He visited Eimeo, Huahine, and Atui; returned to Rarotonga in October; and soon afterwards sailed for England, with his wife and family, arriving there on the 12th of June, 1834, after an absence of nearly eighteen years.

It was not, however, with any thought of taking his hand from the plough, of abandoning the work to which he had solemnly devoted himself, that he had returned to England. He was not insensible to the pleasure of seeing once more his native land, of revisiting the scenes of his early youth and manhood, of renewing the old associations; but his chief object was to advocate the cause of missionary effort, and interest the Christians of England in the rising Christian settlements of the South Seas. As a deputation from the London Missionary Society, he made a laborious progress through the principal towns of England, addressing large public meetings, and wherever he went awakening enthusiasm by his transparent sincerity, and riveting attention by the force of his natural eloquence. But this was not the only means he took of promoting the prosperity of the South Sea Missions. He obtained, after various conferences, the consent of the Directors of the London Missionary Society to the establishment of a self-supporting Theological College at Rarotonga, for the education of native missionaries; to the foundation of a school at Tahiti, in which the sons of the chiefs and others might obtain a superior education, while it also served the purpose of a Normal Institution for the training of native schoolmasters; and to the supply of adequate resources for strengthening existing missions and planting the Cross of Christ in places where it was still unknown. He also engaged the Bible Society to print the Rarotongan New Testament. Writing in 1835, he says:—

"Superintending the press is very laborious work; I have, however, 10,000 tracts of various kinds completed. The journeys of the Israelites, Bunyan's Pilgrim, and other works are in hand. I am also fully engaged in public. Within the last two months I have preached and spoken between sixty and seventy times. I trust great things may be accomplished for the mission, a deeper interest awakened in the South Sea Islands, and the means obtained of extending our labours as far as New Guinea." It was at this time, too, that he prepared, with some needful literary assistance, that most fascinating of books, his "Narrative of Missionary Enterprise in the South Sea Islands." In April 1837 it was given to the public, who at once received it with signal favour. The copy which lies before us is one of the "fourth thousand" issued in the same year. By September 1838, 7500 copies had been sold of a book published at twelve shillings. A new edition was then issued of 6,000 copies, which were quickly disposed of, and in April 1840 a cheap edition appeared, which in three years reached a sale of 24,000. The book is now a portion of the standard literature of the Christian Church; and the good it has effected, the zeal it has stimulated, the energy it has sustained, who shall pretend to estimate? It has well been said of it that it contains a history of Gospel propagation unequalled by any similar narrative since the Acts of the Apostles.

A favourite scheme with Mr. Williams was to obtain a missionary ship in the place of the old and unseaworthy *Messenger of Peace*, which was unfitted for the longer voyages he contemplated on his return.* With the sanction of the Directors, an appeal for the necessary funds was issued in December 1837, and the response was so liberal and so prompt that in the following spring he was able to purchase a beautiful brig, the *Camden*, for £1,600. Her repairs and outfit cost about £1000, all raised by voluntary contributions. It should be added that the corporation of the city of London voted a gift of £500. As soon as she was ready for sea, Mr. Williams prepared to embark for the scene of his Christian labours. Accompanied by his wife,

---

* While in England he visited the Carpenters, at Bristol, and Mary Ann Carpenter writes of him as having "deep and enlarged religious convictions, great benevolence, a gift of tongues, handicraft-skill, and some of Brother Martyn's way-wisdom and simplicity."

his son, and his son's wife, and a band of missionaries and their wives, destined to take up the work of evangelization in Raiatea, Tahiti, Rarotonga, and Samoa, he set sail from Gravesend on the 11th of April, 1838. The voyage proved an eminently agreeable one, and on the 1st of July the missionary ship anchored in Simon's Bay, Cape of Good Hope. She made no long delay, resuming her voyage on the 19th, and on the 10th of September she entered Sydney Harbour. Here Mr. Williams renewed old friendships, and established an Australian Auxiliary of the London Missionary Society. But he was naturally eager to reach his beloved islands, and on the 25th of October again set sail, anchoring in the picturesquely beautiful bay of Pangopango, in the island of Tuluila, on the 23rd of November. Afterwards he proceeded to Upolu, where the Samoans received him with an enthusiastic welcome. Having re-organised the missionary settlements in the Samoa group, he directed his course to Rarotonga, dropping anchor off Avarua on Monday, the 4th of February.

"We had long been anxiously expecting his arrival," writes Mr. Buzacott, "and when our patience was nearly exhausted, a brig was seen off the island with strange colours flying, and the natives immediately said, 'It is Williams.' As soon as she had dropped anchor, I hastened off to welcome our beloved brother's return to a place to which he ever felt so peculiarly attached. I will not attempt to describe my feelings on witnessing such a cargo of missionaries and Testaments, and especially on finding that some of them were to remain and assist us in this group. As the morning was unfavourable, they would not all land immediately, and therefore, taking our letters from dear absent friends, only Mr. Williams and three others accompanied me to the shore. By this time the beach was completely lined with natives, their countenances expressive of the greatest joy, anxiously waiting to give Williams a hearty welcome; and it was a considerable time ere we could squeeze our way through the crowd, who appeared to be very happy in again shaking hands with their old friends."

A week was spent at Rarotonga in incessant work, and then Mr. Williams set out for Tahiti, with the missionaries intended for that important station. On the 26th of March he left

Tahiti, on a visit to the various islands of the Friendly Group; and called, in succession, at Eimeo, Huahine, Raiatea, Borabora, and other places, finding at each station abundant cause for thankfulness to God. On the 2nd of May we find him back at Upolu, where he continued to reside for several months, superintending the labours of its Christian community, and preparing for an evangelizing expedition to the western archipelagoes of Polynesia. After a tender parting with his wife and attached disciples, a parting not without sad forebodings—for it was known that he was going amongst a savage population—Mr. Williams set sail on the 4th of November, and after touching at Savaii and Rotuma steered for the New Hebrides.

On the 17th, the *Camden* arrived off the island of Fatuna. It appeared to be one great and rugged mountain mass, which fronted the sea with perpendicular cliffs. No low land was seen in any direction, and at first it was thought that the island was uninhabited. On nearing the coast, however, the voyagers discovered cultivated patches on the sides of the hills, and little low huts grouped among the trees. At length a couple of canoes approached, in one of which were four men, tolerably well-made and well favoured. Their complexion was neither black like that of the negro, nor brown like that of the Polynesian, but of a sooty colour. Their faces were thickly smeared with a red pigment, and a long white feather was stuck in the back of the head. The lobe of the ear was pierced and rendered large by the repeated introduction of a piece of wood, until it was sufficiently extended to receive a piece of an inch or more in diameter. Into this hole a number of tortoiseshell rings, from two to six or eight, were introduced by way of ornament. The cartilage also of the nose was pierced, and, in many instances, having been stretched too much, was broken. One of the islanders was induced to go on board the *Camden*, where he was kindly treated, and attired in a gay red shirt, which pleased him immensely. In the evening he was landed, and the beginning made, as it was hoped, of a friendly intercourse with the natives.

In Mr. Williams's journal occurs the following entry :—

"Monday morning, 18th. This is a memorable day, a day which will be transmitted to posterity, and the record of the events which have this day transpired will exist after those who have taken an active part in them have retired into the shades of oblivion, and the results of this day will be . . . ."

This is the last entry in Mr. Williams's diary, and probably these were the last words he ever wrote. The date "Monday morning" appears, however, to be a slip for "Monday *evening*," and the entry refers to the day's auspicious work at the island of Tauna, the chiefs of which had given him a very friendly reception, and agreed to provide for a couple of Christian teachers. The visit to Tauna extended over two days, and was marked by several pleasing incidents, which encouraged Williams to hope that a field had been found in the New Hebrides where the seed of God's truth could be sown, and patiently watched and watered in hope of harvest blessings.

About one o'clock on the 19th, the *Camden* set sail, and stood northward to the island of Erromanga, reaching its southern side sufficiently early in the evening to run along the coast for some miles to the westward, until, as the darkness fell, the rocks and bays could no longer be discerned, and the vessel was put about to lie-to during the night.

At daylight, on the 20th, she ran down to the south side, and before noon reached Dillon's Bay. Seeing a canoe paddling along in shore, with three men in her, Mr. Williams ordered the whale-boat to be lowered, and embarked in her with Captain Morgan, Mr. Harris, and Mr. Cunningham, two missionaries, and four hands. On speaking to the men in the canoe, they found them to be a different race of people to those at Tauna, shorter of stature, and darker of complexion; they were wild in appearance, and churlish in manner. Mr. Williams made them some presents, and endeavoured to persuade them to come into his boat, but in vain.

The missionaries then pulled up the bay, some of the natives on the shore running along the rocks at a distance. Observing a beautiful valley, brightened by a crystal stream, they drew towards the beach to see if they could get some fresh water. Mr. Harris, asked if he might land, and Mr. Williams assenting, he did so and sitting down, the natives closed round him, and brought him some cocoa-nuts. After a short interval, Mr. Williams landed, accompanied by Mr. Cunningham, and divided a few pieces of coloured print among those nearest to him. They soon strolled a short way inland, directing their course up the side of the brook. The looks and manners of the savages, however, were far from reassuring; and Mr. Cunningham remarked to Mr. Williams that probably they had to dread their revenge in consequence of a former quarrel with strangers, in which, perhaps, some of their friends had been killed. Mr. Williams did not reply, being at the time engaged in repeating the Samoan numerals to a crowd of boys, one of whom was saying them after him. Mr. Cunningham, who was a few paces ahead, observed some shells of a species new to him; he picked them up, and was putting them in his pocket, when he heard a yell, and almost simultaneously Mr. Harris rushed out of the bushes about twenty yards in front of him. It was a case of *sauve qui peut*. Mr. Cunningham shouted to Mr. Williams to run, and sprang forward through the natives gathered on the bank of the stream, who, staggered, perhaps, by the suddenness of his onset, immediately gave way. Looking round, he saw Mr. Harris fall in the brook, and the water dash over him, while a number of savages were beating him with clubs. Mr. Williams hesitated for a moment,—a moment only, but it was too much to lose. Instead of making for the boat, he ran directly down the beach into the water, pursued by a savage, probably intending to swim off until the boat picked him up. But the beach being steep and stony, he missed his footing and fell backward, the savage dealing him several blows with a club on the arms and over the head. He twice dashed his head under water to avoid the club with which his fierce pursuer stood prepared to strike him the moment he arose. Mr. Cunningham, who had reached the boat, threw a couple of stones, which for an instant retarded the progress of another native, who was close behind; but he recovered himself immediately, rushed upon Mr. Williams, and, some others coming up, all was over.

"Though every exertion was used," says Mr. Cunningham, "to get up the boat to his assistance, and though only about eighty yards distant, before we got half the distance our friend was dead, and about a dozen savages were dragging the body on the beach, beating it in the most furious manner. A crowd of boys surrounded the body as it lay in the ripple of the beach, and beat it with stones, till the waves dashed red on the shore with the blood of their victim. Alas! that moment of sorrow and agony, I almost shrieked in distress. Several arrows were shot at us, and one passing under the arm of one of the men, passed through the lining of the boat and entered the timber. This alarmed the men, who remonstrated that, having no firearms to frighten the savages away, it would be madness to approach them, as Mr. Williams was dead; to this Captain Morgan reluctantly assented, and pulled off out of reach of the arrows, where we lay for an instant to consider what we should do, when it was proposed that we should, if possible, bring up the brig, now about two miles distant, and, under cover of two guns which she carried, to land, and, if possible, to obtain the bodies, which the natives had left on the beach, having stripped off the clothes. We hastened on board and beat up for the fatal spot; we could still perceive the white body lying on the beach, and the natives had all left it, which gave us hope of being able to rescue the remains of our friend from the ferocious cannibals. Our two guns were loaded, and one fired, in hopes that the savages might be alarmed, and fly to a distance; several were still seen on a distant part of the beach. Shot we had none, but the sailors collected pieces of iron, etc., to use if necessary. Our hopes were soon destroyed, for a crowd of natives ran down the beach and carried away the body, when we were within a mile of the spot. In grief we turned our backs and stood from the fatal shores. We had all lost a friend, and one we loved, for the love he bore to all, and the sincerity with which he conveyed the tidings of peace to the benighted heathen, by whose cruel hands he had now fallen."

Thus died John Williams: sealing with his blood that noble and devoted testimony to the truth as it is in Christ which he had borne for so many years with admirable constancy of purpose and purity of motive. According to the teaching of the Church there are three kinds of martyrdom: "The first, both in will and deed, which is the highest; the second, in will but not in deed; he third, in deed but not in will." Or as Keble expresses it:—

> "One presses on, and welcomes death;
> One calmly yields his willing breath,
> Nor slow, nor hurrying, but in faith
>   Content to die or live:

> And some, the darlings of their Lord,
> Play smiling with the flame and sword,
> And, ere they speak, to His sure word
>   Unconscious witness give."

Williams belonged to the first and highest order: he knew the peril of his enterprise, and confronted it willingly, for the sake of human souls and his love of the cross of Christ.

BOOK IV.

PRISON REFORM.

CONDITION OF OUR PRISONS IN THE 18TH CENTURY
JOHN HOWARD.
MRS. ELIZABETH FRY.

PRISON REFORM.

WHEN and where John Howard was born, biographers do not seem able to determine; but it was probably at Enfield, and some time in the year 1725.

His mother died while he was still an infant, and as he was of a sickly constitution, he was sent to a cottager residing on his father's estate at Cardington, near Bedford, to grow strong in the pure country air. He took a great liking to the healthy, picturesque village, and in after life it became his favourite place of abode.

In due time he became old and robust enough for school, and was sent first to one academy, and then to another, going through the superficial curriculum which was then in vogue, but acquiring a very imperfect knowledge of his own language, and none of any other. At the age of sixteen or seventeen he was apprenticed to a wholesale grocer in Watling Street, London. Probably his father wished him to gain some spirit of order and acquaintance with common affairs, for there was no need of his undertaking anything in commerce or trade, and as he was allowed a servant, a couple of saddle horses, and private apartments, it is certain that his apprenticeship involved him neither in hard work nor privation. Soon afterwards his father died, and Howard came into the enjoyment of an ample estate. His natural prudence and acquired habits of business now served him in good stead. He plunged into none of the dissipations favoured by the young men, the *jeunesse dorée* of his time; but, to improve his knowledge of the world, and refine his taste, set out upon a tour through France and Italy. On his return, he took lodgings at Stoke Newington, for his health was still delicate, and devoted himself to study, taking up the subjects of Medicine and Natural Philosophy. The religious feelings which his father had cultivated in him now took a more serious and decided form. Sprung from a

Nonconformist family, he cherished Nonconformist principles, and joined the denomination known as the Independents; but at no time in his life did he exhibit the prejudices or partialities of sectarianism. When he had no opportunity of attending a place of Dissenting worship, he freely joined in the service of the Church of England; and Dr. Aikin sententiously observes, that "though he was warmly attached to the interests of the party he espoused, yet he had that true spirit of Catholicism, which led him to honour virtue and religion wherever he found them, and to regard the *means* only as they were subservient to the *end*."

Suffering sometimes makes men hard and cruel; in others, it opens the source of human feeling. It has been said of the poet that he learns in suffering what he teaches in song; and in like manner the philanthropist is taught to sympathize with affliction by his own bitter experiences of pain or trouble. So it was with John Howard: in his hours of anguish he learnt to feel for the sorrows of his kind, and thenceforth endeavoured to relieve them. A pure and living spirit of charity was kindled in his heart, and the religious convictions to which he tenaciously clung helped to sustain and develop it. He not only extended his hand to those who appealed to his benevolence, but sought out the stricken and distressed in their obscurity; remembering, as he distributed his alms, that "it is more blessed to give than to receive."

It would seem to have been in accordance with this principle that, after recovering from his long and severe illness, he offered his hand in marriage to his landlady, to whose care he believed the preservation of his life was due. As he was only twenty-four, and the lady, a widow, fifty-two, we may reasonably conclude that, in this instance, his benevolence was carried to an unwise extreme. The marriage, however, proved happier than he deserved; and for three years the oddly-assorted couple lived together in unclouded tranquillity. Mrs. Howard died in 1755; and the bereaved husband sought a solace for his grief in foreign travel. He embarked for Portugal in 1756, on board the *Hanover* packet, but was captured by a French privateer, carried to Brest, and, with the crew and the rest of the passengers, was flung into prison.

"In the castle at Brest," he says, "I lay six nights upon straw; and observing how cruelly my countrymen were used there, and

SUPPOSED BIRTHPLACE OF JOHN HOWARD.

at Morlaix, whither I was carried next, during the two months I was at Carpaix upon parole, I corresponded with the English prisoners at Brest, Morlaix, and Dinan; at the last of those towns were several of our ship's crew, and my servant. I had sufficient evidence of their being treated with such barbarity that many hundreds had perished; and that thirty-six were buried in a hole at Dinan in one day. When I came to England, still on parole, I made known to the commissioners of sick and wounded seamen the sundry particulars, which gained their attention and thanks. Remonstrance was made to the French court; our sailors had redress; and those that were in the three prisons mentioned above were brought home in the first cartel ships. A lady from Ireland, who married in France, had bequeathed in trust with the magistrates of St. Maloes sundry charities, one of which was a penny a day to every English prisoner of war at Dinan. This was daily paid, and saved the lives of many brave and useful men."

On his return to England his attention was at first directed to Cardington, his paternal estate, upon the extension and improvement of which he determined. He purchased an adjoining farm; and, residing upon his property, spent his days in supervising the necessary alterations, promoting the welfare of his tenants, and ministering to the wants of the poor and dependent. His leisure he employed in literary pursuits; and having been elected a Fellow of the Royal Society (May 13, 1756), contributed three papers to its "Transactions."

On the 25th of April, 1758, he married again, and this time through affection rather than gratitude. This second Mrs. Howard is described as possessing, in no ordinary degree, all the softer virtues of her sex; "not deficient in personal attractions, amiable in her disposition, and ardent in her affection; ever conforming herself to her husband's wishes, and cheerfully seconding the execution of all his plans." But she was of a frail constitution, and her health giving way, was ordered to try the more genial air of the south coast. Howard accordingly purchased the estate of Watcombe, near Lymington, where he resided for three or four years; and then, the expected improvement in his wife's health not having taken place, he returned to his beloved Cardington.

There he resumed his interrupted plans; he enlarged and embellished his house, re-arranged the grounds, and laid out the gardens in the new style which "Capability" Brown and other reformers had recently introduced. A beautiful avenue of trees, which encircled his whole demesne, was one of its most attractive features. This still and shady grove was his favourite resort; and in its pleasant solitude he spent many a lonely hour in devising, and many a social one in communicating to his friends, when devised, those "glorious schemes of benevolence, which will never cease to impart to every spot his footsteps are known to have traversed on so merciful an errand, a charm more powerful than, without the magic influence of some such genius of the place, can dwell in nature's loveliest or sublimest scenes." This, however, was not his sole place of retirement. In a sequestered part of the grounds he caused a rustic building to be erected, a fabric made up of the roots and trunks of trees, with a thatched roof. Its door and windows, we are told, were "Gothic;" admitting light enough for studious reading, but excluding all distracting glare. A monitory hour-glass occupied a bracket in the interior; and places were also provided for a model, some memorial of his former travels, and a female figure, represented in a contemplative attitude. A small bookcase enclosed some favourite volumes; amongst them, the works of Flavel, Hervey, Young, and Milton, and some popular treatises on philosophical subjects. The following inscription faced the visitor as he entered the door :—

> "O solitude, blessed state of man below,
> Friend to our thoughts and balm of all our woe;
> Far from thronged cities my abode remove
> To realms of innocence and peace and love.

> "That when the sable shades of death appear,
> And life's clear light no more these eyes shall cheer,
> Its work may be fulfilled—its prospects won—
> By virtue measured, not a setting sun."

It must not be supposed that Howard led a solitary or ascetic life, for though his sobriety of manners and orderly habits unfitted him for the riotous living then too common among the rural gentry of England, he received his true friends with a hospitality at once cordial and grateful. He always maintained a genial intercourse with several of the first persons in his county who knew and respected his worth. "Indeed," says Dr. Aikin, "however uncomplying he might be with the freedoms and irregularities of polite life, he was by no means negligent of its received forms; and though he might be denominated a man of scruples and singularities, no one would dispute his claim to the title of a *gentleman.*"

Howard seems to have been an exemplary landlord, though with a disposition to exercise his authority somewhat arbitrarily, or at least not in accordance with our modern ideas of the liberty of the subject. Dr. Aikin represents it as the cardinal object of his ambition, that the poor in his village should be the most orderly in their manners, the neatest in their persons and habitations, and possessed of the greatest share of the comforts of life, that could be met with in any part of England. And as it was his disposition to carry everything he undertook to the greatest pitch of perfection, so he spared no pains or expense to effect his purpose. He began by building a number of neat cottages, to each of which he allotted a small portion of garden ground and other conveniences. "In this project," says Dr. Aikin, "which might be considered as an object of taste, as well as of benevolence, he had the full concurrence of his excellent partner. I remember his relating that once, having settled his accounts at the close of a year, and found a balance in his favour, he proposed to his wife to make use of it in a journey to London, or any other gratification she chose. 'What a pretty cottage it would build!' was her answer, and the money was so employed. He was careful to place in these comfortable abodes the soberest and most industrious tenants he could find, over whom he ruled with the directness of a paternal despot. He provided them with employment, assisted them in distress and sickness, and educated their children. In order to preserve their morals, he agreed with them that they should regularly attend their several places of worship, and abstain from public-houses and from such amusements as he considered pernicious. And obedience to these rules he somewhat tyrannically enforced by making them tenants at will. Patriarchal discipline of this type would hardly find admirers or supporters in the present day; but it appears to have been attended with excellent results. Cardington, which at one time was infested with poverty and wretchedness, soon became one of the neatest and prettiest villages in the kingdom; exhibiting all the gracious signs of competency and content, which are the natural rewards of virtuous industry."

This life of peaceful and not unprofitable simplicity was darkly overshadowed on the 31st of March, 1761, by the death of his amiable wife Henrietta, a few weeks after the birth of a son. It had been well if her offspring had died with her, for he lived only to be a reproach and an affliction to the father whose mistaken ideas of education crushed his young feelings, blighted his sympathies, and forced his feet into that downward path which leads the unhappy victim to destruction. Howard's theory of education was based upon a principle; but then, unfortunately, it was an erroneous one; and if we argue from false premises, our inferences will necessarily be false. Coleridge, in some exquisite lines, has told us that if—

> "O'er wayward childhood thou wouldst hold firm rule,
> And sun thee in the light of happy faces,
> Love, Hope, and Patience, these must be thy graces,
> . And in thine own heart let them first keep school.
> For as old Atlas on his broad neck places
> Heaven's starry globe, and there sustains it, so
> Do thou upbear the little world below
> Of education—Patience, Love, and Hope."

Howard, on the other hand, thought that Fear was the leading motive. He was of opinion that obedience was the first condition on which the teacher must insist, and to secure it resorted to a rigorous exercise of authority. Restraint, chastisement, compulsion—these were the methods of his rule. And with the natural result, in his boyhood his son was slavishly submissive and compliant, but in his youth, throwing off the yoke, he became a hopeless profligate. No strong secret sympathies bound him to his father; no gracious associations endeared to him his home. He plunged into the temptations which he had previously shunned,—not from principle, but terror; was hurried into gross sensualities; an intellect never very strong broke down beneath the stress laid upon it; and his last years were passed under the fatal shadow of insanity. The truth must be told, that Howard, in his domestic relations, permitted himself that benevolent despotism which he practised in his relations towards his tenantry.

Howard's health again failing, he shut up his mansion at Cardington, placed his son in a boarding-school at Cheshunt, and started for the Continent in the summer of 1769. Landing at Calais, he struck across France to the classic shores of Geneva, and thence proceeded to Milan. There he was much shocked by what he conceived to be the irreligious spirit of the Italians. In his journal, under the date of November 26th, the following entry occurs:—

"Having bought an Italian Almanack, I counted the Holy days in Italy—thirty-one besides the fifty-two Sabbaths. Oh! how is pure religion debased in these countries—preventing on so many days the providing for a family by work, and allowing every species of wickedness at little cabarets on the Sabbath-days! How different to the primitive sacred Sabbath! When men leave the Holy Word and set up their own inventions, God often leaves them—then how do they fall! Blessed be God who has called us Protestants out of darkness into His marvellous light! Make me more sensible, more thankful, O my God! How much reason have I to bless God for the Reformation! How is religion debased into show and ceremony here in Italy! Twenty saints' days near together at Christmas! poor creatures prevented from getting their daily bread, thousands idling and miserable in the streets."

Again, on the 30th, he writes from Turin:—

"My return without seeing the southern parts of Italy was after much deliberation. I found a misimprovement of a talent spent for mere curiosity, at the loss of many Sabbaths; and as many donations must be suspended for my pleasure, which would have been, as I hope, contrary to the general conduct of my life; and which, on a retrospective view on a death-bed, would cause pain as unbecoming a *disciple of Christ*, whose mind should be formed in my soul;—these thoughts, with distance from my dear boy, determine me to check my curiosity. Oh, why should vanity and folly, pictures and baubles, or even the stupendous mountains, beautiful hills, or rich valleys, which ere long will all be consumed, engross the thoughts of a candidate for an everlasting kingdom! A worm ever to crawl on earth, whom God has raised to the hope of glory, which ere long will be revealed to them who are washed and sanctified by faith in the blood of the Divine Redeemer!

Look forward, O my soul! How low, how mean, how little is everything but what has a view to that glorious world of light, life, and love! The preparation of the heart is of God. Prepare the heart, O God! of Thy unworthy creature, and unto Thee be all the glory through the boundless ages of Eternity!

"This night my trembling soul almost longs to take its flight, to see and know the wonders of redeeming love, join the triumphant choir, sin and sorrow fled away, God my Redeemer all in all. Oh, happy spirits that are safe in those mansions!"

In spite of the exaggeration of this language, Howard's Christian sincerity is not to be doubted; but the limitation of his views and the narrowness of his intellectual scope are strikingly illustrated by the fact that his journals, which are full of those morbid self-communions, contain no reference to the beauties of Nature, and the masterpieces of Art, with all their rare grace and charm, which everywhere surround the traveller in Italy. In truth, up to this time Howard stands before us as simply an English country gentleman, with warm religious feelings bordering upon Calvinism, some slight amount of culture, a few very strong opinions and rigid theories, much sobriety of temper, and practical common sense. An excellent landlord, so long as his tenants do not dispute his authority; and an affectionate father, so long as his son yields an implicit obedience. But as yet we find little to distinguish him, except his piety, from his brother squires; and no reason why he should have become known beyond his immediate circle. He had found no special work in life to do; and it seemed probable that his career would be spent in alternate residences at Cardington and visits to the Continent. For a man to rise above his fellows, if he have not the impulse of genius, he must have an object or a powerful motive. Howard as yet had not discovered the object, or acknowledged the motive. His mission had not devolved upon him; and he groped his way through the world with an almost Pharisaic conviction that he was doing his best, and an occasional chant of humiliation, when he remembered his faults, follies, and sins.

The work that was intended for him to do came to him in 1773, when he was nominated High Sheriff of Bedfordshire. The office was one which was generally held as conferring dignity rather than imposing a duty, but Howard was too honest to accept the honour without discharging the responsibilities. The county gaol was under his jurisdiction,—that gaol of Bedford in which John Bunyan had composed his wonderful allegory of "The Pilgrim's Progress." He paid it a visit; he observed the miserable condition of its wretched inmates; and then the aim and purpose of his life rose suddenly upon him. Prison reform had been advocated as early as 1701, when Dr. Bray, as representing the Society for Promoting Christian Knowledge, had visited Newgate and other prisons, and in a published essay described the crime **and cruelty** and mismanagement which he found **prevailing in** them. But nothing came of it. In 1729, a Parliamentary Committee inspected the Metropolitan prisons, and brought **to** light a number of atrocities, which temporarily shocked the public conscience. But nothing came of it. The work **was one** which could be done only by a man in earnest; a man **with** the necessary leisure, with adequate means; of a resolved and patient temper; and a believer in the divine law of Charity. Such a man was John Howard, who—

> "Touched with human woe, redressive **searched**
> Into the horrors of the gloomy jail;
> Unpitied and unheard where Misery moans;
> Where sickness pines; where thirst and hunger burn,
> And poor Misfortune feels the lash **of Vice**."

Howard himself has **told** us **how** he was led to embark upon the enterprise which has invested his life with so pure and permanent an interest, and rescued his name from the oblivion that must otherwise have absorbed it.

"The distress of prisoners," he says, "of which there are few who have not some imperfect idea, came more immediately under **my** notice when I was sheriff of the county of Bedford, **and** the circumstance which excited **me** to activity **in** their behalf, was the seeing some, who, by the verdict of juries, were declared not guilty; some **on** whom the grand jury **did not** find **such an** appearance of **guilt** as subjected them to **trial**; and **some** whose prosecutors **did not** appear against them; after having been confined **for months,** dragged back to gaol and locked up again till they **should pay** sundry fees to the gaoler, the clerk of assize, etc.

"In order to redress this hardship, I applied to the justices of the county for a salary to the gaoler in lieu of his fees. The Bench were properly affected with the grievance, and willing to grant the relief desired, but they wanted a precedent for charging the county with the expense. I therefore rode into several neighbouring counties in search of one; but I soon learned that the same injustice was practised in them; and looking into the prisons, beheld scenes of calamity which I grew daily more and more anxious to alleviate. In order, therefore, to gain a more perfect knowledge of the particulars and extent of it, by various and accurate observation, I visited most of the county gaols in England."

Howard began this tour of inspection in November. First he visited the neighbouring prisons of Huntingdon and Cambridge, then went farther afield, north, and south, and west, and east. At Northampton the poor prisoners were allowed neither bedding nor even straw. At Leicester the cells were damp, dark, and offensive. At Nottingham, "down twenty-eight steps are three rooms for criminals who can pay. Down twelve steps more are deep dungeons cut in the sandy rock, very damp." Stafford, Lichfield, Warwick, Worcester,—of all, the dreary record was the same. At Gloucester he found that Robert Raikes had undertaken the work of reform. He completed this, his first tour, at Aylesbury, and returned to Cardington to rest. But what he had seen preyed upon his generous spirit, and in ten days he resumed his survey, resolved, when his facts were all marshalled and prepared, to agitate for a redress of the existing evils.

At Salisbury, coal was allowed to the prisoners, but as they had no chimneys in the wards, they kindled their fires on a raised brick in the middle, and endured the smoke as best they could. "Just without the prison gate," says Howard, "is a round staple fixed in the wall; through it is put a chain, at each end of which a debtor, padlocked by the leg, stands, offering to those who pass by, nets, laces, purses, etc., made in the prisons. At Christmas, felons chained together are permitted to go about, one of them carrying a sack or basket for food, another a box for money.' Truly, we have in some things improved upon the usages of our forefathers! At Horsham was a prison with small rooms, but no court for air or exercise. No straw was allowed; the inmates slept upon the boards. Howard adds that, when he and the keeper entered, they saw a heap of rubbish. The prisoners had been two or three days undermining, and had planned a general escape for that night. "Our lives," he says, "were at their mercy; but, thank God, they did not attempt to murder us and rush out."

At the inner door of the prison at York, Howard saw liquors handed to those who seemed to have had enough before. Formerly there was no water in this prison, except when there was too much, that is, in a very high flood of the Ouse. "The felons' court," he says, "is down five steps; it is too small, and has no water; in it are three cells, in another place nine cells, and three in another. The cells are in general about seven and a half feet by six and a half, and eight and a half feet high, close and dark, having only either a small hole over the door, or some perforations in it of about an inch in diameter, not any of them into the open air, but into passages or entries. In most of these cells three prisoners are locked up at night; in winter for fourteen or sixteen hours; straw on the stone floors; no bedsteads. There are four condemned rooms, about seven feet square. A sewer in one of the passages often makes these parts of the gaol very offensive."

Is it to be wondered at that the young offender who passed into one of these torture-chambers, half ashamed, half penitent, emerged from it a hardened and desperate criminal? Can one imagine any process better adapted to fill the heart with rage against all mankind, and to silence the faint whispers of an uneasy conscience?

After visiting Lincoln, Ely, Norwich, Ipswich, and Colchester, Howard went to London. The county gaol at Southwark he describes as "having eighteen large rooms, yet not sufficient for the number of prisoners. No bedding, no straw, no infirmary, no chapel."

Through Devonshire the indefatigable philanthropist made his way into Cornwall. The gaol at Lancaster he thus describes:—

"Though built on the large green belonging to the old ruinous castle, it is very small. The prison is a room or passage, $23\frac{1}{2}$ feet by $7\frac{1}{2}$, with only one window, 2 feet by $1\frac{1}{2}$: and three dungeons or cages on the side opposite the window: these are about $6\frac{1}{2}$ feet deep; one 9 feet long; one about 8 feet; one not 5 feet: *this last for women*. They are all very offensive. No chimney; no water; no sewers; damp earth floors; no infirmary. The court not secure; and prisoners seldom permitted to go out to it. Indeed, the whole prison is out of repair, and yet the gaoler lives distant. I once found the prisoners chained two or three together. Their provision was put down to them through a hole (9 inches by 8) in the floor of the room above (used as a chapel); and those who served them there often caught the fatal fever. At my first visit I found the keeper, his assistant, and all the prisoners but one sick of it, and heard that a few years before many prisoners had died of it, and the keeper and his wife in one night."

We need not go further. In each prison which Howard visited he found the same great evils existing, and the result of his tour was the collection of a mass of evidence, which, when brought before a committee of the House of Commons, excited the greatest astonishment. Some measures were thereafter enacted in 1774, which ensured the payment of prisoners' charges out of the county rates, and provided more effectually for the sanitary regulation of the gaols. These were the first steps towards the Prison Reform on which Howard had set his heart, and encouraged him to continue his well-directed labours. The services which he had rendered to humanity were too conspicuous to be overlooked; and the thanks of the House of Commons were unanimously voted.

With renewed activity, Howard took up his self-imposed mission, in the discharge of which he manifested a remarkable patience, and a power of endurance which is surprising, when we consider how much he had suffered from ill-health. For in Howard's time none of those facilities existed which now make English travel so delightful. The highways were lamentably ill-kept, and infested with robbers and mendicants; and the traveller's progress was slow and laborious. With an energy that never tired, Howard proceeded from town to town, and gaol to gaol, witnessing scenes of oppression and cruelty which shocked his generous heart. In the noisome dungeon of Morpeth he found three miserable creatures chained down, and deprived of everything but just so much food as would sustain their wretched life.

At Newcastle, the prisoners confined there during the assizes, men and women, were huddled together for four or five nights in a dirty damp dungeon of the old Castle, in which, as it was roofless, the water, in a wet season, stood some inches deep.

The county gaol at Chester was one of the worst in the kingdom. "Down eighteen steps is a small court," says Howard, "which was common to debtors and felons. It is lately divided; but the high close pales which separate the two courts, now so very small, deprive both debtors and felons of the benefit of fresh air: the former, in their free ward, the pope's kitchen; the latter in their day room, the king's kitchen. Both these are six steps below the court: near the former is the condemned room. Under the pope's kitchen is a dark room or passage: the descent to it is by twenty-one steps from the court. No window; not a breath of fresh air; only two apertures with grates in the ceiling into the pope's kitchen above. On one side of it are six cells (*stalls*), each about eight feet by three, with a barrack bedstead, and an aperture over the door about eight inches by four. In each of these are locked up at night sometimes three or four felons. They pitch these dungeons two or three times a year: when I was in one of them, I ordered the door to be shut, and my situation brought to mind what I had heard of the Black Hole at Calcutta."

A great and pleasing contrast was presented at Maidstone. There the gaoler received a salary, instead of making what profit he could from bad liquor sold to the prisoners. The fees of liberated criminals and of supposed culprits, when acquitted, were discharged from the county funds. A comparatively liberal allowance was made to felons, though Howard did not think it was judiciously apportioned; for each had a quart of beer and eighteen ounces of bread a day, while no provision of the same kind was made for the poor debtors. "The baker who serves the felons," says Howard, "sells thirteen loaves to the dozen, and debtors have amongst them every thirteenth loaf."

The work in which Howard was engaged made a large demand on his humanity. He incurred no slight risk in visiting these fever-haunted cells; and those for whom he exerted himself so bravely and patiently belonged to a class with which the public have little sympathy. It seemed, indeed, almost a matter of course that harsh treatment should be meted out to the felon, and it required all Howard's energy and perseverance to bring about an improved state of public feeling. It was not then accepted as a patent and obvious truism, that the very worst thing you can do with a criminal is to place him in circumstances and associations which absolutely preclude his amendment. As for the poor debtors, the world regarded them with indifference, if not with suspicion. They had failed, and the world has no pity for failure. Some, perhaps, had failed through unavoidable misfortunes; but the prosperous are not prone to make distinctions in their judgments. It is enough that you have not succeeded; and nothing is so hard to be forgiven as want of success. Thus Howard, in his benevolent crusade, met with little of that encouragement which is derived from the approval and support of your fellows, and by not a few he was regarded with a pity as contemptuous as that which a wise world lavished upon Don Quixote.

Even in the metropolis, the centre of the light and learning of the country, under the very eyes of the Government, and within sight of the educated, refined, and intelligent classes, the condition of the prisons was such that in our day it would provoke an explosion of popular indignation. Something, indeed, had been done in the way of amendment in 1729, as we have already stated, but how much more remained to be done the reader may infer from Howard's plain unvarnished description of the debtors' prison, the Fleet. It was divided, he says, into four floors, or, as they were called, *galleries*, besides the cellar floor, which was called Bartholomew Fair.

"On the first floor, the Hall Gallery, to which you ascend by eight steps, are a chapel, a tap-room, a coffee-room (lately made out of two rooms for debtors), a room for the turnkey, another for the watchman, and eighteen rooms for prisoners. Besides the coffee-room and tap-room, two of these eighteen rooms, and all the cellar-floor, except a lock-up room to confine the disorderly, and another room for the turnkey, were held by the tapster, who bought the remainder of the lease at *public auction*.

"On the first gallery are twenty-five rooms for prisoners. On the second twenty-seven: one of them, parting the staircase, is their committee room. At the other end, in a large room over the chapel, is a dirty billiard table kept by the prisoner who sleeps in that room. All the rooms I have mentioned are for master-side debtors. The weekly rent of those not held by the tapster is 1s. 3d., unfurnished. They fall to the prisoners in succession; thus, when a room becomes vacant, the first prisoner upon the list of such as have paid their entrance fees takes possession of it. When the prison was built the warder gave each prisoner his choice of a room according to his seniority as prisoner. If all of them be occupied, a new comer must hire of some tenant a part of his room, or shift as he can. Prisoners are excluded from all right of succession to the rooms held by the tapster, and let at the high rents aforesaid. The apartments for common-side debtors are only part of the right wing of the prison. Besides the cellar (which was intended for their kitchen, but occupied with lumber and shut up) there are four floors. On each floor is a room about 24 or 25 feet square, with a fire-place, and on the sides seven closets or cabins to sleep in. Such of those prisoners as swear in court that they are not worth £5, and cannot subsist without charity (of them there were at one of my visits sixteen, at other times not so many), have the donations which are sent to the prison, the begging-box, and the grate.

"I mentioned the billiard-table. They also play in the court at skittles, mississippi, fives, tennis, etc.: and not only the prisoners, but I saw among them several butchers, and others from the market, who are admitted here as at any other public house. The same may be seen in many other prisons, where the gaoler keeps or lets the tap.

"Besides the inconvenience of this to prisoners, the frequenting a prison lessens the dread of being confined in one. On Monday night there was a wine club; on Thursday night a beer club, each lasting usually till one or two in the morning. I need not say how much riot these occasion, and how the sober prisoners, and those that are sick, are annoyed by them.

"Seeing the prison crowded with women and children, I procured an accurate list of them, and found that where there were 243 prisoners, their wives (including women of an appellation not so honourable) and children were 475."

Howard's statement is fully borne out by contemporary evidence. A few years prior to his visit, a poem, entitled "The Humours of the Fleet," was published by a debtor named Dance, the son of the once-famous architect of Guy's Hospital. In its rude ryhmes the author describes the various inmates of this "poor but merry place," and the pastimes in which they find amusement; some playing at rackets in the court, others at whist, billiards, or backgammon indoors; while—

> "Some, of low taste, ring hand-bells, direful noise!
> And interrupt their fellows' harmless joys:
> Disputes more noisy now a quarrel breeds,
> And fools on both sides fall to loggerheads:
> Till, wearied with persuasive thumps and blows,
> They drink to friends, as if they ne'er were foes.'

No attempt seems to have been made by the authorities of the prison to preserve peace or decorum, but the prisoners themselves maintained some semblance of order, by a rough-and-ready kind of Lynch law, offenders being forcibly carried to the common yard, and punished beneath the pump.

> "Such the amusement of this merry jail,
> Which you'll not reach, if friends or money fail;
> For ere its threefold gates it will unfold,
> The destined captive must produce some gold.
> Four guineas at the least for different fees
> Completes your *Habeas*, and commands the keys;
> Which done and safely in, no more your bled.
> If you have cash, you'll find a friend and bed;—
> But that deficient, you'll but ill betide,—
> Lie in the hall, perhaps, or common-side."

As early as 1691 an effort had been made to reform the debtors' prisons of England by one Moses Pell, whose "Lives of the Oppressed" is, he says, "a small book as full of tragedies as pages; they are not acted," he continues, "in foreign nations, among Turks and infidels, papists and idolaters, but in this our own country, by our own countrymen and relations to each other; not acted, time out of mind, by men many thousands or hundred years agone, but now at this very day, by men once living in prosperity, wealth, and grandeur; they are such tragedies as no age or country can parallel." The contents of this little volume, which include reports from sixty-five debtors' prisons, fully bear out the truth of this announcement.

Fielding, the novelist, in his "Amelia," draws a vivid sketch of the condition of another great London goal. He represents an ignorant Justice as committing "Mr. Booth" to Bridewell, upon a charge of assulting a watchman, when he had interfered simply to prevent an outrage by two men of fortune, who bribed the constable to let them escape. He goes to prison; a number of people surround him in the yard, and demand "garnish," and the keeper explains to him that it is customary for every new prisoner to treat the inmates with "something to drink,"— a phrase which seems to have been the great shibboleth of eighteenth-century England. But the young man has no money, and the keeper looks on complacently while the vagabonds strip him of his clothes. All persons sent to Bridewell, whatever the character of their offences, were placed under exactly the same discipline. There, street robbers, who were certain to be hanged, were enjoying themselves over a pipe and a bottle of wine; the man without a shilling in his pocket had the prison allowance of a penny loaf and a jug of water. Felons and debtors were in a few cases separated; but, as a general rule, prison discipline in those "good old times" made little, if any, distinction between a burglar and a bankrupt.

In truth, a prison, as Howard's exertions proved conclusively, was a scene of shameless extortion and barbarous oppression. In such places as the Fleet, the King's Bench, and the Marshalsea, and in not a few of the provincial gaols, drunkenness, lewdness, and vice of every kind were permitted and even encouraged, for the gaolers, profited by their prevalence. Gambling was countenanced in all its ruinous varieties. A prison, instead of being a school of reform, was a den of iniquity. The duped there learned to dupe and cheat in his turn, the knave grew more skilful in his knavery; and each, when released, went forth a bolder and more unscrupulous proficient in the artifices of deception and the ways of crime.

Having inspected the most important prisons in England, the untiring philanthropist crossed the Welsh border. We find him at Flint late in June, 1774, and before the end of July he had visited Ruthin, Carnarvon, Dolgelly, Montgomery, Presteign, and Ludlow; returning by way of Worcester and Oxford to his quiet retreat at Cardington. He resumed his chivalrous labours on the 28th, the special object of inquiry in this, his second expedition, being the condition of the Bridewells or Houses of Correction and the town as distinguished from the county gaols. He found it as bad as the condition of the larger establishments. At Taunton nearly one-half of the prisoners had recently been swept away by the gaol fever,—a rough and expeditious mode of gaol delivery, not very creditable to the humanity of Christian England. At Marlborough, "all the rooms," he says, "are on the ground floor; and by a sewer within doors they are made very offensive, especially the men's night room; in which, when I was there first, I saw one dying on the floor of the gaol fever. The keeper told me that just before, one had died there, and another soon after his discharge. Upstairs are the rooms for those who pay. No court; no water accessible to prisoners; no straw. Allowance to petty offenders, none; felons two pennyworth of bread a day." The greater a man's delinquencies the larger seems to have been the allowance made him, and the more generous his treatment; so that, in effect, a premium was offered on crime.

The Bridewell at Hereford is "quite out of repair. Indeed, it is not only ruinous, but dangerous. In the day-room there was a large quantity of water from the roof. No fireplace; offensive sewers; no court; no water; no stated allowance; no employment; keeper's salary £10. Six prisoners, whom I saw there at my first visit, complained of being almost famished. They were sent hither from the assize a few days before to *hard labour* (as the sentence usually runs) for six months. The Justices had ordered the keeper to supply each of them daily with a twopenny loaf: but he had neglected them. They broke out soon after."

Passing over Bath, Hereford, Monmouth, Brecon, Cardigan, Haverfordwest, Carmarthen, Cambridge, Usk, Berkeley, Bristol, Taunton, Bridgewater, Exeter, Bodmin, Lostwithiel—names which indicate the great extent of country traversed by Howard—we pause at Plymouth, where the town gaol almost literally realized Milton's picture of Pandemonium as—

> "A dungeon horrible on all sides round;
> No light; but rather darkness visible

>   Served only to discover sights of woe,
>   Regions of sorrow, doleful shades, where peace
>   And rest can never dwell."

We transcribe Howard's description of it:—

"Two rooms for felons; and a large room above for debtors. One of the former, the *clink*, seventeen feet by eight, about five and a half feet high (so that its inmates could not stand upright), with a wicket in the door seven inches by five, to admit light and air. To this, as I was informed, those men who were confined near two months under sentence of transportation, *came by turns for breath*. The door *had not been opened for five weeks* when I with difficulty entered to see a pale inhabitant. He had been there ten weeks under sentence of transportation, and he said he had much rather have been hanged than confined in that noisome cell. No water; no sewer; no court. The gaolers live distant: they are the three serjeants at mace. Fees 15s. 10d., no table. Allowance to debtors, none but on application; felons, two pennyworth of bread a day. No straw."

Through Dorsetshire and Hampshire Howard passed into Sussex, and thence retired to Cardington, to enjoy another brief interval of repose, after traversing fifteen counties and painfully inspecting fifty prisons. We are told that a prophet is not honoured in his own country; but Howard's philanthropy, in its utter unselfishness, had moved the admiration of his neighbours, and many of them desired to see him sent to Parliament as their representative. Accordingly, he was induced (in 1755) to stand candidate, in conjunction with Mr. Whitbread, to represent the borough of Bedford. Two worthier or more competent representatives could not have been found; but, after a sharp and spirited contest, their two opponents were returned.' Mr. Whitbread and Mr. Howard petitioned the House to order an inquiry into the circumstances of the election; and, in the event, Mr. Whitbread and one of the sitting members were declared duly elected. We think, with Dr. Aikin, that Howard's failure on this occasion was a fortunate circumstance for the good cause he had espoused; for if he had obtained a seat in the Commons, his plans of prison reform would have necessarily been limited within a very great measure; and the collateral inquiries, which, to the signal gain of humanity, he afterwards adopted, could never have existed.

He now resumed his travels through the counties of York, Lancaster, and Warwick, visiting the Bridewells of Folkingham and Huntingdon on his way, and inspecting that of Aylesbury on his return. Between the 6th and 16th of December he explored many of the prisons in Essex, Suffolk, Norfolk, Cambridgeshire, and Hertfordshire, and closed the record of charity for 1774. Early in the following year he set off for Scotland; then crossed the Channel to Ireland; and having ascertained, by close personal inspection, the condition of almost every prison in the United Kingdom, he resolved upon giving to the world the results of his long and various experience, and to suggest what seemed to him necessary and essential reforms in the treatment of criminals. But when he began to prepare his notes, it occurred to him that much information useful to his purpose might be collected abroad, and, laying aside his papers, he resolved upon travelling over France, Flanders, Holland, and Belgium.

Leaving England in the middle of April, 1775, he speedily arrived at Paris, where he made an unsuccessful effort to penetrate into the interior of that fortress of tyranny, the Bastile, which, within a few years, was to throw open its gates at the summons of an infuriated populace and disgorge its victims. He gained admission, however, to the Grand Châtelet, the Petit Châtelet, and Fort l'Evêque. From France he crossed into Belgium, and thence proceeded to Holland. He was much surprised and highly delighted by the prisons of Brussels, in which the requirements of humanity had carefully been considered. The management and discipline of the *Maison de la Force*, at Ghent, surpassed, however, anything he had before seen, and earned his unqualified praise. At Bruges, Antwerp, and Rotterdam he was not less pleased.

At Delft he found some of his visions of prison reform anticipated. "There were nearly ninety," he says, "in the House of Correction; men and women quite separate, all neat and clean, and looking healthy. They told me their allowance was five stivers a day. All employed on a woollen manufacture; women spinning, carding, etc.; some weaving, from coarse to very fine cloth;

EARNEST LIVES.] HOWARD IN FRANCE. [*Face p. 292.*

their task, to earn thirty-five stivers a week. Some earn a small surplus, but they have only half of it. A burgomaster, to whom I mentioned that circumstance, said it was the truth. They do not put more than eight or ten men to work in one room; for where large numbers are together one idle person corrupts more; and there is not generally so much work done. Here, also, if a prisoner has behaved well for a few years, and given proofs of amendment, the magistrates begin to abridge the time for which he was sentenced. One whom I saw very cheerful told me the cause of his joy was that a year had lately been taken from his term."

Howard returned to England with his views on prison reform confirmed, and in some directions enlarged. He could not devote such prolonged and assiduous attention to the condition of prisoners without being led to reflect upon the causes which filled them with inmates. Foremost amongst these was the law of imprisonment for debt, which inflicted upon the unfortunate, the careless, and the fraudulent exactly the same punishment; and, when it was most needful that men should labour to retrieve the past, doomed them to compulsory idleness. Next came the Draconian character of the English statute-book, which might almost be said to have been written in blood. "Death" was inscribed upon every page. For the man who steals a purse, death; for the man who took his victim's life, death. Well might Howard speak of them as "sanguinary laws," and express his belief that their revisal and repeal would lead to the diminution of crime. How could men be expected to regard the sanctity of human life, when they saw the same value set on a man and a rabbit? When poor wretches, guilty of nothing more than some petty larceny, were hurried to "Tyburn tree," the spectator could not but feel an emotion of pity. The design of the law was counteracted, because, says Paley, it had a tendency which sinks men's abhorrence of the crime in their commiseration of the criminal. No axiom is more incontestable than that "crime thrives upon severe penalties."

The appalling frequency of death punishments for even trifling offences, and the large number of offenders who died of gaol fever, may be understood from the following table, which is one of Howard's:—

	Sentenced to death.	Pardoned, transported, or died in gaol.	Executed.
Shoplifting, riot, and twelve other minor crimes	240	131	109
Defrauding creditors	3	—	3
Returning from transportation	31	9	22
Coining	11	1	10
Forgery	95	24	71
Horse-stealing	90	68	22
Highway robbery	362	111	251
Housebreaking	208	90	118
Murder	81	9	72
	1121	443	678

Notwithstanding the protest of Howard, very little was effected towards reform in our criminal laws until the subject was taken up by Sir Samuel Romilly in 1808, who, in that year, carried a Bill for the abolition of the punishment of death for privately stealing from the person to the value of five shillings. He continued his exertions, supported by Wilberforce and Buxton, for several years, and the work was afterwards taken up by Sir James Mackintosh and Brougham. In 1833, the movement had so far influenced public opinion, that a royal commission was appointed, and, in 1837, the commissioners recommended the remission of the death-penalty in twenty-one out of thirty-one cases in which it could still be exacted. The Government adopted the recommendation, and brought it before Parliament, when Mr. Ewart moved an amendment confining the penalty of death to deliberate murder only, but lost it by the narrow minority of *one*. In 1861, by the Criminal Law Consolidation Act, this object was attained; and capital punishment restricted to cases of treason and murder. Let it be remembered that, in this work of wisdom and mercy, John Howard was one of the first to put his hand to the plough. Howard, too, was one of the first to deprecate public executions, which, as Paley had already taught, had a direct tendency to harden and deprave the public feelings. Commenting upon the miserable scenes of bravado and ostentation which were enacted at Tyburn, he writes:—"An execution day is too much, with us, a day of riot and idleness; and it is found, by experience, that the minds of the populace are rather hardened by the spectacle than affected in any salutary manner."

Howard returned from the Continent, with a rare wealth of facts and experiences, in July 1775. After a short rest at Cardington, he resolved on a second tour throughout the length and breadth of England, in order to keep alive the growing feeling of public indignation, and afford relief to the victims of misfortune or oppression when suitable opportunities presented themselves. Leaving home on the 8th of November, he revisited the gaols of Huntingdon, Oakham, Leicester, Nottingham, Derby, and Stafford. Thence he continued his explorations in the counties of **Lancaster, Chester, Salop,** Montgomery, Radnor, Worcester, Hereford, **and Monmouth.** Afterwards we find him going from Gloucestershire, through Somersetshire and Devonshire, into Cornwall. From Launceston his noble activity hurried him back to Dorchester, in the prison of which he found an epidemic of small-pox raging. The first day of 1776 found him at Reading, and the 6th at Northampton, so little time did he lose in the course of his benevolent expeditions. And in succession, never growing disgusted or discouraged by the monotony of his unwelcome task, he visited the prisons at Daventry, Coventry, Chesterfield, Sheffield, and Thirsk. Thence he struck northward to Berwick-upon-Tweed, and crossed the breadth of England westward to merry Carlisle; after which he passed through Appleby and Kendal, Wakefield, Gainsborough, and Spalding, Wisbeach, Ipswich, Woodbridge, and Beccles, visiting the prison in each town.

On his way southward he took a day or two's rest at Cardington, and, starting again on the 14th of February, traversed the shires of Hereford, Kent, Sussex, Hants, and Dorset, before he made his way to the Metropolis. There he carefully inspected Newgate, the Bridewell, the Savoy, and other places of ill repute, before embarking on a second continental journey, which occupied the months of June, July, and August. He observed at Geneva an enlightened system of prison management in operation. "Felons," he says, "have each a room to themselves, that they may not," said the keeper, "tutor one another." None were in irons: they were kept in rooms more or less strong and lightsome, according to the crimes they were charged with. But the prisons are in general very strong. "The rooms are numbered, and the keys marked with the same numbers. In most of them a German stove. The common allowance sixpence a day."

In Holland, he says, the Government " do not transport convicts, but men are put to labour in the rasp houses, and women to proper work in the spin-houses, upon this professed maxim, *Make them diligent and they will be honest.* The rasping logwood, which was formerly the principal work done by the male convicts, is now in many places performed at the mills much cheaper, and the Dutch, finding woollen manufactures more profitable, have lately set up several of them in those Houses of Correction. In some, the work of the healthy prisoners does not only support them, but they have a little extra time to earn somewhat for their better living in prison, or for their benefit afterwards. Great care is taken to give them moral and religious instruction, and to reform their manners, for their own and the public good. The *Chaplain* (such there is in every House of Correction) does not only perform public worship, but privately instructs the prisoners, catechizes them every week, and I am well informed that many come out sober and honest."

Howard's reflections upon what he had seen abroad are well worth quoting, in illustration of the calm judgment and strong common sense which were his characteristic mental gifts.

"When I formerly made the tour of Europe," he says, "for the benefit of my health, which I did some years ago, I seldom had occasion to envy foreigners anything, either as it respected their situation, religion, manners, or government. In my late journeys to view their prisons, I was sometimes put to the blush for my native country. The reader will scarcely feel, from my narration, the same emotions of shame and regret as the comparisons excited in me on beholding the difference with my own eyes; but, from the account I have given him of foreign prisons, he may judge whether a desire of reforming our own be visionary: whether idleness, debauchery, disease, and famine be the necessary, unavoidable attendants of a prison, or only connected with it in our ideas, for want of a more perfect knowledge and more enlarged views. I hope, too, that he will do me the justice to think that neither an indiscriminate admiration of everything foreign, nor a fondness of censuring everything at home, has influenced me to adopt the language of a panegyrist in this part of my work, or that of a complainant in the rest. Where I have commended, I have mentioned my reasons for so doing; and I have dwelt, perhaps, more minutely upon the management of foreign prisons because it was more agreeable to me to praise than to condemn. Another motive that induced me to be very particular in my account of foreign Houses of Correction, was to counteract a prevailing opinion among us, that compelling prisoners to work, especially in public, is inconsistent with the principles of English liberty; which, with a strange absurdity, taking away the lives of numbers of our countrymen, either by the hands of the executioner, or by diseases which are almost inevitably the result of long confinement in our close and damp prisons, seems to be little regarded. Of such force is custom and prejudice in silencing the voice of good sense and humanity! I have only to add that, fully sensible of the imperfections which must attend the cursory survey of a traveller, it was my study to remedy that defect by a constant attention to the one object of my pursuit alone, during the whole of my two last journeys abroad."

After another tour through a considerable portion of England, Howard betook himself, early in 1777, to Warrington, where his friend Dr. Aikin, a physician and a litterateur,—joint author with his sister, Mrs. Barbauld, of the once-famous "Evenings at Home,"—resided. He desired his assistance in preparing for the press the materials he had so laboriously and conscientiously collected. At Warrington he remained during the whole time his book was in the printer's hands. His mode of living at this time might have shamed many an anchorite. He rose at two, and devoted five hours to the revision of his proof-sheets. At seven he dressed, finished breakfast by eight, betook himself immediately to the printing-office, where he remained for several hours. Leaving with the workmen at one, he generally took a stroll in the outskirts of the town, having first stored his pocket with bread and dried fruit, which, with a glass of cold water, formed his dinner-fare. The evening he spent with Dr. Aikin, or some other friend, and returning to his lodgings, refreshed himself with a little tea or coffee, and retired to rest.

The book so conscientiously prepared was at length finished; and, with a dedication to the House of Commons, was published in the month of April. Notwithstanding Dr. Aikin's labours of revision, it exhibits little literary skill, but is a plain straightforward record of Howard's actual experiences,—a description of what he had seen and verified,—chiefly remarkable, apart from the philanthropic bearings of its subject, for the extreme care with which all the details are presented. The reader feels that every statement is authentic; that there is no exaggeration; and perhaps the thought crosses his mind that, in the hands of a practised writer, the story might easily have been told in such a way as to have lighted a flame of indignation from one end of England to the other. But Howard deliberately sets aside his many opportunities for sensational effects; he appeals to the judgment, and not the imagination; his case is so strong, that he thinks it unnecessary to heighten it by any rhetorical graces, if such he had had at his command.

Howard's book was not without result. Its exposures attracted the attention of the legislature, and some improvements were at once introduced into the administration of our prisons, though not that thorough reform which Howard had proved to be necessary. Feeling that the mind of the public must still be directed to the subject, he set out in April 1778 on another continental tour. At Amsterdam he met with an accident, which disabled him for several weeks; but as soon as he was declared convalescent, he resumed his mission of charity. For the works of art and the memorials of antiquity which "renowned" many of the cities he visited, the single-minded philanthropist seems to have had no eyes; all his thoughts centred in the prisons and Bridewells, in which crime and misfortune found an asylum or a place of punishment. Through Holland he passed into Germany, which was then disturbed with rumours of war between the Emperor and the King of Prussia. He visited Berlin, and the famous fortress-prisons of Spandau, Prague, and Vienna. In the great prison of the Austrian capital, La Maison de Bourreau, he saw an affecting sight. "There are," he says, "many dungeons. As usual, I inquired whether they had any putrid fever, and was answered in the negative. But, in one of the dark dungeons down twenty-five steps, I thought I had found a prisoner with the gaol fever. He was loaded with heavy irons, and chained to the wall; anguish and misery appeared with clotted tears on his face. He was not capable of speaking to me, but on examining his breast and feet for *petechiæ*, or spots, and finding he had a strong intermitting pulse, I was convinced that he was not ill of that disorder. A prisoner in an opposite cell told me that the poor creature had desired him to call out for assistance, and he had done it, but was not heard."

This incident has been introduced by the amiable versifier, Hayley, whom our forefathers elevated into a poet, in his curious " Ode to Howard :"

> " When, in the dungeon's loathsome shade,
> The speechless captive clanks his chain,
> With heartless hope to raise that aid,—
> His feeble cries have called in vain ;
> Thine eye his dumb complaint explores ;
> Thy voice his parting breath restores ;
> Thy cares his ghastly visage clear
> From death's chill dew, with many a clotted tear,
> And to his thankful soul returning life endear." *

---

* The finest compliment ever paid to Howard was paid by Burke in his speech at the Bristol election in 1780 :—" I cannot name this gentleman," he says, " without remarking that his labours and writings have done much to open the eyes and hearts of mankind. He has visited all Europe, not to survey the sumptuousness of palaces, or the stateliness of temples ; not to make accurate measurements of the remains of ancient grandeur, nor to form a scale of the curiosities of modern art ; not to collect medals, or to collate manuscripts ; but to dive into the depths of dungeons ; to plunge into the infections of hospitals ; to survey the mansions of sorrow and pain ; and to take the gauge and dimensions of misery, depression, and contempt ; to remember the forgotten, to attend to the neglected, to visit the forsaken, and compare and collate the distresses of all men in all countries. His plan is original, and it is as full of genius as it is of humanity. It was a voyage of discovery ; a circumnavigation of charity. Already the benefit of his labour is felt more or less in every country. I hope he will anticipate his final reward, by seeing all its effects fully realized in his own. He will receive, not by retail, but in gross, the reward of those who visit the prisoner ; and he has so forestalled and monopolised this branch of charity, that there will be, I trust, little room to assist by such acts of benevolence hereafter."

In this anticipation Burke was sadly mistaken. That Howard's exertions effected a considerable reform is undoubtedly true, and his is the glory of having made the subject one of general and permanent interest. But the buses in our debtors' prisons continued down to their abolition in 1844, as Dickens has shown in his " Pickwick Papers ; " while the reader of Charles Reade's " Never too Late to Mend," which was based upon parliamentary

At Vienna Howard dined with Sir R. Murray Keith, the English ambassador. The conversation turned upon the torture, when a German gentleman who was present observed that the glory of abolishing it in his own dominions belonged to the Emperor. "Pardon me," replied Howard, boldly; "his Imperial Majesty has abolished one kind of torture only to establish in its place another more cruel; for the torture which he abolished lasted, at the most, but a few hours, while that which he has appointed lasts many weeks, nay, sometimes years. The poor wretches are plunged into a noisome dungeon as bad as the Black Hole at Calcutta, from which they are taken out only if they confess what is laid to their charge." "Hush!" said the ambassador, "your words will be reported to His Majesty." "What!" replied he, "shall my tongue be tied from speaking truth by any king or emperor in the world? I repeat what I asserted, and maintain its veracity." A profound silence ensued; but everyone present, we are assured, admired the courageous plain speaking of "the man of humanity."

---

papers, knows that our criminals were subjected to gross tyranny and cruel oppression even to a very recent date.

A poet of a very different calibre to Hayley—the poet of "The Task"—celebrates Howard in his poem on "Charity—"

> "I fear the shame
> (Charity chosen as my theme and aim),
> I must incur, forgetting Howard's name.
> Blest with all wealth can give thee, to resign,
> Joys doubly sweet to feelings quick as thine;
> To quit the bliss that rural scenes bestow,
> To seek a nobler amidst scenes of woe;
> To traverse seas, range kingdoms, and bring home
> Not the proud monuments of Greece or Rome,
> But knowledge, such as only dungeons teach,
> And only sympathy like thine could reach;
> That grief, sequestered from the public stage,
> Might smooth her features and enjoy her cage;—
> Speaks a divine ambition, and a zeal
> The boldest patriots might be proud to feel.
> Oh that the voice of clamour and debate,
> That pleads for peace till it disturbs the state,
> Were hushed in favour of thy generous plea,
> The poor thy clients, and Heaven's smile thy fee

Proceeding into Italy, Howard visited the celebrated *Carceri*, or dungeons, of Venice. There were between three and four hundred prisoners, many of them confined for life in these dark and loathsome cells. He asked some who had been imprisoned for years whether they would prefer the galleys with all their horrors, and was answered eagerly in the affirmative, because the galley-slaves enjoyed *light* and *air*. The *Carceri* were connected by the famous *Ponte dei Sospèrè*, or Bridge of Sighs, with the prisons of the *Sotto Piombi*, *i.e.*, "under the leads," situated at the top of the Ducal Palace. Here, from 1820 to 1830, was confined the Venetian Tyrtæus, the patriotic poet Silvio Pellico, who, in his book, *Le Mie Prigione*, has revealed the secrets of his prison-place. They are terrible enough, those dark, stifling, miserable cells: but far more appalling are the *Pozzi*, or dungeons, in the lower stories, which can be reached only by obscure and intricate passages. The lowermost tier are dark as Erebus, dark with a darkness which can almost be felt; so that one wonders if the mind exposed to their unutterable horror could long retain its balance. Each is square, with a kind of slab to serve for the prisoner's bed; and here, in a swampy cell, the walls of which dripped with water, the unhappy captive, innocent, perhaps, of every crime, except that of being unfortunate,—ignorant, very often, of what offence he was accused, was doomed to linger through the wretched years, until madness released him from the power of memory, and the bitterness of regret; or death mercifully took him to its welcome repose. The modern apologists of the Venetian oligarchy pretend that the poor wretches doomed to these awful dungeons were all abandoned criminals; but even if their hypotheses were better founded than they can show them to have been, what shall we think of the lenity of a government which inflicted even on the vilest the torture of a slow and gradual death!

From Venice Howard went to Florence, passing through Padua, Ferarra, and Bologna; thence to Leghorn and Loretto, and next arrived at Rome, where the condition of the prisons did no credit to the Papal Government. He says:—

"There are eighteen strong rooms for the *men*, which are close and offensive; each of them having but one window for admitting light and air. These rooms are never opened without an order from the governor of the city. There were thirty-six prisoners. They are not permitted to go out of their rooms at any time but for examination. Some, having been confined there many years, appeared with pale sickly countenances, but none were in irons. There is a chamber for distracted prisoners, in which were seven miserable objects. I wish I could say I had seen no torture chamber.

"Besides the torture-chamber, at one corner of this building were placed a pulley and rope, by which malefactors, with their hands behind them, were pulled up; and, after being suspended for some time, were inhumanly let down part of the way, when, by a sudden jerk, their arms were dislocated.

"The State prisoners are confined in the Castle of San Angelo, the ancient *Mausoleum Hadriani*."

As to the galleys at Civita Vecchia, Howard writes:—

"The slaves condemned to them are confined for different times, according to the nature of their crimes: but the shortest time is three years, for vagabonds, who are generally employed on board the pontoons in clearing the harbour. For theft, the term is never under seven years. Persons convicted of forgery are always confined for life; and if found guilty of forging bank-notes or any instruments by which large sums have been lost, they are punished with an iron glove. Prisoners for life are chained two and two together" [a circumstance of which Bulwer Lytton has made effective use in his novel of "Lucretia"]; "those for *limited terms* have all a single chain, and, at their first arrival, of the same weight; but when they have no more than one or two years to serve, they have only a ring round their leg, which is lessened as the end of their time approaches. For escapes, they are obliged to finish their first condemnation, and then receive a fresh one for the same time as the former; but if the first was for life, the same is renewed, and they receive from a hundred to two hundred lashes a day for three days after their arrival."*

---

* No improvement had taken place in the Roman prison system when Fowell Buxton visited the Holy City half a century later. Writing of the prison of Civita Vecchia, he says:—"It is an old and strong fortress close by the sea, containing 1,364 desperate-looking criminals, all for the most aggravated offences,"—some rendered more brutal, if possible, by their enforced intercourse and communication with one another. "We went, first, into a vaulted

After revisiting the prisons in Switzerland, Howard rapidly traversed Germany, and proceeded, by way of Frankfort, Cologne, and Aix-la-Chapelle, to Liège, which, in the annals of inhumanity, as recorded by our philanthropist, occupies an evilly conspicuous place. Once more we must let Howard speak for himself, and in his own simply expressive language describe the atrocities of its prison system.

"The two prisons at Liège," he says, "the *old* and the *new*, are on the ramparts. In two rooms of the *old* prison I saw six cages, made very strong with iron hoops, four of which were empty. These were dismal places of confinement, but I soon found worse, in descending deep below ground from the gaoler's apartments. I heard the moans of the miserable wretches in the dark dungeons. The sides and roof were all stone. In wet weather, water from the fosse gets into them, and has greatly damaged the floors. Each of them had two small apertures, one for admitting air, and the other with a shutter over it strongly bolted, for putting in food to the prisoners. One dungeon larger than the rest was appropriated to the sick. In looking into this with a candle I discovered a stove, and felt some surprise at this little escape of humanity from the men who constructed these cells.

---

room, with a low ceiling, as I measured it, thirty-one yards long, twenty-one broad. There was light, but obscure. A good deal of the room was taken up by the buttresses which supported the arches. The noise on our entrance was such as may be imagined at the entrance of hell itself. All were chained most heavily, and fastened down. The murderers and desperate bandits are fixed to that spot for the rest of their lives; they are chained to a ring fastened to the end of the platform, on which they lie side by side, but they can move the length of their chain on a narrow gangway. Of this class, there were upwards of 700 in the prison; some of them famed for a multitude of murders; many, we are told, had committed six or seven; and indeed, they were a ghastly crew,—haggard, ferocious, reckless assassins. I do not think that the attendant gaoler very much liked our being there. A sergeant, in uniform, was ordered to keep close by me; and I observed that he kept his hand upon his sword, as he walked up the alley between the adjacent platforms.

"There was a fourth room at some distance, and our guide employed many expedients to divert us from going there. . . . This was worse than any of the others: the room lower, damper, darker, and the prisoners with, if possible, a more murderous look. . . . The mayor afterwards told us, that he, in his official capacity, knew that there was a murder every month among the prisoners. I

"The dungeons in the *new* prison are abodes of misery still more shocking; and confinement in them so overpowers human nature, as sometimes irrevocably to take away the senses. I heard the cries of the distracted as I went down to them. One woman, however, I saw, who (as I was told) had sustained this horrid confinement forty-seven years without becoming distracted. The cries of the sufferers in the torture-chamber may be heard by passengers without, and guards are placed to prevent them from stopping and listening. A physician and surgeon always attend when the torture is applied, and on a signal given by a bell, the gaoler brings in wine, vinegar, and water, to prevent the sufferers from expiring. 'The tender mercies of the wicked are cruel.' Thus, in the Spanish inquisition, the physician and surgeon attend to determine the utmost extremity of suffering without expiring under the torture."

At Antwerp, he writes, "there are two rooms for citizens; and upstairs there is a cage, about six feet and a half square, into which criminals are put before the torture. A criminal, while he suffers the torture, is clothed in a long shirt, has his eyes bound, and a physician and surgeon attend him, and when a confession is forced from him, and wine has been given him, he

spoke to a good many of them, and, with one exception, each said that he was condemned for murder or stabbing. I will tell you one short conversation:— 'What are you here for?' said I, to a heavy-looking fellow, lying on his back at the end of the room. He made no answer; but a prisoner near him, with the sharp features and dark complexion of an Italian, promptly said, 'He is here for stabbing' (giving a thrust with his hand to show how it was done). 'And why is he in this part of the prison?' 'Because he is incorrigible.' 'And what were you condemned for?' 'For murder.' 'And why placed here?' '*Sono incorrigibile*' (I am incorrigible). In short, this prison combines together, in excess, all the evils of which prisons are capable. It is, as the mayor said, a sink of all the iniquity of the State. The Capuchins certainly preach them a sermon on the Sunday, and afford them an opportunity of confession; of which, if the prisoners avail themselves, the priests must have enough to do. The sight of it has kindled in my mind a very strong desire, that the old Prison Discipline Society should make a great effort, and visit all the prisons of the world. I had hoped that sound principles of prison discipline had spread themselves more widely, but I now fear that there are places, and many of them, in the world, in which it is horrible that human beings should live, and still more horrible that they should die."—*Memoirs of Sir Thomas Fowell Buxton*, pp. 496, 497.

is required to sign his confession; and about forty-eight hours afterwards he is executed.

"In a small dungeon is a stone seat, like some I have seen in old prison towers, in which it is said that formerly prisoners were *suffocated by brimstone* when their families wished to avoid the disgrace of a public execution. No person here remembers an instance of this kind, but about thirty years ago there was a *private* execution in the prison."

In the early part of 1779, Howard undertook another survey of the prisons in Cornwall, Somerset, and Devon. A fortnight's rest at Cardington, and then he was off to Oxfordshire and Buckinghamshire. With brief intervals of rest, the spring was occupied in visiting the prisons in various parts of England; June and July were devoted to Ireland and Scotland; and the rest of the year this ubiquitous man, who almost emulated the Wandering Jew in activity, spent in North Wales, in the eastern counties, and in Bedfordshire. The notes collected during these and other expeditions, which in all had covered eleven thousand miles, he prepared for the press, and proceeded to Warrington to print them, as before, with Dr. Aikin's assistance. Under the title of "An Appendix to the State of Prisons," and in the form of a quarto volume of 220 pp., he published them in the early part of 1780; and at the same time he gave to the world a pamphlet descriptive of the horrors of the Bastile, translated from the narrative of one who had experienced them.

Howard appears to have thought nothing done while anything remained undone. His wanderings had not touched the north of Europe, nor had the influence of his mission of charity extended thither. In May, 1781, he resolved to remedy this omission; crossed to Ostend, then proceeded to Bremen and Hamburg, and in July arrived at Copenhagen. In Denmark he found the whipping-post recognized as one of the institutions of the country, and ascertained that for some offences a curious punishment had been instituted, that of the Spanish mantle,—a kind of band, narrow at the top, which was placed over the delinquent's head and shoulders, reaching down to his knees. Both at Copenhagen and Stockholm he discovered that the prisons were in a very unsatisfactory state. Proceeding into Russia, he witnessed at St. Petersburg the infliction of the punishment of the knout.

"August 10th, 1781. I saw two criminals, a man and a woman, suffer the punishment of the knout. They were conducted from prison by about fifteen hussars and ten soldiers. When they arrived at the place of punishment, the hussars formed themselves into a ring round the whipping-post, the drum beat a minute or two, and then some prayers were read, the populace taking off their hats. The woman was taken first, and after being roughly stripped to the waist, her hands and feet were bound with cords to a post made for the purpose, a man standing before the post, and holding the cords to keep them tight. A servant attended the executioner, and both were stout men. The servant first marked his ground and struck the woman five times on the back. Every stroke seemed to penetrate deep into the flesh. But his master, thinking him too gentle, pushed him aside, took his place, and gave all the remaining strokes himself, which were evidently more severe. The woman received twenty-five, and the man sixty. I passed through the hussars, and counted the number as they were chalked on a board; both seemed but just alive, especially the man, who yet had strength enough to receive a small donation with some signs of gratitude. They were conducted back to prison in a little waggon. I saw the woman in a very weak condition some days after, but could not find the man any more."

The knout-whip was a formidable instrument; fixed to a wooden handle, one foot in length, were several thongs, about two feet long, twisted together; to the end of these was fastened a single tough thong of about eighteen inches, tapering towards a point, and capable of being changed by the executioner for a fresh one when too much softened by the victim's blood.

From St. Petersburg, Howard, though suffering from ague, hurried to Moscow. Thence he proceeded to Breslau, and from Breslau to Berlin, and from Berlin to Hanover. On his way to the latter city an incident occurred characteristic of Howard's John Bullism. He came to a very narrow part of the highway, where only one carriage could pass at a time; and, to prevent a collision, postilions entering at each end were required to blow their horns by way of notice. Howard's postilion obeyed the rule; but, after pushing forward a considerable distance, they met a courier, travelling on the king's business, who had coolly ignored it. The courier ordered Mr. Howard's postilion to turn back; but Mr. Howard remonstrated that he had complied with the regulations while the other had violated it, and, therefore, should insist on prosecuting his journey. Relying on an authority which, in Prussia, was supreme above rules and regulations, the courier indulged in high words and menaces, but in vain. As neither was disposed to yield, they sat still for a long time in their respective carriages; until the courier at length gave up the point to the imperturbable Englishman, who would on no account renounce his rights.

Our humane traveller again made acquaintance with the prisons of Holland and Flanders, and having accomplished a journey of 4,465 miles wholly in the cause of charity, returned to England towards the close of the year 1781.

Having spent his Christmas at Cardington, and made arrangements for the further education of his son, he began, on the 21st of January, 1782, his third general inspection of English prisons. It is unnecessary for us to follow his steps in this philanthropic journey. Afterwards he went to Scotland; then crossed to Ireland, where the University of Dublin honoured him with the complimentary degree of D.C.L.; returned through North Wales to Shrewsbury; thence to Birmingham; and onwards to London. He spent a few summer days at Cardington, and then struck into the south-western counties. Still unwearied, the philanthropist hastened away to Scotland, and re-inspected its principal gaols,—the second visit in the same year. Again he visited Ireland, North Wales, South Wales, Gloucestershire, Oxfordshire, Hampshire, and Bedfordshire. After a brief stay at Cardington he turned his face northward, and revisited the Yorkshire gaols. We find him, later on, in Staffordshire; towards the end of November, in Kent and Sussex; in December, in Gloucestershire, Oxfordshire, and Berkshire, closing the exertions of a year, during which he had travelled upwards of 8,000 miles, in London. Altogether apart from the noble motives which actuated him, and the benefits he conferred upon suffering humanity, one cannot but admire the dauntless courage and surpassing energy which sustained him during these extensive and prolonged journeys. If we bestow our praise on the traveller who accomplishes a voyage round the world for scientific objects, or to gratify his love of novelty, shall we not reserve some eulogium for him who, in the sweet name of Charity, undergoes such extraordinary exertions and carries out such laborious, continuous, and almost incredible expeditions?

On the 31st of January, 1783, Howard embarked at Falmouth in quest of "fresh fields and pastures new." As one of his biographers puts it, Charity had now conducted her "chosen servant" through all the European countries excepting Spain and Portugal. To the latter he had long since directed his course, but it was not to labour or to disperse relief in the sphere which had been determined; his progress therefore was arrested, and by the discipline of experience he learned to sympathize with the special objects he had been selected to relieve. Now his purpose is in accordance with that appointed, and shall therefore be accomplished. He goes as the almoner of charity to the prisoner and the captive, the messenger of mercy to the outcast.

From Lisbon, crossing the Spanish frontier, Howard travelled, by way of Badajoz and Toledo, to Madrid. At Valladolid he endeavoured to obtain admission to the prisons of the Inquisition, but while allowed to inspect the council chambers and offices, into the more secret recesses was not allowed to set his heretical feet. None but prisoners, he was told, passed their dreadful threshold. "I would willingly become one for a month," said Howard, "if the permission might be granted on that condition." Three years, he learned, was the shortest space for which any were consigned to the worse than sepulchral gloom of those awful chambers. He was assured, moreover, that their wretched inmates were beyond the reach of compassion. Piteous wails might be uttered within their walls, but no appeal disturbed the "deathlike stillness" around their doors.

His European tour, this year, included France, Holland, and Belgium, and was conducted with characteristic energy and alacrity. He returned to England on or about the 23rd of June. In a journey through Ireland he was accompanied by his son. About the middle of August he crossed over to Holyhead, and thence made his way to his estate at Cardington. It was at this period that his domestic peace was first clouded over by the discovery of his son's profligate habits. To wean him from them Howard sent him to Cambridge, entered him at St. John's College, and placed him under the special care of one of the Fellows.

A new mission of humanity was undertaken by the philanthropist—few have ever better deserved this exalted title!—in the course of 1785. He resolved to "confront death in its most frightful form," and, at the risk of his life, to avert from his fellows the scourge by which so many thousands had perished. In other words, he decided to enter upon a personal investigation of the means, if any, by which the progress of that terrible epidemic, significantly known as "the plague," might be averted; and, for that purpose, to visit the lazarettos of Europe.

The plague may be described as a singularly malignant epidemical fever, the seat of which appears to be the countries bordering upon the eastern extremity of the Mediterranean. In the 14th century we first hear of its introduction into England under the name of the Black Death. In the three following centuries it frequently visited Western Europe. In England its last appearance was in 1665, when it ravaged London with awful severity. In 1720 it swept away nearly half the population of Marseilles; but since 1790 it has been almost unknown in the western countries of Europe, and is now confined to Egypt, Syria, Greece, and Turkey. The exact character of the disease defies medical research. A subtle and mysterious poison is absorbed into the blood, the composition of which and the condition of the tissues it almost immediately alters. Few of those attacked by it recover. It is one of the most fatal as well as disgusting of the maladies which afflict mankind; and the extent of its ravages may be inferred from the number of victims who fell in London alone during the visitation of 1665:—in June, 590; in July, 4,129; in August, 20,046; in September, 26,230; in October, 14,373; in November, 3,449; in December, about 950.*

---

* In Professor's Wilson's "City of the Plague" occurs an impressive description of the outbreak of the pestilence:—

"Like a thunder-peal
Once more a rumour turned the city pale;
And the tongues of men, wild-staring on each other
Uttered with faltering voice one little word.

Armed with a list of queries, supplied by his medical friends, Drs. Aikin and Jebb, Howard sailed for Holland in November 1785. It was his object to begin his inquiries at Marseilles, but knowing how jealously the French watched over their Levantine commerce, he foresaw that to gain access to the lazaretto of that port would be a difficult task. He solicited, therefore, the good offices of the Foreign Secretary, Lord Carmarthen. At Utrecht he received a despatch informing him that his request was refused, and that he was prohibited from entering France at all. But Howard never abandoned a settled resolve; and considering that any report of lazarettos which omitted a description of that of Marseilles would resemble the play of "Hamlet" without Hamlet, he determined on making a personal inspection, or sacrificing himself in the attempt. Proceeding by way of Dort, Antwerp, and Brussels, he reached Paris in a few days. To avoid detection he retired to an obscure hotel, having taken his place by the Lyons diligence which started on the following morning. At an early hour he went to bed, and about midnight, was aroused by a violent knocking. On throwing open the door, a servant entered, with a

> 'The plague!' Then many heard within their dreams
> At dead of night a voice foreboding woe,
> And rose up in their terror, and forsook
> Homes, in the haunted darkness of despair
> No more endurable. As thunder quails
> Th' inferior creatures of the air and earth,
> So cowed the Plague at once all human souls,
> And the brave man beside the natural coward
> Walked trembling. On the restless multitude,
> Thoughtlessly toiling through a busy life,
> Nor hearing in the tumult of their souls
> The ordinary language of decay,
> A voice came down that made itself be heard,
> And they started from delusion when the touch
> Of Death's benumbing fingers suddenly
> Swept off whole crowded streets into the grave.
> Then rose a direful struggle with the Pest!
> . . . . . . Then the Plague
> Stormed, raging like a barbarous conqueror;
> And hopeless to find mercy, every one
> Fell on his face, and all who rose again
> Crouched to the earth in suppliant agony."
>
> (Pp. 145—147.)

candle in each hand, preceding a man in black clothes, with a sword at his side, who in a voice of authority demanded if his name were not Howard. "Yes; and what of that?" he replied. "Did you come to Paris in the Brussels diligence, accompanied by a man in a black wig?" He paid no attention to such trifles, was the answer; and the intruder then withdrew. Howard was not again disturbed, and at the appointed hour set off for Lyons, travelling in the character of an English physician. From Lyons he made his way to Marseilles, where his friend, the Rev. Mr. Durrand, at once said to him,—"Mr. Howard, I have always been glad to see you until now. Leave France as fast as you can; I know they are searching for you in all directions." Here, too, he ascertained that the man in a black wig, who travelled with him to Paris, had been sent as a spy by the French ambassador at the Hague, and that his not being arrested was due to the accidental circumstance that the prefect had left Paris for the day, and had given orders that no arrests should be made until his return. The timorous advice of his friend Howard rejected, and he contrived to gain admission to the lazaretto, and all the particulars he required.

Hearing of an interesting prisoner in the galleys at Toulon, Howard set off to visit him. He says:—"Protestants are not compelled to attend mass. The last person who was confined for his religion was released about eight years ago. There is but one slave here who now professes himself a Protestant, and his name is François Condé. He has been confined in the galleys forty-two years, for being concerned with some boys in a quarrel with a gentleman (who lost his gold-headed cane) in a private house in Paris. The boys were apprehended, and this Condé, though only fourteen years of age, and lame of one arm, was condemned to the galleys for *life*. After four or five years he procured a Bible and learned by himself to read; and becoming, through close application to the Scriptures, convinced that his religion was *anti-Christian*, he publicly renounced it, and declared and defended his sentiments. Ever since he has continued a steady Protestant, humble and modest, with a character irreproachable and exemplary, respected and esteemed by his officers and fellow-prisoners. I brought away with me some musical pipes of his turning and tuning. He was in the galley appropriated to the infirm and aged; and these, besides the usual allowance of bread, have an additional allowance from the king of nine sous a day."

Howard next visited the prisons and hospitals at Nice, Genoa, and Leghorn, at Pisa and Florence. At Rome the Pope honoured him with an interview, and on taking leave, clasped his hand, uttering the well-known words:—"I know you Englishmen do not value these things, but the blessing of an old man can do you no harm."

From Malta Howard addressed a letter to a friend, which may be quoted as a specimen of the plain and practical style of his correspondence:—

"I have paid two visits to the Grand Master [of the Knights of Malta]. Every place is flung open to me. He has sent me what is thought a great present, a pound of nice butter, as we are here all burnt up, yet peas and beans in plenty; melons ripe, roses and flowers in abundance; but at night tormented with millions of fleas, gnats, etc. . . . One effect I find during my visits to the lazarettos, viz., a heavy headache, a pain across my forehead, but it has always quite left me in one hour after I have come from these places. As I am quite alone, I have need to summon all my courage and resolution. You will say it is a great design, and so liable to a fatal miscarriage. I must adopt the motto of a Maltese baron, *Non nisi per ardua*. I will not think my friend is amongst the many who treat every new attempt as wild and chimerical, and as was first said of my former attempt, that it would produce no real or lasting advantage; but I persevere 'through good report and evil report.' I know I run the greatest risk of my life. Permit me to declare the sense of my mind in the expressive words of Dr. Doddridge—'I have no hope in what I have been or done.' Yet there is a hope set before me. In Him, the Lord Jesus Christ, I trust. In Him I have strong consolation. These days (Sundays) I go little out. I have the notes of several sermons and my Bible with me. It is a pain to see in almost all the churches, in large gold letters, 'Indulgentia Plenaria,' and before the crucifixes, on canvas or stone, in the street, with *Qui elucidant me vitam eternqm habebunt;* and poor creatures, starved, and almost naked, putting into the box grains, five of which make one halfpenny.

"I am, I bless God, pretty well; calm, steady spirits. All see at the inns, etc., that I leave the mode of travelling, and try to oblige me, but I inflexibly keep to my mode of living, with regimen or low diet. The physicians in Turkey, I hear, are very attentive at the time the plague is there.

"In many instances, God has disappointed my fears, and exceeded my hopes.

"Remember me to any of our friends. A share in your serious moments. Thanks for kindnesses shown to mind and body."

By way of Zante and Smyrna, Howard proceeded to Constantinople, where, with the courage of Christian benevolence, he penetrated into hospitals in which the plague raged so destructively that even the physicians durst not enter them. The report of his medical skill had reached one of the highest officials of the Porte, whose daughter was afflicted with a disease which had baffled the best Turkish doctors. He prescribed and restored her; and if the grateful father then looked upon her benefactor with wonder, his refusal to accept of a purse of 2000 sequins (about £2,000) as compensation, and his determination to take nothing more than a dish of grapes from his garden, did not lessen his admiration.

From Constantinople to Scio, and thence to Smyrna, was Howard's next course. At Smyrna he embarked on board a vessel bound for Venice. Having touched at the Morea for water, they had no sooner put to sea again than they were attacked by a Tunisian privateer. A sharp engagement took place, in which the Moors, as the stronger party, seemed likely to prevail. There was a large cannon on board; it was loaded to the muzzle with spikes, nails, and other missiles, pointed by Howard; and just as the corsair was about to close, was discharged with such effect that she sheered off, and put about.

On his arrival at Venice, he was detained in the lazaretto for upwards of forty days, his ship having arrived from a plague-stricken port. While in this "city of the sea," once so proudly entitled "The Queen of the Adriatic," he gained a good deal of information in reference to its despotic form of government, and he has put on record two very striking anecdotes.

A German merchant who had visited Venice on business

supped every night at a small inn, in company with a few other persons. One evening an officer of the State inquisition called upon him, ordered him to follow, and to deliver up his trunk, after having put his seal upon it. The merchant, to his inquiries into the meaning of so strange a procedure, received no reply, except that the officer put his hand to his lips as a signal for silence. He then muffled his head in a cloak, and guided him through different streets to a low gateway, through which he was ordered to pass; and, stooping down, he was conducted through various subterranean passages to a small, dark apartment, in which he was confined all night. The next day he was ushered into a larger chamber hung with black, having a single wax-light and a crucifix on its mantelpiece. After remaining for two days in absolute solitude, he suddenly saw a curtain drawn, and heard a voice questioning him concerning his name, his business, his companions, and particularly whether he had not, on a certain day, been in the society of certain individuals, and heard an Abbé, who was also named, make use of expressions which were accurately repeated. At last he was asked whether he should know the Abbé if he saw him, and on his replying in the affirmative, a long curtain was drawn aside, and there was his body dangling on a gibbet! After this melodramatic business, wholly unworthy of a powerful government, the German merchant was dismissed.

Again: a senator of the republic was called up from his bed one night by an officer of the inquisition, and commanded to follow him. Obeying the summons, he found a gondola in waiting near his door, and was rowed out of the harbour to a point where another gondola was fastened to a post. Upon this he was ordered to embark; and, the door being open, was led into the cabin, where a dead body with a rope round its neck was shown him, and he was asked if he knew it. Shaking in every limb, he answered that he did. He was then carried back to his house, and nothing more was ever said to him upon the subject. The body he had seen was that of his children's tutor, who had been secretly removed from his house that very night and strangled. The senator, delighted with this young man's conversation, was accustomed to treat him with much familiarity, and in his unguarded moments communicated to him some political matters of no great importance, which he, thoughtlessly, repeated to others. For this imprudence he paid with his life, while his patron's indiscretion was punished with a significant warning.

Howard relates these stories, not upon his own authority, but upon that of his friends. They have so romantic an air about them that one is disposed to relegate them to the world of fiction.

Crossing the Adriatic to Trieste, Howard hurried on to Vienna, where he was admitted to an interview with the emperor. Without pausing for rest or refreshment he traversed 500 miles, on his way into Holland; and from Amsterdam sailed for London in the early days of February, 1787.

In the following month he resumed his inspection of the London prisons, and afterwards of those of Guildford and Kingston. On the 28th of May, as if rest were to him an impossibility and a curse, he crossed to Dublin, where he found that no improvements had been effected in its prison-system. The prisons of Scotland were next visited; and the remainder of the year was spent in desultory expeditions. Opposite Stafford gaol were three ale-houses, which led Howard to make a remark in his "Second Book on Prisons," which, *mutatis mutandis*, might be applied to our own times:—

"The great and increasing number of ale-houses that I observe in my tours through this kingdom I cannot but lament, as it is one great and obvious reason why our prisons are so crowded both with debtors and felons. Many magistrates are sensible of this evil, yet so dreadfully supine and timid as to grant fresh licences (often at the intercession of their interested clerks), in which their conduct is highly culpable. It should be remembered that it is the spirit of our laws, and therefore the duty of magistrates, by every means to *prevent*, if possible, the commission of crimes."

For the sixth time Howard visited Ireland, on his mission of charity, in 1788. Afterwards the London prisons were again inspected, with the mortifying result that he could find no improvement in their condition. It cannot, indeed, be said of Howard that he initiated any decided or comprehensive reform, or was the originator of any memorable legislative enactment. Perhaps his signal merit was, that he kindled in the heart of the English nation a spirit of humanity, a sentiment of compassion and benevolence, to which it had hitherto been a stranger. His example was so noble and so singular that it drew the general attention, and created in the minds of many a desire to imitate it, a longing to walk in the path of charity which he had so patiently and bravely trod. Such a man becomes, unconsciously to himself, a leader, a pioneer, in whose steps thousands and ten thousands follow. He is as a light shining in a dark place, the rays of which are reflected in every direction. Who could behold this man so undauntedly pursuing his philanthropic career, month after month, and year after year,—seeking the squalidest and most unwholesome dens, breathing the same atmosphere as the most obdurate felons, travelling from land to land, and town to town, without feeling that he presented a new, a striking, and a glorious comment on that law of charity which the Christian religion so strongly enforces?

His "Account of the Principal Lazarettos in Europe" appeared in February 1789. It offers the same characteristics of accuracy and plainness and earnestness as his former work. In it he announced his intention of "revisiting Russia, Turkey, and some other countries, and extending his tour in the East." He added: "I am not insensible of the dangers that must attend such a journey. Trusting, however, in the protection of that kind Providence which has hitherto preserved me, I calmly and cheerfully commit myself to the disposal of unerring wisdom. Should it please God to cut off my life in the prosecution of this design, let not my conduct be uncandidly imputed to rashness or enthusiasm, but to a serious, deliberate conviction that I am pursuing the path of duty; and to a sincere desire of being made an instrument of more extensive usefulness to my fellow-creatures than could be expected in the narrower circle of a retired life.

On this, his last journey, the issue of which he seems to have anticipated, Howard set out early in July, 1789. From Amsterdam, which he reached on the 7th, he proceeded to Utrecht, entered Germany by way of Osnaburgh; traversed Hanover and Brunswick; visited Berlin; and through Memel and Mittau, entered the empire of Russia at Riga. Next we find him at St. Petersburg. He visited Cronstadt on the 9th of September, and afterwards struck inland to Moscow, the "holy city." Hearing painful accounts of the Russian military hospitals, and hopeful of alleviating the wretched condition of their inmates, he accomplished the long and dreary journey to Crementschuok, on the banks of the Dnieper, and thence to Cherson, in Little Tartary. While engaged there in his unremitting labours of benevolence, and in daily attendance upon the sick, he was solicited to visit a young lady, residing about sixteen miles from the town, who had been attacked with an infectious fever. He complied, ordered the appropriate remedies, and paid her another visit on an occasion when the rain fell heavily and the cold was intense, and as no vehicle could be obtained, he was compelled to ride the whole distance on an old dray-horse. A day or two afterwards he himself was attacked with the fever, and to dispel it, had recourse to that powerful but dangerous remedy known as James's powder. His illness increased rapidly. A Russian physician was called in, but his skill proved unavailing. Confronting his end with the calm courage of a Christian, this martyr to charity passed away in peace at eight o'clock in the morning of January 20th, 1790, aged sixty-four.

In the record of his noble work, his alms, and all his good endeavours, he being dead yet speaketh; and his memory is still green among us.

The fame of the warrior survives through many generations; that of the poet, as the minds of men daily become more fitted to receive his teaching, will probably expand and deepen; the artist and the musician are remembered by their works; but the philanthropist, however great and splendid his effort and his self-denial, must not expect that his name will be cherished by posterity. Little of what he does is seen by the public eye; and if it were, it would hardly attract the public attention, because it is necessarily unpretentious and unadorned. Therefore, we can well believe that many readers will fail to identify the noble woman to whom Crabbe refers in the following lines :—

> " One I beheld, a wife, a mother, go
> To gloomy scenes of wickedness and woe;
> She sought her way through all things vile and base,
> And made a prison a religious place :

> Fighting her way—the way that angels fight
> With powers of darkness—to let in the light . . .
> The look of scorn, the scowl, the insulting leer
> Of shame, all fixed on her who ventures here;
> Yet all she braved; she kept her steadfast eye
> On the dear cause, and brushed the baseness by."

The reference here is to Mrs. Elizabeth Fry, the heroine of Prison Reform, the "motive" of whose life of high benevolence and Christian duty we find in the beautiful words she uttered on her death-bed:—

"I can say one thing: since my heart was touched at the age of seventeen, I believe I have never awakened from sleep, in sickness or in health, by day or by night, without my first waking thought being how best I might serve the Lord."

Elizabeth Fry was the third daughter of John Gurney, of Earlham, Quaker, and of his wife Catherine, a lineal descendant of the Quaker Apologist, Robert Barclay. She was born at Norwich, on the 21st of May, 1780.

As a child she was very quiet and timid; in look and manner gentle, and as her mother said, "dove-like," but with a large fund of tenacious pride at heart. It was easier to bend than break her; she would give way to a kind word, but if she silently rebelled against a command, nothing could constrain her into obedience. She was distinguished beyond most children by her insight, tact, and resolve to think for herself; altogether an uncommon child, yet not one of any apparent ability, and so weak and physically ailing that she could not apply herself to study. She had, however, her refined pleasures; she was passionately fond of flowers, and a born "collector," delighting in accumulating little treasures of shells, butterflies, and other natural curiosities. Her religious feelings were very profound in childhood; and it was noticed that when her mother in the evening read the usual portion of Scripture and a Psalm, she would sit in a kind of rapt and solemn silence. For her mother, a very fair and amiable woman, she cherished an extraordinary affection. She never willingly left her side; and at night she would often wake and weep from a fear that this beloved mother might die and leave her. She would watch her when asleep, with an anxious dread lest she should cease to breathe, and awaken

ELIZABETH FRY IN NEWGATE.

no more from that slumber which she supposed to resemble death. In this morbid apprehension there was something of a presentiment or unconscious prophecy; for when she was only twelve years old, her mother was taken from her,—a blow which she felt even to the day of her own death. Thirty-six years afterwards she spoke of it with evident pain.

Years passed away, and Elizabeth Gurney developed into a fair tall maiden, of slender and graceful figure, and attractive countenance. She was a bold and skilful equestrian; she sang well and danced well; was by no means averse to admiration, and took a very unquakerlike interest in dress. The "meetings" of the Friends she attended reluctantly, and as often as she could pleaded ill-health as an excuse for absence. The religious impressions of her childhood had yielded to worldly influences. By degrees, however, her better nature began to struggle against them. She was really of too true and noble a temper long to delight in the trivial aims and amusements of society, though the conflict was sharp enough while it lasted, and makes her record of this period of her life an interesting psychological study. She describes with graphic faithfulness her alternations between doubt and belief, seriousness and levity, the desire for higher and purer things, and the not unnatural contentment of youth with the petty pleasures of the day. Most of us have gone through a similar experience; not all of us, perhaps, have emerged from it so successfully as Elizabeth Gurney,—perhaps because we had not the courage to make so uncompromising an analysis as she did of her thoughts and feelings.

Let us take two or three extracts, which will give us an insight into her mental condition:—

"Monday, May 21st, 1797. I am seventeen to-day Am I a happier or a better creature than I was this time twelvemonth? I know I am happier; I think I am better. I hope I shall be much better this day year than I am now. I hope to be quite an altered person; to have more knowledge, to have my mind in greater order, and my heart too,—that wants to be put in order as much, if not more, than any part of me, it is in such a fly-away state; but I think, if ever it settled on one object, it would never, no, never, fly away any more; it would rest quietly and happily on the heart that was open to receive it."

"June 20th. If I have long to live in this world, may I bear misfortunes with fortitude; do what I can to alleviate the sorrows of others; exert what power I have to increase happiness, try to govern my passions by reason; and strictly adhere to what I think right."

"July 7th. I have seen several things in myself and others I never before remarked; but I have not tried to myself. I have given way to my passions, and let them have command over me. I have known my faults, and not corrected them; and now I am determined I will once more try, with redoubled ardour, to overcome my wicked inclinations. I must not flirt, I must not even be out of temper with the children; I must not contradict without a cause; I must not mump when my sisters are liked, and I am not; I must not allow myself to be angry; I must not exaggerate, which I am inclined to do; I must not give way to luxury; I must not be idle in mind; I must try to give way to every good feeling, and overcome every bad. I will see what I can do; if I had but perseverance, I could do all that I wish. I will try. I have lately been too satirical, so as to hurt sometimes; remember it is always a fault to hurt others."

"July 11th. Company to dinner. I must beware of not being a flirt: it is an abominable character; I hope I shall never be one, and yet I fear I am one now a little. Be careful not to talk at random. Beware, and see how well I can get through this day, without one foolish action. If I do pass this day without one foolish action, it is the first I ever passed so. If I pass a day with only a few foolish actions, I may think it a good one."

"August 6th. I have a cross to-night. I had very much set my mind on going to the oratorio; the Prince (William Frederick, Duke of Gloucester) is to be there, and by all accounts it will be quite a grand sight, and there will be the finest music; but if my father does not like me to go, much as I wish it, I will give it up with pleasure, if it be in my power, without a murmur. . . . I went to the oratorio; I enjoyed it, but spoke sadly at random: what a bad habit!"

Self-knowledge is the first step to self-control. Elizabeth Gurney, it is evident, was not ignorant of her faults, and in her effort to overcome them required only some good influence to steady and support her. That influence she found in the teaching of William Savery, an American Quaker, who, early in 1798, was on a visit to England, and on the 4th of February officiated at the Friends' Meeting-House in Norwich. The impression which he produced upon Elizabeth is thus described by her sister Richenda :—

"On that day," she says, "we seven sisters sat as usual in a row under the gallery. I sat by Betsy. William Savery was there. We liked having yearly meeting friends come to preach ; it was a little change. Betsy was generally rather restless at meeting, and on this day I remember her very smart boots were a great amusement to me : they were purple, lined with scarlet.

"At last William Savery began to preach. His voice and manner were arresting, and we all liked the sound; her attention became fixed; at last I saw her begin to weep, and she became a good deal agitated. As soon as meeting was over, I have a remembrance of her making her way to the men's side of the meeting, and having found my father, she begged him if she might dine with William Savery at the Grove, to which he soon consented, though rather surprised by the request. We went home as usual, and, for a wonder, we wished to go again in the afternoon. I have not the same clear remembrance of this meeting; but the next scene that has fastened itself on my memory is our return home in the carriage. Betsy sat in the middle, and astonished us all by the great feeling she showed. She wept most of the way home. The next morning William Savery came to breakfast, and preached to our dear sister after breakfast, prophesying of the high and important calling she would be led into. What she went through in her own mind I cannot say, but the results were most powerful and most evident. From that day her love of pleasure and of the world seemed gone."

This was not entirely the case ; Elizabeth's Gurney's spiritual difficulties were not so easily got rid of. She herself was conscious that the victory was not yet won. On the evening of the day so memorable in her life-history she wrote :—" My imagination has been worked upon, and I fear all that I have felt will go off. I fear it now, though at first I was frightened that a plain Quaker should have made so deep an impression upon me; but how truly prejudiced in me to think that, because good came from a Quaker, I should be led away by enthusiasm and folly. I wish the state of enthusiasm I am now in may last, for to-day I have felt that *there is a God.*"

The "impression" was not very "deep." Two days afterwards she went to Norwich, where the evident admiration of some officers revived her not unnatural feeling of girlish vanity. She returned home "as full of the world as she went to town full of heaven!" Much agitated by conflicting emotions, she proceeded to London on a visit to a relative. Of course she was taken to Drury Lane Theatre, and for the first time had a glimpse of the magic world of the stage, with its picturesque parodies rather than faithful representations of real life, its exaggeration and its poetry. But whether her expectations had been too highly raised, or whether her mind was not in a condition to sympathize with mimic passions, certain it is that she was disappointed; and though the best actors and actresses of the day played on this occasion, she actually wished the performance over. Afterwards she saw "Hamlet" and "Bluebeard," and was better pleased: but "I do not like plays," she frankly writes; "I think them so artificial, that they are to me not interesting, and all seems so—so very far from pure virtue and nature." But if the theatre did not engage her fancy, she retained her partiality for the dance, and, as she frankly owns, for a little pungent gossip.

"March 26th. This morning I went to Amelia Opie's (the novelist), and had a pleasant time. I called on Mrs. Siddons, who was not at home; then on Dr. Batty; then on Mrs. Twiss, who gave me some paint for the evening. *I was painted a little.* I had my hair dressed, and did look pretty, for me. Mr. Opie, Amelia, and I went to the opera concert. *I own I do love grand company.* The Prince of Wales was there; and I must say I felt more pleasure in looking at him than in seeing the rest of the company or hearing the music. I did nothing but admire his Royal Highness; but I had a very pleasant evening indeed.

"March 27th. I called with Mrs. H. and Amelia on Mrs. Inchbald (the novelist and dramatist). I like her vastly; she seems so clever and so interesting. I then went to Hampstead, and stayed at our cousin Hoare's until the 12th of April. I returned to Clapham. My uncle Barclay, with great begging, took us to the opera. The house is dazzling, the company animating, the music hardly at all so, the dancing delightful. He came in, in the middle of the opera; I was charmed to see him—I was most merry—I just saw the Prince of Wales. Tuesday, my dearest father came to London! We dined at the . . . and went to a rout in the evening. Friday, I had a pleasant merry day with Peter Pindar (Dr. Walcot, the satirist). Monday, I went with my father and the Barclays to Sir George Staunton's (secretary in Lord Macartney's embassy to China)."

"April 16th. I arrived at home with my father, after paying a few more visits."

This would seem to have been Elizabeth Gurney's last, as well as her first, plunge into the gaieties of fashionable life. William Savery's teaching had not been ineffectual, and her heart, which was sound enough at the core, inclined more and more towards the Christian practice. For a long time her rest at night was disturbed by a singular and painful dream, as of a stormy sea breaking upon her with angry billows that threatened to sweep her away. But when the long conflict was at an end, and she triumphed in the consciousness of absolute peace of mind, "a change came o'er the spirit of the scene." The sea broke in loud waves as before, but she stood safe beyond its fury, and thenceforth it ceased to harass her. Elizabeth Gurney regarded the change as an omen from above, and a prefigurement of her future fate; devoutly hoping "not to be drowned in the ocean of the world, but permitted to mount above its waves, and remain a steady and faithful servant to the God whom she worshipped."

She now began to visit the poor and sick in Earlham and Norwich; she read the Bible to them, she taught the children. A school at home, which began with one boy, increased to such an extent that she had to accommodate the pupils in a vacant laundry, and before long they numbered seventy, whom she instructed and controlled without any assistance. Gradually she gave up what had hitherto been her principal amusements, music and dancing; adopted the quaint simplicity of Quaker dress; and fell into the not less quaint usages of Quaker speech. Those unnecessary sacrifices were not made without a struggle. When asked by her friends to sing or dance, she hesitated to refuse, yet could not consent without a feeling that she was doing wrong. On one occasion, meeting an old acquaintance, whom she felt unable to address in the plain speech of the Friends, she actually ran away. At last her sense of duty conquered; and while we think she was mistaken, we cannot but admire her steadfastness in what seemed to her the path of right. Mistaken, we mean, in regarding as sinful the innocent amusements which grace and heighten daily life, and, in the case of music at least, elevate the mind and purify the heart; but not mistaken in withdrawing from what her conscience condemned. Any occupation that seems to us unlawful, we are unquestionably bound to relinquish, however innocent it may be in itself or may appear to others.

In 1800 Elizabeth Gurney was married to Mr. Joseph Fry, a London merchant, and, of course, one of the Friends. She then removed to St. Mildred's Court, in the City, where her husband and his brother conducted an extensive business. In her domestic duties she realized a pure and constant happiness, and in the course of nine years five children came to share her affection and occupy her mind. In 1809 the family removed from the turmoil of London to the rural tranquillity of Plashet, a quiet Essex village; and to one so keenly alive to the beauties of Nature the change was very welcome. But she did not abandon herself to sentimental enjoyment. She quickly interested herself in the condition of the country people; established a girls' school on the Lancastrian system; distributed soup in the winter to the deserving poor; administered simple medicines when needed; and supplied them with good warm clothing at a very cheap rate. A number of Irish had settled down about half a mile from Plashet; and their quick emotional nature responded with the deepest gratitude to her thoughtful benevolence. We are told that she exercised a wonderful influence over them. "She had in her nature a touch of poetry, and a quick sense of the droll; the Irish character furnished matter for both. Their powers of deep love and bitter grief excited her sympathy; almost against her judgment, she would grant the linen shirt and the boughs of evergreen to array the departed, and ornament the bed of death. She frequently visited Irish Row, never but to do good or administer consolation. Gathering her garments round her, she would thread her way through children and pigs, up broken staircases and by narrow passages, to the apartments she sought; there she would listen to their tales of want or woe, or of their difficulties with their children, or of the evil conduct of their husbands. She persuaded many of them to adopt more orderly habits, giving little presents of clothing as encouragements; she induced some to send their children to school, and, with the consent of the priest, circulated the Bible amongst them. On one occasion, when the weather was extremely cold, and great distress prevailed, being at the time too delicate herself to walk, she went alone in the carriage, literally piled with flannel petticoats for Irish Row; the rest of the party walking to meet her, to assist in the delightful task of distribution."

Her charity was extended with equal forethought and earnestness to the gipsies who yearly visited the neighbourhood. Moreover, she had early recognised the benefits of vaccination, and having learned how to perform the operation, she was accustomed to visit the whole parish at stated intervals, for the purpose of gratuitously vaccinating the children.

Admirable as was this work, however, it differed in little from the work undertaken and accomplished by hundreds of English gentlewomen in their respective spheres of influence; and had Elizabeth Fry never gone beyond their boundaries, her name would probably have remained unknown to the world at large. She herself was conscious that something yet remained to be done, though for awhile that something assumed no definite shape. She was conscious of powers undeveloped, of gifts unused. At last she began to grope her way towards the light, to feel that she was called upon to deliver the "oracles of God" among her co-religionists. She hesitated long; apprehensive lest she should be misled by a warm imagination; influenced probably by a natural womanly reluctance; but, towards the close of 1810, the death of her father finally determined her. By his bedside she had poured forth her soul in eloquent utterances of prayer and thanksgiving; and on her return to Plashet, believing that the work was not her own doing, nor at her own command, she publicly took upon herself the office of the ministry. The fervour of her thoughts, the copiousness and beauty of her language, and the enthusiasm of her devotion, soon showed that she had not mistaken her calling. She held her audiences spell-bound; and men not of her own creed, men prejudiced against the public ministrations of women, were constrained to own the power of her eloquence and the contagion of her zeal.

In November, 1812, Mrs. Fry and her family removed to St. Mildred's Court for the winter. Soon afterwards, she was induced by some of her friends to visit the female prisoners in Newgate. It was indeed time that someone took an interest in their unhappy condition. In two wards and two cells, the entire superficial area of which did not exceed 190 yards, three hundred women and children were confined; some tried and convicted, others as yet untried; but all showing the same misery, herding together, in rags, without bedding or beds, cooking, washing, living, sleeping, starving, grumbling, fighting, and blaspheming in these four small rooms. The governor himself shrank from entering the women's part of the prison; it was an Alsatia of filth, misery, and sin. Into this terrible scene passed Mrs. Fry, accompanied by Miss Anna Buxton, like a ray of celestial light. She paid three visits,—on each occasion distributing the much-needed relief.

It was not, however, until Christmas, 1816, that she entered upon what we may call the real work of her life,—prison-reform. She then began a regular series of visits to the female prisoners in Newgate. Observing that the children were pining for want of air and exercise, she addressed herself to the mothers, and so stirred up their better feelings that they agreed to co-operate with her in establishing a school. An unoccupied cell was granted for the schoolroom; Mary Connor, a young girl committed for theft, was appointed schoolmistress; and the school was opened for children and young persons under twenty-five years of age. Many applicants had to be refused for want of room. A friend who accompanied Mrs. Fry on one of her visits writes:—"The railing was crowded with half-naked women, struggling together for the front situations with the most boisterous violence, and begging with the utmost vociferation. She felt as if she were going into a den of wild beasts, and she well recollects quite shuddering when the door was closed upon her, and she was locked in with such a herd of novel and desperate companions.

One of these desperate women rushed round the prison yard with arms extended, tearing everything of the nature of a cap from the heads of the other women, and 'yelling like a wild beast.'" Yet she afterwards became a decent woman, and married respectably —a brand snatched from the burning.

To a woman of Mrs. Fry's refined tastes and delicate nurture, these prison-scenes must have been painfully repulsive. "It was in our visits to the school," she writes, "where some of us attended almost every day, that we were witnesses to the dreadful proceedings that went forward on the female side of the prison,— the begging, swearing, gaming, fighting, singing, dancing, dressing up in men's clothes; the scenes are too bad to be described, so that we did not think it suitable to admit young persons with us." But while conscious of a feeling of profound disgust, even of loathing, Mrs. Fry resolutely persevered with the "work of noble note" she had taken upon herself so chivalrously. She saw that a reform was urgent, and felt that it was her mission to effect it; and she was too sagacious a woman to suppose that it could be effected except at the cost of much self-sacrifice. If it be true that revolutions cannot be made with rose-water, it is no less true that reforms were never achieved by kid-glove philanthropists. To carry healing to the sick, and comfort to the distressed, we must go down into the pool, like the angel at Bethesda, and trouble the waters. "Do not stir Camarina" is the maxim of the selfish or the ignorant; of the man who cries, "After me, the deluge," or of him who would sleep in apathy on a powder magazine.

With great perseverance, and in spite of many discouragements, Mrs. Fry succeeded in forming "An Association for the Improvement of the Female Prisoners in Newgate," whose objects were: "To provide for the clothing, the instruction, and the employment of the women; to introduce them to a knowledge of the Holy Scriptures, and to form in them, as much as possible, those habits of order, sobriety, and industry, which may render them docile and peaceable whilst in prison, and respectable when they leave it." The members laboured under Mrs. Fry's direction with great good will, and with very considerable success. At the end of ten months, Mrs. Fry thus sums up the result:—

"Our rules have certainly been occasionally broken, but very seldom; order has been generally observed. I think I may say we have full power amongst them, for one of them said it was more terrible to be brought up before me than before the judge, though we use nothing but kindness. I have never punished a woman during the whole time, or even proposed a punishment to them; and yet I think it is impossible, in a well-regulated house, to have rules more strictly attended to than they are, as far as I order them, or our friends in general. With regard to our work, they have made nearly twenty thousand articles of wearing apparel, the generality of which are supplied by the slop-shops, which pay very little. Excepting three out of this number of articles that were missing, which we really do not think owing to the women, we have never lost a single thing. They knit from about sixty to a hundred pairs of stockings and socks every month; they spin a little. The earnings of work, we think, average about eighteenpence per week for each person. This is generally spent in assisting them to live, and helping to clothe them. For this purpose they subscribe out of their small earnings of work about four pounds a month, and we subscribe about eight, which keeps them covered and decent. Another very important point is the excellent effect we have found to result from religious education; our habit is constantly to read the Scriptures to them twice a day; many of them are taught, and some of them have been enabled to read a little themselves. It has had an astonishing effect; I never saw the Scriptures received in the same way, and to many of them they have been entirely new, both the great systems of religion and of morality contained in them; and it has been very satisfactory to observe the effect upon their minds. When I have sometimes gone and said it was my intention to read, they would flock upstairs after me, as if it were a great pleasure I had to afford them."

To find employment for so many idle hands was no light task. It occurred to one of Mrs. Fry's coadjutors that they might supply the convict settlement of Botany Bay with stockings and other articles of clothing. She called on a large export firm in Fenchurch Street, and stating her desire to carry off from them this branch of their trade, she asked their advice. With noble generosity they entered heartily into her object, and undertook to supply the work.

A gentleman who visited Newgate after Mrs. Fry had begun her philanthropic labour, speaks warmly of the almost miraculous transformation that had taken place. "I was conducted," he says, "by a turnkey to the entrance of the women's wards. On my approach, no loud or dissonant sounds or angry voices indicated that I was about to enter a place which, I was credibly assured, had long had for one of its titles that of 'hell above ground.' The courtyard into which I was admitted, instead of being peopled with beings scarcely human, blaspheming, fighting, tearing each others' hair, or gaming with a filthy pack of cards for the very clothes they wore, which often did not suffice even for decency, presented a scene where stillness and propriety reigned. I was conducted by a decently-dressed person, the newly-appointed yards-woman, to the door of a ward, where, at the head of a long table, sat a lady, belonging to the Society of Friends. She was reading aloud to about sixteen women, prisoners, who were engaged in needlework around it. Each wore a clean-looking blue apron and bib, with a ticket, having a number on it, suspended from her neck by a red tape. They all rose on my entrance, curtsied respectfully, and then, at a signal given, resumed their seats and employments. Instead of a scowl, leer, or ill-suppressed laugh, I observed upon their countenances an air of self-respect and gravity,—a sort of consciousness of their improved character, and the altered position in which they were placed. I afterwards visited the other wards, which were the counterparts of the first."

This reform was, in a great measure, due to the magnetism of Mrs. Fry's personal influence. In her way, she had something of that power over her fellows which the world has seen in a Pericles, a Julius Cæsar, a Charlemagne, a Bruce, a Napoleon; a power springing, perhaps, from the confidence of the individual in himself or in his mission. Being apprised on one occasion that some gambling was still carried on, she called the offenders before her, and desired them, little thinking they would consent, to give up their cards. To her surprise, five packs were at once surrendered, with earnest expressions of contrition. But while this reform, like every reform, owed much to the reformer, we must not forget that she was aided largely by the reformed, who were quick to understand that the new system contributed greatly to their comfort. It is a mistake, we believe, to suppose that any considerable number of people take an interest in disorder and anarchy. The instincts of the many are always in favour of a settled rule, **because only** under such a **rule are** individual interests secure.

Before this happy epoch, it **had** been the "use and wont" of the female convicts, on the eve of their departure for Botany Bay, to tear down, burn, **and** destroy everything. But now they left the prison like people clothed, and in their right mind. Mrs. Fry and her associates accompanied them to Deptford, saw them embark, divided them into classes, superintended the election of monitors, distributed Bibles, supplied working materials, and arranged a school for the children. The working materials were a little difficult. There were one hundred and twenty-eight convicts, and what could they be set to *do?* At last, patchwork **was suggested.** Application was made to the Manchester houses in **London,** and a large quantity of coloured prints was freely **contributed.** Some of the quilts "created" by the ingenuity **of the** convicts **sold for a guinea each** at Rio de Janeiro. For five **weeks** the transport **ship lay in the** river. Then **came** the moment of departure. Mrs. Fry **stood** at the cabin door, attended by her friends and the captain; the women on the quarter-deck, opposite **to them.** The sailors, anxious to see all that took place, crowded **into** the rigging, climbed upon the capstan, or mingled in the **outskirts of** the group. The silence was profound, while, in her **clear musical** voice, Mrs. Fry **read** a chapter from the Bible. **The** crews of the neighbouring **vessels,** attracted by the novel scene, bent over the bulwarks, and listened, apparently **with** attention. She closed the holy Book, knelt down on the **deck,** and implored **a** benediction on the work from that God who, though one may sow and another water, **can** alone give the increase. Many of the women wept bitterly, all seemed touched; and when this Good Samaritan left the ship, they followed her with **tear-filled eyes and** fervent blessings, until her boat passed up the crowded **river, and was lost to** sight.

For some years Mrs. Fry continued her philanthropic exertions, **but not, let us** admit, to the neglect of her domestic duties. **The** double burden was heavy, but in her Christian enthusiasm she found the strength to **bear** it. And it seems to us that when God gives us work to do, He also gives us the needful energy to do it. The beauty and unselfishness of Mrs. Fry's motives were shown very strikingly by the modesty with which she bore the great reputation that accrued to her. Whether Queen Charlotte spoke to her in public at the Mansion House, or her name was mentioned in Parliament with praise and honour, or the most distinguished personages of the day attended her addresses to the women in Newgate, she was still the same unassuming, calm, and retiring Christian gentlewoman. It was not in England only that her work was known and valued. It lent an impetus to prison reform in Paris, Tunis, Berlin, Amsterdam, St. Petersburg. The Russian Czarina, in a transport of admiration, exclaimed: "How much I should like to see that admirable woman, Madame Fry, in Russia!" There is a wonderful fertility in a good deed.

We shall not dwell on Mrs. Fry's wise efforts to procure the abolition of capital punishment for crimes affecting property, or on her untiring exertions to promote the religious education of the poor. The special work of her life was the reform, on rational and humane principles, of the interior administration of our prisons; and in this direction she was not inferior to John Howard. She devoted to it her talents, energies, and her means: happier than many workers, she was permitted to witness the successful result of her labours. As we have hinted, her influence was felt both at home and abroad; her example encouraged many noble women to follow in the same path of well-doing, and, as ragged-school teachers and district visitors, to help forward the amelioration of the condition of the "lower orders." She herself was indefatigable: accompanied by her brother, Joseph John Gurney, she personally visited and examined the prisons, lunatic asylums, penitentiaries, and refuges of the United Kingdom, and, afterwards, the most important institutions of a similar kind on the Continent. Her experience enabled her to recommend many beneficial changes in the construction and internal arrangement of prisons, as well as in the transportation and treatment of convicts.

But wherever distress, or poverty, or ignorance was to be found, Elizabeth Fry saw a motive for exertion. She did not pass by on the other side; she waited upon the sufferer, and with her own hands bound up his wounds. No case of wretchedness came to her notice that she did not attempt to relieve. No poor suppliant ever poured his sorrows into her ear in vain. She seemed to live only for others; her career was one lofty epic of well-doing. Thus, during a visit to Jersey in 1833, rendered necessary by domestic affairs, she contrived to reform the prison and hospital, and establish a district society. A day at Freshwater, in the Isle of Wight, in the neighbourhood of the Coast Guard Station, suggested to her the great and good undertaking of providing libraries for all the Coast Guard Stations in Great Britain,—an undertaking bristling with difficulties, but in which she abated not one jot of perseverance until it had been successfully accomplished. The reader will observe that in all her schemes Mrs. Fry was eminently practical. She was no believer in Utopia, moral or political; her plans were always considered carefully, and involved neither impossibilities nor improbabilities; her attention to details was worthy of a great administrator. Her courage was wonderful, and so was her tact. She never yielded to prejudices, but she did not unnecessarily excite them. Hence it happened that all her reforms were carried to a successful issue with the cordial co-operation of the authorities whom they concerned. Nor did she go out of her way in search of a vocation: she did the duty which lay close to her hand, and she entertained no romantic or exaggerated theories of "woman's mission." A woman's primary duties she regarded as centred in her home and household; but she was not the less convinced that for all a wider field of usefulness lay open. She appreciated, and practised, the usual charities of gentlewomen: their visits to the sick, the destitute, and the aged, their supervision of the village school; but she deeply regretted that so few carried their Samaritanism no further,—that they did not follow the widow and disabled when driven by necessity to the workhouse, or take charge of the workhouse school, that resort of the orphaned and forsaken; less attractive, perhaps, than the school of the village, but even more requiring oversight and attention.

Many scenes in Mrs. Fry's varied career have a special and attractive interest. Our limits, however, will allow us to put only one before the reader, but that will sufficiently illustrate her admirable qualities of moral intrepidity, enthusiasm, and humility.

On the 31st of January, 1842, the King of Prussia met Mrs.

Fry at Newgate, and afterwards lunched with her at Mr. Fry's country house at Upton. The account of the day's proceedings runs as follows:—

"We set off about eleven o'clock, my sister Gurney and myself, to meet the King of Prussia at Newgate. I proceeded with the Lady Mayoress to Newgate, where we were met by many gentlemen. My dear brother and sister Gurney and Susannah Corder being with me was a great comfort. We waited so long for the king that I feared he would not come; however, at last he arrived, and the Lady Mayoress and I, accompanied by the sheriffs, went to meet the king at the door of the prison. He appeared much pleased to meet our little party; and after taking a little refreshment, he gave me his arm, and we proceeded into the prison and up to one of the long wards, where everything was prepared; the poor women round the table, about sixty of them, many of our ladies' committee, and some others; also numbers of gentlemen following the king, sheriffs, etc. I felt deeply, but quiet in spirit—fear of man much removed. After we were seated, the king on my right hand, the Lady Mayoress on my left, I expressed my desire that the attention of some, particularly the poor prisoners, might not be diverted from attending to me reading by the company there, however interesting, but that we should remember that the King of kings and Lord of lords was present, in whose fear we should abide, and seek to profit by what we heard. I then read the twelfth chapter of Romans. I dwelt on the mercies of God being the strong inducements to serve Him, and no longer to be conformed to this world. Then I finished the chapter, afterwards impressing our all being members of one body, poor and rich, high and low, all one in Christ, and members one of another. I then related the case of a poor prisoner, who appeared truly converted, and who became such a holy example; then I enlarged on love and forgiving one another, showing how Christians must love their enemies.

"After a solemn pause, to my deep humiliation and in the cross, I believed it my duty to kneel down before this most curious, interesting, and mixed company; for I felt my God must be served the same everywhere and amongst all people, whatever reproach it brought me into. I first prayed for the conversion of prisoners and sinners generally, that a blessing might rest on the labours of those in authority, as well as the more humble labourers for their conversion; next I prayed for the King of Prussia, his Queen, his kingdom, that it might be more and more as the city set on the hill that could not be hid; that true religion in its purity, simplicity, and power might more and more break forth, and that every cloud that obscured it might be removed; then for us all, that we might be of the number of the redeemed, and eventually unite with them in heaven in a never-ending song of praise. All this prayer was truly offered in the name and for the sake of the dear Saviour, that it might be heard and answered. I only mention the subject, but by no means the words.

"The king then gave me his arm, and we walked down together; there were difficulties raised about his going to Upton, but he chose to persevere. I went with the Lady Mayoress and the sheriffs, and the king with his own people. We arrived first. I had to hasten to take off my cloak, and then went down to meet him at his carriage door, with my husband and some of our sons and sons-in-law. I then walked with him into the drawing-room, where all was in beautiful order, neat, and adorned with flowers. I presented to the king our eight daughters and daughters-in-law, our seven sons and eldest grandson, my brothers and sisters, . . . and afterwards presented twenty-five of our grandchildren. We had a solemn silence before our meal, which was handsome and fit for a king, yet not extravagant—everything most complete and nice. I sat by the king, who appeared to enjoy his dinner perfectly at his ease, and very happy with us. We went into the drawing-room after another solemn silence and a few words which I uttered in prayer for the king and queen. . . . We had then to part. The king expressed his desire that blessings might continue to rest on our house."

We have alluded to Mrs. Fry's continental journeys. She visited France in 1836; Paris in 1838; France and Switzerland in the following year; Holland, Northern Germany, and Denmark in 1841. We find her at Paris in 1843, when she visited the great women's prison at Clermont-en-Oise. On her return she fell ill, and thenceforward a deep shadow of physical pain and mental sorrows afflicted her. Her old friends passed away, and she lost some of her grandchildren, her kith and kin, and finally a beloved son. Her last public appearance was on the 3rd of June, 1845; but she was not able to stand; she could only address the meeting seated. Growing feebler and feebler, she was removed in July to Ramsgate, for the benefit of the sea-air; but it was impossible to arrest the rapid decline both of mind and body. On the 13th of October it was evident that the great change was close at hand. One of her daughters, who sat reading Isaiah to her, heard her murmuring, in a low but distinct voice :—" Oh, my dear Lord, help and keep Thy servant!" These were her last words. She sank into a state of unconsciousness, and so remained, until on the following morning she peacefully expired.*

---

* "All that was mortal of Elizabeth Fry," says Miss Kavanagh, "now rests by the side of her little child, in the Friends' burying-ground at Barking; but her name, her deeds, her spirit are with us still. Who shall estimate not only the good which she did, but that to which her example led? How noble, how generous, was the use she made of the personal beauty, exquisite voice, ready eloquence, and many talents with which she was gifted? The extremes which met in her character gave her greater power. Timid, daring, prudent, enthusiastic, practical, equally alive to the beautiful and the humorous, Elizabeth Fry was eminently fitted for her task. She possessed an insight into character and a power of control which enabled her to influence almost every one who came within her sphere." We have drawn the materials of our sketch from the "Life of Mrs. Elizabeth Fry," by Mrs. F. Creswell, edit. 1868.

BOOK V.

"THE POOR ARE ALWAYS WITH US."

VINCENT DE PAUL: HIS LABOURS ON BEHALF OF THE POOR.
ENGLISH SISTERS OF MERCY: MISS SIEVEKING; MRS. MOMPESSON.
AN ENGLISH GENTLEMAN AMONG THE POOR: EDWARD DENISON.
AMONG THE SICK: "SISTER DORA."

"THE POOR ARE ALWAYS WITH US."

IN a peasant's cottage at Pouy, near Dax, a small village situated on the high open ground that lies at the foot of the Pyrenees, was born, on the 24th of April, 1576, to Jean de Paul, and his wife Bertranda, a male child, whom they christened Vincent.

Jean de Paul was a peasant farmer, of the type so dear to Irish land reformers; the few acres of ground were his own which he laboriously cultivated, with the assistance of his wife, and, as they grew up, of his six children. Of the four boys, Vincent was the third, and as soon as his years permitted he was engaged like the others in the work of the little farm. His special duty was to take charge of his father's sheep, and lead them to the pasture. The solitary hours which thus fell to his lot he improved by meditating upon the pious lessons inculcated by a devout mother. A venerable oak grew on the grassy plain where the sheep wandered; its hollow trunk he converted into a little oratory, where much of his time was spent in prayer; its branches sheltered him from the summer sun and the autumnal rains.

His father was quick to detect in him, not only his early piety, but signs of a more than ordinary intelligence; and feeling that it would not be right for such qualities to be wasted in the farm and pasture,—hoping, perhaps, that they might prove of pecuniary benefit to the family,—he sent him, at the age of eleven, to the Franciscan convent at Dax. Here his mental gifts were rapidly developed; and his progress was so rapid that, four years later, the chief magistrate of Pouy received him into his house as tutor to his children; a position which enabled him to continue his studies without being a burden on his parents. To the great satisfaction of his patron, and to his own signal gain, he remained in it for five years, years of intellectual growth and contented usefulness. Then, in December, 1596, acting on the advice of his friend and employer, he separated himself from the world by receiving the tonsure and the four minor orders. Resolving to devote himself wholly to the service of God in His Church, he repaired to Toulouse, in order to master the science of theology. In December, 1598, the young student was ordained deacon; and on the 23rd of December, 1600, being then in his twenty-fifth year, he was admitted to the priesthood. It is worth noting that he discharged the duties of this high office for *sixty years*, his death taking place on the 27th of September, 1660.

I have spoken of it as a "high office;" and indeed, to expound the "oracles of God" to his fellow-men, to deliver to them the great message with which our Lord entrusts His chosen ambassadors, is a solemn responsibility, which none should lightly undertake or carelessly discharge. Each of us, it is true, has, in his sphere of life, and according to the measure of his powers, a duty to fulfil towards the community of which he is a member; but that which falls upon the priest, or pastor, has, at all times and among all peoples, been rightly regarded as of supreme weight and sacredness. Such it was considered by Vincent de Paul. Writing, in after years, to a friend, he says of the priesthood:—"It is the most exalted condition that there can be upon this earth, and that which it was our Lord's will to choose and to exercise. For myself, if, when I had the rashness to enter it, I had known what it was, as I do now, I had much rather have been a labourer and tilled the ground, than have engaged myself in so awful a profession; and this I have said more than a hundred times to poor country people, when, in order to encourage them to be contented, and live as they ought, I have told them that I considered they were happy to be in that state of life; and indeed, the older I grow, the more I am confirmed in this opinion, because I discover every day how far I am from the perfection to which I ought to have attained."

After his admission to the priesthood, Vincent did not immediately secure a charge, and to provide for his support he again accepted a situation as tutor at Buzet. Here he gathered round him a number of pupils, children of good families; and by his conscientious devotion to their mental and moral education, so won the confidence of their parents, that when he returned to Toulouse to continue his theological studies, they desired him to take their children with him. That his educational work might not interfere with the work of self-culture, he deprived himself of many hours usually given to sleep and recreation.

So far his life had given no promise of special distinction, and had it continued in the same groove, his biographer would have had no story to relate, however signal might have been its influence for good in the circle of which he was the centre. In 1605, he had occasion to visit Marseilles, and then the first noteworthy event in his career occurred; an event which, disastrous as it was in itself, proved to be the door that opened up to him his true work in the world. Returning from Marseilles by sea, he was captured by Turkish pirates, despoiled of all he possessed, and carried with his fellow-passengers to Tunis to be sold into slavery. "After they had stripped us," he writes, "they gave to each a pair of drawers and a linen coat and cap, and walked us about the town, whither they had come for the express purpose of selling us. Having paraded us through the streets with chains on our necks, they led us back to the ship, in order that purchasers might see who ate heartily and who did not, and to show them, moreover, that our wounds were not mortal." [Vincent had been wounded by an arrow.] "This done, we were taken back to the market-place, where merchants came to inspect us, exactly as men do who want to buy a horse or an ox. We had to open our mouths and show our teeth; they felt our sides, examined our wounds, made us walk, trot, run, lift heavy weights, and wrestle, that they might judge of our individual strength, and they subjected us to a thousand other indignities."

Vincent was sold to a fisherman, who, however, soon disposed of him to a pretended physician and alchymist. At the end of ten or eleven months this man died, bequeathing his slave, with his other property, to a nephew, who sold him to a renegade Christian, from Nice. As he was carried away to labour on an inland farm, where the tropical heat caused him severe suffering, and the heavy toil overtasked his energies, it seemed, at first, as if his fate in life were permanently fixed; but every man's future is a problem the solution of which must be left to time. One of the renegade's wives (he had three) observed, with a feeling of compassion, this patient and gentle labourer, so evidently superior to his unfortunate condition. She began to talk to him, and it was inevitable but that their conversation should turn upon Vincent's favourite theme, the love of Christ. One day she asked him to sing some of the Christian songs of praise. The remembrance of the captive Israelites in their Babylonian exile pressed upon him, and he began, through his tears, the psalm, "By the waters of Babylon;" after which he sang or chanted the "Salve, regina," and many others, which gave her wonderful pleasure. That evening she told her husband he had done wrong in abandoning his religion, of the excellence of which she had been persuaded by Vincent's account of his God, and by the hymns he had sung in her presence. In these, she said, she so delighted that she could not believe that the Paradise of her fathers, the Paradise of the Koran, could equal, in its glory and joy, the sweet calm and satisfaction of soul she had felt while listening to the Christian's praises of his Lord and Saviour.

Her simple speeches went home to her husband's heart, and thenceforth he looked eagerly for an opportunity to escape to France, where he might resume his profession of the Christian faith. It was not until June, 1607, that the opportunity presented itself; then he and his family, accompanied by Vincent, crossed the Mediterranean in a small boat, and on the 28th landed safely at Aigues-Mortes. They repaired without delay to Avignon, and the apostate was publicly received back into the communion of the Church. Vincent afterwards accompanied the pro-legate to Rome, and was introduced to the dignitaries of the Pontifical Curia, who formed so high an opinion of his prudence and judgment that they entrusted him with a confidential mission to Henry IV. He was thus on the road to high preferment, but the profligacy of the French Court so shocked the simple-minded Christian priest that he quickly withdrew into retirement, and sought the tranquil shelter of the oratory. He appears at this time to have gone through that terrible trial of doubt and despondency which so many souls have suffered like a baptism of fire. But he emerged from it victorious, and hastened to busy himself with the cure of souls in the little suburban village of Clichy. There his poor and humble flock soon learned to regard him as a friend and father, and Clichy became a kind of "model parish," where the people, it was said, "lived like angels"—so great is the influence of one earnest, devoted Christian spirit!

Years afterwards Vincent himself bore witness to their pious living. "The good people of Clichy," he said, "were so obedient to me, that when I recommended them to attend confession on the first Sunday of every month, to my great joy none were missing. Ah, I used to say to myself, how happy thou art to have such good people; the Pope is not so happy as I am! One day the first Cardinal de Retz inquired, 'Well, Monsieur, how do you progress?' 'My lord,' I replied, 'I am more happy than I can say.' 'Why so?' 'Because I have such good people, and so obedient to everything that I tell them, that I say to myself that neither the Pope, nor you, my lord, are so happy as I.'"

At the urgent request of his ecclesiastical superior, Vincent reluctantly left this pleasant sphere of labour, and undertook the duties of chaplain and tutor in the family of the Count de Joigny, a scion of the illustrious house of De Retz. He continued to discharge them for a period of about twelve years, until his pupils had grown up from boyhood into manhood, and under his wise and prudent care had been thoroughly fitted to play their parts on the world's stage with dignity. It is easy to understand, from what we have already seen of his character, with its happy combination of modesty, tenderness, and gentle wisdom, that he would secure the affectionate and trustful regard of all who came under his influence. His, indeed, was one of those natures—not, alas! too common,—in the sunshine of which others seem spontaneously to put forth their better qualities. There was about him a singular personal charm and attractiveness, that was felt by men of the highest rank as well as of the lowest, by the cultured not less than by the ignorant. This charm arose in part from his Christian humility, from his absolute forgetfulness of self; in part, from the exquisite refinement of manner due to a cultured mind and a sympathetic temper.

Not only was he "unwearied" in all the duties of his chaplaincy, and in his work as a tutor, but he watched with tender vigilance over the welfare of the servants of the Count's large household. In sickness he waited upon them, in health he instructed them; he catechised them, he composed their differences, he gave them opportune and prudent counsel. The little leisure that remained to him after all these labours were accomplished he devoted to the care of the peasants and workmen round about; and in this way he was led to the organization of that special system of religious enlightenment which under the name of " Missions " has recently been introduced into the English Church. One day he was sent for to attend a poor man living in one of the Count de Joigny's villages; he was dangerously ill, and according to the custom of the Catholic communion, wished to make his confession. His neighbours described him as a man of good character, religious habits, and irreproachable life. Vincent, however, soon discovered that all this fine seeming did but conceal "a heavy load of deadly sin" upon his conscience; a load which, but for Vincent's knowledge of the human heart, and his power of gaining the full and entire confidence of all who consulted him, he would have carried, unconfessed, and unrepented of, into the Eternal Presence.

Vincent was led by this occurrence to meditate on the apathetic condition of the masses, and to devise some means of awakening them to a sense of their religious duty. As a first step in this direction, he held, on the 25th of January, 1607, a special service in the parish church of Folleville; and so great was the effect of his address, such were the numbers who sought spiritual consolation and advice, that he was obliged to send to Amiens for assistance. In the work of preaching, teaching, and catechizing, three priests and himself were busily engaged for several days, and in all the villages round about they reaped an abundant harvest. Such was the origin of the evangelizing agency of "Missions," which has so often been beneficial in infusing new vigour and vitality into the Church.

With the exception of four months in 1617, which he spent in Christian work at Chatillon, Vincent remained an honoured member of the family of De Joigny until the death of the Countess in 1625. By her will this admirable lady devised an annual sum of 16,000 livres for the establishment of a Society of Mission Priests, whose special responsibility should be, the evangelization of the peasantry and general population of rural France. Not long before her decease, she and her husband had obtained from the Archbishop of Paris, brother of the Count, an old disused collegiate building, called the Collége des Bons Enfans, which they fitted up as a home and centre for this Society. The foundation and endowment were both made over to Vincent de Paul, who was appointed Superior; and in him was vested the power of choosing and electing every year as many ecclesiastics as the revenues of the foundation would bear. The conditions attached to the deed of endowment were:—That these ecclesiastics should devote themselves exclusively to the care of the poor in rural districts, and to this end should bind themselves not to preach, nor to administer the Sacrament, in any town where there was a bishop or archbishop, or a civil court of justice, except in cases of manifest necessity; that they should live in common, under the obedience of Jean Vincent de Paul, and after his decease, of their Superior, under the name of the Company or Congregation of Priests of the Mission; and that they should hold a mission every five years throughout the demesnes of the Count and Countess de Joigny, and also afford spiritual assistance to convicts.

Along with the post of Superior of the Mission College, Vincent held that of spiritual director to the Convent of the Visitation, which had recently been established by Madame de Chautal at Paris, and also that of Chaplain-General of convicts and galley-slaves. In the last-named capacity he visited Marseilles, in order to inspect the galleys and inquire into the condition of the wretches confined on board of them; it was probably much worse than that of the inmates of the very worst prisons in Europe, and this, too, at a time when prison administration was but another word for cruel oppression. "Pitiable beyond words," we are told, "was the state of things which he found there. Reckless misery, blank despair, and blasphemy combined, seemed to make of the Bagne a hell upon earth." Moved with feelings of the deepest compassion for these unhappy creatures, Vincent addressed all his energies to the task of ameliorating their condition. Hitherto, the sole thought of those entrusted with the administration of the criminal law had been *punishment;* of the *reformation* of the criminal no idea had crossed their minds. So long as he underwent the chastisement ordained for his offence they were satisfied: that he could be restored to society as a penitent and a useful member, they had never regarded as possible or within their purview. It is the glory of Vincent de Paul that he anticipated the prison reformers of the next century. He endeavoured to revive in the heart of the criminal a consciousness of right and wrong, while he secured their confidence by his evident compassion for their sufferings and his patient hearing of their complaints. Patience and Sympathy! Ah, these are the golden keys that unlock the most obdurate bosom! It was not that Vincent de Paul was a man of genius,—though, unquestionably, he was largely endowed with the faculty of organisation,—but he possessed those two grand sweet virtues, which are as powerful as genius, and without which genius loses its command of the hearts and minds of men.

An extraordinary illustration of this patience and sympathy, approaching even to the sublime, is recorded by the good man's biographer. I know not whether we can accept it as authentic, though the Abbé Maynard seems to entertain no doubt. Among the inmates of the galleys at Marseilles was a young man, stricken almost to death by the agonizing reflection that his wife and children were utterly destitute, and by his consciousness that he was innocent of the crime with which he was charged. Vincent de Paul was satisfied of his innocence, and prevailed upon the officer of the gang to set him free, offering himself as a substitute. That his inquiries into the state of the galleys might be the fuller and the more independent, he had concealed from everybody his real name and position; so that none knew who it was that rose to such a height of self-sacrifice. For several weeks, it is said, Vincent worked in chains with the rest of the gang, until the Count de Joigny, surprised at his long silence, made inquiries which led to his discovery and release. During this period of voluntary humiliation he contracted, we are told, a disease which, for many years of his life, proved a terrible torture; and his ankles bore to the day of his death the marks of the pressure of his self-imposed chains.

Returning from Marseilles, after his release, Vincent de Paul passed through the town of Mâcon on his way to Paris. He had no sooner entered it than he was surrounded by a crowd of clamorous beggars, who, at that time, held the town practically at their disposal, and levied blackmail upon the orderly portion of the population. They were so numerous and so audacious that the authorities feared to repress their outrages, lest they should break out into open rebellion, and involve the town in anarchy. Vincent de Paul, as we have hinted, was one of those rare men who possess the gift of organization; one of those at whose touch disorder magically melts into order, and at whose voice the most mutinous are brought back under the influence of law. Though he was but a passing traveller, he could not see such a state of things without an immediate effort to remedy it. First securing the support of the civil and ecclesiastical authorities, he proceeded to collect the most reputable inhabitants of the town and to form them into an association, pledged to restore order. A list was then made out of all the beggars; their circumstances were investigated, and they were divided into two classes—the professional mendicants, who lived by ruffianism, and the suffering poor, whom their necessities constrained to ask for alms. For the latter, assistance was provided suitable to their different needs; to the former a regular distribution was made, contingent on their observance of various simple rules; such as that they should present themselves every Sunday at one particular church, and that they absolutely refrained from public or private begging. The arrangement of all the details of his plan occupied Vincent for three weeks, and then he went on his way, followed by the grateful praises of the inhabitants of Maçon. Happy would it be if for every Augean stable in the **world** such a Hercules could be found as Vincent de Paul!

Resigning the place which he had happily held for so many years in the Count de Joigny's family, Vincent took up his residence as Principal in the Collége des Bons Enfans. At this time he was about forty-nine years of age, and he is described as a man of average stature, well-knit, with a large head, and rather bald. His forehead was high, broad, and commanding; **his** eye keen; his demeanour grave, but gentle. By constant self-discipline he had so conquered a natural austerity of manner, and so acquired an attractive grace and mildness, that it was scarce possible, men said, to find any who could make religion more comely in the eyes of the world, or more easily gain souls to Christ. He was not a man of great intellectual force, of an original and creative mind; but he was capable of conceiving lofty ideas, and possessed the faculty of developing them into action. He was slow in deliberation and cautious in judgment; never committed himself to an enterprise every detail of which **had not** been carefully considered; nor offered an opinion on a subject until he had examined it from every point of view. Like Marlborough, he never lost his serenity; his resources were always and entirely at his command; and his patience was as inexhaustible as his energy. He was a man of few words; speech to him was silvern, and silence golden; but when he spoke it was always with firmness, distinctness, and a natural eloquence. Innovations in religion, and, in fact, changes of all kinds, he strongly disliked; and unconsciously he acted on the principle of the old Latin saying, " Quieta non movere."

If I were to adopt the plan of writers who compile books upon Representative Men, and label each with a particular virtue or mental qualification, I should put Vincent de Paul before the reader as a type of *Charity*. This was the dominant inspiration of his life, his guiding motive, the principle underlying all his thoughts and actions. The majority of men undoubtedly consider themselves charitable, and, perhaps, in a limited way, are really so; that is, they will fling a penny to a beggar, or contribute some small sum to a " deserving case." But Vincent de Paul's charity reached a far higher standard, expanded in a much broader development. To the poor, the distressed, the feeble, he gave *himself*. His conception of Charity is embodied in the following passage from an address he delivered to the members of his Community: " Let us love God, my brethren," he said, " but let it be at the cost of the labour of our arms and of the sweat of our brow; for very often these frequent acts of the love of God, of delighting in Him and longing for Him, and other such affections of a fervent heart, though in themselves very good and desirable, are nevertheless to be regarded with suspicion when they do not lead us to the practice of an active love. ' Herein,' our Lord says, ' is my Father glorified, that ye bear much fruit.' It is to this we must look: there are many who, having attained to a composed and well-regulated exterior, and to an inner man filled with great thoughts of God, rest there, but when it comes to deeds, or there is occasion for them to act, they stop short. They pride themselves upon their warm feelings; they content themselves with the sweetness of their communion with God in prayer; they can speak of these things with the tongues of angels; but if there be occasion to work for God, to suffer, to mortify themselves, to instruct the poor, to seek the lost sheep, to dispense with some comfort, to welcome sickness or any other misfortune, alas! they are no longer there, their courage fails them. No, no, let us not deceive ourselves: all our work consists in doing (*Totum opus nostrum in operatione consistit*)."

But Vincent de Paul's charity went still further. He carried it into his judgment of man's character and motives. He put the best construction upon all that was said and done. His philanthropy was so fervent, so real, that he desired to render to every one the duties and services of charity. And this, because he constantly bore in mind the fact that men are all children of the same Father, and saw Him in them, whosoever and whatsoever they might be. King or noble, bishop or priest, merchant or artisan, Dives or Lazarus,—in each he saw the image of our Lord; and, therefore, each had a claim upon his honour, his love, and his duty.

On the growth of his association of Mission Priests, on the increase of their members and the extension of their sphere of labour, it is unnecessary for me to dwell. Enthusiasm, in a good cause, when sustained and guided by what one may call the practical faculty, almost invariably does something more than "deserve" success; it accomplishes the results it desires, and even grander results than its most sanguine visions had anticipated. The old Collége des Bons Enfans soon proved inadequate to the accommodation of Vincent's little army of Christian workers; and in 1632 he transferred them to the large disused conventual buildings which had at one time served as the lazar or leper house of Paris. From this date to 1660, the last year of the founder's earthly career, no fewer than seven hundred "missions" were held by priests from S. Lazarus alone, while branches of the Society were established in as many as six-and-twenty of the French dioceses.

The next important work undertaken and carried out by Vincent was the establishment of a system for the better training and preparation of candidates for holy orders; the necessity for such a system having been impressed upon him by his own observations of clerical apathy and negligence. "He used to say that as ,a conquering general, if he would keep possession of the

towns which he has taken, must leave strong garrisons behind
him; so, after Satan had been driven from his strongholds, it was
very necessary for faithful soldiers of Christ to occupy the ground:
and that, unless good and earnest priests could be provided to
care for and help on the souls which had been won for God, it
was almost certain that they would fall back again, and their last
state be worse than the first; and yet he was well aware, from his
own acquaintance with the clergy in country places throughout
the length and breadth of the land, as well as from the complaints
which reached him from all sides, how few such were to be
found." With Vincent de Paul, to recognise an evil was to
devise a remedy for it. He perceived clearly that he could not
depend upon the existing generation of clergy, who had grown
accustomed to the old groove, and were wedded to the ancient
traditions; his work must be prospective; he must seize upon the
young men then coming forward as candidates for the ministry,
and endeavour to breathe into them a loftier spirit, to animate
them with a higher sense of the sacredness and solemnity of their
duties. His plan was, to require that all who desired to receive
holy orders should be carefully instructed in the necessary studies,
should make a spiritual retreat for some days before ordination,
and go through a course of moral theology. It was taken up at
once by the Bishop of Beauvais and the Archbishop of Paris;
and as it extended, Vincent established Retreats for Ordinants at
S. Lazarus, receiving five times a year, for a period of eleven
days, as many as from seventy to ninety men, who were entertained as welcome guests, and lodged and boarded free of
expense.

The happy influence exercised by these "Retreats" Vincent
acknowledged with a grateful heart; but he had a keen perception
of the weakness of human nature, and apprehending that the
good impressions and resolutions acquired and made in the calm
retirement of S. Lazarus might only too readily glide away in
rude contact with the world, he sought for some means of sus-
taining and confirming them until they assumed a character of
permanency. After much reflection, he instituted for this purpose
a weekly conference; and every Tuesday the young priests assembled at S. Lazarus to discuss the nature of their solemn duties,
and the graces necessary for a faithful discharge of them. Out

of these gatherings grew a confraternity or guild, the members of which were bound to assist one another under certain fixed conditions; thus, they visited those who were sick, and in case of the death of any one of their number, the survivors followed him to the grave. They were required to rise at a certain hour, to spend at least half-an-hour a day in silent prayer, and daily to read, kneeling and bare-headed, a chapter of the New Testament.

We now arrive at the third, and perhaps the greatest, of Vincent de Paul's philanthropic achievements, the one in right of which he finds a place among our "Good Samaritans"—the institution of "Sisters of Charity." His first movement in this direction was made as early as 1617, during his brief residence at Chatillon. Deeply moved by the mass of poverty and indigence around him, and struck by the want of all order and definite effort in the attempts to relieve it, he collected a body of workers, whom he called a "Confraternity of Charity," for the purpose of providing the sick poor, at their own houses, with proper care and nursing. Any devout women, married or unmarried, were admitted into this Confraternity, who, for the love of God and His poor, were willing to enter upon the work, and to pledge themselves to a regular and systematic discharge of it. By degrees, these charitable Sisterhoods spread over all the land, as they almost invariably sprang up in places where Vincent and his lazarists had held a Mission; a proof of the eminently *practical* character of Vincent's religious teaching; of the manner in which he insisted that Faith should confirm itself by Works. Their supervision, therefore, assumed the proportions of an onerous charge, and Vincent, who had already too many burdens to sustain, looked around him for some capable assistant to whom he could entrust it. At last he found the helper he needed in a Madame Louise Legras, an affluent widow, who desired to dedicate herself wholly to God's service.

"From her youth," says her English biographer, "she had been of a serious and philosophic turn of mind: so much so, that her father gave her a classical education, as the only one worthy of her gravity and intellect. But her soul soared beyond the things human learning professes to teach: she longed to enter a religious order; and she would have done so, but that her health proved too delicate for the austerities of the cloister. Even in the world she led a life of retirement, charity, and self-denial; and from the first years of her marriage she belonged to the poor and to the sick of her parish. She visited them in their illnesses, gave them medicines and relief, attended on them, made their beds, consoled or exhorted the sorrow-stricken or the dying, and shrank from no task, not even from the laying out of the dead. In the fervour of her zeal, Madame Legras wished, in placing herself under the spiritual guidance of Vincent, to take a vow of devoting herself henceforth to the poor; but, with his cautious dislike of anything resembling precipitation, he forbade her to do so for four years: during which he put her zeal and charity to repeated trials."

The Romish clergy are not generally credited with any special scrupulousness in their efforts to make converts or gain adherents; but nothing is more remarkable about Vincent de Paul than his absolute straightforwardness, and his anxiety at all times that none should join him who had not measured the full extent of the responsibilities they undertook. It was owing to this wise honesty that few, if any, of his helpers, when once they had put their hand to the plough, drew it back again; that few, if any, fell out of the ranks, disgusted with or overborne by the hardness of the service. Not until he had thoroughly tested the constancy of purpose of Madame Legras did he offer her the supervision of his Confraternities of Charity. She accepted it gladly, and in an earnest spirit; and thenceforth, every summer, she visited the different villages where they were established, examining into their progress, and instructing and encouraging their members. At first they had been limited to the rural districts; but in a country where no Poor Law existed, no government or national organization for dealing with pauperism, the need for them was quite as urgent in the towns, and especially in the capital itself. Several Parisian ladies, therefore, obtained Vincent's permission to form themselves into an association under the same rules and regulations as those which governed his Sisterhoods. But it was soon found, as evidently Vincent had anticipated, that full reliance could not be placed upon ladies of rank and position; in some cases their husbands objected to the work they had undertaken; in others the ladies themselves grew weary of its monotony or unpleasantness. Then they began to devolve their duties upon their servants, who did not always attend very strictly to the orders they had received, or, at all events, failed to show—as that class of individuals so very generally fail to show—the love, the sympathy, and the tenderness more eagerly coveted by the poor, and more keenly appreciated by them, than any material relief.

To meet this difficulty Vincent looked around him for pious women who would give up their whole lives to the care of the sick; who would accept it as an honourable vocation and a service unto God: women whom no social ties would distract in the performance of their duties, and in whose intelligence and fidelity a reasonable confidence might always be placed. It was in 1635 that his search first proved successful; and he had then the good fortune to meet three or four "Sœurs de la Charité," under the general superintendence of Madame Legras. He required of them that they should undergo a careful training in nursing the sick, in preparing and administering medicines, and other useful and necessary details; and, further, he accustomed them to habits of obedience and devotion. The work grew rapidly, because it met a "felt want," and met it in a practical and reasonable manner. The seed sown by Vincent ripened into a noble harvest which has spread over many lands. His "Sisters of Charity" were the direct ancestresses of our Sisters of Mercy, Sisters of the Poor, District Visitors, and the like. Madame Legras was the first of a long line of noble women, of whom, in our own day, we have seen such bright and beautiful examples as Miss Aikenhead, Sister Dora, and Florence Nightingale. To women,—such women as felt no vocation for a married life, but were nevertheless disinclined to immure themselves in the unprofitable life of the cloister,—women with a capacity for usefulness and a talent for administration, if they could but find appropriate fields for their exercise,—this new organization proved scarcely less beneficial than to the rich and poor for whose benefit it was called into existence. This is the advantage of all good and noble work: it entails a benediction upon the workers as well as upon those for whom they work.

In the following century, as I have elsewhere written, no fewer than four-and-thirty establishments of Sisters of Charity existed in Paris alone; and they were also to be found in Italy, Spain, Poland, and the Netherlands, in America, and even in India.

Neither Vincent nor Madame Legras had at the outset any conception of the grandeur of the enterprise they had, with so rare a sagacity and so chivalrous a benevolence, initiated. And, in truth, no reformer can ever see the full extent of his reform, or estimate aright its abundant possibilities. Could Columbus, when he revealed the Western World to the eager eyes of Europe, have anticipated, even in his wildest dreams, the vast issues of his discovery? In every "work of noble note" the increase comes from God. As for Vincent de Paul, he did what all of us ought to do—the task that lay close at hand to be done, without thought of the future; and he did it admirably, with rare prudence and good sense, and a careful adaptation of the means to the end. He did not attempt too much, nor did he ask too much of the agents he employed. Gradually he enlarged his design and extended his sphere of action, until almost every branch of philanthropic effort fell within the range of his Sisterhoods; but nothing was done hastily, nor without mature consideration.

The regulations which he laid down for the observance of the Sisterhoods bore the stamp of his practical turn of mind. The Sisters were subjected to a probation, a preliminary trial, of five years; after which they took the vows of obedience, chastity, and poverty; but they took them for one year only, so that if they repented of the weight of the burden, they might be at liberty to get rid of it. Nor could they renew them without the permission of the Superior, who took every opportunity of reminding them of the nobleness of the vocation to which these vows were the solemn and sacred introduction. "A Sister of Charity," he would say, "has need of a higher degree of virtue than the members of the austerest religious order. There is no order of religious women which has so many and such arduous duties to perform; inasmuch as the Sisters of Charity must in themselves discharge almost all the offices of other Orders. In the first place, they must labour after their own perfection, with as much earnestness as the Carmelites; next, they nurse the sick like the nurses of the Hôtel Dieu and other hospital sisters; and lastly, they undertake the education of young girls, like the Ursulines. . . . They must remember," he would add, "that although they are not nuns, that condition not being suitable for the works of their vocation, for that very reason, because they are more exposed than those who are cloistered and shut out from the world, they require a loftier and severer virtue. Their monasteries are the homes of the sick; their cells are hired rooms; their cloisters, the streets of the city or the wards of the hospital; instead of a barred gate to protect them, they have the fear of God; and for a veil, holy modesty. Hence, they must in all places endeavour to behave with at least as much reserve, self-control, and edification, as regular nuns use in their convents; and to obtain of God this grace, they must labour to acquire all the virtues commended to them by their rules, and particularly a deep humility, a perfect obedience, and a great detachment or separation from their fellow-creatures. And, specially, they must exercise any possible precaution to preserve perfect purity of body and soul."

To some ears a ring of Romanism will be perceptible in this advice, but, nevertheless, it is, on the whole, very broad and generous and wise. Vincent continued, in the instructions which he addressed to the Sisters :—

"Lest the spiritual offices they render should interfere with the bodily services they are bound to give,—a thing which might easily happen, if by too long staying with one patient they allowed others to suffer through neglecting to give them their food or medicine at the proper hour, they must be very careful in the management of their time, and the arrangement of their work, according to the number and needs of their patients, great or small. And since in the evening their duties are not generally so urgent as in the morning, they may choose that time for the instruction and exhortation of their patients, particularly when administering to them their medicines.

" In their attendance upon the sick they must make God their sole thought and object, and thus they will become indifferent alike to the praises they may receive or the hard words that may be dealt out to them, except that they will turn both to good account, inwardly rejecting the former, and humbling themselves in the knowledge of their own nothingness; and welcoming the latter, in honour of the revilings of the Son of God upon the Cross by those very men who had received of Him so many favours and graces.

" No gift, however small, must they accept from the poor whom they assist. They must beware of thinking that the poor are in any way obliged to them for the services they render; seeing that in very truth, it is they themselves who are indebted to the poor. For through that small charity which they bestow not of their substance, but only of a little care, they make to themselves friends, who shall one day have a right to receive them into everlasting habitations. And even in this life they receive, through the poor on whom they wait, greater honour and truer satisfaction than they could have dared to hope for in the world: of this they must be careful to make no improper use, but rather to abase themselves in the consciousness of their own unworthiness.

"They will remember that they are called Sisters of Charity,— that is, sisters whose profession it is to love God and their neighbour; and that, therefore, besides the sovereign and supreme love they must have for God, they ought to excel in the love of their neighbours, and especially of their companions. Accordingly, they will avoid all coolness and dislike towards any, and, at the same time, all special friendships and attachments to some above others; since these two vicious extremes are sources of division, both in communities and among private persons, if they dwell upon and entertain them. And should it happen that they have quarrelled among themselves, they must ask pardon of one another, at the very latest before they retire to rest.

"Moreover, they will bear in mind that they are called 'servants of the poor,' which, in the eyes of the world, is one of the lowest conditions, to the end that they may always have a low opinion of themselves, and reject immediately the least thought of vain-glory which might arise in their minds, if they hear any good said of their works, remembering that it is to God that all the glory is due, because He alone is the author of them.

"They will be very faithful and exact in following their Rule, and all the laudable customs which have hitherto been observed in their mode of life, particularly those which concern the perfecting of their own happiness.

"But not the less must they remember that, whenever necessity or obedience requires it, they must always prefer the service of the poor to their devotional practices, inasmuch as, in so doing, they are leaving God for God."

Vincent was too wisely liberal to enforce upon the Sisters a rule as rigid as that which prevails in the cloister. The obligations imposed upon them were of a different order: namely, to rise all the year round at four in the morning; to pray twice a day; to live with extreme frugality; to drink no wine, except in illness; to minister to the sick even in the loathsomest diseases; to watch throughout the night by the bed of the dying; to live shut up within the dull walls of an hospital; to breathe air heavy with infection; to endure with calmness, and even to welcome with rejoicing, fatigue and danger, sickness and death. It will be seen that the Sisters took upon themselves a burden of no light weight, but it was one which God gave them strength to bear, and in the bearing of it there was joy and blessing and honour.

To Vincent de Paul the heroism which was thus quietly manifested was a constant source of wonder and loving admiration, though it was he himself who had called it into being. His feelings are best described in his own words, which he addressed to the Mission Priests in 1658. At the request of the French queen, Anne of Austria, he had sent four Sisters to attend upon the wounded soldiers at Calais, and two of them had succumbed to fatigue:—"I recommend to your prayers," he said, "the Sisters of Charity whom we sent to Calais to assist the wounded. Four went, and two—the strongest—have sunk beneath the burden. Imagine what four poor girls can do for five or six hundred sick and wounded soldiers! Is it not affecting? Do you not consider it an action of great merit before God, that women should, with so much courage and resolution, go amongst soldiers to relieve them in their need; that they should voluntarily subject themselves to so much fatigue, and even to disease and death, for the sake of those who braved the perils of war for the good of the State? We see how these women were filled with zeal for the glory of God and the succour of their fellow-creatures! The queen has honoured us by writing and asking for more Sisters to be sent to Calais, and four leave to-day for that purpose. One of them, about fifty years of age, came to me last Friday at the Hôtel Dieu, where I was then staying. She said that, having learned that two of her Sisters had died at Calais, she came to offer herself to go in their place, if I would allow it. 'Sister,' I replied, 'I will think about it.' See, my brethren, the courage of these women, thus to come forward like victims, glad and willing to render up their lives for the love of Jesus Christ and the good of their neighbour. Is not this admirable? In truth, I know not what to say, except that they will judge us on the great day of the Lord. Yea, they will be our judges, unless we are as ready as they to expose our lives for the love of God."

From the beginning of 1649 the infirmities of old age began to press heavily upon our indefatigable philanthropist, whose charity was so broad and so true because it was a charity inspired by a profoundly religious feeling. He was no longer able to move about on foot or on horseback, but was compelled to use a little carriage. He grieved deeply at being constrained to yield himself this indulgence, but a still greater grief was his inability to kneel. No failure of energy, however, no abatement of zeal, could be detected in his discharge of the multifarious works of mercy, charity, and religion that devolved upon him. Never was there greater need of his spirit of enthusiastic benevolence and his power of organization; for the war had desolated the provinces of Champagne and Picardy; and the Mission priests, under his direction, were severely taxed in their heroic endeavours to feed the hungry and clothe the naked, to shelter the homeless and bury the dead. For more than three years this colossal work fell almost entirely upon Vincent and his disciples. And when it was happily ended, for this apostle of Christian charity yet remained another loving and charitable task. In 1653 a wealthy Parisian citizen consulted him on the best means of employing a large sum of money which he desired to devote to God's service. It was to be placed entirely at Vincent's disposal: the sole condition being that the donor's name was never to be revealed. The trust was one he could not refuse; and after meditation and prayer, he proposed to expend it in founding a Hospital or Almshouse for aged and necessitous artisans. The donor approved of the suggestion; and accordingly Vincent purchased and fitted up suitable premises for the accommodation of twenty men and as many women, under the title of the Hospital of the Name of Jesus.

His weakness continued to increase as year after year was added to his record. Before his end came he experienced the hard trial of losing three of his dearest friends—a M. Porlail, who had been his life-long helper, his secretary, and assistant-superior; a certain Abbé de Chandenier, whose Christian fellowship he had held as a very precious thing; and Madame Legras, his right hand in carrying out the organisation of the sisterhoods of charity. With eighty-four winters on his head, the venerable Superior might well long to follow his beloved friends to their rest, and he was often heard to sigh,—" For how many years, O Lord, have I abused Thy grace! Alas! I live too long, since there is no amendment in my life, and my sins are multiplied according to the long procession of my years." And again, on hearing of the departure of any of his mission-priests, he would say :—" Thou leavest *me*, O God, and callest to Thyself Thy servants. I am one of those tares that spoil the good grain Thou gatherest, and here am I still, uselessly cumbering the ground. Well, well, my God, *Thy* will be done, not mine."

However long deferred, the summons of death must come at last. About noon, on the 25th of September, 1660, the aged Father fell suddenly into a deep sleep. For some time he had suffered attacks of drowsiness; but this one was so profound and calm that, on his awaking, an attendant remarked upon it. " Ay," said Vincent, " it is the brother who has come beforehand, while we are waiting for the sister."* On the day following, Sunday, after hearing mass in the chapel, and communicating, as was his custom, he was seized with a stupor and lethargy, from which it was impossible to rouse him, except for brief intervals. The physician acknowledged that no remedies could further avail, and advised that the last rites of the Church should be administered. Vincent revived sufficiently, however, to utter a few words of benediction on the members of the congregation, absent as well as present. In the evening, the last Sacrament was administered. His feebleness was so great that it was thought safer not to undress him, and he spent the night in his chair, in sweet and tranquil communion with his heavenly Father. Of the various ejaculations repeated to him, the one which seemed to please him most was the " Deus adjutorium meum intende ; " and whenever he heard it he would respond, " Domine ad adjuvandum me festina." A Retreat was at this time being held in the Home, and the priest

---

* We are reminded of the poet Shelley's lines :—

" How wonderful is Death,
Death and his brother Sleep!"

who conducted it obtained permission to take leave of the aged saint, for whom he had always cherished a deep affection. He asked his blessing on all the associates of the weekly Conferences, and his intercession to obtain them grace; so that the fire of holy zeal which his words and example had kindled and kept alive might not be quenched after his departure. Vincent answered, "Qui cœpit opus bonum, ipse perficiet." These were his last words, and they explained the motive of his life—an absolute forgetfulness of self, and an entire devotion to the glory of his Divine Master.

A few minutes later, at half-past four o'clock on the morning of Monday the 27th of September, 1660, he passed away, bequeathing to posterity that most precious of all legacies, a glorious example.

It was the distinctive merit of Vincent de Paul, whose life we have thus briefly sketched, to open up to women a new and adequate vocation, one particularly adapted to their special gifts, one in which all their graces of character could fitly be utilised. Many lives, which might otherwise have been wasted, have thus been made profitable to themselves and to others. The womanly virtues—meekness, obedience, purity, tenderness, patience—are just those which are most necessary to the successful accomplishment of the work of charity; and women succeed so much more fully than men in labours among the sick and distressed, because they are so much more sympathetic. Even their physical qualifications are an advantage—the light tread, the delicate touch, the soft voice. Again, they have a wonderful power of endurance, and night after night they will watch by the bedside of the invalid, always on the alert, always attentive, always patient and gentle; when men would have succumbed to fatigue, and in their weariness grown irritable or negligent. It was a happy day for the poor and suffering when a new sphere of duty was revealed to women as the active agents of organised charity.

Commenting upon the career and character of Amelia Sieveking, her biographer justly remarks that, though all women cannot be, nor is it necessary that they should be, exactly what she was, yet can they strive to imitate her in her truthfulness, her faithful performance of duty, her conscientiousness and self-control, the earnestness which she carried into the smallest matters, the diligence with which she followed every good work, her severity towards herself, her mildness and discretion towards others. She was possessed with the spirit of Vincent de Paul; her life, like his, was a grand illustration of compassionate and ministering love, of the highest and purest charity; and in the Protestant Church she sought to found such an association of women, devoted to benevolent work, as he had founded in the Roman. In the history of female effort and endeavour we know of no more stirring chapter than that which records her long labours in the Cholera Hospital of Hamburg. It was in October 1831 that the plague of Asiatic cholera swooped down, in fearful severity, upon the city of Hamburg. Unterrified by its ghastly concomitants, she immediately tendered her services to the hospital authorities. They were accepted, and for eight weeks she waited upon the sufferers with indefatigable vigilance, soothing them in their agonies, and receiving their dying injunctions and wishes. The entire superintendence of the men's wards, as well as of the female ward, and the general supervision of the attendants, were placed in her hands. We may gather some idea of the onerous nature of her daily duties from a letter she wrote to her mother :—

"In the morning," she says, "I have to see that, before the physician's visit, all the wards are cleaned, the beds made, and that everything is in proper order. Three times a day—morning, afternoon, and evening—I visit the sick-beds in company with the physician, the surgeon, and the apothecary, when Dr. Siemssen gives to each the directions belonging to our respective departments. In the women's ward, of course, I have to pay particular attention to all the medical orders, as I am responsible there for their exact fulfilment. In the men's wards my special duty is only to observe what diet is prescribed, according to which I draw up the daily bill of fare for the housekeeper. Not unfrequently, too, I have to read the necessary notice of his admission to the relatives of the sick man, as the patients are often brought in unknown to their family. The linen of the wards is also under my charge. At present I also occasionally take part, when I see any need for it, in the actual nursing of the men; but if the number of our patients should greatly increase, I should be obliged to do less of this even in the women's ward, as the general superintendence would be of more importance, and would give me full occupation; but it would then be of great use to me that I have thus acquired experience in the treatment of patients."

Only those who know something of hospital life, and something too of the terrible character of choleraic disease, can fully appreciate the courage, resolution, and truly heroic patience displayed in the performance of such delicate and difficult duties. What was very striking in Miss Sieveking's character was her thorough simplicity of mind, her entire unconsciousness that she was doing a good and a great work. It seemed to her the work she was called upon to do, and as a matter of ordinary duty she did it, and did it with all her powers. "On the whole," she writes, "I am certainly at present called to the work of Martha rather than Mary; but this is quite right. It is enough if the Lord will but employ me in His service; the mode I leave entirely to Him. If I could but perform the labours of Martha with the quiet mind of Mary! but I am far from attaining this at present. Now and then, too, I find an opportunity for practising something of Mary's work, when it is suitable, which certainly happens very rarely. I read aloud portions of some religious book to my nurses and patients, and in the convalescents' wards I have been requested by some to procure them something to read. I gave them various little selections of prayers, and sent to the Christian Circulating Library for some other works of a more entertaining character. The following day I was greatly pleased at being voluntarily asked by some of the readers for a Bible, that they might look out the text referred to, and I immediately procured two for them."

The following extract illustrates her surprising energy and vigour:—" I continue very well in health, and it is really remarkable what a degree of physical strength is given me from above. Thus, last night, when a sick woman was brought in who required close attendance, I did not get to bed until four o'clock in the morning; at half-past six I had to rise again, and at seven my coffee was brought, but at eleven I had never yet found a moment in which I could drink it; and with the exception of the time when I was writing out the list of diets, half-an-hour at dinner, half-an-hour in the afternoon, when I had a cup of tea in my own room, and half-an-hour in the evening, when I read aloud from a devotional work in my own ward, I have never sat down ten minutes together in the whole day; and yet I feel no trace of fatigue. And my dear mother must not imagine this to be the result only of excitement; my mind is perfectly quiet and composed; indeed, I feel better when there is a great deal to do; an inactive life in an hospital would be indeed something terrible."

In later years she spoke with much frankness of her motives and experiences during this episode of her career:—" While in the hospital," she said, " I received many letters telling me of the judgment pronounced by various people on my conduct, and though a few praised me, for the most part I was blamed. I was particularly sensitive to blame in this case, for though I certainly did seek the glory of God in the first place, yet I cannot deny that sometimes the thought had glided into my mind that people would admire my self-sacrifice. Instead of that, it was, 'She wants to do something remarkable; she wants to set up for a martyr,' and all this was very good for me. But if I was humbled by the answer of men, I was but confirmed in my resolve to persevere until I had overcome all hindrances and fairly solved the problem before me. I was called an enthusiast, but it was by prayer that I conquered, and never have I regretted the step I then took. From that time, too, I determined never in future to stand in dread of the opinions of men, or to allow them to destroy my peace."

The great work of Miss Sieveking's life was the foundation of an order of Sisters of Mercy in the Protestant Church. With pain and regret she had observed that the Protestant system offered no such employment for the charitable energies of women as the Roman; and that they were thus deprived of what for themselves could not be other than a valuable spiritual training, while the poor and destitute were left without the aid and counsel they so sorely needed. She saw that in hundreds of instances unmarried females were debarred from doing the good to which their hearts inclined them, because they had not the assured position and official sanction which a definite organization, under the sanction of the Church, would provide. And it was her conviction that many a soul, struggling anxiously towards the pure and the true, but let and hindered by external or internal influences, would, in such a vocation, find the strength and support it needed, and be prevented from sliding back into the slough of worldliness. What society required was, in her belief, an organization for the relief of the poor and destitute; and she held that such an organization could be worked more beneficially and effectively by her own sex than by men. Such, indeed, was the case in the Primitive Church; in which women of good repute were encouraged to devote themselves to the Church's service, to visit the poor, nurse the sick, and teach the female catechumens.

Stolberg says of Vincent de Paul, that he had one noteworthy custom. "This man, who undertook and executed such a colossal mass of work, used to begin very slowly; slowly laid his foundations, examined long what the will of God might be; but when once convinced what it was, he went forward with irresistible power, and God granted him results as speedy as they were fruitful." Miss Sieveking was of the same mind as Vincent de Paul. Her scheme of a Protestant Sisterhood she meditated with devout care, pondering every detail, and anticipating every objection; and in 1832 it took actual form and shape. Started at first by her individual energy, the Association was soon reinforced by the energy and goodwill of kindred spirits; so that in one year the number of working members increased from fourteen to twenty-five. The rules of the Sieveking Association were gradually adopted by the numerous guilds and sisterhoods that sprang out of it, and those now operating in connection with the various Protestant Churches must all be traced back to this one original.

Without the purest courage, without the loftiest enthusiasm, and that faith and hope which are its main elements, Miss Sieveking could never have accomplished the work she did. The reader, we think, will feel a blush of shame as he reads her simple account of the labours of a single day. "I get up," she writes, "at half-past four, and am busy for the school-children until six. I take my breakfast while I am at work. At six I start for the city, arriving at the Town Hall about a quarter after seven. Here there are generally about twenty or more poor people waiting to speak to me. This lasts till half-past eight, when I go to our own house and look through any notes that have come for me, or prepare something more for my school, and if there is any time left before lessons begin, I take another walk, either to call on some of the poor people, or go on their errands to the doctor for the poor, and guardians, and the like. At ten o'clock my little ones come to me, and stay until nearly two. At half-past two I go to the Free School, where I give religious instruction till half-past three. The time from half-past three till five is filled up with errands or writing for the Association. At five some of my former scholars assemble, and first I hold a regular Bible lesson with them; then we drink tea and converse, and towards the end of our time I generally tell them anything likely to interest them in the way of literature or general subjects. At eight o'clock they separate. Meantime the visiting reports from the ladies of the Association have been sent in. These reports, upwards of a hundred in number, have to be looked through, many things to be taken note of, and the visits newly apportioned. This work employs me as long as I can keep awake, but I cannot finish it for bed-time."

Such was a day in Miss Sieveking's busy life. But of course it signifies an amount of labour which few persons would be justified in undertaking, because few would have the physical or mental energy requisite to carry it out. Moreover, it leaves no time for self-culture, or private devotion, or kindly intercourse with friends. We may work, however, in Miss Sieveking's spirit without implicitly or servilely adopting her method.

Among her later achievements were the building of a model lodging-house, and the establishment of a children's hospital. Both were eminently successful, as were all Miss Sieveking's projects; partly because they were always so thoroughly matured, and partly because everything she did was done at the right time. Much good work is ruined by over-haste, and much by inopportuneness. It is useless to sow the seed until the field is ready. Meanwhile her Association prospered largely, and she lived to celebrate its twenty-fifth anniversary; when the great idea which had filled her whole soul and animated her whole life, the devotion and consecration of her sex by works of love and living charity, had ripened into a great fact, into a blessed reality.

"Every great and commanding movement in the annals of the world," says Emerson, "is the triumph of enthusiasm." But in the present time enthusiasm is greatly sneered at and depreciated.

This new departure is a pitiful and discouraging sign. For what *is* enthusiasm but an earnest devotedness towards some high purpose?—an eager belief in the value of some special object, a constant effort to attain the heights of spiritual and intellectual endeavour? What is it but an emotion of the heart, a passion of the soul? What is it but the life and force and power which make men and nations capable of doing great things, or of suffering and waiting? In the eyes of the Pharisees our Lord was an enthusiast: so was St. Paul in the eyes of Festus. And were not the Christians of the first two centuries enthusiasts, amid the fires and wild beasts of Rome? Are not all men enthusiasts who, at the risk of their hearts' blood, and in despite of the bitterest suffering, strive to purify, to better the world? How all such reformers and philanthropists are laughed at by the cynical philosophers of these latter days, when a cold and self-satisfied indifference to all unselfish exertions or generous impulses is represented as the highest phase of a wise man's wisdom! The old shibboleths of loyalty and truth and patriotism and self-sacrifice,—in a word, every phase and form of enthusiasm,—are derided and dishonoured by the disciples of the new philosophy. Yet let us not shrink back ashamed from the worship of the pure and beautiful. Let us not shut our hearts against those sweet purifying influences which flow from a desire to live a noble and an upright life. Let us not fail to keep before our eyes an Ideal, to which it shall be our constant effort and yearning to attain. Let us never refuse to share in any work which has for its object the elevation of humanity. Where would this world be but for the enthusiasm of its reformers, philanthropists, teachers? What but enthusiasm has set up the cross of Christ in the islands of the wide southern seas? What but enthusiasm has consolidated the fabric of our constitutional freedom? What but enthusiasm has covered our and with schools and raised the common people out of a slough of apathetic ignorance and degradation? And it is this same enthusiasm, with all its cleansing and ennobling vitality, that each one of us should carry into his daily life, so that it may give breadth and height to our thoughts, an inspiration to our industry, and dignity to our manhood.

It must have been enthusiasm, the highest, purest enthusiasm, which strengthened and supported Mompesson during his experiences of the plague at Eyam. Most of us have read of St. Carlo Borromeo's heroic devotion when the pestilence ravaged Milan, how he bent over the beds of the death-stricken, and administered food and medicine and the consolations of religion while breathing the fatal air of infection; but few, perhaps, have heard of the humble English pastor, who played as noble a part, though on a less conspicuous stage. William Mompesson was Rector of Eyam, a picturesque Derbyshire village, between Chatsworth and Buxton, when the plague last visited England (1665). He had been married only a few years, and by his wife, a beautiful young creature of twenty-seven, had two lovely children, a boy of three and a girl of four years of age. When the terrible pestilence showed itself in the village, he at once sent away his little ones; but his wife would not leave him, and the two remained to share the dangers and trials of their people. Mompesson was a brave and thoughtful man; he fully appreciated the peril of the situation, and set to work with calm resolution to confront it. To London he sent for the remedies most in vogue; and to the Earl of Devonshire at Chatsworth he wrote, to promise that the villagers should not cross the boundaries of their parish, so as to spread the contagion, if he would provide that food, provisions, and other necessaries should, at regular times, be deposited at certain points on the hills around, whence they might fetch them, and leave the proper payment. Further, all letters should be placed on a stone, and duly fumigated, or passed through vinegar, before they were sent into circulation. The Earl readily assented to these propositions, and for seven dreary months Eyam was thus fenced off from the outer world—remote and alone, like some island in the far-off melancholy main.

The Eyamites, inspired by their pastor's example, behaved heroically. They submitted without a murmur to this rigid seclusion; and though among the rocks and dales of that part of Derbyshire escape would have been easy, not one of them, it is believed, made an attempt to pass the prescribed boundary.

Mr. Mompesson, as a sanitary precaution, held his services out of doors. The spot which he selected for this purpose is still pointed out. A torrent in the winter dashes down a cleft in the rugged hill-side in the middle of the village; in the summer its bed is dry. Towards the village the ascent is clothed with soft velvety turf, and sprinkled with rowan and hazel and elder, and made musical by the songs of birds. On the other side the slope is steep, and broken with sharp rocks, which here start up into uncouth columns and spires, there form into irregular archways, hung with ivy and leafy growth. One of these rocks, which was hollow, and could be entered from above like a gallery, served Mr. Mompesson as pulpit and reading-desk, and his congregation seated themselves on the green banks opposite. Twice on Sundays Mr. Mompesson read prayers and preached; he read prayers also on Wednesdays and Fridays; and every day, on a hill above the village, he read the funeral service over the victims of the plague, allowing no obstacle or hindrance to interfere with his performance of these sacred and solemn duties.

His wonderful faith supported him; and though, in addition to those services, he paid continual visits to the sick, and nursed and fed them, and prayed with them and cheered them, he preserved his health unshaken. Four-fifths of his parishioners, in spite of all his cares and precautions, were carried to the silent hill-side cemetery, but he still retained his energy and vitality. It was not until his wife was taken that he lost heart. Her illness was very brief; for fatigue and anxiety had so reduced her strength that she could offer no long resistance to the enemy. She was often delirious; but when she was too much exhausted to endure the exertion of taking cordials, her husband would implore her to try for their children's sake, and she lifted herself up and made the effort. She bore her agonies with a serene patience, and died calmly, repeating the responses to her husband's prayers with her latest breath. To Mompesson her departure was like the going out of a great light. Left alone amongst the dead and dying, he felt as if his own end were close at hand, and in writing to his patron, Sir George Savile, spoke of himself as his "dying chaplain," and commended to his generosity his "distressed orphans." But he was quite resigned and peaceful. "I thank God," he wrote, "that I am willing to shake hands in peace with all the world; and I have comfortable assurances that He will accept me for the sake of His Son; and I find God more good than ever I imagined, and wish that His goodness were not so much abused and contemned."

It was in August that Mrs. Mompesson died. For two months longer the pestilence prevailed, and the bereaved servant of God, supported by his devout enthusiasm, continued his ministrations among the sick and discharged his pastoral duties towards the living. Gradually the extreme violence of the scourge abated; the victims grew fewer daily; and at last there came a day when the hand of the destroyer ceased to smite. After the 11th of October there were no fresh cases; and Mr. Mompesson set to work to burn all woollen stuffs in the place, lest the infection should linger among them. Writing on the 20th of November, he states some particulars of the terrible character of the visitation. "The condition of this place," he says, "hath been so dreadful, that I persuade myself it exceedeth all history and example. I may truly say our town has become a Golgotha, a place of skulls; and had there not been a small remnant of us left, we had been as Sodom, and like unto Gomorrah. My ears never heard such doleful lamentations, my nose never smelt such noisome smells, and my eyes never beheld such ghastly spectacles. Here have been seventy-six families visited within my parish, out of which died 259 persons."

Who can doubt but that it was his holy enthusiasm which strengthened and sustained William Mompesson through the full course of his dreadful, arduous labours? It is a notable fact that their severity did not permanently affect his health; he lived to a ripe old age, dying, full of years and honours, in 1708.

Miss Kavanagh has preserved for us the record of a noble woman, whose labours among the sick and poor were not less worthy than those of our Derbyshire pastor. In or about 1752, Anne Marie Gilbert Auverger was born at Château-Giron, a little town of Brittany. Her philanthropic tendencies—if I may use so big a phrase in association with one so simple and unassuming—manifested themselves at an exceptionally early age; she was only fifteen when her parents, at her urgent request, placed her as boarder with the Sisters of Mercy who ministered to the sick of Vitré. It was understood that she desired to devote her life to this holy work. She remained at Vitré for a year, patiently availing herself of every opportunity of learning, so to speak, her profession, and accustoming herself to face the most loathsome forms of disease,—and only those accustomed to hospitals know what loathsome forms disease sometimes assumes! On returning home she petitioned that, as most in accordance with her tastes and her future calling, she might wear plain brown gowns; and when some persons objected to this simplicity, and to her caps, which were not becoming, they said, for so young a maiden, she answered with a smile,—" I wish to save up all my charms for heaven. The fashions here do not please me; I hope to be better adorned there than you are now." This speech savours a little, perhaps, of exaggeration; but there was true wisdom in her reply to a sister who censured her habitual liveliness, and told her "she was very merry for a girl so devout." " Religion," said she, "is not melancholy; one cannot but feel happy in the service of so good a master as God."

At all events, her service was cheerfully and constantly rendered. After morning prayer, she daily distributed bread and gave out work to a large number of the poor. She spent the afternoon in visiting the sick, disregarding all obstacles of weather or distance; carrying the sunshine of her presence into the remotest cottages, and into the squalidest stables, where wretched peasants, men, women, and children, less valued than cattle, perished of cold and hunger. In the evening she taught four pauper children.

The repute of her good works brought her the means of accomplishing and extending them. Liberal givers poured their donations freely into her hands; made her their almoner: they gave the money, she the time, the labour, and the thought. In the years 1769 and 1770 Brittany suffered severely from a treble visitation of scarcity, severity of weather, and contagious disease. The Marquis de Château-Giron, a nobleman of wealth and benevolence, employed this young girl, then only in her seventeenth year, as the steward of his charities: he had heard of her enthusiasm, her energy, her sympathy with the suffering, and felt well assured that the moneys entrusted to her would be prudently employed.

Anne Auverger did not limit her zealous exertions to cases of physical distress. Her compassion for the sinner was even greater than her pity for the sufferer; and towards the weak and erring of her own sex her charity was boundless. With the courage of a transparently pure soul, to whom all things were pure, she visited them in their abodes, boldly penetrating into the very haunts of vice; she spoke to them with pathetic candour; and though her warnings were not always heeded, she was never insulted,—the most abandoned were constrained into silence in her presence. She wisely aimed at prevention as well as cure, and to do away with the temptations of poverty and idleness, hired a house for the reception of friendless young girls, boarding and lodging them, providing them with employment, and carefully superintending their conduct. One of them, by some clandestine agency, was beguiled into a place of evil repute. As soon as she was apprised of the circumstance, she hastened to the den, boldly entered it, smote its owners with brave pitiless words of reproach, and rescued her *protégée*, for whom she immediately procured a situation in the country. When this incident became known, some fastidious natures professed to be horrified, and informed Anne Auverger that the world disapproved of her conduct. "The world!" she exclaimed; "we must let the world speak: it condemns everything which seems to censure its own selfish maxims."

In 1771, a contagious fever ravaged Château-Giron, and Anne multiplied her noble labours. Day after day she waited upon the sick with her usual fearlessness and zeal. But the effort proved too much for her strength. In her weakened condition the fever seized upon her; she was unable to resist it; and after an illness of only five days she departed, leaving behind her a memory of singular beauty and brightness, and the name, which at so early an age she had gloriously won, of "The Mother of the Poor."

It is now universally admitted that the "Open Sesame" by which one may hope to get at the hearts of the poor is sympathy. A sympathetic word or look is more prized by the distressed and suffering than any alms. It is an acknowledgment of the tie which binds all humanity together. The poor feel no gratitude for the gift that is bestowed by the cold and indifferent hand that tells of a cold and indifferent nature; they feel no gratitude for that mechanical charity, that system of grants and doles, by which society too often endeavours to compound with its conscience and dispense with the necessity of individual exertion. No, what the poor crave and appreciate is sympathy; but there can be no sympathy where there is no knowledge. And how is this knowledge to be obtained? Between the rich and the poor in England yawns a gulf almost as impassable as that which in the parable separates Dives and Lazarus. They form "two worlds," wholly distinct and apart from each other in their feelings, tastes, ideas, sentiments, and needs; having no points of attraction, but rather of repulsion. Writers upon India tell us that the great difficulty of the British Government is its inability to get at the real opinions of its Indian subjects; between the Hindoo and the Englishman rises a barrier of ignorance which prevents the growth of an intelligent and practical sympathy. We know nothing of the millions whom it is our lot to govern. Such, in England, is, on the whole, the position of the "upper classes" towards the lower. They have little, if any, knowledge, and certainly only a superficial knowledge, of the currents of thought and feeling by which they are swayed.

Upon this lamentable fact hinges the plot of a striking novel recently published, "All Sorts and Conditions of Men," in which the hero and heroine are represented as conscious of its existence, and as chivalrously bent upon obtaining a real and thorough acquaintance with the lower orders by the expedient of living among them. They abandon their social habitat, and in fictitious characters descend from the one world to the other; submit themselves to entirely new conditions of life; and divest themselves as far as possible of their old associations. What is here so ingeniously portrayed as a romantic enterprise was, to a certain extent, actually undertaken and carried out, less than twenty years ago, by a philanthropic member of the "privileged class;" and his heroic work was done in the very part of London,—Stepney, the east-end,—in which the authors of the novel referred to place the scene of their ingenious inventions. "Two millions of people, or thereabouts," as they remark, "live in the east-end of London." Yet "they have no institutions of their own to speak of, no public buildings of any importance, no municipality, no gentry, no carriages, no soldiers, no picture-galleries, no theatres, no opera,—they have nothing." There is no grace or beauty to brighten their lives and refine their tastes. The "respectable" streets are dull and monotonous, narrow thoroughfares, with rows of small brick houses on each side, distinguished by their uniformity of ugliness. As for the poorer and less reputable highways and byways, their unloveliness, their squalor, is almost beyond belief. An artist condemned to spend his whole life in this miserable region would, we think, soon go mad—mad with disgust and despair—mad with a sense of the depths to which humanity degrades itself.

It was, however, in the centre, or almost the centre, of this strange region that Edward Denison took up his abode in the autumn of 1866. The spot he chose is called Philpot Street, and it lies between the din and dinginess of the Commercial Road and Mile-end Road. For the son of a Bishop, a scholar who had gained high University honours, a man of culture and refinement, an athlete who had rowed in "the eight" of his college, was a good shot and a skilful horseman, no more unpromising residence could apparently be selected. But he went there voluntarily, and he went there on "a mission," a self-imposed mission, characteristic of the generosity of his temper and the enthusiasm of his character. For some years his attention had been gravely directed to the condition of the lower classes. He had studied them abroad, during his travels in France, Italy, and Switzerland; and at home he had sought to grapple with many of the problems which their habits and manners involve. He was no theorist or sentimentalist, however, and would not advance a step without some knowledge of the ground which he was treading. He soon arrived at the conclusion that to know the poor you must live among them; and as one of the visitors or almoners of the Society for the Relief of Distress, he resolved to live among those who inhabited the Stepney district of East London.

Here is his own account of his field of labour:—

"Stepney is in the Whitechapel Road, and the Whitechapel Road is at the east end of Leadenhall Street, and Leadenhall Street is east of Cornhill; so it is a good way from fashionable and even from business London. I imagine that the evil condition of the population is rather owing to the total absence of residents of a better class—to the dead level of labour which prevails over that wide region, than to anything else. There is, I fancy, less of absolute destitution than in the Newport Market region; but there is no one to give a push to struggling energy, to guide aspiring intelligence, or to break the fall of unavoidable misfortune. . . . It is this unbroken level of poverty which is *the* blight over East London; which makes any temporary distress so severely felt, and any sustained effort to better its condition so difficult to bring to a successful issue. The lever has to be applied from a distance, and sympathy is not strong enough to bear the strain. It was as a visitor for the Society for the Relief of Distress that I first began my connection with this spot, which I shall not sever till some visible change is effected in its condition. What a monstrous thing it is that in the richest country in the world large masses of the population should be condemned by an ordinary operation of nature annually to starvation and death! It is all very well to say, How can it be helped? Why, it was not so in our grandfathers' time. Behind us as they were in many ways, they were not met every winter with the spectacle of starving thousands. The fact is, we have accepted the marvellous prosperity which has in the last twenty years been granted us, without reflecting on the conditions attached to it, and without nerving ourselves to the exertion and the sacrifices which their fulfilment demands."

Denison undertook a two-fold duty,—he was a helper and a teacher. He carried to the distressed and suffering the assistance they needed in food, medicine, and clothing; he advised them on the better ventilation of their houses; he gave to some of the most deserving a start in life. But besides and above this, he laboured to raise the intellectual status of the community and to awaken their spiritual nature. All that he did had the religion of Christ as its basis; the Bible was the book from which his teaching was mainly drawn. He felt that a man was immeasurably elevated in the scale of humanity when he became a Christian. One of his schemes was the establishment of an evening class of instruction for working-men, and it proved very successful. His hearers hung delightedly on his lips while he traced to them the course of the Gospel history, illustrating it from his large stores of miscellaneous knowledge. "Why," he said,—" why don't the clergy go to the people as I propose to go? What is the use of telling people to come to church, when they know of no rational reason why they should; when, if they go, they find themselves among people using a form of words which has never been explained to them; ceremonies performed which, to them, are entirely without meaning; sermons preached which, as often as not, have no meaning, or, when they have, a meaning intelligible only to those who have studied theology all their lives?"

The interest excited by these weekly scriptural lectures was not ephemeral: it extended and deepened. Of one of the later he writes:—"I am warming to my work here. I gave them fifty minutes last night on the text, 'Not forsaking the assembling of ourselves together;' and though I am confident they understood nearly all I said, it might perfectly well have been addressed, with some modifications, to an educated audience. I preached Christianity as a society, investigated the origin of societies, the family, the tribe, the nation, with the attendant expanded ideas of rights and duties; the common meal the bond of union; rising from the family dinner-table to the sacrificial rites of the national gods; drew parallels with trades unions and benefit clubs, and told them flatly they would not be Christians till they were communicants."

He flavoured his lectures with plentiful quotations from Wordsworth, Tennyson, and the poets generally, believing that, if his hearers did not wholly understand them, they would catch here and there a beautiful image or thought, and be pleased by the melody of the verse. While he infused so true a religious spirit into his teaching, he was far from being an advocate of voluntary, that is, denominational, education. In truth, his experience convinced him of the complete inadequacy of the system to meet the national wants. And thus, some years before the Elementary Education Act was passed, which has covered England with Board Schools, he wrote:—"I comfort myself with the confident hope that we are even at the threshold of State secular education. Elementary mental training is but making the jar; it is no argument against the jar that you don't know what may get into it unless you are allowed also to fill and solder it up. People must have a very queer notion of human nature who fancy that a mind which has been taught to think will be a less fit receptacle of Divine Truth than one which is incapable of thinking. I am inclined to say with the Roman Emperor, when he was told the Christians were about to destroy a temple, 'Let the gods defend themselves.' I feel it a blasphemy even to think that God's truth can suffer by the extension of man's truth."

Indiscriminate charity was one of the evils against which our reformer resolutely set his face. "If we could but get one honest newspaper," he says, "to write down this promiscuous charity and write up sweeping changes, not so much in our poor-law theory as in our poor-law practice, something might be done. . . . Things are so bad down here, and that giving of money only makes them worse. I am beginning seriously to believe that all pecuniary aid to the poor is a mistake, and that the real thing is to let things work themselves straight; whereas by giving alms you keep them permanently crooked. Build school-houses, pay teachers, give prizes, frame workmen's clubs, help them to help themselves, lend them your brains; but give them no money except what you sink in such undertakings as these.

"The remedy is, to bring the poor-law back to the spirit of its institution—to organise a sufficiently elastic labour test, without which no out-door relief can be given. Make the few alterations which altered times demand, and impose every possible discouragement on private benevolence. Universal administration of poor law on these principles for one generation would almost extirpate pauperism."

But it is a question whether this arbitrary drying-up of the springs and sources of private charity would not have an injurious moral effect. Charity is twice blessed; it blesses the giver as well as the recipient; it expands his sympathies and spiritualises its aim. To interfere with it would be to favour the growth of individual selfishness; and we cannot but believe that the morality of the nation would eventually suffer. Promiscuous charity no doubt deserves the severest censure: in truth, it is not charity, but laziness; to inquire into the merits of every case would be a serious trouble, and it is easier to satisfy one's conscience by a general bestowal of alms. But private benevolence need not be, and very often is not, promiscuous charity; and we may encourage the former, the true Samaritanism, without encouraging the latter, which is simply its counterfeit.

For several months Mr. Denison continued to labour in the field he had chosen, though at times he felt very profoundly the depression arising from its unchanging unloveliness. "My wits," he writes on one occasion, "are getting blunted by the monotony and ugliness of this place. I can almost imagine—difficult as it is—the awful effect upon a human mind of never seeing anything but the meanest and vilest of men and man's works, and of complete exclusion from the sight of God and His works—a position in which the villager never is, and freedom from which ought to give him a higher moral starting-point than the Gibeonite of a large town." He carried on his weekly lectures with increased enthusiasm as he perceived that they grew in popularity. He visited the sick, he organised schools, he taught the children, he "interviewed" the local authorities, he promoted the sanitary improvements of the neighbourhood. All this was good and useful work; but no doubt the *best* work was done by the mere fact of his presence—the presence of a refined, cultivated, God-fearing gentleman—in such a district. In Spenserian phrase—he made a sunshine in a shady place. He was an example, of which everybody could recognise the significance and beauty; an ideal to which many, we can well believe, were fain to make their little efforts to rise. If there is anything of good in the practice of the Christian virtues, his self-denial, his active benevolence, his generous devotion, his purity of life and speech, could not but exercise a happy influence. We can well believe that if his chivalrous conduct found any considerable number of imitators, the gulf of which we have spoken as separating almost hopelessly the rich and the poor would soon be bridged.

It was not possible, perhaps, that a man of Mr. Denison's social position, with his many duties and responsibilities, should always be able to isolate himself among the poor of East London; and yet we can hardly help regretting that his singular and beautiful experiment was not of longer duration. But his friends and relatives, and among them his uncle, the Speaker of the House of Commons, were urgent that he should enter into Parliamentary life, and he at length consented to become a candidate for Newark. He was elected; but he made no conspicuous figure in the House of Commons, notwithstanding his unquestionable mental power. And this because his interest in political questions was merely speculative, while in social questions it was active. "The problems of the time," he wrote, "are social, and to social problems must the mind of the Legislature be bent for some time to come." It was to these his own mind was given. He cared very little for the strife of parties, for the fierce contentions between the "ins" and the "outs." He had no political ambition; what he wanted was to see the condition of the poor ameliorated, and the national life of England made purer and happier.

Into what special channel his activity would have finally been directed it is impossible to say. With his large views and broad sympathies, his abilities, force of character, and wide experience, we cannot doubt but that he would have made his mark in his time had he lived long enough. One would have supposed that for a man of such exceptional gifts God would have had some exceptional work to do; but His ways are not as our ways, and for all we know, Denison's work was, by his life in that East-End London district, to set an example and a pattern. However this may be, his physical strength gave way beneath repeated attacks of congestion of the lungs, and in the autumn of 1869 his illness assumed so serious a character that he was ordered to winter at Cannes, or take a voyage to Australia. As the latter alternative seemed to offer the fuller opportunities for the acquisition of knowledge, it was accepted. But during the outward voyage he sank very rapidly, and on January 26th, 1878, within a fortnight of his landing at Melbourne, he passed away, in his thirtieth year. To a man of such brilliant promise, so prematurely cut short, we may say—

> "Thy leaf has perished in the green,
> And, while we breathe beneath the sun,
> The world, which credits what is done,
> Is cold to all that might have been."

At the village of Hauxwell, near Richmond, in Yorkshire, was born, on the 16th of January, 1832, Dorothy Wyndlow Pattison, the daughter of the Rev. Mark Pattison, rector of Hauxwell. As a child she was very delicate, but was distinguished by the sweet equableness of her temper, and by her love of fun and mischief. Her faculty of observation was very fully developed, and in her tenacious memory she accumulated a constantly increasing number of facts and particulars to be made use of in after life. There seemed no reason to suppose at that time that her career would have in it anything extraordinary; yet a judge of character, taking note of her strong will, her fortitude, her self-control, her quiet reserve of power, would have seen that for an extraordinary career she was in every way fitted. Her devotion of herself to others was early manifested. As she grew in years, she grew in strength; became a good and daring horsewoman, riding across country and following the hounds with true Yorkshire zest; and gradually developed into a tall, strong, and very handsome creature, with a great capacity for humour, a merry laugh, and an incessant activity. In height she was about five feet seven inches; she was beautifully proportioned, with small and finely-formed hands. Her features were almost Greek in their regularity; the forehead was wide and high; the mouth small, with exquisite red lips, which, when they parted, disclosed a perfect set of pearly teeth; **her** dark-brown eyes, somewhat widely apart, shone with **eloquent** expression; and her hair, of the same colour as her eyes, **waved** all over her head in crisp curls. A more fascinating woman one seldom meets with; for in addition to this rare personal beauty, she possessed a wonderful charm of manner,—that almost magnetic influence which is virtually irresistible.

The finer faculties of her nature seem to **have been first** awakened by Miss Florence Nightingale's work during the Crimean War; and if her father had consented, she would have joined the band of devoted women who went out as nurses. Her longing, however, for a more stirring and **more** useful career than the home-life afforded did not subside; **and** after her **mother's** death, in 1861, she was left free to gratify it, Mr. Pattison refrain**ing from** further opposition. The first essay was as a village schoolmistress at Little Woolston, near Bletchley, where she remained for three years. But the post did not bring out all **her** capabilities; she felt, to use her own expression, that she was not doing her utmost,—and on **her** recovery from a severe illness, induced by daily toil and night nursing, she entered the Sisterhood **of the** Good Samaritans, whose head quarters were at Coatham, near Redcar, **in** Yorkshire. **This** was in **the** autumn of 1864. The training to which she was immediately subjected tested with sufficient harshness her sincerity **of** purpose. She made beds cleaned and scoured floors and **grates**, swept **and** dusted, and finally "**did the** cooking" in the kitchen at Coatham. But it was coarse work, and, as it seems to us, useless work, which could have been done as well, or perhaps better, by a hired "help"; and was, at all events, wholly unworthy of Dorothy Pattison's fine intellect and many gifts. We rejoice when she was finally established in the Cottage Hospital at Walsall; for we feel that then she had at last discovered her true sphere of labour (1865).

She had a great deal to learn, for she had had no regular training in the art of nursing, but she had the will and the capacity. Her special ambition was to prove a good surgical nurse; and her tenacious memory and keen faculty of observation assisted her in discerning the character of wounds and the exact position of fractures. Her coolness, courage, and talent gave her an immediate command over the rough men, colliers and operatives, who were her principal patients, while her beauty and her charm of manner and her ready sympathy drew their hearts towards her, so that they became her willing slaves. Constitutionally able to bear, without disgust or shrinking, the terrible details of loathsome diseases and ghastly accidents, her profound pity for human suffering gave a lighter touch to her skilful hand and a warmer light to her beaming eye. She moved to and fro in the hospital wards like an angel sent down from Heaven to bless and to save. The wounded bore their agony more patiently when she looked upon them; the dying yielded their last breath more calmly if she sat by their side. A beautiful and a fascinating woman, to whom was open the path of wedded life, with its fair prospects of domestic happiness, she deliberately chose a lot which brought her into hourly contact with pain and affliction in their most repellent aspects, because she felt that in such a lot she could best exercise her varied powers, and lift up others to her own moral height. And she accepted it with so much enthusiasm, and with so fine an aptitude, that "Sister Dora" soon became a household word in Walsall, and a type of self-sacrifice and ardent Christian zeal.

Walsall, as everybody knows, is a large and populous town situated on the borders of "the Black Country," amid a labyrinth of tall chimneys, which vomit forth clouds of smoke and tongues of flame, darkening the heavens with a pall of lurid gloom, and filling the atmosphere with a pungent odour. Here, on the brow of a hill, a new hospital was erected in 1867, and placed under the charge of Sister Dora, who, out of her private means, had given liberally towards its erection. It contained twenty-eight beds, but, at need, could accommodate a larger number; and was so arranged that the entire nursing could be done by one person, if that person possessed Sister Dora's activity of mind and body.

The three wards into which it was divided opened upon one another in such a manner that when she read prayers she could be heard distinctly by the inmates of all. The out-patient department was connected with it by a glass passage, which Sister Dora's taste converted into a greenhouse. The hospital windows overlooked a garden, and a breadth of green turf, and clusters of trees and shrubs, which defied the smoke. At the bottom of the hill ran the South Staffordshire railway, and the passage of the trains afforded a constant amusement to the patients, especially to those connected with the railway, who were able to recognise the driver of each passing engine by his peculiar and characteristic whistle.

In 1868 the hospital was opened, under the personal superintendence of Sister Dora. The same year was marked by an outbreak of small-pox in Walsall, which added greatly to her labours, as, after her hospital-work was done, she sped from house to house to tend the unhappy sufferers. "One night," says her biographer, "she was sent for by a poor man who was much attached to her, and who was dying of what she called 'black-pox,' a violent form of small-pox. She went at once, and found him almost in the last extremity. All his relations had fled, and a neighbour alone was with him, doing what she could for him. When Sister Dora found that only one small piece of candle was left in the house, she gave the woman some money, begging her to go and find some means of light, while she stayed with the man. She sat on by his bed, but the woman, who had probably spent the money at the public-house, never returned; and after some little while, the dying man raised himself up in bed with a last effort, saying, 'Sister, kiss me before I die.' She took him all covered as he was with the loathsome disease, into her arms, and kissed him, the candle going out almost as she did so, leaving them in total darkness. He implored her not to leave him while he lived, although he might have known she would never do that. It was then past midnight, and she sat on, for how long she knew not, until he died. Even then she waited, fancying, as she could not see him, that he might be still alive, till in the early dawn she groped her way to the door, and went to find some neighbours."

Than this the annals of heroism present few finer instances of generous and self-sacrificing courage. Is it wonderful that a woman capable of such deeds became the idol of the poorer classes of Walsall,—that the rough, rude men who wrought in its coal-pits and iron-works would have died for her, as she would have died for them? No doubt there was some slight alloy of baser metal in the gold. Sister Dora was proud of her power, and not insensible to the homage she received. But against this admixture of human weakness she strove very resolutely; and after all, it does but bring her nearer to our sympathies. Otherwise she had been something too perfect, too pure and good for human nature's daily food; whereas it is as a woman, with a woman's tenderness and devotion, and something of a woman's foibles, that we love to regard her.

To what is known as conservative surgery, a surgery that seeks to save rather than to cut away the diseased or broken limb, Sister Dora paid special attention, and in this department she attained a remarkable degree of success, owing, I think, to her patience and tenacity, and womanly dexterity and delicacy of manipulation. A fine vigorous young man was brought into the hospital one night, whose arm had been torn and twisted by a machine. The doctor pronounced immediate amputation indispensable. Observing the sufferer's look of despair, and moved by his agonized lamentation, Sister Dora scrutinized the wounded limb very carefully. "Oh, Sister!" exclaimed the man; "save my arm for me, it's my right arm!" She turned to the surgeon. "I believe I can save it if you will let me try." "Are you mad? I tell you it's an impossibility; mortification will set in in a few hours; nothing but amputation can save his life." To the anxious patient she said, simply: "Are you willing for me to try and save your arm, my man?" His consent was rapturously given. The doctor walked angrily away, saying: "Well, Sister, remember it's your arm: if you choose to have the young man's death upon your conscience, I shall not interfere; but I wash my hands of him. Don't think I am going to help you." Heavy as the responsibility was, she accepted it, encouraged by the patient's evident confidence in her; and for three weeks she watched and tended his arm, and prayed over it, day and night. At the end of that time, catching the doctor in one of his most amiable moods, she asked him to examine the limb; and with no little reluctance, for no professional man likes to be proved in the wrong, he complied. There it was, straight, firm, and healthy!

SISTER DORA.

"Why, you have saved it!" cried the doctor, "and it will be a useful arm to him for many a long year."

We shall not attempt to describe Sister Dora's feelings, in which a sense of triumph was not unnaturally mixed with thankfulness; or those of the patient, who thenceforth became one of her loyalest admirers. He went by the name of "Sister's Arm," and after he ceased to be an in-patient, constantly came to have his limb looked at,—that is, to gaze on the noble and devoted woman who had done him so great a service.

Not the least remarkable of her qualifications was her tact. She managed her patients with as much address as the most experienced diplomatist could handle the Powers on the political chessboard. A man who had been brought into the hospital seriously hurt, swore all the time she was dressing his wounds. "Stop that!" said she, abruptly; and the man did stop, only to begin again when the pain returned. "What's the good of it?" said Sister Dora; "*that* won't make it any easier to bear." "No, but I must say something when it comes so bad on me, Sister." "Very well, then, say 'poker and tongs.'" And "poker and tongs" was adopted by the ward in place of unseemly oaths.

Her genial humour and love of fun diffused a pleasant atmosphere through the Hospital. She would invent games for the boys, and sometimes sit down with a patient at chess or draughts. Men of the working classes have very little genuine amusement in their lives; hard work and dull homes weigh upon them with a constant pressure; and the monotony of dulness which surrounds them is, I think, one of the painfullest results of nineteenth-century civilisation. Judge then of the freshness and novelty of the scene which that Hospital presented! A beautiful and cultivated woman, who knew how to preserve her dignity, whom they instinctively felt to be immeasurably above them, could yet joke and laugh with them every day, could raise their spirits by her delightful humour, had always a ready answer to their questions, and inspired them with a pure and wholesome merriment of which previously they had had no conception. "Make you laugh!" said a big Irishman; "she'd make you laugh when you were dying!" Truly, she realized the graceful words of the ward, and made a sunshine in a shady place!

From Miss Lonsdale's admirable biography of "Sister Dora"

we borrow the following account of an average day's work at Walsall Hospital, as recorded by one of Sister Dora's lady-pupils :—

Sister Dora used to come down into the wards at half-past six in the morning, make the beds of all the patients who were able to get up, and give them their breakfasts, until half-past seven, when it was time for her own breakfast. The bright, sunshiny way she always worked, with a smile and a pleasant word for every one, was in itself a medicine of the best kind. She would quote proverbs or apt pithy sayings, and she often asked questions which would set all the men thinking—such as "What is a gentleman?" By the time she came back into the wards, they would have their answers ready. "To go to church with a gold watch in your pocket" constituted a gentleman, according to one man. "To be rich and well-dressed, and have a lot of fellows under you," was another answer. Some men were more thoughtful, and said, "Nay; that won't make a gentleman." But although most of them knew what a gentleman was *not*, they found a great difficulty in defining what he *was*. Then would Sister Dora, while she was dressing the wounds, or going about her work, give them her own views on the subject, and show how a man could be rich and well dressed, and yet be no gentleman. She told me once that she often cried when she went to bed at night to think how many good words she might have spoken in season to her men. She used generally to invent some queer nickname for each of them, in order that they might (as she said) the sooner forget their former lives and associations, if those had been bad. Thus one man would always be spoken of as "King Charles" (even having it written upon his egg for breakfast), because his face suggested Charles the First to Sister Dora. "Darkey," and "Cockney," and "Pat," and "Stumpy," would answer to no other names. Rude, rough fellows, of course, constantly came in; nobody had ever seen such a woman as this before, so beautiful, so good, so tender-hearted, so strong and so gentle, so full of fun and humour, and of sympathy for broken hearts as well as for every other kind of fracture, and the best friend that many of these poor maimed men had ever known. She was the personification of goodness and unselfishness to them; skilful and rapid in her work,—a great matter where wounds are concerned, and in a place where there was much to be done and few people to do it. After her own breakfast she read prayers on the staircase, so that all the patients in the three wards could hear and join. Then came the daily ward work—the washing of breakfast-things and of patients, and the dressing of wounds. At half-past ten o'clock there were usually several out-patients, who came regularly to have their wounds poulticed or lanced, or otherwise attended to. The doctor generally appeared about eleven, and went his rounds. At twelve came the patients' dinner, at which Sister Dora attended minutely to every detail, and always carved herself. Then she read prayers in the little general sitting-room, the lady-pupils, if there were any, and the servants only attending.

"Then followed dinner for the nurses, a very movable feast; sometimes put off for an hour or more, and sometimes omitted altogether, as far as Sister Dora herself was concerned, if any visitors whom she was obliged to see, or any accidents came in, at that time. Out-patients, who were treated every day, began to arrive at two o'clock, and truly their 'name was legion,' when it was no uncommon event for sixty or a hundred persons to pass through the little rooms in the course of an afternoon. It was a most interesting sight to watch Sister Dora with her out-patients. They had the greatest confidence in her skill, and with good reason. All faces brightened whenever she approached; she generally knew all about them and their circumstances—had perhaps nursed some of the family before as in-patients, and she always had a word of sympathy and advice for each. The doctors got through their part of the work quickly, for they passed on to her such minor operations and dressings as are entrusted to experienced dressers in large hospitals. The setting of fractures, and even the drawing of teeth, when no surgeon was present, were common operations to her. Her bandaging was so good that a surgeon at Birmingham called upon all his students to admire, and to study as a model of excellence, the bandaging of a man's head, which was her handiwork. The treatment of the out-patients often took between two and three hours, so that the in-patients' tea at five o'clock had sometimes to be prepared by the servants, when neither Sister Dora nor her pupils could be spared. About half-past five or six the nurses had their own tea; but it was rarely

that Sister Dora got a quiet meal, for either some one would
come tapping at the door, saying 'she was wanted,' or the
surgery bell would ring, as, indeed, it often did all day long.
'There is no peace for the wicked,' she would say, as she got up
to do whatever was needed. After tea she went into the wards
again, and this was the time to which her patients looked forward
all day. She would go and talk to them individually, or a
probationer would play the harmonium, and they would sing
hymns, she joining with her strong, cheery voice, while she
washed up the tea-things. Some of the patients would play at
games, in which she occasionally took part. She had a way of
inducing the men to wait on each other, and many of them did
this, besides a great deal of work in the wards. She always
had a devoted slave in some boy, whose ailments kept him
a long while in the hospital. A poor diseased boy called Sam,
who was about ten years old when he came, served her with
preternatural quickness and intelligence. One morning his arm
was so painful that, instead of getting up as usual, he covered
his face with the bed-clothes, and sobbed as noiselessly as he
could underneath them. Sister Dora was obliged that morning
to fetch the various articles she needed herself—cotton wool,
syringes, bandages, ointment, old linen, etc., which Sam usually
looked out, and put in order ready for her use. 'Tell Sam I do
miss him,' she said. *How* his tears ceased, and his face beamed
all over with delight, when her words were repeated to him! He
instantly dressed himself, and ran to fulfil his daily office. He
followed her about like her shadow, and was never so happy as
when doing something for her. She used to amuse herself by
consulting him occasionally, saying, ' **Now, Doctor!** ' (such was
his nickname), 'what would you do in this case?' Sam would
promptly reply, 'Iodine paint,' or 'Zinc ointment,' or whatever
he thought he had observed that she used in similar cases.

"A boy about seventeen years of age, whom Sister Dora called
'Cockney,' because he had been 'dragged up,' as he expressed it,
in London, came in with an injury to his leg from a coal-pit
accident. He seemed to have no one belonging to him, and his
leg was long in healing, partly because, short of strapping him
down, it was impossible to keep him from hopping continually
out of bed, when he ought to have been quiet. He was possessed

with a spirit of fun and mischief, and would have made a capital clown in a pantomime or a circus. Jests and jokes flowed from him spontaneously on all occasions. He gave a great deal of trouble, but everybody liked him. One of the nurses whom he plagued most remarked, 'I wonder Sister Dora has not had more influence for good over him.' After he had left the hospital, he came up one day to the out-patients' ward, and waited long for a sight of 'Sister,' saying afterwards, 'Isn't she beautiful! That is what I call a real lady.' How could any one, indeed, live with her without realizing how much there was to love and **admire?** and will not the recollection of her **beautiful** life and ministry prevent many a man from falling into 'that worst of scepticisms, a disbelief in human goodness'? '**Cockney,**' probably, will often look back with regret on the 'Christian tent,' as he called the hospital where it was his good fortune to be taken. By eight o'clock wounds had been dressed for the night, and the **patients'** supper was served. Sister Dora read prayer always, even when, as sometimes happened, her many **duties and** labours **had** so delayed her that most of the patients were asleep, for she said, 'The prayers go up for them all the same.' Just before bedtime **came** her own supper, when she would **often** be **very merry, and would relate** her many remarkable experiences **with intense fun and drollery.** Her keen sense of the ridiculous must have preserved her from much weariness of spirit. This was the time to which the lady-pupils looked forward, and when they expected to enjoy themselves, but they were not unfrequently disappointed. Sister Dora would just **look in at** the door and say, 'I am going to bed; I don't want any supper to-night.' This often happened on Fridays or during Lent, and how she managed to get through such constant **hard** work upon the very meagre diet she allowed herself was a marvel. Her life was one long self-sacrifice. '**We** *ought* to give up our lives for the brethren,' she said, and **she** acted upon her convictions."*

We have **already** hinted that Sister Dora **was not a "perfect character," but** a life which was one long self-sacrifice may be allowed **to counterbalance** many imperfections. I wonder whether the **Good Samaritan was a "**perfect character"? Maybe that at

---

* "Sister Dora." A Biography, by Margaret Lonsdale, pp. 93-100.

home he displayed, to the critical eyes of his own household, some glaring weaknesses,—infirmities of temper and of purpose, arrogance, self-will, or indecision; but for all that he kept alive in his heart the flame of charity, and when he fell in with the poor and afflicted, he did not pass by on the other side. And, therefore, we may believe that much was forgiven to him. Shall we not forgive something to Sister Dora? She was, we are told, a person of strong, almost violent prejudices, as a woman of such strength of character assuredly would be,—robust in her failings and foibles as in her virtues. She grudged others a proper share of work; she was over-impatient of feebleness or hesitancy; she loved her own way, and took care to have it; she was a little too fond of showing her physical strength, and a little too conscious of her superior capacities. Let all this be granted, and she remains a noble woman, of a type peculiar, I think, to England. Shrewd common-sense she combined with a highly imaginative temperament. Her piety was sincere, deep, and unostentatious. Her charity was boundless; her self-abnegation immense. She was a glutton of work, that is, of work in a good cause; and every unoccupied minute she regarded as a minute lost. Let us take her, then, as she was—a woman of rare gifts and powers, but not without some flaws of character, and yet thank God that He gave us such a pattern to live by.

A pattern and an example! It is the peculiar felicity of men and women of the type of Sister Dora that they help their fellow-creatures, not only by their own efforts, but by the efforts of those whom their life and teaching have inspired. Sister Dora's sphere of individual action and direct personal influence was comparatively limited; it did not extend, in her lifetime, beyond Walsall; but who shall pretend to compute the range of her *indirect* influence? How many have been inspired by her example? In how many hearts has the seed ripened which fell, day after day, from her lavish hands? Well, she lived for us as well as for others; and cannot we profit by her life? The reader shrugs her shoulders contemptuously; she replies, "We can't *all* be Sister Doras; we can't *all* superintend a Cottage Hospital, and tend the sick, and dress the wounded, and straighten the limbs of the dying." True; but we can all take of her spirit of pure philanthropy, her Christian charity, her deep devotion, and with these high graces

adorn our own little lives. We can be Good Samaritans in our own small circles, in our neighbourhoods, by our own firesides. There is no greater mistake than to believe no work good unless it is done on a large scale. Mary Magdalene's pot of ointment is as precious in the Master's eyes as St. Paul's prison-chains. Sister Dora herself was too sagacious not to see that her way could not be, and ought not to be, every woman's way. To a friend who had asked her opinion of woman's work, she said:—
"I feel pretty much like Balaam of old, as if I should give quite the contrary advice to what you wanted of me; to wit—you would like me to urge women working in hospitals, etc. I feel more inclined to harangue about women doing their work at *home*, being the helpmeet *for* man, which God ordained, and not doing *man's* work. Then, when they have faithfully fulfilled their home duties, instead of spending their time in dressing, novel-reading, gossiping, let them spend and be spent."

In our experience we have frequently noticed the dangerous delusion possessing young minds, that work to be good work must be heroic; that one must follow in the missionary's steps, and carry the Gospel of Christ into savage lands, or take charge of a hospital,—or at the least assume the robes and rules of a Sisterhood,—if one would merit and receive the Saviour's commendation, "Well done, thou good and faithful servant!" We have called it a dangerous delusion, because those overmastered by it are prone to sink into apathetic indolence,—to do nothing, because the work which lies close at hand is not grand enough for their lofty ideas. Ah, friends, let us take hold of that which lies close to our feet; let us do it in our best way; and finish it off as best we can, assured that the benediction of heaven will descend upon it. Those are fine hopeful words of Joubert's:—
"Whether one is an eagle or an ant in the intellectual world matters little; what *is* essential is to have one's place marked there, one's station fixed, to belong decidedly to a wholesome and regular order. A small talent, if it keep within its limits, and rightly discharge its task, may reach the goal just as well as a greater one." And the spirit in which we should address ourselves to our labour has been well described by Archbishop Trench:—

"Not as though we thought we could do much,
Or claimed large sphere of action for ourselves ;

> Not in this thought—since rather it be ours,
> Both thine and mine, to ask for that calm frame
> Of spirit, in which we know and deeply feel
> How little we can do, and yet do that."

In February, 1875, a fresh visitation of small-pox afflicted the town of Walsall; and to induce the poor to send their cases to the Epidemic Hospital, erected for that purpose, Sister Dora volunteered to take charge of it. Thence, in the following month, she wrote to a friend the following characteristic letter:—

"MY DARLING . . . .

"Your letter, which I received last night, made me cry: it was so long, so full of affection, and I had never seen anyone all day beyond my patients to speak to. My darling, you must not come; if anything should happen. You are a very likely subject to take it, and this place smells of pox from the moment you open the door. You must not fret. I rejoice that He has permitted one so unworthy to work for Him; and oh, if He should think me fit to lay down my life for Him, rejoice, rejoice, at so great a privilege! My heart is running over with thankfulness, and as I toil on I seem to hear the still, small voice, 'Ye did it unto Me.' . . . Oh, don't talk about my life. If you knew it, you would be down on your knees crying for mercy for me, a sinner. How God keeps silence so long is my wonder. Remember me at Holy Communion . . .

"If things were only going on well at the Hospital I should not mind, but . . . . is so naughty again. . . . The text and verse for to-day are so beautiful—' I will allure her, and bring her into the wilderness, and speak comfortably to her.'

> 'Once more He speaks—no stern rebuke,
>   No anger in the word—
> "Is it so hard to turn from all,
>   And walk with Me, thy Lord?
> Come; thou hast never heard My voice
>   As thou shalt hear it now;
> I have no words for brighter days
>   Like those the dark ones know!"'

Now, is not that beautiful? One man is blind with the pox. Another, a woman, is very delirious; she tried to escape last night;

it took myself and the porter to hold her down. That fellow is very good; he scrubbed the kitchen floor only this morning to save me. You would laugh to see me washing my babies. Poor things! they are smothered in pox. I am obliged to put them into a warm bath. . . . They are getting quite fond of me; but they do make washing. We have all that to do besides the night nursing, so you may fancy!

"I am writing this while waiting for my potatoes to boil. My bedroom and sitting-room is getting to look quite gay with flowers. I find time to read to my patients. They have scarcely ever heard of Jesus, and they are so ill they cannot attend to much. You must write again. I have no one to speak to, no time to read, and my letters are company at meal-times. I really wish you could take a peep at me; I am very bright and happy, and like this hospital better than the other. I have also much under my eye. Of course there is not the change of work, and no time for breathing a mouthful of fresh air. Faithful Murray comes every evening, and does my messages, etc. I believe he would not mind taking the small-pox for me to nurse him! Remember me most kindly to your husband. Kiss all my darling children.

"Believe me your affectionate

"SISTER DORA."

To me, the most remarkable episode in Sister Dora's career seems her ministration to the sufferers by the Burchells explosion in October, 1875. Eleven men, one Friday afternoon, were seated underneath the furnace, when an explosion took place, and a cataract of molten metal, seething and glowing, dashed down over them. In their agony and sudden alarm, they leaped into the neighbouring canal; but being, with some difficulty, rescued, they were conveyed to the hospital. The spectacle presented by their charred bodies was singularly awful. They were so burnt and disfigured as scarcely to retain the semblance of humanity. Some, in their deadly thirst, cried out, "Water! water!" A few were dying painlessly, their wounds having literally annihilated sensation; others moaned or shrieked, "Sister, come and dress me!" "*Do* dress me!" "Oh, you don't know how bad I am!" She answered,—"Oh, my poor men! I'll dress you all, if you'll give me time." To each she administered a glass of brandy, and then endeavoured to undress them; but the flesh was so burnt away that it was almost impossible to cut off their clothes.

So frightful were both sight and smell that the medical men of the town, who were promptly on the scene, suffered from constant sickness, and could hardly stay in the ward. Ladies who had proffered their assistance were driven away, overcome by their sensations; but Sister Dora, true to herself and her mission, never flinched. For ten days she tended the sufferers with unflinching fortitude, and did her best to alleviate their miserable condition, and to smooth for them the path to the grave. Only two recovered. One of these, named Cassity, describes her as going from bed to bed, talking, laughing, and even joking with the victims; sitting by their bedsides, and seeking to divert their thoughts from themselves by telling them stories. "She was with us," he said, "almost night and day;" and after all had died, except himself and a man named Ward, she would still come down twice or thrice in the night to see that these two were doing well. Cassity described her as, in cap and slippers, silently going round at two in the morning, from bed to bed, with a soft smile on her face. "It did you good only to look at her." Cassity, as he related his simple tale, would bare his burnt and shrivelled arms in testimony to the wonderful skill and patient attention of his nurse. Every time he mentioned "Sister Dora" he stood up, and reverently pulled his forelock, as if he had pronounced the name of a saint or an angel, which he was scarcely worthy to utter. "What we felt for her I couldn't tell you; my tongue won't say it."

Cassity went by the name of "Burnty." His feet were so much injured that he never expected to walk again; but Sister Dora assured him that he would certainly be able to do so, and, accordingly, before he left the hospital, sent him to be measured for a pair of boots, which was to be her parting gift. "Well," said the woman at the boot-shop, "I wouldn't be such a softy as to think you'll ever be able to wear a pair of boots with those feet." Greatly discouraged, Cassity returned to the hospital. "You'll wear out many pairs of boots, my Burnty," said Sister Dora. "And so I have," said Cassity; "she was right enough. But it was all along of *her*, who never left my burns a day all those months, without looking to them with her own hands."

Our first impression, on reading Miss Lonsdale's biography of this remarkable woman, was, we confess, that it was greatly exaggerated in colouring and tone; but a medical friend, who resided at Walsall during the period of Sister Dora's reign, assures us that it nowhere exceeds the literal truth. He speaks of Sister Dora as fascinating in the extreme; and as distinguished by the highest qualities of womanhood, as well as by those which men are apt to regard as almost exclusively belonging to their own sex. Courage and tenderness were fairly blended in her heroic nature. Of her generosity one must speak as highly as of her fortitude; of her brightness of disposition as of her patience; while her capacity for self-sacrifice was deepened and strengthened by her profound and unaffected piety. That she was "a clever woman" goes without saying; she had a natural gift of organization, a remarkable quickness of perception, and an extraordinary fertility of resource. In society she must have achieved quite a brilliant reputation; but a more lasting and a purer fame will be hers as "Sister Dora," of the Walsall Cottage Hospital.

We gather a few more anecdotes from Miss Lonsdale's pages.

Sister Dora, like most sunny and sanguine natures, was singularly successful in extracting amusements from what the world calls trifles, and in an hour's walk in the streets would find matter enough for the diversion of her patients for many a day. She had a great spontaneity of spirit, and loved to share her pleasures with others. One day, she fetched her lady-pupil to see a case in the out-patients' ward; and, with laughing eyes, exclaimed, "I have often heard the old saying, 'a hair of the dog that bit you,' but never before saw the remedy applied." She pointed to a dog-bite, on which a mass of *hairs* had been plastered, whether of the offending animal, or of some other dog, did not clearly appear.

On another occasion, a woman, who had been roughly handled by her brutal husband, came up to the hospital with a severe cut on her head. While she dressed it, Sister Dora listened with keen sympathy to the woman's simple narrative of her troubles, and her determination to go before the magistrates on the following morning, and prefer a charge against her husband. "Are you quite sure now to go?" asked the Sister. "Yes; I can bear such treatment no longer." Thereupon Sister Dora began to bandage the head much more elaborately than the wound required, and, observing her lady-pupil's look of surprise, remarked aside, with a look of keen enjoyment, "I think the husband will get an extra week for my beautiful *second* bandage."

A clerical eye-witness of Sister Dora's work for three years (1871 to 1874) has put on record his views of her character, all confirming the impression that she was a woman of extraordinary gifts and graces. "She had," he says, "a bright, ready wit, and a playful irony that never wounded, but often had the effect of stirring up some poor, feeble-spirited patient, bracing him like a tonic. . . . There was a man whom she induced to become quite a leader of the responses at prayers, by saying that his very name, Clarke, ought to make him help the parson. Poor fellow! Clarke had to lie many weary weeks with a shattered leg, and often he grew desponding. Fragments of bone used to work through the skin to the surface, and Clarke used to keep these splinters in a box. She used to rally him about *his bones*, and many a time made all in the ward laugh by asking Clarke 'to show his bones to some visitor.' She always tried to make Sunday a day of extra brightness, and the same at Christmas and Easter. (On these days there used to be full choral services held in the hospital). On the evening of New Year's Day she used to give an entertainment to the inmates, and as many old patients as she could accommodate. These festivals were most enjoyable. There was first a kind of 'People's evening,' or 'Penny readings entertainment,' and the patients seemed to forget their pains; and good humour and bright faces filled the great ward where it was held. Before it was ended, some one generally gave an address to the patients. Then came supper, to which all who could move off their beds sat down, and those who could not were well cared for. Many a poor fellow now at work in coal-pit and work-shop will long remember those evenings of bright and innocent mirth.

"She sometimes had patients who were utter sceptics. She soon found them out, and was always very careful, and used much tact in dealing with them. She knew that they were scanning her conduct, and would judge of Christianity more or less by the way she presented it to them in her daily actions. Many who came in scoffers went out convinced that Jesus was the Christ. I know none who were not convinced that she, at least, was true and good. One hard sarcastic Scotchman spoke to me about her just before he left the hospital. He was one of those working-men who are not uncommon in towns—men who have imbibed Tom Paine and Voltaire through secondary sources, and are bitterly prejudiced against Christianity and its professors, especially parsons. He told me he had watched her carefully while he lay there, and gave as his emphatic verdict, 'She's a noble woman; but she'd have been that without her Christianity!'"

He forgot that, at all events, her Christianity made her *nobler*. But was it true? Would she have been what she was "without her Christianity"? Was it not her Christianity which taught her to sympathize with the poor and suffering, with the feeble and distressed? The ancient world produced no such women as Sister Dora; because its creeds did not teach the beauty and sublimity of a life of self-sacrifice, of that "Altruism" which spends and is spent for the sake of those who fall in life's battle, and would perish of their wounds by the wayside, if the "Good Samaritan" did not perceive and bind them. While the keynote of the old philosophy is Endurance, that of the Christian teaching is Self-sacrifice; and Sister Dora, in her short but beautiful career, elevated the heathen virtue by blending it with the Christian.

One grand example of her faithful heroism must not be omitted. She took an active part in one of those admirable religious movements which the Church calls "missions," held in Walsall, in November, 1876, and conducted a special effort organised for the rescue of the wretched women who crowd the streets of a great town at night,—a class from whom the happier and purer of their sex generally shrink with loathing and disgust. In the course of her work she passed, with two companions, into a "slum," or narrow court of particularly evil repute. Pausing before a small house, which was brilliantly lighted, they looked in at the window, and saw a circle of women gathered round a table, and evidently receiving orders from an ill-looking man, apparently their master. She knocked at the door; no answer. She knocked a second time; and a man's voice growled, "Who's there?" "Sister Dora," was the reply. Then came a volley of oaths, and the question, "What do you mean by coming here at this time of night?" "Open the door," she replied; "it's Sister; I want to speak to you." Still swearing, the man obeyed. She paused on the threshold, and addressed him with much compassion in her look and tones. "Why, Bill, what possesses you to treat me like this? Don't you remember what you told me the last time you came up to have that head seen to?" Growls and oaths were the only reply, with orders to "Be quick, and say what she wanted."

"I'll tell you what I want," answered Sister Dora, advancing into the room, and holding out her hand, first to one woman and then to another; and as they crowded round her, she addressed them severally. "Well, Lizzie," or "Mary, how are you?" and "I've seen you before—did up your arm last winter twelvemonth —but I can't put a name to you;" or "You came up to see me two months ago." Then, speaking to them all, "I want you to go down on your knees with me now, this moment, and say a prayer to God." To the astonishment of the two clergymen, the whole party knelt with Sister Dora, while from a full heart she appealed to the Divine Father on behalf of her "brothers and sisters." As the man rose from his knees, he turned to her in a shamefaced manner, saying,—"I'm very sorry, Sister, I was so rude to you. I didn't mean it: you've been good to me." "Then," was the quick reply, "if you're sorry, will you do what I ask you?" "That I will." "I want you, and all these women here, to come with me into a room we've got hard by, and to listen to something some friends of mine have to say to you there." The man at once complied, and all repaired to the little mission-room, which was quickly filled.

Night after night, the waifs and strays, the fallen and the miserable, of Walsall assembled in this temporary place of worship. As many as thirty-five of the fallen women of the town were sometimes assembled; all gathered in by Sister Dora's unassisted exertions. They dropped in by twos and threes, most of them very quiet, and were received by Sister Dora with a few words of encouragement and sympathy. "There was something very touching," says an eye-witness, "in her treatment and attitude towards them. No condescension, no 'stand apart, for I am holier than thou;' but yet, though she was so gracious and sisterly, they seemed to feel that she was rather a pitying angel than one of their own sex. It seemed to me that she knew them nearly all *by name;* and she told me that she had doctored nearly all of them at different times. Many of them used to seek her only after nightfall, but she was ever ready to help, and never scorned them. I know not whether I need dwell on the service. There were three clergymen present. The service began with a hymn, which many of them joined in. Prayer followed. Then two short addresses were given, and were listened to intently, and not without evident emotion on the part of some. Earnest appeals were made to them to forsake their present courses, and offers of guidance and assistance to such as should resolve to do so. When the service was over Sister Dora spoke to each of them as they left, and obtained promises that they would come again. A second service was held, and seemed even more successful than the first. Several stayed behind at its close to speak with the clergy and Sister Dora. Three, I believe, were eventually rescued (I can only speak of *one* myself). Many of them seemed to feel themselves 'tied and bound with the chain of their sins,' but yet they had no strength to get free. Some of them were little better than slaves to some tyrant—some 'Bill Sikes,' who treated them like a dog, and whom yet they clung to with dog-like fidelity.

"For some weeks after the mission Sister Dora still continued her labours amongst these poor sinners. Every Sunday night there was a late service held, and, braving no small risks amidst the drunken and dissolute, Sister Dora indefatigably visited their homes, and *compelled* them to come in. Sister Dora always paid these visits alone. One visit she described to me. It was a much better house than any she had been in before—most of them being mere cottages—and the occupant was evidently superior to most of her neighbours in education. She was well-dressed, and when she asked in a stately manner, 'To what am I indebted for the pleasure of your visit?' Sister Dora owned that she felt almost inclined to leave without delivering her soul. She began her difficult task, and was met at first with quiet, civil-spoken contempt; but her heart warmed as she reasoned and pleaded, and her words became inspired, and before she left the woman broke out into sobs, and they knelt together in prayer.

"It was work at times not unaccompanied by personal risk, but I have met few persons more utterly fearless. She came back to where I was waiting for her after diving into one of the rookeries, and told me she had had a narrow escape. She had encountered a ruffian inflamed with drink, who burst out into a torrent of wild blasphemy, and threatened to have her life. He was quieted at once by his partner in sin, who said, 'Shut up, you fool! it's Sister Dora.' He even muttered some apology. Two of the women who had attended some of the services at the room were seized soon after by the police on a charge of robbery, and locked up. Sister Dora visited them frequently in the cells. Like her Master, she seemed never to despair of a human soul. The 'lost' were those whom she knew that He came to seek and save."

Sister Dora's death was not less remarkable than her life. In her last hours she displayed the fortitude and reticence of Emily Brontë, accompanied by that Christian faith which, unhappily, Emily Brontë lacked. It was in the course of the winter of 1876-77 that she first became aware of the existence of a disease which must ultimately, and at no distant date, prove fatal. Her medical adviser thought it possible that surgical aid might postpone the result for awhile; but she knew too much of the uncertainty attending all such measures to be willing to submit to the necessary treatment. Imposing absolute silence on her physician, she resolved to let the disease take its natural course, her desire being to continue her work as long as possible. Into that work she threw herself with redoubled ardour. It seemed her determination to get out of her body and mind their utmost capacity. Sternly repressing all signs of suffering, which none who looked upon her mature beauty and fine form suspected, she addressed herself to her various tasks with an energy and an ardour such as even she had never before exhibited. She was unwilling that a single opportunity should be lost, a single duty set aside, a single responsibility neglected. "I grudge every moment," she would say, "I must spend in taking care of this body." Necessarily her friends could not understand this apparent impetuosity, this unresting fervour, and frequently remonstrated with her, fearing lest the sword should wear out its sheath. She visited all the towns and villages within ten miles of Walsall, until she was recognized by all as a "ministering angel," who brought with her help and a balm for the sin-laden soul as well as the disease-stricken frame.

One night, the hospital doctor hastily summoned her to the case of a child in the last stage of diphtheria. As a last chance he performed the operation of tracheotomy, making an incision in the child's throat, and inserting a tube in the hope of relieving the suffocation. Sister Dora knelt down by the bed, put her mouth to the incision, and deliberately drew from the child's throat the poisonous membrane which was choking it. The child recovered; and Sister Dora suffered for three weeks from diphtheritic sore throat.

One night, Sister Dora, who had retired to bed much earlier than usual, was aroused from a sound sleep by the night-nurse:— "Sister, Sister, do get up! there's a man in the house, and I can't get him out! We shall all be killed!" Sister Dora hastily threw on her clothes and ran downstairs, where she found a flashy-looking man, with conspicuous rings and watch-chain, standing in the hall. Was not that, he enquired, the Cottage Hospital? "Yes," she replied, "and will you tell me your business here?" He thought, was the answer, he could be accommodated with a bed. "Oh, dear, no! we only give sick people beds here." "Well, anyhow, I've come," rejoined the fellow, "and I mean to stay." "Two people," said the Sister, "have to be consulted about that, and I, for one, do not mean to let you."

He advanced towards her, and she hoped that, in the dim light, he could not see how her trembling frame gave the lie to her bold words. "Do you think," said he, "*you're* going to prevent me from spending the night here if I choose?" "Of course I can't prevent you from staying in the passage; but you will have to force your way past me before you get any farther;" and there, on the last step of the staircase, she extended her arms across as a barrier. The man coolly seated himself on a bench in the hall. Meanwhile, their dialogue was disturbed by a series of frantic cries from the night-nurse:—"Sister, do leave him and come upstairs; we shall all be murdered—we shall indeed!" to which she received for answer, "Hold your tongue, you goose!" ("I could have beaten the woman," said Sister Dora afterwards, when telling the story).

For some considerable time she and her unwelcome visitor watched each other; and she was beginning to fear that he really meant to carry out his threat of spending the night in the hospital, when he made "a sudden dart down the passage" towards the kitchen. But her alertness foiled him, and in a moment her tall

form barred the way. Then he turned round with the remark,—
"You're a brave one—I've accomplished what I came for; I
wish you good evening," and so departed, leaving Dora to bolt the
door behind him, and assail the night-nurse with reproaches for
her indiscretion in admitting the man, and displaying afterwards
such a nervous spirit. A few weeks after this strange incident,
Sister Dora received an anonymous letter of apology, enclosing a
donation of one pound for the hospital funds. The committee
made every possible effort to detect the offender, but in vain;
probably he was some reckless fellow who had made a bet to try
an experiment on Sister Dora's reputed courage.

Her courage was shown much more strikingly in the silence
with which she endured the torture of the cancer that was slowly
killing her. She dressed the wound, which daily grew larger, herself. In the closing days of September, 1878, she went to London
with a view of studying Professor Lister's method of treating
wounds; but the visit was cut short by her illness. She hastily
returned to Birmingham, and thence was carefully removed to
Walsall, as she had expressed a desire to die " among her own
people." Her doctor consented to preserve her secret, and it was
made known only to an old servant, when, from increasing weakness, she was no longer able to dress the wound with her own
hands. Why she insisted upon this mystery is not very clear,
unless we ascribe it to an excessive sensitiveness, or some morbid
dislike to have it known that she, Sister Dora, suffered from such
a disease. Even her own sisters she would not allow to nurse her.
On her deathbed she derived great pleasure from the repetition
of some of Faber's hymns, saying, that "often, when her heart
had felt cold, she had sat down on the floor before she went to
bed at night, to repeat and refresh herself with them, and that they
had been the dearest companions of her solitary life."

Towards the end of November her condition grew much worse,
though her extraordinary vitality still struggled against the disease,
and supported her under its tortures. On the 27th she wrote, or
rather dictated, to a friend,—" My cough is terrible; it will not
cease, and I am so troubled with sickness. . . . Do pray for me,
dearest, that I may have patience to endure unto the end whatever He shall lay upon me, and that, when I pass through the

dark valley, He may fold me in His arms. Write to me when you can, for I do like a letter, to feel that I am not cut off from the outer world." Again, on the 30th :—" How can I thank you for the sweet, loving letters which find their way so continually to cheer my sick-bed! And they do cheer it, for they speak of such true heart-sympathy, entering into, and thinking of, all my pains and sufferings. Pray that my patience may not fail. . . . My nights are most distressing, owing to the cough, and now I care for nothing except water, which is my one cry all day long; so I think I cannot live long upon that."

A clergyman who frequently visited her writes:—" On two occasions she put a word in my mouth. One Sunday afternoon she asked me what my evening sermon was to be about. I told her. She said, 'Tell them to work while it is called to-day, for the night cometh, when no man can work.' It was the day when the annual collections were made for the Cottage Hospital, and in the course of my appeal on its behalf, I gave her message. The other occasion was a Sunday evening, when all the cabmen in the town had promised, at Sister Dora's request, to attend our mission-room service. Before evening service I was with her, and she said, 'Oh, speak to them on this text, "What think ye of Christ?" Make it ring in their ears.'

"They all came except two, who were unavoidably away on duty, and I preached from the text suggested. She had great sympathy with 'poor Cabby.' Every year she used to give them all some small present—a warm muffler, a pair of driving-gloves, or something of the kind. Before her illness, she had ordered about thirty pairs of warmly-lined gloves, intending them for a Christmas-box; but when it became evident that she would scarcely live till Christmas, she asked me to call the men together and present the gloves, with a few words from her. They were much affected, and in their rough but hearty way tried to express their feelings, giving me messages of affection to convey to her, and in every way showing their sorrow at the thought that she would never be amongst them again."

A friend who was very frequently with her writes:—

"I shall never forget the unselfishness, brightness, and patience with which she bore her long trial. (The last stage of her illness lasted eleven weeks.) Often, when she was suffering so much that I was afraid to do anything but watch her silently, she would ask some question about my home concerns, and go on talking of them with as much interest as though she were perfectly free from pain. One of her greatest pleasures was reading letters from her friends, and dictating answers to them, in which she would make as little as she truthfully could of her own sufferings, and show the liveliest interest in any little thing that concerned her friends. Her sufferings were sad to see; but even when she was moaning with pain which, she said, was like the cutting of a knife, she would go on dictating, as best she could, between her moans. At other times she was so drowsy that she would fall asleep before the letter was finished, or while I was reading to her; this distressed her even more than the pain, and she would beg me most earnestly to keep her awake. I do not think she had the times of extreme happiness which some people have felt when near death, for she said, 'The suffering is so real, so present, I seem scarcely able to think of the future happiness.' . . . Her sorrow was, that she could not realize God's presence more, and her fear was lest she should seem impatient. She spoke most decidedly against the idea that we need any one to go between the soul and Christ, and I shall never forgot her bright, beautiful smile as she listened to the words, 'He that believeth on Me hath everlasting life,' saying, with the deepest earnestness, 'That is just what I want.' . . . I feel that I cannot give you any true idea of those last hours that I spent with her, or of the vivid remembrance I have of her, as her brave and loving spirit waited for the moment when God would call her to the full, unclouded daylight of eternity, into the dawn of which she seemed already to have entered."

But we will linger no longer over these death-bed details. It is evident that Sister Dora's Christian courage did not desert her in her last hours, though she had her occasional fits of depression, due, no doubt, to her growing weakness; and that she faced the inevitable future with the stern resolution which was part of her character. That the end was very near all saw on Saturday, December 21st, and her old servant came to wait upon her dear mistress through the last sad hours. Sister Dora repeatedly said, "Oh, I hope I shall sing my Christmas carol in heaven," and her hope was fulfilled.

On Monday night the pain was almost more than she could bear; and early on the following morning, the 23rd, she said, "I am dying; run for Sister Ellen." Her servant endeavoured to soothe her: "Our Blessed Lord," she said, "is standing at the gates of heaven to open them for you." She was no longer in want of consolation; all the dread and darkness of the future had vanished. "I see Him there," she answered; "the gates are opened wide." When the physician had exhausted all the remedies for her relief that science could afford, she said to her attendants, "I have lived alone, let me die alone;" and she repeated the words, "Let me die alone," until they were compelled to leave her, one friend remaining outside to watch through the open door. She lingered for some hours, apparently without pain. And about two p.m. the anxious watcher knew, by a sudden and slight change of position, that the long struggle was over—the battle at an end—and that the brave, pure spirit of Sister Dora had passed "behind the veil."

O mystery of life and death! How it would smite our hearts, and weigh down our souls, but for such examples of faith and hope as we find in those servants of the Cross who live and die like Sister Dora!

Hazell, Watson, and Viney, Printers, London and Aylesbury.

www.ingramcontent.com/pod-product-compliance
Lightning Source LLC
Chambersburg PA
CBHW030558300426
44111CB00009B/1030